# PC Magazine Take Word for Windows to the Edge

# PC Magazine
# Take Word
# for Windows
# to the Edge

**Guy Gallo**

**Ziff-Davis Press**
**Emeryville, California**

| | |
|---|---|
| Development Editor | Valerie Haynes Perry |
| Copy Editor | Jan Jue |
| Technical Reviewer | Edward Mendelson |
| Project Coordinator | Bill Cassel |
| Proofreader | Aidan Wylde |
| Cover Design | Ken Roberts |
| Book Design | Laura Lamar/MAX, San Francisco and Stephen Bradshaw |
| Screen Graphics Editor | Dan Brodnitz |
| Technical Illustration | Cherie Plumlee Computer Graphics & Illustration |
| Word Processing | Howard Blechman and Cat Haglund |
| Page Layout | Adrian Severynen and M. D. Barrera |
| Indexer | Ted Laux |

This book was produced on a Macintosh IIfx, with the following applications: FrameMaker®, Microsoft® Word, MacLink®*Plus*, Aldus® FreeHand™, Adobe Photoshop™, and Collage Plus™.

Ziff-Davis Press
5903 Christie Avenue
Emeryville, CA 94608

ISBN 1-56276-079-3

Manufactured in the United States of America
⊕ The paper used in this book exceeds the EPA requirements for postconsumer recycled paper.
10 9 8 7 6 5 4 3 2 1

# CONTENTS AT A GLANCE

Bonus Disk

# TABLE OF CONTENTS

# Part 2    WordBasic

**Part 3     An Encyclopedia of Tips**

# INTRODUCTION

IN THE OLDEN DAYS, COMPUTER PROGRAMS RESEMBLED KNOWN THINGS. A database stored information in distinct fields, categorized alphabetically, much like paper forms in a file cabinet. Spreadsheets arranged numbers on a grid that looked, not coincidentally, like a ledger. Word processors arranged text as had typewriters: characters per line, lines per page.

As personal computers have become more powerful, and software design has evolved from character-based to graphical, software programmers have invented new ways for a program to "think" of its data. A database, for instance, can have "depth," with the relationships among items surpassing simple alphabetical arrangement. Second-generation spreadsheets possess sophisticated number crunching tools that go beyond the ledger metaphor. Word processors now borrow more from the typesetting machine than from the typewriter.

The difficulty is this: As computer programs become more powerful, conceiving new relations and new paradigms for handling information, users often find their conceptual hold slipping, the familiar approaches, based on older models, no longer providing guidelines to aid in learning and using the program.

To fully exploit the power of an advanced application, the user must approach with fresh eyes, willing to learn the specific vocabulary, the unique methodology, of the program. Many new software applications require a shift in perspective, a new conceptual orientation. Word for Windows is one such program. It is, most definitely, not a typewriter.

The frustration of learning a complex program can lead a user to dismiss the more advanced features as mere "bells and whistles," fancy stuff better left to the expert with time to spare. *Take Word for Windows to the Edge* is not simply a catalog of advanced features or neat tricks. This book will guide you through the conceptual underpinnings, the fundamental assumptions and paradigms, of Word for Windows. At the other end, Word's design will make more sense, its features, both basic and advanced, will acquire a coherence. You will have the understanding and tools necessary to make Word perform more efficiently.

## Purpose

*Take Word for Windows to the Edge* will increase your productivity. It will make Word more flexible, more powerful, and more specifically tailored to your particular requirements and habits. Writing is an idiosyncratic activity. We all bring to the task of putting words together our own peculiar idea of process, organization, document management, and end product. There are as many ways to approach composition, be it a letter or an annual report, as there are writers. It is the particular grace of Word that it can be customized to suit your preferences.

Enhanced productivity should be understood as more than simply saving time or doing more work. It should also mean better work. This book hopes to make Word more than a time-saving tool. Any word processor, sufficiently understood, will produce documents faster than a typewriter. The ultimate goal of this book is not more documents, but better documents. It will provide insights into the design of Word, in the form of conceptual discussions, example utilities, and usage tips, that can be applied, in practical ways, to transform Word from a word processor into a tool that enhances writing rather than simply recording it, that automates the tedious to leave more room for the creative.

A secondary, or perhaps ancillary, goal is to make using Word more fun. That may seem a frivolous ambition for such a book. But when a complex program is more fully understood, and the user no longer fears the tool—when it can be mastered rather than mastering—the work itself, and not the software, becomes paramount. An increased mastery of the tool cannot help but minimize the anxiety and tedium normally associated with the mechanics of composition. The goal is not simply to make Word more enjoyable, but to make it transparent to the process of writing itself, for its tools to be put in the service of creativity.

It should be stated here as well that the concepts, utilities, and tips gathered and presented in this book are the product of extensive familiarity with Word. I am not a programmer. I am not a computer writer. I am a writer. And what I know of Word I know because I use the program. What I hope the book will provide is a view into the program that will benefit any user, no matter how experienced, no matter how new. It will demonstrate ways of using Word that will make it simpler, faster, and more enjoyable to produce documents of any size or complexity.

Every document has two lives: as a draft and as a product. That is, the document in process, known only to the writer, and the finished, formatted, printed, and distributed public text. This book will discuss both aspects of document creation with Word, examining the ways in which it can be tailored to ease the input of data, and the ways in which the final output can be polished.

## Organization

*Take Word for Windows to the Edge* is organized into three main sections. Included with *Take Word for Windows to the Edge* is a disk containing over 50 original macros, each of which is described aand annotated in detail in the WordBasic chapters.

## Part 1: Fundamentals of Word's Design

The first section will take the basic design concepts of Word and explain what they are, how they are related, and how these essential elements can be mustered to create a uniquely customized version of Word, tailored to your (or your company's) particular needs.

The major topics of this conceptual discussion will be

- The inherent flexibility of Word's design

- Changing default behavior in menus, keystrokes, and commands

- Adding new functionality through macros

- Using styles to enhance both the process and the product

The unifying concept in this first section is the template: what it is, what it controls, and what it contains.

## Part 2: WordBasic

This section will delve more deeply into the mysteries of Word's "macro language." For the beginner it will describe the simplest way to use WordBasic: the macro recorder. From there it will detail modifying recorded macros and creating macros from scratch.

Not intended as a replacement for the Microsoft WordBasic manual, *Using WordBasic*, Part 2 will touch on the fundamentals of the language's features, and provide several hints and tips for simplifying macro creation.

## Part 3: An Encyclopedia of Tips

This section will illustrate the theoretical concepts of Parts 1 and 2 with annotated macro examples. These examples will solve specific problems. You will learn how to modify built-in commands, how to replace built-in commands with macros, how to add new functionality via WordBasic, and how to combine WordBasic, styles, glossaries, and fields in custom templates.

In addition, a chapter will be devoted to tips on optimizing Word, avoiding pitfalls, and circumventing limitations.

Note: There are also seven appendices containing useful reference material.

 ## What's on the Disk

Here is a sampling of the types of macros on disk, that illustrate the power of WordBasic:

- **Macros That Add Commands Microsoft Left Out**—Such as, WinArrangeTwo and WinCascadeAll

- **Macros That Enhance Built-in Commands**—Such as, ControlRun and FileOpen

- **Macros That Add Complex Features to Word**—Such as, BackUpThisDoc and CopyMacro

- **Utility Macros**—Such as, ChangeTool and gLib

- **Sample Templates**—The sample disk also contains six templates that are created in Chapter 12.

Refer to Appendix G for specifics on how to use the disk.

## Assumptions

This book is not intended as a tutorial or a reference. It assumes you are familiar with Word for Windows and are comfortable with the geography and terminology. It does not, however, assume that you are a programmer or a computer professional.

If you have never built a custom template or designed an application macro, it would be advisable to read Parts I and II before examining the example macros. In those sections the essential information for understanding WordBasic will be explained in detail.

If you are already familiar with templates and macros, these sections will still prove useful in elucidating how to unify the various concepts and tools in Word.

## Conventions

When you are prompted for input, the characters to be typed will appear in boldface type. For example:

Type **My dog has fleas**

New terms will appear in italic:

*Templates* are extremely powerful.

Navigating the menus in Word will be specified in one of two ways; either by specifying the menu sequence:

Select File, New

or by specifying the name of the command macro to execute:

Select FileNew

Note: The similarity between these two ways of specifying a menu selection is not coincidental, as I will discuss in Chapter 1.

Within macro listings, WordBasic reserved words will be formatted in boldface type. For instance:

```
Sub Main
Beep
MsgBox "My dog has fleas"
End Sub
```

Macros that are included on disk can be found in a file named to correspond to the chapter in which the macro is discussed. For example, all of the example macros from Chapter 7 are located in the disk file CH07MACS.DOC. The source code for a macro that is also included on disk will be marked with an icon and a margin note:

**DISK**
AutoExecBackup—
Possible AutoExec
macro to backup
NORMAL.DOT

## References

The following Microsoft publications about Word will be referred to from time to time:

- *Microsoft Using WordBasic*    *Using WordBasic* is the Word for Windows 2.0 Technical Reference. It contains detailed information about WordBasic statements and functions and about macro programming in general. It is free for the asking from Microsoft (a card was included in the box, and the number for ordering is listed in Appendix F).

  Note: The current version of *Using WordBasic* was based, in part, upon an earlier tutorial/guide written by WexTech Systems. I was one of the authors of that earlier book. Therefore, any similarity in tone and/or emphasis you might notice between the two books is not accidental. Some of the ideas and examples in this book are elaborations of work done for WexTech.

- *Microsoft Word User's Guide*    The *Word User's Guide* is the general Word for Windows manual. Specific chapters will be referenced.

**Customization, Translucence, and Macros**

**Templates Explored**

**Template Properties Affecting Text**

**Interface Properties**

1

**Fundamentals of
Word's Design**

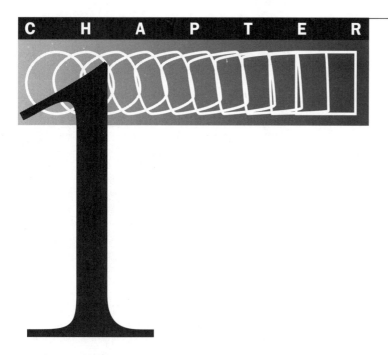

C H A P T E R

1

# Customization, Translucence, and Macros

THE DESIGNERS OF WORD FOR WINDOWS HAVE CREATED A RICH AND COMplex program that many people would consider perfectly sufficient as is, right out of the box, with no modification. At first glance it may be difficult to imagine what might be added. But no matter how many features a program has, no matter how deeply considered a given function might be, someone, somewhere, can think of another, or a better, or a faster way to do things. No program can be all things to all people. Program designers know this. They leave themselves elbowroom. They build in a solution: *customization*.

## Customization

You will find some form of customization in even the simplest program. Specifying a data path, a user name, or color preferences are all customizations. To give a *very* primitive example, the DOS DIR command has a series of command-line switches. If you want a wide display you append /W to the command; if you want to pause the display you append /P. These options are, in fact, customizations. Or, to use a Windows example, think of the File Manager. You can specify the font to be used or whether the file display should be lowercase.

In developing a complex program such as a word processor, a program development team has two options in their struggle to please as many people as possible. They can try to anticipate every possible variation in how the program will be used and then attempt to provide solutions approximating these predictions. Or they can make the program flexible.

Word for Windows takes the second route with a vengeance. Virtually every aspect of Word for Windows can be accessed and altered or replaced. This may seem excessive. It isn't. This may seem daunting. It won't be by the time you finish working with the examples in this book.

## Translucence: How the Inner Workings Shine Through

The most unique aspect of Word for Windows is that it allows you to "see behind" its surface. The consequence of seeing behind the scenes is the ability to alter even Word's most basic functions. Before going on to examine the ramifications of this design in detail, let me demonstrate translucence as it applies to Word.

When we think of the various editing functions of a word processor, such as searching for text, formatting a page layout, loading a new file, or saving a file to disk, we normally think of commands. The user presses a given key sequence or selects the appropriate menu item, and the program executes the instructions (performs the command). For many new computer users this looks a lot like magic, a special kind of voodoo. The actual procedure, the code that executes when the key is pressed or menu selected, is hidden deep in the bowels of the program, never to be seen, never to be questioned, never to be changed. In most programs these basic-level commands are arranged in an immutable order and perform in an immutable manner. However, in Word even the basic editing commands are available for scrutiny and alteration.

For instance, take the command to search for text. If you select Find from the Edit menu you will see the following dialog box:

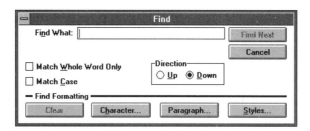

This is the normal way of accessing the EditFind command. To demonstrate the way in which Word allows a user to see behind the scenes, let's access this same command in another manner.

First, if you are following along in Word, cancel the Find dialog box. Now select Macro from the Tools menu. After the Macro dialog box appears, press Alt+C. This will bring up the following dialog box:

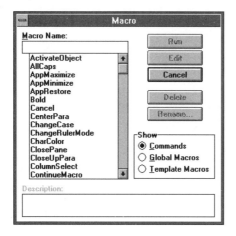

This display is most important—it goes to the heart of the principle of translucence. The list it contains should look familiar. Each item in the Macro Name list box corresponds to one of those normally inscrutable, magical commands.

If you browse through the Macro Name list, you will notice two remarkable things. First, each of the commands can be called, or run, from this dialog box. To demonstrate this, scroll to EditFind in the list, highlight it, and click on the Run button. You will see the same dialog box as the one presented when you selected Edit, Find from the menu. This is remarkable because it clearly illustrates the strict connection between functions that are normally called commands and what Word calls a *macro*. That is, each function, every command, possesses a corresponding *command macro*. Second, you will notice that when you select any one of these command macros, the Edit button becomes available. What this means, essentially, is that you can access, examine, and alter any command macro. The ramifications of this will become clear in Chapter 5 where we will examine in detail the process of changing a built-in command macro. For now, suffice it to say that the ability to change how a built-in command macro functions is one of the most powerful customization tools that Word provides.

And, conversely, you can deduce the name of a command macro by the location of the command on the menu: To open a file you select Open from the File menu, therefore it is no surprise that there is a command macro named FileOpen. This correspondence between a command macro's name and its location in the menu geography is no accident, and becomes extremely useful when programming in WordBasic.

To make this connection between editing functions and command macros clearer, let's take a moment to examine a further correspondence: that between a command macro's name and its location on Word's menu. For instance, the FileNew command macro is executed when you select New from the File menu. EditSearch is the name of the command macro that corresponds to Search on the Edit menu. ToolsOptionsView corresponds to the View sub-submenu on the Options submenu of the Tools menu. Figure 1.1 shows this connection by using the FileNew command as an example. What you should note is that you can find a command macro's location by parsing the name according to capitalization: FormatStyle implies Style on the Format menu.

In sum, the list of command macros is actually a list of the commands that make Word work. The programmers have done a remarkable thing: They have allowed the user access to the normally hidden inner workings of the program. I term this quality in Word *translucence*. In Word not only can you add new commands by creating macros (which will be explored in the next section), but you can also alter the built-in command macros. By way of contrast, most computer programs are opaque. You are given a set functionality presented in a set order. You may be able to supplement the given commands, but you cannot normally replace the given functionality.

**Figure 1.1**

Connection between a macro name and its menu location

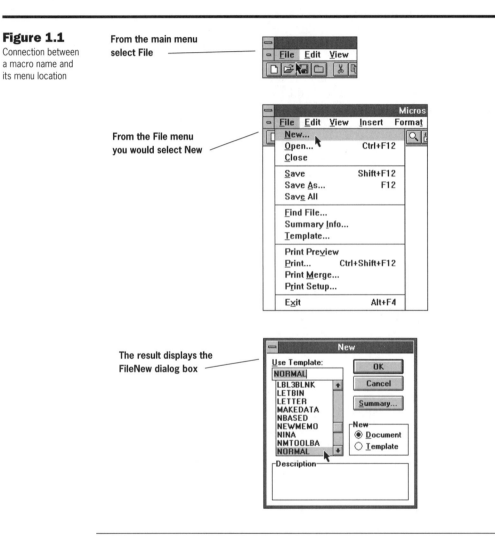

From the main menu
select File

From the File menu
you would select New

The result displays the
FileNew dialog box

This book will teach you how to make the most of translucence. You will learn how to alter built-in commands, how to supplement them with new commands, and how to organize their use most efficiently.

# Introducing Macros

You may have noticed a curious thing in the foregoing paragraphs. The word "command" was used interchangeably with the phrase "built-in macro" or "command macro." And further, you may have noticed that in the list of commands brought up by selecting Tools, Macro, the heading for the list was "Macro Name." Before proceeding it would be well to explain what is meant by this ubiquitous term "macro," and what it has to do with the editing commands in Word.

I have no idea who first used this word in connection with computer programming. "Macro" means "large" and normally refers to the Big Picture—it's the opposite of "micro." Perhaps the best way to think of this catchall computer-speak word is precisely as a catchall. Small, repeated functions and tasks are gathered under a single, specifically defined, easily accessible command called a *macro*.

Take the EditFind command discussed earlier. When you execute this "macro" a window pops up asking you, among other things, for the text to find and whether or not the case of the search text should be matched precisely. In this example, there are two functions joined together under a single command:

- Looking for the text specified

- Determining if it contains the proper mix of upper- and lowercase

Deep within Word there are two distinct sections of program code that are called upon to do this double task. The EditFind macro has combined them to accomplish this multiple-step task at once. From this perspective, one should consider any computer program an organized collection of macros, written and structured by a programmer. It is the particular virtue of Word that neither the macros themselves, nor their placement and organization in the program, are set in stone. It is one of this book's tasks to demonstrate how Word's inherent flexibility can be tapped for greater enjoyment and productivity.

In addition to altering the built-in command macros, users can create *custom macros* in order to extend Word's functionality. Custom macros are created by recording a series of actions, by writing from the ground up, or a combination of both. Creating and editing custom macros will be detailed in Chapter 5.

# Access Methods

Every command in Word has two parts: the macro that executes the command, be it a built-in macro programmed by the creators of Word or a custom macro created by the user, and the manner in which that macro is called. There are three ways in which a macro can be called:

- By selecting an item from the menu

■ By pressing a keyboard sequence

■ By clicking on a toolbar icon

These should be thought of as *access methods*.

Word contains a set of default access methods to execute the most frequently used built-in command macros. These defaults are manifested when you install Word, as well as in the structure and arrangement of the menu, the choice of icons and macros for the toolbar, and in the default shortcut key assignments. However, any of these default access methods can be altered to suit your (perhaps idiosyncratic) preferences. This ability to change the interface presented to the user is the first hallmark of Word's flexibility, and the first evidence that translucence translates into customization power.

As an introduction to Word's customization potential, let's step through making one change in each access method category.

### Menu Change

The dialog box used to change the various screen tools, such as the status bar and scroll bar, is usually accessed through three menu levels: Tools, Options, and View. Let's place a command on the View menu (a logical choice) to more easily access this important dialog box.

**1.** Select Tools, Options (Alt+O-O).

**2.** Press M in order to display the ToolsOptionsMenu dialog box:

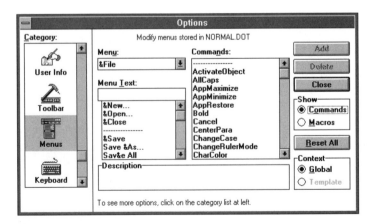

**3.** Press Alt+O to bring up a list of the internal commands.

**4.** Press Alt+N to move to the list of commands. In the list of commands, find ToolsOptionsView. (Hint: Pressing T will move to the start of commands beginning with the letter "t.")

**5.** Press Alt+U to move to the list of main menu items.

**6.** Press Down Arrow until View is highlighted.

**7.** Press Tab.

You are now in the edit box for the text that will actually appear on the menu once you complete the addition of this access method. The ampersand refers to the letter that will be placed on the menu as underlined and as the speed key for that menu. By default you will now see &Tools Options View... in the Menu Text edit box.

**8.** Type **&View Preferences**.

**9.** Press Alt+A to add the new menu item.

You now have a new menu item beneath the View menu. This item will display the ToolsOptionsView dialog box, where you can change various settings relating to the view of your document. Press Alt+V-V to see the result of the above change.

## Keyboard Change

In order to alter the keyboard shortcut sequence that calls a macro that toggles DraftView:

**1.** Select Tools, Options (Alt+O-O).

**2.** Press K in order to display the ToolsOptionsKeyboard dialog box:

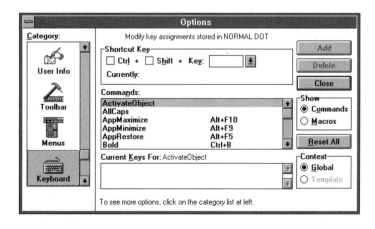

**3.** Press Alt+O to bring up a list of the internal commands.

**4.** Press Alt+N to move to the list of commands.

**5.** In the list of commands, find ViewDraft.

**6.** Press Ctrl+Shift-D. This will change the display in the Shortcut Key box to the unassigned keystroke, Ctrl+Shift-D.

**7.** Press Alt+A to add the new keyboard assignment.

You now have a keyboard access method that will toggle Draft Mode on and off. Press Ctrl+Shift-D several times to demonstrate the effect of this toggle.

## Toolbar Change

The toolbar is a great addition to Word for Windows. However, I take exception to the command macro assigned to the very first icon on the toolbar. By default, the first icon, which looks like a blank page, executes the command FileNewDefault, creating a new, blank document. However, this icon assumes that every new document should be based on the default settings (as they are defined in the global customization template named NORMAL.DOT. If you don't know what global customization, or template, or NORMAL.DOT are, bear with me. NORMAL.DOT is briefly explained in the next section; all three terms are covered more fully in the next chapter.) Me, I like more choices than the default. I want this icon to run the same macro run by the FileNew menu item. So, to change the toolbar:

**1.** Select Tools, Options (Alt+O-O).

**2.** Press T to display the ToolsOptionsToolbar dialog box:

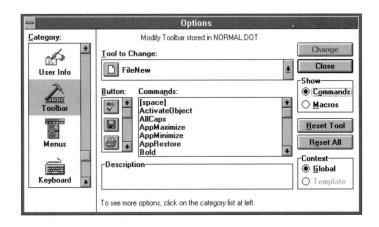

3. Press Alt+O to bring up a list of the internal commands.

4. Press Alt+T to choose which tool to change. Since we are changing the first tool, we are already there.

5. Press Tab twice to move to the list of commands.

6. Find FileNew (hint: press F eleven times). Press Alt+A to change the tool.

Now when you click on this icon you will be presented with a list of templates to choose from.

## Where Do the Changes Live?

We have just made three changes. But what have we changed? If you select File, SaveAll, you will be prompted with the following message:

What does this mean? If you respond Yes—which you should for the purposes of this exercise—you will see, on the status line, the message

```
Word is saving NORMAL.DOT...
```

It means the access method changes we just made constitute changes to the macros and the commands they affect: ToolsOptionsView, ViewDraft, and FileNew. It also means those changes will be saved to the file named NORMAL.DOT. This is a special type of Word document called a *template*. Specifically, NORMAL.DOT is the "global" template. It contains all of the customizations that you wish to have sway over most documents, in most situations, most of the time. Customizations stored in the global *context* will have authority unless they are specifically contravened by customizations contained in the local template.

The previous sentence contains more than it may seem at first glance. It bears repeating: *Customizations stored in the global context will have authority unless they are specifically contravened by customizations contained in the local template.* Memorize that. It will be a crucial concept in all that follows. Before the significance of this statement will have full impact we must spend some time exploring the general concept of templates and the related, all-important concept of context. These ideas are so central to the customization aspects of Word for Windows that they deserve their own chapter.

CHAPTER

2

## Templates Explored

ENTRAL TO THE EFFECTIVE USE OF WORD FOR WINDOWS IS AN UNDERstanding of templates. Most simply put, templates are the single most significant aspect of the program. Many people use Word without ever fully understanding what a template might add to their own use of the program. They do so, in my opinion, mainly because the documentation for Word works hard to avoid concepts that might be foreign or difficult for the new user. This documentation strategy is at odds with the inventive design of the program. It's almost as if the designers don't know what a good thing they've created.

## What Is a Template?

Every document created in Word for Windows is based on a template. If you select File, New, you are prompted to choose which template to use in creating a new document. By default (that is, if you simply press Enter) the template used is NORMAL.DOT. This template, in which all global preferences are stored, has one special power: It rules when no other template is active. And if there is another template active that does not explicitly contravene the customizations held in NORMAL.DOT, those global preferences continue to rule. This concept of *rule*, or *scope*, is an important one, and it will be explored in more detail in Chapter 4. But for the moment NORMAL.DOT should simply be considered one of many templates. Now it's time for some definitions.

A *template* is a specialized Word for Windows document, normally, but not necessarily, named with the extension .DOT (DOcument Template). It contains instructions for various properties, some affecting text layout and formatting, and others affecting the interface, which are passed on to any document based on that template.

It's really a rather simple concept. A template in Word for Windows is the same as a template in any other parlance: a guide to be used in the creation of another object. The template determines certain aspects of the new object. The object created based upon a Word template is a document.

In general, you should think of a template as a container in which you can store customizations that control text and formatting properties, and customizations that affect the way in which Word operates.

When you create a document based on a template, or load a document that was previously associated with a template, in effect you are "loading" both the document and the template into Word. The document is visible for editing. The template remains in the background, holding various elements at the ready. But you should realize that the template is, in fact, somewhere in memory, waiting to be used, waiting to be altered.

## Text Properties

A template determines several default characteristics about a document *at the time of its creation.* These "starting point" text properties fall into three main categories:

- Layout information such as margin settings, orientation, and page size.

- Style definitions such as font, font size, emphasis attributes, and indentation for paragraphs.

- Default text, or boilerplate, that will be automatically inserted into all new documents based on that template. This can include multiple paragraphs of complexly formatted text, header and footer information, fields, bookmarks, or pictures.

## Interface Properties

A template can also determine several aspects of *how Word operates* when you are editing a document based on that template. These template-bound interface customizations also fall into three categories:

- Glossary information, that is, boilerplate not automatically inserted into the text, but held at the ready, stored with the template, and accessible with an abbreviation

- Customized versions of the built-in command macros or user-macros

- Access Method customizations the user may have created

# The Standard Templates That Word Installs

When you install Word for the first time, the setup program copies a collection of templates to your hard disk. Below is a table of the templates that ship with Word and a short description of the type of document they are used to create:

| Template | Use |
| --- | --- |
| ARTICLE2.DOT | Article manuscript |
| DATAFILE.DOT | Used with Print Merge to create form letters |
| DISSERT2.DOT | Academic dissertation |
| FAX.DOT | Fax cover sheet |

| LETBLOCK.DOT | Block-style letter |
| LETMDSEM.DOT | Modified semiblock-style letter |
| LETMODBK.DOT | Modified block-style letter |
| LETPERSN.DOT | Personal letter |
| MAILLABL.DOT | Mailing labels |
| MEMO2.DOT | A business memo |
| OVERHEAD.DOT | Overhead projection presentation |
| PRESS.DOT | Press release |
| PROPOSAL.DOT | Formal business proposal |
| REPLAND.DOT | Report in landscape orientation |
| REPSIDE.DOT | Report with sideheads |
| REPSTAND.DOT | Report in portrait orientation |
| TERM2.DOT | Academic term paper |

Simple instructions about how to use these templates are provided in Chapter 37 of the *Microsoft Word User's Guide.*

These templates should not be viewed as unalterable, immutable tools. Rather, you should look on them as starting points for your own customized set of templates. No matter how cleverly designed no template created by someone else can anticipate all the various and variable aspects of your particular setup. On the simplest level, for instance, you may not have a font called for by the template, or you may prefer a different font. Although this book will not provide a detailed analysis of the individual templates that ship with Word, the chapters that follow will give you a greater understanding of how these templates work, what they contain, and how they can be modified to suit your own preferences.

## The Global Template: NORMAL.DOT and First Glance at Context

When you load Word for the first time, an additional template is created named NORMAL.DOT. This is a very important template. As stated above, NORMAL.DOT is the template used when you create a new document and do not specify a custom template. The customizations stored in NORMAL.DOT are termed "global" and, as stated in Chapter 1, they rule all documents unless contravened by a customization contained in a custom template.

The specific ways in which this fact will affect the design and creation of templates will be demonstrated with specific examples in Chapter 4. However, I'd like to offer a few general definitions and comments.

The term *focus* will be used throughout what follows. You see focus every time you change applications in Windows: the title bar changes to the color reserved for the "active" application. In Word, when you move from one document window to another, the same change in the document title bar occurs. In addition, the blinking insertion point is moved to the active document. The document that contains the insertion point is said to have the focus.

The focus, in turn, determines which customizations are in effect. For instance, if the focus is on a template based on NORMAL.DOT, only the customizations contained in NORMAL.DOT will be available. If you switch the focus to a document based upon LETBLOCK.DOT (to take a random "for instance"), the customizations available will be both those contained in LETBLOCK.DOT and those in NORMAL.DOT that are not contravened by a LETBLOCK.DOT customization.

Another way of stating this is: the focus determines the currently active context, either global or template. When in a document based upon a custom template (that is, when in a template context), the global customizations "show through" unless they are blocked by contradictory customizations defined in the template.

Word dynamically alters which customizations are available depending upon the context. This is an incredibly powerful facility. It allows you, for instance, to have multiple template-based documents loaded at the same time, each with its own unique customizations. Switching from one document to another will change which customizations will be available. Though this concept may seem rather heady when described theoretically, it will become evident when implemented.

## Where Templates Live and How To Move Them

The Word installation process copies the predefined templates into the same directory that contains the program files. The directory proposed by the setup program is C:\WINWORD.

The setup program tells Word where to find the available templates by creating a setting in your WIN.INI file named *Dot-Path*.

You can view this setting in one of two ways: You can load WIN.INI into the Notepad application and search for the phrase "Microsoft Word 2.0," or you can access a listing of all Word related WIN.INI settings by displaying the ToolsOptionsWinini dialog box (Alt+O-O-W). In Chapter 13 we will discuss the various Word settings stored in WIN.INI.

To some, it seems messy to have DOT files and program files jumbled up in the same directory. If you prefer a more segregated organization of your hard disk, you can move your templates to their own subdirectory.

1. Using File Manager, create a directory to hold all your templates—for instance, C:\WINWORD\DOT.

2. Move all the DOT files found in the Word directory to this new subdirectory.

3. And finally, change the Dot-Path setting in WIN.INI to point to the new subdirectory.

The next time you load Word, FileNew and FileTemplate will display a list of templates found in your new Dot-Path.

The fact that you can change the Dot-Path setting from within Word, using ToolsOptionsWinini, allows you to have, if you require, multiple directories containing templates. You might, for instance, have a set of templates for personal use and one for business use. There is one limitation in changing the Dot-Path from within Word, however: the NORMAL.DOT that was initially loaded remains loaded even after you've changed the active Dot-Path. To pass control to a new NORMAL.DOT you would have to change the Dot-Path and then exit and reload Word.

You should also be aware that although Word assumes all your templates are stored in the Dot-Path directory, it is possible to base a document on a template found in any directory simply by specifying the full path designation of the template.

Note: It is also possible to base a new document upon an existing document. After invoking FileNew, simply type the full path name of the "model" document instead of selecting a template. The document itself will be inserted (as if it were template boilerplate) into the new document. The styles and layout information will be copied into the new document. The new document will inherit whatever template is attached to the existing document.

## Changing a Template's Properties

In chapters to follow we will explore in more detail the various properties and customizations that can be created and/or altered and stored in a template. But first it is important to understand how changes are made to a template.

There are two ways to change a template property: You can make the change in the document based on the template and instruct Word to save the changes to the template, or you can make the change directly to the template.

## Making Template Changes from within a Document

Many settings that are stored in a template can be modified while editing a document. For example, select the Format, Page Setup menu item and press Alt+M to bring up the following dialog box:

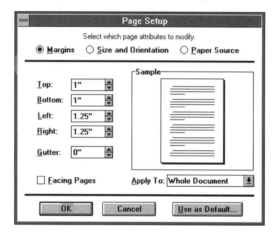

Notice the button in the lower right: Use as Default. If you make any changes to the margins and then click on this button, you will see the following message box:

If you do not click on Use as Default, the margin settings will only be changed in the document itself. If you explicitly choose Use as Default, the margin settings will be changed in both the document and the underlying template.

There is a parallel option available when you alter style information. When you execute FormatStyle and click on the Define button you will see a check box, Add to Template, at the bottom of the dialog box:

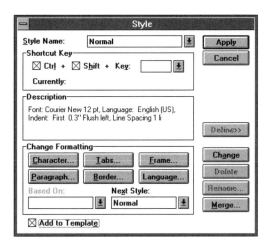

When this option is checked, all changes to existing styles or new styles will be saved to the underlying template as well as to the document.

### Editing a Template Directly

Some template settings can only be modified directly within the template in question. For this reason it is important to make sure now, before proceeding, that you understand how to open a template for direct editing: *Opening a template requires precisely the same steps as opening a document, with a single exception. Instead of looking for all .DOC files, you are looking for .DOT files.* You can change the file specification in the FileOpen dialog box either by typing \*.**DOT** directly, or by choosing Document Templates (\*.DOT) from the List Files of Type drop-down list box.

## Summary: Definitions

An understanding of templates is fundamental to virtually all customizations in Word for Windows. Before I present detailed discussions of each of the six template properties, here is a list of basic concepts and definitions concerning templates:

- A template is a special form of document. It can be loaded into Word and edited the same as any document. This is significant since you may wish to make some modifications directly to the template.

- Templates are stored, by default, in the program directory (where WINWORD.EXE resides); they can optionally be moved to a unique directory, a practice that will be covered in Chapter 13 (see *Microsoft Word User's Guide*, page 797).

■ Changes made to a template determine the nature of all *subsequent* documents based on that template; changes are not retroactive—they do *not* automatically alter already existing documents.

■ Most template customizations can also be changed from within a document; that is, changes made to a document—such as changes in font information, or margin information—can optionally be saved to the underlying template.

■ Completely changing the underlying template, that is, attaching a different template altogether, does not automatically change the ruling text characteristics; attaching a different template does, however, change the ruling customization features—for example, macros, glossaries, and access customizations automatically change when a different template is attached; font, layout, header, and footer information do *not* change with a change in template.

■ With text and layout attributes the template is used as the model, but as soon as a document is created, you should imagine that those attributes are actually copied into the document.

■ Macros, glossaries, and access customizations, on the other hand, travel with the template; they are not copied into the document.

**C H A P T E R**

# 3

# Template Properties
# Affecting Text

I N THIS CHAPTER WE WILL EXPLORE THREE PROPERTIES OF A TEMPLATE THAT should properly be seen as text- and formatting-related tools: layout, styles, and boilerplate. These template properties directly affect the document itself, providing default formatting information and potentially, default text.

# Layout

Layout information is perhaps the most fundamental property carried by a template. Every document must have margin settings, and every document must have an orientation as landscape or portrait. Elements of layout can be directly applied to the document *without reference to any template*. However, when properly used, a template gives you a standard starting point for a class of documents.

## Margin Settings

For example, you may wish to have 1.5″ left and right margins for all documents written as letters. In this case you would change the margin settings in the template LETTER.DOT. All subsequent letters based upon that template would begin with a left and right margin of 1.5″.

Such a change would be effected by bringing up the FormatPageSetup-Margins dialog box (by selecting from the menu or pressing Alt+T-U-M), shown in Figure 3.1.

**Figure 3.1**
FormatPageSetup dialog box (Margins selected)

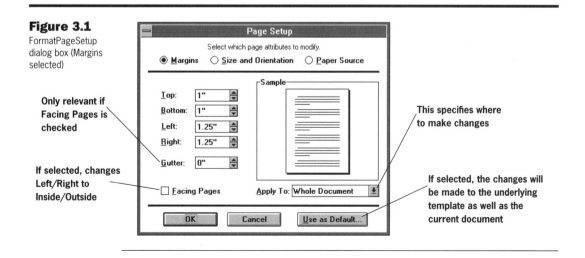

Only relevant if Facing Pages is checked

If selected, changes Left/Right to Inside/Outside

This specifies where to make changes

If selected, the changes will be made to the underlying template as well as the current document

If you are making this change from within an existing document, you would click on Use as Default to transfer the modifications to the template. If you are editing the template directly, selecting OK would be sufficient.

The drop-down list box at the lower right, labeled "Apply To:", determines what portion of the document will be affected by the margin change. The options are Whole Document, This Point Forward, and, if you are in a multisection document, This Section.

As you change the left and right margin settings, you will notice that the *greeked* lines representing text displayed on the sample page change width. This illustrates a significant difference between Word (and many other advanced word processors) and the machine most people are familiar with, the typewriter. If you are accustomed to working on typewriters you might imagine line formatting in terms of characters per line. With a typewriter one thinks of a line as a set number of characters, the left margin as "the number of spaces to skip," and the right margin as "the place to ring the bell." If a page is 80 characters wide and the left margin is set at 10 and the right at 70, then each line can contain 60 characters. Not so with Word. Here we think of margins in terms of a measurement in from the left and right edges of the page. The length of the line is whatever is left after subtracting the margin measurements from the page width. A standard 8.5-inch-wide page, set with 1.25-inch left and right margins, has a line 6 inches wide.

The number of characters that fit within the boundaries is no longer set. With the increased use of proportionally spaced fonts and the flexibility of computer-generated point sizes, the number of characters is now completely a function of how many characters in a specific font will fit in a line of a given length.

Similarly, the number of lines that will fit on a page is a function of line height, line spacing, and font point size. Word defines the printable area of the page with the following equations:

```
Printable Page Height = Page Height - (Top Margin + Bottom Margin)
Printable Page Width = Page Width - (Left Margin + Right Margin)
```

Word calculates all this in the background and provides a best fit for every font, taking into consideration all the variables such as page height and width, indentation specifications for a paragraph style, and font characteristics. In this way Word is much more like a typesetting machine than it is like a typewriter. Used in combination with paragraph formatting and styles, the margin settings discussed here provide precise control over the layout of text on a page.

**NOTE.** *If you click on the Facing Pages check box, the edit boxes for left and right margins change to Inside and Outside. Changing the inside setting allows you to alter what is known as the* gutter margins *for pages that will be printed on both sides of a sheet of paper. Think of this as the margin closer to the binding. Changing the outside margin affects the white space between the text and the nonbound edge of the document.*

## Size and Orientation

Also on the FormatPageSetup dialog box are three option buttons, placed across the top. In the above example the button next to "Margins" was selected. If you select Size and Orientation (or press Alt+S) the dialog box changes to what is shown in Figure 3.2.

**Figure 3.2**
FormatPageSetup
dialog box (Size and
Orientation selected)

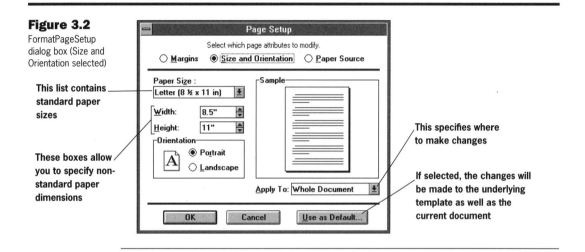

This list contains standard paper sizes

These boxes allow you to specify non-standard paper dimensions

This specifies where to make changes

If selected, the changes will be made to the underlying template as well as the current document

On this screen you can alter the page size specification for the document and determine whether the document will be sent to the printer in portrait or landscape orientation.

New to version 2.0 of Word for Windows is the ability to mix portrait and landscape in the same document. You can easily see an example of mixed portrait and landscape by clicking on the toolbar's envelope icon and selecting Add to Document. This command inserts a landscape section that contains the envelope data at the beginning of the document.

## Paper Source

The third button on the FormatPageSetup dialog box, Paper Source, is useful if you want the first page of a document to be fed from a different paper tray than the rest. This option is illustrated in Figure 3.3.

A good example of this would be a multipage letter where the first page needs to be printed on letterhead stationery, but the rest of the pages do not. In such a case you might want to feed the first page manually and subsequent pages from the default tray.

The paper source options listed for first page and other pages depend entirely on which printer you have installed. For example, if you have a laser printer installed, you will see Default Tray, Upper Tray, Manual Feed, and Envelope.

**Figure 3.3**
FormatPageSetup
dialog box (Paper
Source selected)

The contents of
these lists will
vary according
to your printer's
capability

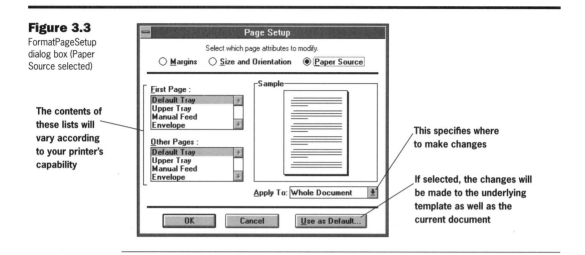

This specifies where
to make changes

If selected, the changes will
be made to the underlying
template as well as the
current document

## Summary: Layout Notes

Layout changes are saved with the document. You can optionally alter the underlying template, as discussed in Chapter 2, by selecting Use as Default. Note that all three of these layout characteristics—Margins, Size and Orientation, and Paper Source—can be applied either to the entire document, or to a portion of the document. How Word defines the possible divisions listed in the Apply To drop-down list depends upon the nature of the current insertion point.

| Insertion Point Position | Apply To Options |
| --- | --- |
| A blinking bar insertion point in a document consisting of a single section | Whole Document, This Point Forward |
| A blinking bar insertion point in a multisection document | This Section, Whole Document, This Point Forward |
| A solid selection marks a block of text | Whole Document, Selected Text |
| A solid selection marks a block of text and spans multiple sections | Selected Sections, Whole Document |

In the case where your choice is This Point Forward, Word will insert a section break before the insertion point. If your choice is either Selected Text or Selected Sections, Word will insert a section break before and after the current selection.

By default Word inserts a section break that also moves the selected text to the next page. For Size and Orientation and Paper Source this is a necessity (since the actual nature of the printing changes). For example, if you wanted a given section of text printed in landscape, you would do the following:

1. Select the text in question.

2. Select Format, Page Setup, Size and Orientation (Alt+T-U-S).

3. Press Alt+L to select the landscape option button.

4. Press Alt+A to move to the Apply To list.

5. Select Selected Text from the drop-down list.

The above example requires that Word move the selected text to a discrete page. However, margin settings can be mixed on the same page. For example, suppose you wanted a specific block of text in the middle of a page to have unique left and right margin settings. You would do the following:

1. Select the text to receive unique margins.

2. Select Format, Page Setup, Margins (Alt+T-U-M).

3. Press Alt+L to move to the left margin edit box and enter a new measurement.

4. Press Alt+A to move to the Apply To list.

5. Select Selected Text from the drop-down list.

This inserts two new section breaks, one before and one after the text in question. However, by default these section breaks also specify page breaks. To change them from Next Page to Continuous section breaks:

1. Select Format, Section Layout (Alt+T-S).

2. Select Continuous from the drop-down list.

3. Move to the next section and repeat steps 1 and 2.

If you toggle into page view by selecting View, Page Layout, you will see that the selected text has new margin indents while remaining on the same page.

# Styles

If layout information is the most fundamental of the template properties, style information is the most frequently used and altered, and perhaps the most flexible. Many writers continually experiment with various fonts, various paragraph indentations, and line spacing. (It's a great way to avoid writing....)

Fortunately, Word makes it a trivial matter to alter character and paragraph characteristics, thereby saving lots of time (drat!) for the work of writing itself.

What is a *style*, exactly? A style contains information about text formatting. It gathers into one easily accessed and easily altered place information about font type, font size, attributes (such as underline or bold), paragraph indentation, line spacing, borders, shading, placement on the page (via frames), and language (French, Spanish, and so on).

In Word it is possible to never realize you are using styles. You can type directly into the program, never using any style other than Normal (the style that is applied by default). You can then manually alter the look of the text, using the Ribbon or ruler bar, to indent text and alter font attributes. But this method has several disadvantages: It takes many more keystrokes. It is likely that when you want to replicate this direct formatting in the future you will have forgotten some of the specifics. And it is much less flexible than a style. If you have a format you will use more than once, it is worth the effort to create a style.

A style allows you to define the paragraph and character attributes once, either in a document or in a template itself, and save that collection of characteristics under a meaningful name of your own choosing.

## Built-in Styles

Word for Windows contains a number of built-in styles. Whether you know it or not, all your Word documents use styles to some degree. In a new template, the number of styles visible in either the FormatStyle dialog box or the Ribbon is four.

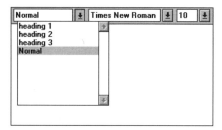

The style named Normal is the style used to format a paragraph when no other style is explicitly applied. Although the above four styles are the only ones visible when you first create a document based upon a virgin template (such as the first document ever created in Word), realize that there are 36 reserved style names. Each of these reserved styles is associated with specific functions or text types in Word. As you add elements to your document, the list of styles grows. For instance, there is a style named annotation reference and another named annotation text. These two styles will not be visible in the style list until you insert an annotation into the current document. Similarly, there are styles for indexes, footnotes, tables of contents, headers, and footers. All of the reserved styles, with the exception of Normal and Normal Indent, are listed with lowercase names. You can more easily distinguish custom styles from the built-in styles if you used mixed case names when defining a custom style. Style names are not case sensitive: specifying "body" or "Body" would apply the same style.

Style names, unlike names for macros, can contain punctuation marks and spaces. The consequence of this is that you could name all related custom styles with a given punctuation mark as the first character. This would group related styles together in the list of available styles. Styles that begin with punctuation marks will also be placed at the top of the list, since punctuation marks come before alphanumerics in alphabetized sort order.

If you would like to see a list of the reserved styles, bring up the Format-Style dialog box (Alt+T-Y), and press Ctrl+Y, followed by Alt+Down Arrow. A reserved style is added to your document's *style sheet* (a list of available styles) only when you explicitly apply that style to a paragraph or you insert an element which requires that style (such as adding a footnote). For some reason known only to a Word programmer, this list of the styles lurking in the background ready for transfer to the document does not include envelope address and envelope return. These two styles are only accessible when you include an envelope in a document.

**NOTE.** *Once a built-in style has been added to the list, it cannot be removed from the document (or template). This can be an aggravation at times, especially since it sometimes happens that the list of styles explodes to include all 36 of the built-in styles even if you have not "asked" for all 36. That is, you have not inserted all of the various functions, index levels, heading levels, and so on, that would call for including all the built-in styles in the list.*

## Custom Styles

The major difference between a custom style and a built-in style is that the user determines everything about a custom style, including name, character and paragraph attributes, and shortcut key. A custom style is not associated with a specific Word element, such as a footer. Another key difference is that a custom style can be deleted or renamed at any time.

The strategic creation and use of custom and built-in styles can greatly enhance both the process of document creation and the final product.

Because of the significance of styles, I would like to spend some time examining their various components by walking through the customization process. I will outline the steps to create a new style (named Quotation in the example) and point out concepts of significance or interest along the way. (If you are completely at ease creating and modifying styles, you might want to skim this section.)

1. Select Format, Style (either via the menu or by pressing Alt+T-Y).

2. Define a new style by pressing Alt+D to expand the dialog box to display the Define portion.

3. Type **Quotation** in the Style Name edit box. (Notice that the Change button has become Add.)

4. To change character attributes, select the Character button or press Alt+C. You will see the dialog box shown below (your specific fonts may vary).

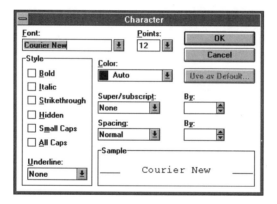

Notice that this screen controls every possible character attribute. There are attributes for emphasis (Bold, Underline, capitalization), copyediting attributes (strikethrough), super- and subscript, Spacing, and the underrated and extremely useful character attributes of Hidden (more on that shortly) and Color.

Since the Quotation style will be used to format quotations in a manuscript, the question becomes, How do we wish such a paragraph to be distinguished from normal text? One possibility would be to format a quoted paragraph in italic. (Another acceptable format would be to decrease the point size.) I like italic. Click on the Italic check box and then on OK.

5. Now press Alt+P to bring up the Paragraph formatting box. You will see the dialog box shown below.

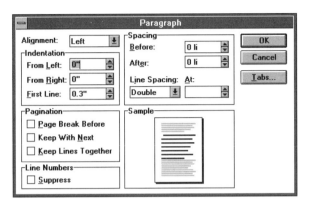

One hallmark of a quotation format is an offset from the left of half an inch; an acceptable additional distinction might be less space between lines.

6. In the From Left edit box enter **.5″**. A quotation should not have a first line indentation, so in the First Line edit box enter **0″**. Press Enter or select OK.

This is a matter of taste, but I don't like my quotations split across pages (and it makes for a better lesson), so I would suggest checking Keep Lines Together. All of the other attributes will be inherited from the Normal style.

Let us assume, for the sake of this example, that you are quoting the famous Frenchman Georges Bataille most of the time.

1. Tell Word to use the French speller and thesaurus by selecting Language from the dialog box shown below and choosing French.

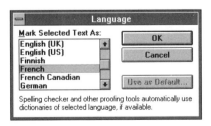

If you don't have the necessary French modules for the spell checker, thesaurus, or grammar checker, and therefore you want Word to completely skip paragraphs formatted as Quotation, you can specify no proofing from the Language dialog box.

**2.** Select OK. This will take you back to the FormatStyleDefine dialog box.

Notice that the Description box now contains the changes entered in the above steps. Also notice the two drop-down list boxes at the bottom of the dialog box: Based On and Next Style. These are extremely powerful items and deserve some explanation; they'll be covered individually in the next two sections.

### The Based On Specification

The Based On specification determines which already existing style to use as the starting point for a new style. This can be extremely useful in managing styles. By default, all new styles are based on Normal. This allows you to modify all the styles in a template by changing the characteristics of a single style (Normal). For example, to change all the styles in a document or template from Times New Roman to Arial, you would simply change that attribute in Normal.

The Based On specification can be used in more complicated ways. For instance, you might have a document that has two distinct types of paragraphs which *always* use different, contrasting, font information. A good example might be the division between body text and headlines or chapter headings, where body text always uses a Roman, serif font (New Times Roman), and headings always use a Modern, sans serif font (Arial). In this case you would define two separate "parent" styles: Body and Headings. New style variations affecting body text would be based on Body. The styles that control outline levels or other special headings would be based on Headings instead of Normal. In this way changes to the body text-associated styles would be independent of changes to heading-associated styles. The inheritance structure of such a document might look like this:

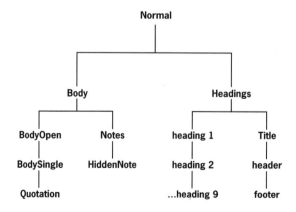

To break the link between a child style and its parent, simply go into the FormatStyle dialog box and delete the Based On style name. This renders the style autonomous.

In a complexly formatted style sheet, basing all styles on Normal quickly becomes unwieldy. The best strategy is to think through the design of a template, determine which styles are related, which should inherit attributes, which should bequeath them, and use Based On to keep the logic that is most easily altered when your design needs change (or you get that fancy new set of fonts).

### The Next Style Specification

Next Style is a feature that makes such good sense, saves so much time, and performs so logically that once you use it you can't imagine why all word processors haven't always had such a feature.

What it does is simple: It determines what happens when you press the Enter key at the end of a paragraph. If the name in the Next Style box is the same as the current style name, nothing much happens. If you are currently typing in a given style, the next paragraph is also that style. This is how most word processors work.

It's when you *change* the style in the Next Style box to something other than the current style that the power of the feature becomes evident. The best example of this feature's utility I can think of is in preparing a play script. A play consists of two types of paragraphs (for the most part): character name and dialogue. Using the Next Style feature, you could enter most of the manuscript without ever applying a style: The Next Style for Character would be Dialogue, and the Next Style for Dialogue would be Character. Every time you press Enter to start a new paragraph you automatically apply the other style.

Essentially, the Next Style feature allows you to control what style will follow the current style when you start a new paragraph. You could specify, for instance, that heading 1 be followed by heading 2 rather than Normal.

Returning to our example, let's alter the Next Style setting for the custom Quotation style.

1. Select Alt+X to move to the Next Style edit box.

2. Type **Normal** (or select Normal from the drop-down list). This will ensure that when you finish entering the quotation, and begin a new paragraph, the style will be reset to Normal. Before finishing the creation of the Quotation style, let's assign it to a shortcut key.

3. Move to the Key edit box (by pressing Alt+Y) and press Q. By default the Ctrl and Shift key modifiers are checked. The above step will assign this style to the shortcut key Ctrl+Shift+Q.

Since we will use this style in many documents based on this template, we must ensure that all the style definitions we've created are saved to the underlying template.

4. Check Add to Template.

5. Save the style information by selecting the Add button. This informs Word to save the style Quotation to the current style sheet and to the underlying template.

   The FormatStyle dialog box remains open, in the event you wish to create another style.

6. Either press Esc or select the Close button, since we do not wish to create another style. The work done in creating the Quotation style has not yet been saved to disk. Word has been informed that both the current document and the underlying template have been altered (a style has been added), but the files themselves have not yet been changed.

7. Select Save All from the File menu. You will be asked if you wish to save changes to the document. You will be asked if you wish to save changes to the underlying template. In real life (as opposed to this example) you will most likely want to respond yes to both queries.

In this example we did not touch on three of the available style options: Tabs, Frame, and Border. They will be discussed in Part III of this book.

## Styles: Miscellaneous Notes

Covering all aspects of style creation and management is beyond the scope of this chapter. Part III will continue the discussion about styles. However, here are a few useful tips:

- **Using the Ribbon**   You can also create a style via the Ribbon. With the Ribbon on, select the properly formatted paragraph, press Ctrl+S to move to the Style drop-down list box on the Ribbon, and type the new style's name. This method is quick and convenient. It has several drawbacks, however. Some of the options available on the FormatStyleDefine dialog box are not available (such as Space Before and Space After) and a style created in this way cannot be added to the template during creation. To do so, you would have to select this new style and click on Add to Template in the FormatStyleDefine dialog box.

- **Using the Color Attribute**   You may have wondered what possible function the Color attribute serves, since your printer (most likely) prints in only one color. For those of us who have not entered the multicolored-document age, this attribute still has utility. I find it useful, for instance, in delineating on-screen section marks between chapters. Used well, the Color attribute can render the structure of your document more legible as you write. I would recommend, for instance, formatting the various heading levels of an outline in different colors. You might want footnotes or annotations in contrasting colors as well.

The color attribute is also useful as a way of marking text for later use, conditional additions to your document, or important sections that you may wish to locate easily. The way to do this is simple: Settle upon a consistent color for a particular class of text, and apply it as you are typing. You can search for text of a specific color by using the EditFind command.

- **Using Hidden Characters** The Hidden character format is extremely useful. Unlike most character formatting, which is often chosen by virtue of what it will add to the final product—the printed copy of a document— hidden text can be used quite effectively to enhance the *process* of writing. For example, you might want to have an easy way to print alternate versions of the same document. In such a case you could create a style named NormalHidden, based on the Normal style and identical to it in every way save one: The new style would include the Hidden attribute. Thereafter, you could format conditional paragraphs in NormalHidden, and then print both versions of the document. (This would be controlled by the ToolsOptionsPrint dialog box, which allows you to toggle the printing of Hidden text on and off.)

Another possible use of the Hidden attribute is the creation of a paragraph style intended only for the writer of the document, a sort of note format, which would display only when desired. The use of hidden text, its advantages and its pitfalls, will be discussed at greater length in Part III.

- **Printing the Style Definitions** You can print a listing of all the style definitions in a document by selecting Styles from the drop-down list box labeled "Print:" on the FilePrint dialog box, as shown below.

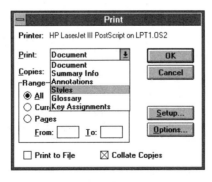

Also note that you can print glossary and key-assignment information from this menu as well.

### Style Sheets versus Templates

In desktop publishing parlance, a style sheet is a list of formatting instructions to be followed in the composition of a document. Other word processors, including Word for DOS, explicitly borrow this terminology. Word for Windows incorporates the concept of a style sheet into the object we are considering, the template. In fact, the list of styles used by a given Word document, the style sheet, resides in two places: in the template and in the document.

When a document is first created, the style sheet in the defining template is passed to the document. Then, once the document has been saved to disk, it has an independent style sheet. That is, it is possible to make changes to the styles in the document without affecting the original style sheet located in the template.

This fact, that a document's style sheet and its originating template style sheet can get out of sync, is significant. It allows you more precise control over the style characteristics of an individual document. This greater flexibility, however, has a price. It requires that you explicitly maintain synchronization if you want all documents based upon a certain template to maintain identical style sheets. (A macro named SyncStyles is included on disk to automate the process of copying style sheets from a document to a template or from a template to a document. See Chapter 10.)

In other word processors, when you attach a second style sheet to a document, it replaces the first one; the styles in the document automatically change. Not so with Word. Remember, the document inherited a style sheet from the original template, but copied that style information to its own, document-specific style sheet. Word provides a way of *merging* styles from different sources. With this facility, it is possible to write a macro that attaches a new template (giving rule to the new template's macros and access methods), and at the same time merges the styles from the template into the document's style sheet. Such a macro is included on disk as FileTemplate.

## Boilerplate Text

Boilerplate will seem a simple concept compared to the intricacies of styles. This section will give you time to catch your breath.

As discussed in Chapter 2, boilerplate is text, common to all documents of a given type, that is, all documents based upon a given template. Such template-bound boilerplate is passed from a template to any document based on that template. Boilerplate optionally includes fields and formatting instructions.

When considering the use of boilerplate text in a template, the first question to ask is this: Is there any text common to *all* documents of a given class? For instance, all letters might have the date and a salutation beginning with "Dear". The second question is: Does the amount of common text warrant setting up a template to carry that text to all subsequent documents in this class?

The most complicated thing about setting up boilerplate in a template is realizing that it must be done *before* creating a document based on that template. To create template-bound boilerplate you must edit the template directly. Unlike the template text properties discussed so far, which could be changed while in a document and optionally saved to the underlying template, boilerplate can only be inserted into the template itself.

To illustrate the use of boilerplate we'll create a new template for a memo named NEWMEMO.DOT.

## Creating a New Template

The following step-by-step instructions for creating a new template may seem basic to an experienced user. But this is such a crucial task in customizing Word, I want to make sure everyone is comfortable.

1. Select New from the File menu.

2. Press Alt+T. (This tells Word to create a new template based on the selected template, NORMAL in this case, rather than a new document.)

3. Press Enter. The result is a template that contains only the default fonts and margins.

   Had you selected a template other than NORMAL as the starting point, then you would begin, not with the defaults, but with whatever style, font, text, macro, and glossary information had been previously stored in that template.

   The title, as displayed on the Word title bar or the document title bar, should be "Template1". Like the default "Document1", this is a temporary file name.

4. Select File, Save. You will be prompted to supply a name for this template.

5. Enter **NEWMEMO**.

**NOTE.** *Notice that as soon as you save a template, Word assumes you wish to save to the directory that contains all of your other DOT files. This directory is referred to as the DOT-Path. Also note that you need not supply the file extension. Word will always save a template with the DOT extension unless you specifically tell it to do otherwise.*

Now comes the fun part: adding boilerplate.

## Entering the Text

Memos have a consistent format that includes several lines of text common to all memos. The first step in creating the boilerplate is to decide what that common text will be. You then enter it, once, and place it on the page, nicely formatted.

1. Type the phrase **Interoffice memo** as the first line in the empty template.

2. Select that phrase using the mouse or the cursor keys.

3. Press Ctrl+P, type **14**, and press Enter to change the point size to 14 points.

4. Press Ctrl+B to make the phrase bold.

5. Press Ctrl+E to center the text on the line.

6. Deselect the phrase by pressing the Right Arrow key.

7. Press Enter and Ctrl+Q, to start a new paragraph and reset it to the Normal style (that is, no longer centered).

8. Press Ctrl+P, type **12**, and press Enter to change the font size to 12 points.

9. Type **From:**, press Enter; type **To:**, press Enter; type **Date:**, press Enter; and type **Concerning:**. You should now have the boilerplate text shown in Figure 3.4.

10. Save the template.

To see how things are progressing, you might want to create a new document based on NEWMEMO. Be sure to return to NEWMEMO.DOT before proceeding with the following sections.

## Adding Headers and Footers

The most basic use of a header or a footer is as the location for page numbers. This is so frequently the only use of headers and footers that Microsoft implemented a dedicated command to place page numbers in a header or a footer (InsertPageNumbers). But it is useful to realize that what this command actually does is automate a process available under the View, Header/Footer menu.

**NOTE.** *The location of the command to create headers and footers is a little idiosyncratic. It is located on the View menu. Some would argue that logically it should be placed on the Insert menu (after all, you insert a header). In the old days of Word version 1 this command was located on the Edit menu. It's almost as if the Word programmers split the difference and decided upon the View menu.*

---

**Figure 3.4**

Stage one of
NEWMEMO.DOT

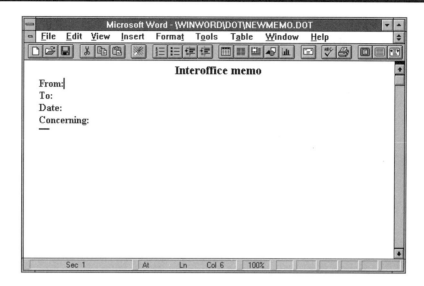

---

Our memo requires only a simple footer that displays the current page
number. To show the relation between InsertPageNumbers and ViewHeader-
Footer, let's insert the page numbers with one and examine the results with
the other. Before starting, so that we are looking at the same screen, make
sure you are in Normal View (by selecting View, Normal, Alt+V-N).

1. Select Insert, PageNumbers (Alt+I-U).

2. Press Alt+B, Alt+C to center the page number within the footer.
   Let's modify the default page number to make it a bit more informative.

3. Select View, Header/Footer (Alt+V-H).

4. Press F to highlight the Footer item in the list box, and press Enter. This
   action will open a Footer edit pane, as shown below:

**Note.** A dedicated
toolbar separates
the footer from the
body of the
document. The
functions of this
toolbar are clearly
explained in the
*Microsoft Word
User's Guide.*

You could now add text to the footer, put a period after the digit, or add
a hyphen on either side.

By default, Word compensates for multilined headers or footers. That is, if in a given section the header extends past what is defined as the top margin, Word will automatically adjust the top margin to accommodate the height of the header. If you want the header to overlap the text, that is, to freeze the top or bottom margin, simply add a minus sign in front of the margin measurement, for example, –1″ instead of 1″.

## Using Fields

To see clearly the connection between the InsertPageNumbers command and manually editing a footer, and to introduce the concept of a field, set turn Field Codes on (Press Alt+V-C).

The Footer edit pane should now look like that shown below:

The command InsertPageNumbers placed a *field* into the footer. The *field code* for the current page number is "{PAGE}". All field codes begin and end in curly braces. Fields will be covered in more depth in Chapter 11, but since they are an integral part of the customizing power of a template, the concept bears some introduction. Definition: a *field* is a special instruction, embedded into a document, which provides an easy way to automatically insert certain types of information. Often the information so inserted is variable, such as the page number or the current time. Fields are documented in Chapter 41 of the *Microsoft Word User's Guide.*

Field codes are entered in one of two ways:

- By inserting the desired field from the InsertField menu (Alt+I-D)

- By inserting the field code characters (the curly braces) by pressing Ctrl+F9 and typing the field code name directly.

To make our page number footer more informative, let's add a field that will display the total number of pages in the current document.

1. Place the insertion point at the end of the existing {PAGE} field.

2. Press spacebar, type **of**, and press spacebar again.

3. Select Insert, Field (Alt+I-D).

**4.** Press N four times. This brings you to the field named No. of pages. Note that the field code proposed is numpages.

**5.** Press Enter.

Our footer, with Field Codes on, now looks like this:

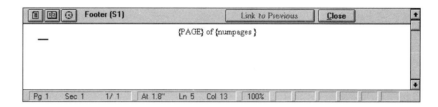

This is a useful combination of fields. It will print page numbers in the format *x* of *y*, where *x* is the current page number and *y* is the total number of pages in the document. For instance, page 2 of a four-page document will have "2 of 4" as the footer.

**6.** Now close the Footer Edit pane by pressing Alt+Shift+C (or clicking on the Close button), and we'll modify the template's boilerplate text to use fields.

**NOTE.** *It is a Windows convention that the underlined character of a command word found on a menu or a dialog box represents the speedkey. For instance, the "F" is underlined in the main File menu, and you access that menu by pressing Alt+F. However, when the command word appears on a toolbar such as the one that appears when editing a footer or macro, the underlined character is pressed in combination with Alt+Shift rather than with Alt alone.*

Fields can be used anywhere in a document, not just in headers and footers. And just as a template that contains header or footer information (including fields such as {PAGE}) will pass that information on to a document, so any boilerplate in the body of the document (including any fields) will be passed on to the document.

There are several ways in which fields can enhance our memo template. The most obvious use would be for the "Date:" line.

**1.** Place the insertion point at the end of the "Date:" line.

**2.** Press Ctrl+F9. This inserts the field code braces.

**3.** Type **date** (fields are not case-sensitive).

**4.** Press F9 to update the field.

You could also insert this field using the InsertField menu. This second method has the advantage of allowing you to alter the format in which the date will display and print. The default date format is controlled by a keyword located in WIN.INI (see Appendix B of *Microsoft Word User's Guide*).

After you insert this field into the template, any document based on this template will automatically have the current date inserted on the "Date:" line. Since {DATE} is a variable field, every time you *open or print* that document, the date will change to reflect the current date.

There are two other date fields you could use: {createdate}, which inserts the date the document was *created*, and {printdate}, which inserts a variable field that is updated with the current date at the time of *printing*.

Another obvious candidate for automation with a field is the "From:" line. You could simply type your name into the boilerplate. But that would lock the template's utility to your particular use. To generalize the "From:" line so that it could be used, for instance, by anyone in your office, you would use the {author} field. This field inserts the current author information exactly as it is entered in the Name field of the ToolsOptionsUserInfo dialog box.

## Using Bookmarks in a Template

Word provides a simple and elegant way to insert a placeholder into a document. Bookmarks are underrated and extremely useful.

Even if you are familiar with bookmarks, you may not realize that they can also be inserted into a template. For instance, in our NEWMEMO.DOT, we could mark the start of the actual memo with a bookmark named StartHere, as follows:

1. Enter a blank line after "Concerning:".

2. Select Insert, Bookmark (Alt+I-M).

3. Type **StartHere**, and press Enter.

A similar bookmark could be created for each of the boilerplate lines.

The reason for placing a bookmark in a template may not be obvious at first glance. The simplest example of a template bookmark's use is creating a new document based on that template, and then immediately moving the insertion point to the point where text editing is to begin. To do this you would press F5 twice, to bring up a list of bookmarks. Selecting StartHere and pressing Enter would move the insertion point to the beginning of the memo.

However, the real cleverness of template bookmarks, and in fact of the fields inserted in the previous section, is most evident when they are combined with a macro.

## Recording an AutoNew Macro for NEWMEMO.DOT

This is getting a little ahead of ourselves, but let's create a macro so that whenever a new memo is created two things happen: All fields are updated, and the insertion point is moved to the beginning of the memo. Don't panic. This particular macro can be created without knowing a thing about WordBASIC; it can be created using only the macro recorder.

1. First, save all changes made to NEWMEMO.DOT.
2. Then create a new document based on NEWMEMO.DOT.
3. Select FileTemplate and press Alt+T. (What this does is ensure that all glossaries and recorded macros will be stored with the template rather than in NORMAL.DOT.)
4. Turn on the macro recorder by selecting Tools, RecordMacro (Alt+O-R).
5. Name the macro to be recorded **AutoNew**, and press Enter. You are now in Record mode. Notice the "REC" that displays on the status line.
6. Select the entire document by pressing Ctrl+NumPad5.
7. Update all fields by pressing F9.
8. Press F5 twice. This should display a list of all bookmarks.
9. Select StartHere, and press Enter.
10. Turn off the macro recorder by selecting Tools, StopRecorder (Alt+O-R).
11. Save the macro to the template by selecting File, SaveAll. (You will be prompted to save the new document, but that's optional. You must, however, answer Yes when asked if you wish to save changes to NEWMEMO.DOT.)

You have just created a useful macro that will be run every time you create a new memo based upon NEWMEMO.DOT. The fact that the macro was named AutoNew is what tells Word to execute it every time a new document is created based on the template. If you examine the macro, you will see that the macro recorder inserted a single instruction for each function executed. The "source code" for this simple macro is the following:

```
Sub Main
EditSelectAll
UpdateFields
EditGoto .Destination = "StartHere"
End Sub
```

EditSelectAll corresponds to pressing Ctrl+NumPad5. UpdateFields corresponds to pressing F9. EditGoTo .Destination = "StartHere" corresponds to pressing F5 twice and selecting StartHere.

Having created this AutoNew macro, which automatically updates all fields and then moves to the start of the memo, you can now add any of a number of other field codes that would further automate the creation of a new memo.

For instance, you might insert a {FILLIN} field on the "To:" and "Concerning:" lines. The {FILLIN} field pops up a small edit box that includes a text description. So, for example, the field code {FILLIN "Enter who this is to:"}, when updated, will display the following dialog box:

You can use a field code to enter the same information in two places at once. For instance, if you inserted the nested field (*nested* meaning there is a field within a field)

{subject{fillin "What does this memo concern?"}}

both in the document and in the Subject field of the FileSummaryInfo command, the response would be inserted in both of those places.

## Summary

In this chapter we have discussed three of the six properties stored in a template: layout, styles, and boilerplate. We have shown how changes to the first two can, optionally, be saved to the underlying template. We have explored editing the template directly to alter the default text (including text generated by fields), which will be passed on to subsequent documents based on the template. And finally, and briefly, we have shown how an AutoNew macro can be used to enhance and automate the utility of these default template properties.

Another way of looking at these three aspects of a template is to consider that they are stored in the template *until a document is created.* Once a document is created based on the template, these properties are, in effect, copied into the document itself.

By contrast, the template properties discussed in the next chapter—properties that can rightly be viewed as changing the interface that Word presents to the user—do not live in the document at all. They are stored in the template, travel with the template, and are never copied into the document. If the underlying template is replaced by another, then these properties, what you might call interface properties, will change to those contained in the new template.

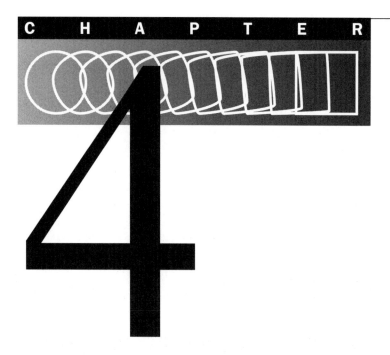

# Interface Properties

I N THIS CHAPTER WE WILL EXAMINE THREE INTERFACE PROPERTIES THAT CAN be stored in a template: macros, access methods to macros (command or user), and glossaries. The customizations discussed in the previous chapter provided guidelines for the layout and formatting of *what* you enter into Word; the customizations described in this chapter affect *how* you enter text into Word. They alter the interface Word presents to the user.

## A Deeper Look at Context

Chapter 1 introduced the concept of a macro and posited that every editing command in Word possesses a corresponding built-in command macro. Further, we discussed the fact that every command possesses two parts: the macro itself and the manner in which that macro is accessed. To illustrate the creation of access methods, examples were given for each type: keyboard, menu, and toolbar. In those examples the access method was created and saved when the ruling template was NORMAL.DOT. It is also significant that none of those examples created a new user-macro. The examples modified (through access methods) built-in command macros.

The next step is to understand two key ideas:

- User-macros, whether created by recording, editing, or a combination of both, *can be template specific.*

- Access method modifications (keyboard shortcuts, menu items, and toolbar icons) affecting either command macros or user-macros can also be specific to a given template.

By template specific I mean the following: The modifications to how Word works—whether it be the availability of a macro itself, or the particular access method created to execute a macro—will only be available *when working on a document based on the template holding the modification.* Put another way: template modifications possess a *context.*

Before going on to examples of the three interface properties that can be stored in a template, let's explore further this idea of where modifications are stored, and when those modifications are available.

### Global versus Local Context

As stated above, every document in Word is based on a template. This is somewhat obscured by the fact that often a document is created for you, for instance, if you start Word without any other command-line parameter, or if you click on the FileNewDefault icon on the toolbar. But it is important to realize that such documents *are* based on a template. They are based on the template named NORMAL.DOT. There is some confusion in terminology because although the template is referred to as "normal," changes that are saved to this template are sometimes, as in the dialog box shown in Figure 4.1, referred to as "global."

---

**Figure 4.1**

FileTemplate dialog box

---

For simplicity's sake, in future, a document based on NORMAL.DOT will be referred to as a *normal based document.* A document based on any template other than NORMAL.DOT will be referred to as *template based.*

The interface properties stored in NORMAL.DOT, that is, the global interface properties, are available at all times. This is the unique feature of NORMAL.DOT. Customizations stored globally are available *even if you don't have a document based on NORMAL.DOT loaded at all.* For example, the changes made to NORMAL.DOT in Chapter 1 would be available even if the only document you had loaded and active was a document based upon NEWMEMO.DOT.

By contrast, if we were to create a customization and store it in the local context defined by NEWMEMO.DOT, those modifications would be available *only when a document based upon NEWMEMO.DOT was the active document.*

To illustrate this concept, let's examine the FileTemplate command. Select Template from the File menu (Alt+F-T). You will see the FileTemplate dialog box shown in Figure 4.1.

This is the command used to change the template associated with the current document. But of special interest here are the three option buttons grouped beneath the heading "Store New Macros and Glossaries as." Any choice made from among these three option buttons is a global setting. It is saved from session to session, and remains in effect until explicitly changed. This setting controls where recorded macros and glossaries are stored.

In my opinion there should be only two choices. The first option—Global—to store all new macros and glossaries globally (in NORMAL.DOT and available to all documents) is dangerous. It encourages bad habits. Unless all of your documents are of a single type you should be encouraged to learn about templates. Having an option to store everything globally encourages an overdependence upon NORMAL.DOT, and might obscure the benefits of templates. Climbing down from the soapbox, I will explain the other two options.

When the second option—With Document Template—is active, all new recorded macros and defined glossaries will be placed in the active template. If NORMAL.DOT is currently the ruling template, the customization will be stored globally. If any other template is active, the macro or glossary will be marked for storage in that template. This might lead to some confusion if you are not already familiar with templates.

The third option—Prompt for Each New—is the most flexible, and, in fact, the most instructive. It is flexible because the user is prompted for the location of each item at the time of its creation. It is instructive because it continually reminds the user that there are two contexts available: global and local. Until you have organized your templates properly, and understand precisely the consequences of storing modifications in them, I would recommend using this third setting.

## Global versus Template Macros

Now it's time to get down to cases and demonstrate the power of template specific customizations, and the extraordinary flexibility that Word provides in its combination of macros, access methods, templates, and context.

To best illustrate these aspects of Word, I propose to step through, once again, the recording of a macro and the creation of an access method. We will create a similar macro in both the global and template contexts and show how the same keystroke can be made to perform a different task dependent upon the location of the insertion point, that is, depending upon its context.

Open two documents, one based upon NORMAL.DOT and one based upon the NEWMEMO.DOT created in Chapter 3. Select Window Arrange All to position the two documents for easy access.

The first step in creating a macro is deciding upon the task to be accomplished. I could now propose a simplistic and useless example, but what would be the fun in that? The examples in this book will strive for utility as well as insight. Even if they are not specifically suited to your needs, they should be easily adaptable. So, let's recall the basic definition of a macro: a series of actions gathered under a single, easily accessible command. One criterion for nomination to macro status is that the series of actions is often repeated. I posit the following, not uncommon, situation:

- You want a standard method for emphasizing a word. For instance, all technical terms should be formatted as Arial 12 point bold italic.

- This attribute will be applied to words or phrases, not to paragraphs, so the creation of a style does not solve the problem.

- This attribute will be the same no matter what the font used for body text.

- The actions involved are applying the font Arial, specifying 12 point type, turning on bold, and turning on italic.

Word does not currently support character styles. That is, styles define both paragraph and character attributes. There is no provision for storing only character attributes under a style name that might be applied only to a portion of a paragraph. To accomplish what is proposed in this example would require a complex sequence of keystrokes—Ctrl+F, Arial, Enter, Ctrl+P, 12, Enter, Ctrl+B, Ctrl+I—or an equivalent number of menu choices or mouse clicks. The solution, once revealed, is simple: Record a macro.

### A Global Macro

In this example we will record a macro that will turn on various character attributes, assign the macro to a keyboard access method, and save the changes globally.

1. With the focus on the normal based document (that is, the insertion point idling in the document based upon NORMAL.DOT), turn on the macro recorder by pressing Alt+O-R. You will be presented with the following dialog box:

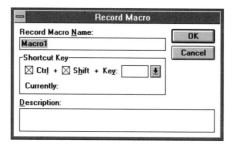

2. Type **SpecialBold** as the macro name.

3. Press Alt+Y to move to the Key edit box and press Z. (I propose Ctrl+Shift+Z as the shortcut key because it is not reserved by Word and is unlikely to be in use.)

4. Press Alt+D to move to the Description edit box. This allows you to enter a phrase describing the macro. This is a good habit to form, as

macro descriptions become increasingly useful the more you use macros. Type **Turns on Arial bold italic 12 pt**.

5. Press Enter or click on OK.

   You are now back in the document. If you have the status bar visible, you will see the phrase REC displayed in the penultimate recessed box. This indicates that you are in Record mode. Every action now performed will be recorded and stored in the macro named SpecialBold.

6. Press Ctrl+F, type **Arial**, and press Enter. This changes the current font to Arial.

7. Press Ctrl+P, type **12**, and press Enter. This changes the current point size to 12.

8. Turn on bold by pressing Ctrl+B.

9. Turn on italic by pressing Ctrl+I.

10. Turn off the macro recorder by pressing Alt+O-R.

   To test the SpecialBold macro:

1. Press Ctrl+spacebar to reset the character attributes to normal.

2. Press Ctrl+Shift+Z and type a phrase.

This simple grouping of formatting actions, gathered in the macro named SpecialBold, will reappear in a later chapter. We will be able to make it significantly smarter when we explore the WordBasic programming language and move from recording to editing macros. But for now it will do to demonstrate the principle of context.

We recorded the above macro in the global context, that is, in a document based upon NORMAL.DOT. When you select FileSaveAll, this macro will be saved to disk in the NORMAL.DOT template. It will be available for every document you load or create. To demonstrate this, move the insertion point to the other document, the one based upon NEWMEMO.DOT, select a word, and press Ctrl+Shift+Z. However, there is a circumstance where this new macro will not be available: *if there is a contravening macro named SpecialBold.*

## A Template Macro

To demonstrate what happens if there are competing versions of a macro in the global and the template context, let us assume that the above definition of special bold is appropriate to every class of documents you can imagine creating *except* a memo. With the focus in the document based on NEWMEMO.DOT, repeat steps 1-5 above. Note that since the active document is based upon a

template other than NORMAL.DOT, you are given a choice as to where to
store the macro (assuming you followed my advice and chose the third option
in FileTemplate; see "Global versus Local" above). You should see the following dialog box:

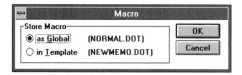

To store this version of SpecialBold in NEWMEMO.DOT rather than
NORMAL.DOT, press Alt+T and Enter. Repeat steps 6-8 above, and then
turn off the macro recorder.

The difference between the global version of SpecialBold and the NEW-
MEMO.DOT version of SpecialBold is that the latter does not apply italics.
To appreciate the consequence of this, and to illustrate the idea of context,
move between the two open documents and execute SpecialBold in each.

1. Press Ctrl+spacebar to reset the character attributes to normal.

2. Press Ctrl+Shift+Z and type a phrase.

In the normal based document the phrase will appear as Arial bold italic 12
point. In the template based document it will appear as Arial bold 12 point.

## Summary: On Context

In addition to creating a macro that may prove useful in your own work, the
above example demonstrates two significant concepts:

■ If there is a macro of the same name in both the global and the template
context, which version of the macro is executed depends upon the location of the insertion point when you call the macro.

■ The same access method—be it keyboard, menu, or toolbar—can perform a different action depending upon the location (the context) of the
insertion point.

It should be clear by now why this aspect of a template—the ability to
store template specific macros—is called an *interface property*. In the above
example a new command and a new keystroke shortcut were added to Word.
We have changed the way the program works. And, most significantly, we
have demonstrated how such a change can be tailored specifically to a class of
documents (all memos) while leaving the interface to all other documents
untouched.

# Creating Custom Access Methods

In the above example we created a keyboard access method when we recorded the two versions of SpecialBold. This power was skimmed over. But its importance should not be underestimated.

In the same way that you can have template-specific text attributes or template-specific macros, you can have template-specific access methods.

In customizing Word to provide the most efficient arrangement of keystroke shortcuts, menu items, and toolbar icons, the following principles should be applied:

- Create a template that will rule a class of documents—for instance, a template for letters, one for memos, one for novels, and one for screenplays.

- Decide what common actions this class of documents calls for repeatedly.

- Decide what functions should be most easily available.

- Decide which of those frequently used functions should be grouped on the menu, which on the toolbar, and which assigned easily remembered keystroke shortcuts.

These same principles should be used when determining how to group styles and macros. Another way of phrasing the question is: Which documents have what in common; are there sufficient similar requirements that will be used frequently enough to warrant gathering the associated styles, macros, access methods, and glossaries into a ruling template?

## Customizing the Toolbar

To illustrate the concept of a context-specific customization more visually, let's make a single change to the toolbar in NEWMEMO.DOT. In the default toolbar the 17th tool is an envelope icon. This tool calls the built-in command macro named ToolsCreateEnvelope. It is unlikely that we will ever be mailing a memo. This button could be put to better use as an access method to a more frequently used function that has a specific value to the class of documents based upon NEWMEMO.DOT.

One candidate for placement on our memo's toolbar might be the macro that calls the thesaurus. To customize the toolbar associated with all memos based upon NEWMEMO.DOT:

1. Make sure the focus is on a NEWMEMO-based document.

2. Select ToolsOptionsToolbar (Alt+O-O-T). The ToolsOptionsToolbar dialog box is described in Figure 4.2.

**Figure 4.2**

ToolsOptionsToolbar
dialog box

List of current toolbar buttons and
associated macros

Scrollable list
of customizable
options

Options buttons
that determine
which macros
to display

Reset current
tool to default

Reset all tools
to default

Option buttons
that determine
the context of
modifications

Scrollable list of
105 toolbar icons

List of macros available for
assignment to the toolbar

Description of the currently
selected macro

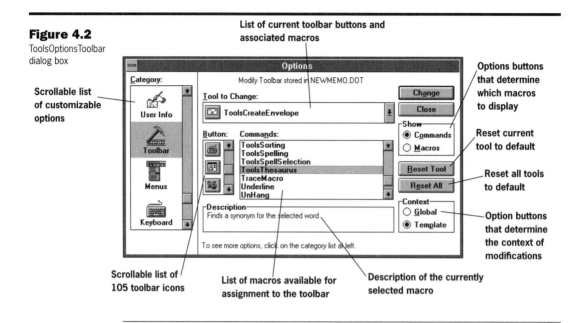

**3.** Press Alt+T to open the list of tools. Think of this as choosing a position on the toolbar. What you will see in this list is the *current button/macro combination that is assigned to that position.*

**4.** Find the envelope icon/ToolsCreateEnvelope item in the Tool to Change drop-down list.

**5.** Press Alt+B to move to the list of buttons/icons (Microsoft calls them buttons, but they are icons).

Let's pause to consider this list of icons. There are 105 icons. The toolbar is new to Word, and the implementation leaves many things to be desired. Foremost among the deficiencies is that you cannot create new icons nor can you modify existing icons. If you browse through this list of button faces, you might be struck by the obscurity of some icons (the microphone , for instance, or the flowchart ), or by the triviality of others (such as the smiley face  or the piggy bank ). None of them stands out as appropriate for our task, an icon that will represent the thesaurus. The closest is 64th in the list. It looks like a dialog box.

**6.** Find and highlight the 64th icon in the list of buttons. It looks like: 

**7.** Press Alt+O so that the built-in command macros are displayed in the list of macros.

The two option buttons in the Show box are both instructive and infuriating. They are instructive because they go to the heart of a significant distinction: that between a command macro and a user-macro. They infuriate me because they do not make the further distinction between global user-macros and template user-macros. For consistency's sake there should be three buttons available in this group: commands, global macros, and template macros.

While we are paused it is worth noting that you can assign a template-specific access method (in this case a toolbar button) to a global macro. That is, the macro to be executed need only be available, whether it is available because it is global or available because it is in the same template as the access method customization is of no consequence.

**8.** Press Alt+N to move to the list of commands ("command macros" in our parlance).

**9.** Locate ToolsThesaurus and select it.

**10.** Press Alt+A to make the toolbar assignment.

**11.** Click on Close to remove the dialog box.

Since changing the toolbar actually changes the visual interface presented to the user, it is useful in graphically illustrating the concept of context. To change the toolbar, select WindowArrangeAll to place the two open documents one atop the other. Now, using the mouse or Ctrl+F6, move between the documents. Notice (see Figure 4.3A) that when the focus is in the normal based document the envelope tool is active; when the focus is the template based memo, the envelope tool changes to our customized toolbar access method for the thesaurus (see Figure 4.3B).

This example points out an exceptional aspect of Word's customization strategy: Several different sets of customizations can be potentially operative at any one time; which is actually operative depends entirely upon the context, upon which template rules the document in which the insertion point is located.

Before moving on to adding and altering menus and keyboard shortcuts, here are a few notes about working with the toolbar.

There are a set number of tool (or icon) positions. Even if you have a high-resolution monitor, and there would seem to be space for more than 30 toolbar icons, you are limited to 30.

Some of the 30 positions on the toolbar are occupied by spaces. When you examine the current toolbar using ToolsOptionsToolbar, you will see that some tools are listed as [space]. You can replace these spaces in the toolbar with other icons and then associate the icon with a macro. Similarly, you will notice that the first macro listed, no matter which macro context is selected, is also named [space]. This allows you to replace the currently selected tool with a space. This is useful in grouping related tools together.

**Figure 4.3**

Icons change to
reflect the change in
focus

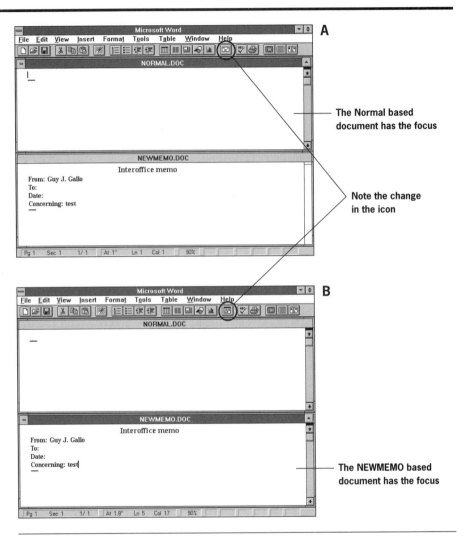

**A**

The Normal based
document has the focus

Note the change
in the icon

**B**

The NEWMEMO based
document has the focus

There is no simple way to insert a tool into the toolbar. This is a glaring limitation in the toolbar implementation. For instance, I often use the SaveAll option from the File menu. I therefore wanted to assign the macro FileSaveAll to the toolbar, and wanted it to be next to the FileSave tool (the disk). But I wanted to keep the space (that is, I didn't want to replace the fourth position, a space, with the new icon, I wanted to place a new icon between positions three and four). To do so requires that you move all the subsequent tools, from position 5 to 30. This is such an arduous task as to make inserting a tool at the beginning of the toolbar impracticable.

However, proving the point of this book's utility, there is a way to do such an insertion "automagically" with a custom macro. I have written a macro, named ChangeTool, which is included on disk, and will be documented in Appendix G. If you are comfortable with macros, you might want to give it a test drive.

The two buttons at the middle right of the ToolsOptionsToolbar (see Figure 4.2) deserve some comment:

- *Reset Tool* resets the currently selected tool to the current normal tool for that position. If you are modifying a template toolbar, it removes the template customization and allows the normal toolbar icon for that position to show through. If you are modifying the global toolbar, it resets the current position to the default for that tool (as Word comes out of the box).

- *Reset All* is a dangerous option. It does just what it says and resets all the tools on the toolbar to whatever the default would be: If you are in a template, it resets to the NORMAL.DOT toolbar; if you are in a normal based document, it resets to the factory defaults. This is dangerous because it is quite possible to unwittingly remove many hours of complex customizing with the click of a mouse. Fortunately, Word prompts you to confirm such a drastic measure. Use with extreme caution.

You will also notice that at the lower right of the dialog box there are two option buttons specifying which toolbar to modify, the global or the template. If you are in a normal document (and therefore there is no template context) the template option will be grayed. This allows you to alter the global toolbar at all times.

If you customize the global toolbar, those customizations will provide the basis for all template toolbars. Think of it this way: If the global tool at position three has been changed, and the local tool at position three has not, then the global customization shows through. If, on the other hand, there is a customized tool at position three in the local template, it takes precedence over the global customization when the template toolbar has rule.

## Customizing the Menu Structure

The menu structure presented to the user is the most frequently used interface. It is also the one access method that many people think of as immutable. Many other programs allow redefining keyboard shortcuts, but very few programs allow you to change the content of their menu system. Modifying which items appear on Word's menu structure should be done cautiously.

(See Figure 4.4 for a graphic description of the ToolsOptionsMenus dialog box.)

**Figure 4.4**

ToolsOptionsMenus dialog box

Scrollable list of customizable options

Drop-down list of the nine top menus; the current selection is the menu being modified

Remove the current item from the menus

Option buttons which determine which macros to display, command or user

Reset all menu items to their defaults

Option buttons which determine the context of modifications

List of the current submenu text descriptions; the edit portion of the combo box contains the current item's text

Description of the currently selected macro

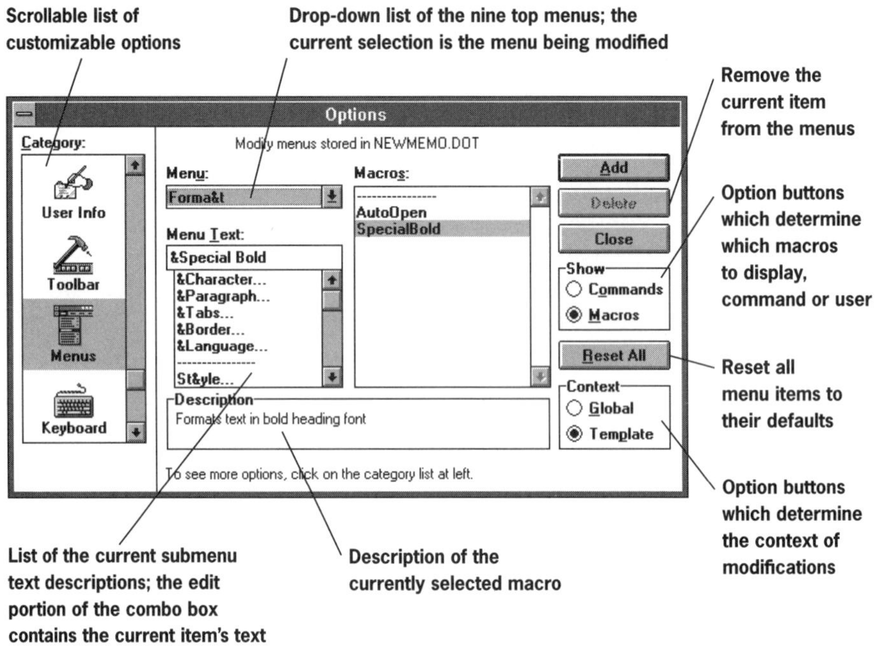

Here is a list of considerations:

- Additions made to the global menu structure will be available in all templates unless they are specifically removed from the template's menu structure.

  For example, if you followed the example in Chapter 2 and added View Preferences to the View menu, that item will be available in a document based upon NEWMEMO.DOT unless you explicitly delete it from the template menu.

- The menu items contained in the default menu, what you might call the *alpha menu*, can be removed.

  This capacity might prove useful if you are customizing a template for a specific use, or for a person who does not want to see all of Word's options. Removing a basic command, at first glance, might seem scary. Where does it go? How do you get it back? The underlying command macro is not removed, it is only removed from the menu. Resetting the

menu is simply a matter of reassigning the command macro to the appropriate menu. Note: Unlike the toolbar customization dialog box, the
menu dialog box does not have a "reset menu item" button. Rather it has
Delete (to remove) and Add (to assign). ToolsOptionsMenus does have
a Reset All button, which can remove all menu assignments (as discussed
above).

- Additional commands, which reference either built-in command macros
  or user-macros, can be added to the bottom of any of the nine top-level
  menus.

It is a good practice to add a divider before adding a new menu item.
Also, as with the toolbar, realize that you can add a template-specific
menu item to access a global macro.

When you select a macro for placement on a menu, Word automatically
suggests the menu text by parsing the macro's name at capitals. The resulting phrase may be nonsense. Be sure to edit the Menu Text to reflect
the macro's function, placing the speedkey marker (the ampersand) at a
location in the phrase that will produce a mnemonic and non-conflicting
speedkey.

- There is, however, a limitation regarding placement: New menu items always gravitate to the bottom of a menu; the alpha menu items always
  gravitate to their default positions.

There is an awkward way around this limitation. Since the alpha menu
items (such as FileOpen or FileSave) automatically move to their default
positions, the only way to insert a custom menu item above an alpha
menu item is to create a user-macro that calls the built-in command. For
instance, if you wanted to insert a macro before FileExit, you would have
to create a user-macro that executed the built-in command macro, and
name it DoFileExit. Then you could remove FileExit from the menu, assign your user-macro to the file menu, and assign DoFileExit as the last
item on the file menu. This solution is acceptable if the number of command macros to be moved in this manner is small. But if you wanted to
put your user macro at the top of the file menu, for instance, you'd have
to create 14 such DoMacroName macros. Very ugly.

- It is not possible, as it is in Excel, to add an additional top-level menu.
  You can, however, through the macro language, rename any of the top-
  level menus.

At all video resolutions there seems to be sufficient room for a custom
top-level menu item between Window and Help. Unfortunately, the designers of Word did not include this ability. And the potentially useful

work-around they did allow, renaming a top-level menu, has a severe limitation.

It is possible to include a WordBasic command in an auto-executing macro that would, for instance, rename Tools to Options. However, this solution involves the following limitation: If you change Tools to Options in NEWMEMO.DOT, it is changed for every other open document as well. That is to say, renaming a top-level menu does not follow the paradigm of context-specific customization. Renaming a top-level menu is always and unchangeably global. In my mind that limitation renders the capability impracticable in all but the most specific of cases.

## Customizing the Keyboard

Word comes with a default set of keystroke shortcuts to access frequently used functions. But like virtually everything else in Word, you can alter existing key assignments and add new key assignments to access either command or user-macros. Like the other modifications discussed in the foregoing sections, these keyboard modifications can be either global or template specific.

This capability should be approached with caution. For one thing, suppose you alter the standard keyboard access methods for built-in commands (for instance, I've switched FileSave and FileSaveAs—by default the former is Shift+F12, the latter F12; I use the former more frequently, so I've defined it as the unshifted function key). Any other user not clued-in to your preferences will be at a loss to understand why nothing works. For another, the keyboard template supplied with Word and the keyboard charts in the manual will no longer reflect the reality of your setup.

**NOTE.** *Any macro (command or user) can have multiple keyboard shortcuts assigned to it at the same time. This brings up a limitation, however: Although the menu item for a macro will automatically display that macro's associated keystroke combination, it will only display the first such shortcut.*

Word allows for keyboard customization in three ways:

■ When you create or modify a style you can also define a shortcut keyboard combination to access that style.

■ When you record a new macro you can define a shortcut keyboard combination to access that macro.

■ You can use the ToolsOptionsKeyboard dialog box to add a new keyboard shortcut or remove an existing shortcut. This third method applies only to macros. To remove a style keyboard shortcut you must do so in the FormatStylesDefine dialog box. The ToolsOptionsKeyboard dialog box is described in Figure 4.5.

**Figure 4.5**
ToolsOptionsKeyboard
dialog box

Scrollable list of
customizable options

A list box of available keys,
modified by check boxes

Adds a new
assignment

Removes
an existing
assignment

Option buttons
which determine
which macro
to display

Reset all key
assignments
in the current
context to
defaults

Option buttons
which determine
the context for
modifications

The current (if any) key
assignment for the
currently selected macro

List of macros available
for key assignment. The
first existing key shortcut
(if any) is listed to the right

```
┌─────────────────────────────────────────────────────────────┐
│ ─                          Options                            │
│ Category:          Modify key assignments stored in NEWMEMO.DOT    │
│  ┌──┐┌─┐   ┌Shortcut Key──────────────────────┐   ┌─────────┐ │
│  │🖌️││↑│   │ ☒ Ctrl + ☒ Shift + Key: [    ] ↓│   │   Add   │ │
│  │  ││ │   │ Currently:                        │   ├─────────┤ │
│  User Info └──────────────────────────────────┘   │ Delete  │ │
│  ┌──┐      Macros:                                 ├─────────┤ │
│  │⚒️│      ┌──────────────────────────────┐↑      │  Close  │ │
│  │  │      │ AutoOpen                     │        └─────────┘ │
│  Toolbar   │ SpecialBold        Ctrl+Shift+Z │    ┌Show──────┐ │
│  ┌──┐      │                              │        │ ○ Commands│ │
│  │📇│      │                              │        │ ⦿ Macros  │ │
│  │  │      └──────────────────────────────┘↓      └──────────┘ │
│  Menus     Current Keys For: SpecialBold          ┌ Reset All ┐│
│  ┌──┐      ┌──────────────────────────────┐↑      └───────────┘│
│  │⌨️│↓    │ Ctrl+Shift+Z                 │        ┌Context───┐ │
│  │  │      │                              │↓       │ ○ Global  │ │
│  Keyboard  └──────────────────────────────┘        │ ⦿ Template│ │
│              To see more options, click on the category list at left. └─────────┘ │
└─────────────────────────────────────────────────────────────┘
```

You may have noticed a similarity among the three dialog boxes associated with these three facilities (FormatStylesDefine, ToolsRecordMacro, and ToolsOptionsKeyboard). They all present a box labeled Shortcut Key such as:

This Shortcut Key edit box provides an easy access to those key combinations that have been reserved for macros and styles. More precisely, you can easily assign a style or a macro to A-Z, 0-9, F1-F12, Ins, and Del modified by the Ctrl key, the Shift key, or the Ctrl+Shift keys in combination. Available key combinations will be noted as [unassigned]. You are protected from assigning a macro to an illegal combination (such as the shifted alphanumerics or the Help key, F1), and you are warned if a previous assignment has already been made to your proposed shortcut (the current assignment will be displayed to the right of the word "Currently").

**Note.** You can print all the user-defined key assignments for the current context by selecting FilePrint and selecting Key Assignments in the Print drop-down list.

Although this method of assigning a keystroke is the most convenient, it is not the most powerful. You can directly modify the keyboard access method for a given macro using the macro language. This fourth way to modify the keyboard is the most flexible, in that you can choose from a wider range of key combinations. In addition to Ctrl and Ctrl+Shift modifiers, you can also access Alt, Alt+Shift, Alt+Ctrl, and even Alt+Ctrl+Shift in combination with alphanumeric, function, and direction keys. This significantly increases the number of possible shortcut keys. The WordBasic command to assign a keyboard shortcut to a macro will be discussed in Chapter 7. And a specialized (and complicated) macro named MacroKey is included on disk and will be documented in Appendix G.

## Using Glossaries

The last item that qualifies as an interface property of a template is a glossary. Like macros and access methods, glossaries travel with the template. Unlike styles and layout information, they are not transferred to the document.

Essentially, there are three types of glossaries:

- Special characters or symbols

- Phrases used frequently in a given class of documents, such as addresses and book titles

- Extended passages of text, such as boilerplate held at the ready for insertion

You can also store pictures and fields in a glossary.

A glossary should be thought of as a special storage place where you can place frequently used text items or larger passages. One of my favorite uses for the glossary is as a temporary storage location for edits. Often, while composing a document, I will place conditional text, sentences that haven't quite passed muster, into a glossary with a long and descriptive abbreviation (such as "TheJunkFromChapterOne").

The rule of thumb, of course, is: The more frequently you foresee using a glossary the shorter the mnemonic abbreviation should be.

### Defining a Glossary

Defining a glossary couldn't be simpler.

1. Type the text to be saved as a glossary.

2. Format the text with the desired attributes (bold, underline, and so on).

3. Select the text to be saved.

4. Select Glossary from the Edit menu (Alt+E-O). Word will present the following dialog box:

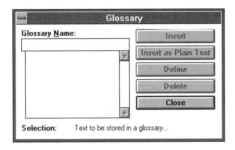

5. Type the desired mnemonic abbreviation and press Alt+D to define the glossary.

6. Press Right Arrow to unselect the text just stored as a glossary entry.

**NOTE.** *If you are working on a template based document at the time of the glossary creation, the storage location for the glossary will depend on the File-Template setting (discussed earlier in this chapter under "Global versus Local Context").*

If a glossary entry already exists for the proposed abbreviation, you will be asked if you want to redefine the existing glossary entry.

For example, if you do a great deal of correspondence with a British financial institution, you would often require the pound sterling symbol. To define such a glossary you would do the following:

1. Select Symbol from the Insert menu (Alt+I-S).

2. Select (Normal Text) in the Symbols From drop-down list.

3. Select, with the mouse or the cursor, the pound sterling symbol (row 5, column 4).

4. Select OK to insert the symbol into the current document.

5. Select the symbol by pressing Shift+Left Arrow.

6. Select Glossary from the Edit menu (Alt+E-O).

7. Type a mnemonic such as l= and press Alt+D to define the glossary. (Note: Glossary abbreviations are not case sensitive: L= and l= are equivalent.)

**TIP.** *If the glossary item is a frequently inserted phrase, you should define it with a trailing space. For example, if you were writing a dissertation on Herman Melville, you might want a set of glossaries to easily reference the book titles, such as:*

| Abbreviation | Text |
| --- | --- |
| cm | *The Confidence Man* |
| md | *Moby Dick* |
| mmd | Melville's *Moby Dick* |
| ty | *Typee* |

*In each of the above cases you would want a trailing space at the end of the phrase so that after inserting the glossary you can simply continue typing the next word without having to insert a space.*

## Inserting a Glossary

There are two ways to insert a glossary into a document. You can either use the ExpandGlossary function key (F3) to expand an abbreviation typed directly into the document or you can choose the abbreviation from the EditGlossary dialog box.

The first method is appropriate for short, often used, and easily remembered mnemonics. So, for instance, to insert the pound sterling symbol, abbreviated as l=, you would type three keystrokes: the abbreviation **l=**, followed by the ExpandGlossary shortcut key F3; to insert the title of Melville's masterpiece, you would type the abbreviation **md** followed by F3.

The above examples might lead you to believe that glossaries would be useful for inserting foreign language letters, that is, diacritically marked characters such as (ê). There's a problem with this. When you type an abbreviation and then press F3, Word assumes that the abbreviation ends at the insertion point and continues backwards to the previous space or punctuation mark. This makes the F3 method of inserting a glossary impractical for typing phrases such as *tête-à-tête*. To demonstrate this:

1. Create a glossary named e^ that will insert ê. Do so by inserting the symbol once from the InsertSymbol dialog and defining a glossary as we did above for the pound sterling symbol.

2. Create a glossary named a` that will insert à.

3. Type **te'** and press F3.

You will get an error message stating there is no such glossary entry. This is because Word is looking for a glossary abbreviation named te', not e'. There is a way around this problem; it is awkward to the point of uselessness, but here it is:

4. Select (that is, highlight using the mouse or the Shift-Left Arrow key) the two-character abbreviation (in this case, e') and then press F3. The glossary will be found and properly expanded.

5. Assuming you have followed the above, and have inserted tê into your test document, now finish the word by typing **te-a`**.

6. Press F3. Note that the à was properly expanded. This is because Word stopped looking for the glossary name when it hit the hyphen.

In short, if the selection is an insertion point, Word assumes the glossary name extends from the current insertion point backwards to the most recent space or punctuation mark. If the selection is a block of text, Word assumes the selection itself is the glossary name.

In such cases, when an abbreviation is in the middle of a word, the more convenient method is to use the EditGlossary command, accessible from the Edit menu. By default this command has no keyboard shortcut. I recommend assigning it to Ctrl+G.

Using EditGlossary to insert a glossary is also appropriate for glossary entries that are less frequently used (and therefore you've forgotten the abbreviation), or which have longer, descriptive names (such as TheJunkFromChapterOne).

EditGlossary is also used to define a glossary. When defining a dialog box, only the Define and Cancel buttons are available. When using this command to insert a glossary entry you will notice three additional buttons: Insert, Insert as Plain Text, and Delete. See Figure 4.6 for an explanation of the EditGlossary dialog box.

Limitation: There is one remarkable inconvenience in the design of this dialog box—there is no segregation of global glossaries and template-specific glossaries. That is, the list of glossaries contains both global and template glossaries. This presents a problem in circumstances where you have carefully defined a series of template glossaries for a specific class of documents and wish to use only those glossaries. If you have a large number of global glossaries, you will find yourself wading through a long list of glossary names. It also can be a problem if you have two versions of a glossary, a global and a template, of the same name. As implemented, this dialog box provides no way to access the global version of a glossary that has the same name as a template glossary, while in a template-bound document. As with macros and access methods, Word searches for a glossary in the current context first, then in the global context. In my opinion there should be a group box of three option buttons to determine which glossaries are displayed: Global, Template (if appropriate), and All.

**Figure 4.6**
Anatomy of the EditGlossary dialog box

List of all available glossaries, both global and template

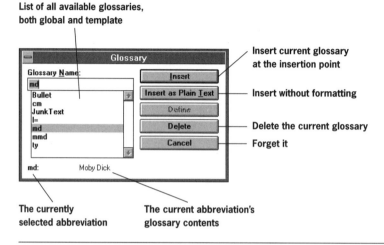

Insert current glossary at the insertion point

Insert without formatting

Delete the current glossary

Forget it

The currently selected abbreviation

The current abbreviation's glossary contents

The difference between Insert and Insert as Plain Text is that the former preserves formatting directly applied to the glossary; the latter inserts only the text, stripping off any formatting instructions.

When you delete a glossary, that is, actually remove the glossary entry from the list of available glossaries, it is not removed from the template until you save all template changes. For a *global* glossary this is when you respond yes to the "Do you want to save the global glossary and command changes?" prompt. For a *template* glossary this is when you respond yes to the "Do you also want to save changes to the document template?" prompt. If you attempt to recover a deleted glossary by answering no, you will also be discarding any other changes made to the global landscape.

If you have a global and a template glossary of the same name, and attempt to delete that glossary, you will delete the template-bound version of the glossary first.

**Note.** You can print all the glossaries for the current context by executing FilePrint and selecting Glossaries in the Print drop-down list.

## Glossaries and Font Information

Deep in the bowels of Word there is a little demon who sometimes makes some weird decisions about font information when you expand a glossary. Therefore, I'd like to spend a moment discussing what assumptions Word makes about a glossary's font information, how that sometimes gets bollixed up, and what you can do to prevent and cure such confusion.

This is what I understand, to date, about glossaries and fonts:

- Word makes a judgment about the base font name *at the time of the glossary's creation* based upon the current normal style font. Usually, if you change the underlying normal style to a different font, glossaries in that context also change in their assumptions.

If the normal style at the time of the glossary's creation is described as Times New Roman, and you subsequently change the style to Courier New, it is possible that glossaries, especially if expanded with the F3 key (as opposed to the EditGlossary menu) will still come in as Times New Roman.

Another potential confusion can result from inserting a global glossary into a template based document. Sometimes the inserted glossary will come in with the global normal font information (Times New Roman, say) rather than the template's normal font information (Courier New, say).

This behavior is somewhat erratic. Some theorize that this is more of a problem if the template in question has a Word 1.*x* lineage (that is, your template was originally created in version 1.*x* and converted when you updated to version 2.0).

- If the glossary contains a paragraph mark, the glossary will preserve all the paragraph formatting information: font name, attributes, indents, and so on (unless you use Insert as Plain Text).

This aspect of glossaries is useful if you are storing large sections of boilerplate.

- If a glossary contains direct formatting, such as italics or bold, those attributes will be preserved when the glossary is expanded (unless you use Insert as Plain Text).

This aspect of glossaries is useful for shorter phrases that contain character formatting, such as the titles used in the examples suggested above.

To avoid the possible problem of a glossary expanding with improper font information (sometimes referred to by the cognoscenti as "phont phunnies"), I suggest the following:

- Do not change the normal style font characteristics in the global context. Word's default font is Times New Roman 10 point. Leave it that way. Although this may seem like an unnecessary restriction, remember that this book suggests organizing documents according to templates in any case. Organize your templates to reflect your predilection for fonts other than Times New Roman 10 point.

- Decide upon a template's style information first, and then define the associated template's glossaries.

- Keep changes to the underlying normal style in the template to a minimum—none at all, if possible.

- If a glossary expands into your document with incorrect font information, select the entire range of the glossary text and press Ctrl+spacebar. Of course, this fix will nuke any direct formatting that might have been stored with the glossary text.

# Notes on Organizing and Using Templates

Word for Windows ships with a number of specialized templates. However, it is unlikely that any template designed and created by someone else will suit your particular needs. Now that you understand what a template contains, and how to modify text and interface properties, I would suggest taking a closer look at the various templates that come with Word.

Managing templates is like any other aspect of file maintenance. You should know what's on the disk. You should probably get rid of those templates you will never use. Winnowing down your DOT-Path makes the File-New and FileTemplate commands easier to use: You won't have to wade through a thick list of cryptic template names to find a template.

I would suggest loading each of the templates you decide might be useful and then fiddling with the styles to make the default font information match the capabilities of your printer and your preferences. And for the purposes of clarity, select Summary Info from the File menu and add or edit the Title field. The text inserted as a title will display in the Description box of FileNew and FileTemplate when a template is selected. An informative title will remind you of the purpose of a template.

## The Global Template (NORMAL.DOT)

Here are a few tips regarding the care and feeding of NORMAL.DOT:

- Do not change the font assigned to the normal style. The reason for this has to do with deep, dark internal secrets about what assumptions Word makes when you cut and paste text between documents, and what assumptions it makes when you expand a glossary.

- Any macro that you determine will be useful in all documents, as opposed to those macros that only affect a class of documents, should be saved globally in NORMAL.DOT.

- Similarly, keyboard assignments or menu assignments that you want to be the universal default should be defined in the global context and saved in NORMAL.DOT.

- The normal toolbar is passed on to every template as the base toolbar. When you customize the toolbar in the global context you have literally changed the default toolbar that is the starting point for all template-specific toolbars.

- Glossaries that you wish to have available no matter what class of document is currently active should be defined in the global context. However, be aware that there may be font collisions when a global glossary defined with one normal style is expanded into a template with a differing normal style. The fewer global glossaries the better.

## Designing a New Template

There are two ways to start the process of creating a new template. The first is to use the FileNew command, select the base template, and choose the Template option button. This will open a blank template and you can make modifications to any of the formatting or interface properties directly on the template.

**NOTE.** *A new template based on NORMAL.DOT will inherit all of the text properties but none of the macros or access methods contained in NORMAL.DOT. A new template based on any other template will inherit all of that template's text properties as well as all of its macros and access methods.*

There is a second, very simple way to create a template. If you have a document, based on any template, in which you have customized the styles directly within that document (that is, you have not saved them to any template at all), you can save the document itself as a Document Template. For instance, let us assume that you have created a document based on NORMAL.DOT, thinking it would be a one-time document. You have created styles and layout information specific to this one document. Then you decide that the work put into creating the styles and layout information should be saved. You could simply

1. Remove all of the text (save what should be presented in all subsequent documents of this class as boilerplate).

2. Select Save As from the File menu.

3. Specify Document Template as the file type.

The above steps would create a new template with all of the style and layout information contained in the document.

**NOTE.** *Creating a template from a document saves only the style and layout information; it does not save either the macros or the access methods into the new template.*

## When To Use a Template Other Than Normal

I'm a bit biased on this question. When your collection of templates is properly defined and organized, there is virtually no reason to base a document on NORMAL.DOT. I use NORMAL.DOT only out of laziness, when creating a scrap document. I always base real documents on a template.

Using a template specially designed for a class of documents has several advantages over basing a document on NORMAL.DOT. You have more precise control over layout and styles. Even if the document created falls between the cracks—that is, does not belong precisely to an already defined class—chances are it has more in common with one of your customized templates than it does with the default settings in NORMAL.DOT. You can control macros, access methods, and glossaries with greater flexibility. Yet you still have access to the customizations, such as global macros or keyboard shortcuts, stored in NORMAL.DOT.

## Disguising a Template as a Document

A template is simply a special form of Word document. This is more true than you may have realized. And it allows a neat trick: disguising a template as a document.

Basically, although Word assumes that all templates possess the extension DOT, and that they are all located in a specific directory, the DOT-Path, in fact you can store a template with any extension, including DOC, and in any directory. When loaded into Word a template looks and behaves precisely like a document.

The advantage of creating a template-document is that all the foregoing interface modifications, which we have discussed as controlling the functioning of Word when working upon a class of related documents, can be made document specific. If you find yourself designing a template that is only used for a single document, it would be appropriate to simply unite the functions of the template (the interface properties) with the document-specific properties (text and text attributes). In essence, a disguised template has all the advantages of a template based document in a single file.

Disguising a template as a document is useful for the following reasons:

- You want to keep a set of glossary definitions united with a single document (rather than with a class of documents).

This can be useful if the document is to be shared among many users. You can thereby distribute the single file rather than the file and an associated template. It is also useful when the document, though similar to other documents of its class, will have many unique glossaries. For example, you might have a FICTION.DOT template for short stories. Your Great American Novel is also based upon FICTION.DOT. You would like to store all 150 of your characters' names in the glossary. You can save them to FICTION.DOT, where they would clutter up the glossary when you're working on short stories; you could create a second template, NOVEL.DOT, based upon FICTION.DOT, and save the glossaries there; or you could disguise the novel document itself as a template and store its associated glossaries directly with the novel.

- You want to distribute a set of macros to another user.

The example documents contained on the sample disk are, in fact, templates saved with a DOC extension. (Other examples of such a hybrid template-document are the files NEWMACROS.DOC and PSS.DOC, distributed with Word.)

To create a disguised template, you can either start from scratch, building a new template from the FileNew dialog box and specifying a name with a DOC extension; or you can select FileSaveAs while editing a document and specify Document Template as the file type. In the first case you will be passing all macros and modifications on to the new template-document. In the second case, you would be passing on only the text and text attributes—macros, access methods, and glossaries would be added subsequently.

**NOTE.** *As soon as you specify Document Template as the file type, Word assumes that you want to store the template-document in the DOT-Path. You must specify a full path name in order to save the template-document in a directory other than the DOT-Path.*

The only disadvantage presented by a template-document is that you cannot save the file to other file types. That is, the file types listed on the FileSaveAs dialog box (such as Text Only, Rich Text Format, or other word processor formats) are no longer directly available. Once saved as a Document Template you cannot save to other formats. To work around this limitation is rather simple, however: Select FileNew, and in the Use Template edit box specify the full path name of the disguised template, including extension. This will create a new document based on the disguised template. All of the existing text in the template-document will be inherited by the new document. You can then FileSaveAs to any other available format.

# Summary: On Template Interface Properties

In this chapter several fundamental concepts were introduced and discussed.

- A macro can be either global or template specific.

- If there are two macros with the same name, which is executed when called depends entirely upon the context of the insertion point at the time of the call. Word searches for the called macro first in the local template (if there is one), then in the global template (NORMAL.DOT), and then among the built-in command macros.

- An access method can be either global or template specific.

- While in a template-based document, if the same access method exists in both the global and the template context, the method as it is defined in the template takes precedence.

- Access methods defined in the global context can be removed from a specific template.

- Glossaries can be either global or template specific.

- While in a template based document, if there is a glossary with the same name in both the global and the template context, the template glossary is expanded.

- There can be several sets of customizations available at any one time. More precisely, the number of customizations *potentially* available is equivalent to the number of different templates activated (by loading template based documents) plus the global customizations.

- Which set of customizations is *actually* available at a given time—that is, which are in effect—depends upon the context, upon where the insertion point is located. The customizations loaded in the active document's associated template will have sway in combination with the global customizations.

- The global customizations are always loaded (even if no normal based document is open) and always available unless contravened by a template customization.

These concepts, when combined with a greater understanding of the macro language, WordBasic, will allow you to design, essentially, your own word processor. Macros, combined with the power of templates, can smooth over rough spots in Word; they can fill gaps and lapses, adding new commands, modifying built-in commands, or combining both to build complex, task-specific applications. In the following chapters we will parse this sometimes daunting phrase, the macro language, explore the basics of macro creation, and demonstrate, with useful, problem solving examples, the incredible power and flexibility WordBasic brings to Word.

**Macro Basics**

**Introducing WordBasic**

**Building Macros—Introduction**

**Program Structure, the Macro Editor, and Debugging**

**WordBasic: Advanced Topics**

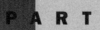

PART

**WordBasic**

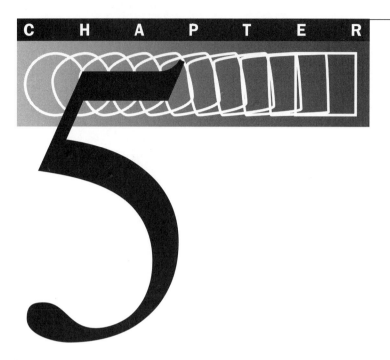

# Macro Basics

*What Is a Macro?*

*The Macro Recorder*

*Introducing the Macro Editor*

*Summary: Macro Basics*

WELCOME TO THE HARDER PART. IN THIS CHAPTER WE WILL EXPLORE macros in greater detail, expanding on examples and ideas found in previous chapters and introducing the fundamentals of macro creation.

At first glance, macros do seem to be more difficult to understand than Word's other customization features, for one reason because each of the other customizations has easy to comprehend analogs in all word processors. Every word processor possesses some facility for modifying margin layouts; most have some way of saving style information; many have boilerplate or glossary features. However, only the more recent advanced word processors have macro languages. Word's macro language is called WordBasic.

## What Is a Macro?

You have probably stumbled upon this phrase "macro language" often in the past. Many computer applications possess macro features of varying complexities. A macro, in virtually all computer applications, is simply a method of automating a specific task or series of tasks into a single, easily accessible command.

Macro facilities come in various flavors. Some simply record a series of keystrokes and assign them to a single keyboard shortcut. You record a series of actions and then play them back, just as recorded. The Recorder application which comes with Windows is one such "macro processor." Other macro facilities allow you to create complex "mini-programs" by combining recorded actions and various control structures usually found in higher-level programming languages. In the next chapter we will explore the features of WordBasic that make it a language, that make it resemble a programming language more than a simple action recorder. In this chapter, we will explore the fundamentals of macro design and the types of problems a macro can solve.

### Built-in Command Macros versus User-Macros

In Word, all commands are alterable "macros." The normal word processing functions, which in other programs are static (or to use the metaphor from Chapter 1, opaque), in Word are called by command macros, and therefore are visible, fluid (or to continue the metaphor, translucent). You can, quite literally, look into the macro that calls EditFind, or ViewDraft, or ToolsOptions-View. And more importantly, you can modify what those macros do when executed.

These command macros should be considered internal. They were designed by the development team, arranged in a specific order on the menus, assigned default keyboard keystrokes. At base, Word consists of the sum of the built-in command macros.

However, WordBasic, whether employed most simply in the form of the macro recorder or more elaborately with the macro editor, allows the user to add new commands or new functionality to existing commands. As you already know, macros on this second tier (those created by the user rather than the programmers of Word) are referred to as custom macros, or user-macros.

## Three Types of User-Macros

As in designing styles or determining the boilerplate contained in a template, the first step in creating a user-macro is to locate the necessity, to characterize the problem, and to determine if that problem is soluble by means of a macro. More simply: What do you want to do; can a macro do it?

Essentially, there are three types of user-macros:

- *Automation*   A macro designed to make often repeated actions conveniently accessible.

- *Extension*   Macros that extend Word's functionality to suit your particular work patterns by adding new commands or altering the way in which the built-in command macros operate.

- *Application*   Macros designed to accomplish a specific, complex task. These macros can be quite large and take on the characteristics of mini-programs.

Of course, these are not hard and fast distinctions. There are extension macros that automate, and automation macros that solve a specific problem. All macros, to one degree or another, partake of all three types. Still, these are useful categories to bear in mind as we approach the design and creation of user-macros.

If there is a series of actions you find yourself repeating over and over, and that series of actions requires a complex sequence of keystrokes or menu choices to accomplish, you have a candidate for what I call an *automation macro*. A macro to solve this kind of problem—repeating easily a complex series of actions—can usually be created with the macro recorder. The example in Chapter 4, in which we created a macro to apply a specific character format, is an example of such an automation macro.

If an internal command macro needs modification to perform precisely to your preferences, you need what I've termed an *extension macro*. For instance, by default the internal macro named FileOpen displays a list of all files with the extension DOC. What if you want it to display a list of all files? You can extend the functionality of FileOpen by writing a user-macro. Later in this chapter we will create a version of FileOpen to accomplish this task.

*Application macros* are less easily characterized. They are larger and require more forethought and design. Application macros do more than automation macros, which collect a series of functions under one name, creating a new command. They do more than extension macros, which extend the functionality of a Word command that already exists. Application macros go beyond both and install what amounts to a new feature.

# The Macro Recorder

There are two ways to create user-macros: recording and editing. Recording is the simpler way to create a macro. Editing a macro is more complex (and therefore more daunting). But even with edited macros, the recorder is often a useful starting point; you can record the basic shape and function of a macro, and then use the macro editor to refine and test.

In the preceding chapters we have used the macro recorder in two examples: the AutoOpen macro for the sample template NEWMEMO.DOT discussed in Chapter 3 and the SpecialBold macro created in Chapter 4. This section will delve into the details of macro recording.

To begin recording a macro the insertion point must be located in a document. That is, you cannot begin recording if a dialog box or menu choice is being displayed. After starting the recording process, by selecting Record Macro from the Tools menu (or pressing Alt+O-R), you will be presented with the dialog box shown in Figure 5.1.

**Figure 5.1**

ToolsRecordMacro
dialog box

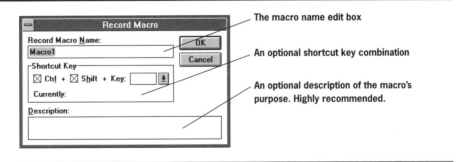

The macro name edit box

An optional shortcut key combination

An optional description of the macro's purpose. Highly recommended.

## Naming a Macro

When you begin recording a macro, Word proposes the name "Macro1." If you record several macros, Word will increment the digit portion of this name. But this default name is hardly informative. You should provide a more useful name. When naming a macro you should bear in mind the following ideas.

Word will preserve the case given to a macro name. If you type all caps, the macro will ever after be displayed in all caps in lists of available macros. If you mix case, the mix will be preserved. Using mixed case is advisable, for one thing because it will create more informative, and more easily read, macro names. For instance, the name "SpecialBold" is more easily read as a combination of the two words "special" and "bold" than is "specialbold." A macro name can be any combination of alphanumerics, with the single proviso that the first position must be a letter, not a number. For instance, Macro1 is legal but 1Macro is not. A macro name cannot contain any punctuation marks. Therefore you cannot include spaces or hyphens or underscores to separate the individual words of a macro's name. You should get in the habit of capitalizing each word of the macro name.

Another convention that can prove useful is to follow the practice the programmers of Word used in naming the built-in command macros. The built-in commands are named according to their general function and their placement on the menu geography. For instance, all macros related to manipulating files begin with the word "File," all macros concerning tables begin with the word "Table." It is a good habit to name a macro descriptively, with multiple capitalized words. For example, in previous chapters, macros were named SpecialBold and RevisionMarksOn. Also, choose macro names with an eye to the purpose and possible menu location of the macro.

## Specifying a Shortcut Key for a Recorded Macro

A macro need not have a shortcut key assigned at the time of its creation. An advantage of assigning a key combination at the start of macro recording is that it's easier to do it now than later. Having a shortcut key combination assigned at the same time as the macro's creation aids in testing the macro. As soon as you finish recording, you can run the macro easily to see that it works as planned.

However, as stated in Chapter 4, the built-in Shortcut Key edit box does not allow access to all legal key combinations. For that reason, I recommend assigning a temporary key assignment at the time of macro creation with the recorder. You can later change this temporary assignment with ToolsOptions-Keyboard, which allows the same range of key assignments as the Shortcut Key edit box, or you can use a more versatile WordBasic command (which will be described in Chapter 7).

Another reason to use a temporary key assignment when first creating a macro is that you may not know which key combination will best suit a particular macro or which combination will best match your own typing style, until after you've used the macro several times. Therefore, settle upon a temporary key combination, some obscure combination like Ctrl+Shift+Z, for all new recorded macros.

## Providing a Macro Description

This is a good habit to develop. The description entered at the time of recording (or editing) a macro will invariably prove useful at a later date. As you accumulate custom macros, especially if your naming conventions prove less than informative, you will come to rely upon the macro description to remind you of the purpose of a given macro. This description is displayed in all of the access method modification dialog boxes, such as ToolsOptionsToolbar. If a macro is assigned to a menu, this description will be displayed on the status bar when the menu text for that macro is selected. It takes a moment more thought, and a teensy bit of typing. The potential payoff is worth the bother.

## What Does the Macro Recorder Record?

What happens after naming, describing, and assigning a shortcut key to the macro depends upon the global setting specified in the FileTemplate dialog box. As discussed in the previous chapter, you can specify that all new recorded macros be stored globally in NORMAL.DOT, or with the current template, or that you be prompted for each. If you have chosen "Prompt For Each New" on the FileTemplate dialog box, you will be prompted for the save location if you are working on a template based document. If you are working in a normal based document, recording will begin immediately since there is no choice as to location. If you have chosen either Global or With Document Template on the FileTemplate dialog box, recording will begin immediately, and the storage location will depend on whether the document is normal or template based.

If you have the status bar displayed at the bottom of the Word screen, you can always tell when the macro recorder is recording. You will see the abbreviation "REC" in the second to last message area:

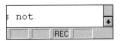

Now comes the interesting part. What's actually happening when you record a macro in Word? Some macro facilities, such as the Recorder application that ships with Windows, transcribe the keys pressed and the mouse movements executed while they are recording. When you play back such a macro you will see the same menu selections and mouse pointer movements, in fast motion to be sure, that you executed during the record process. This is not the case with a macro recorded with Word's macro recording facility. Word does not record keystrokes; it records the results of keystrokes. This is an important fact.

For example, if you record the keyboard sequence Alt+F-T, what you have recorded is not the literal sequence of keystrokes, but the result of those keystrokes: the FileTemplate macro is executed. When you play back this macro, you will not see the File menu. Word will immediately display the File-Template dialog box.

The Word macro recorder does not record mouse movements or mouse button clicks. It does record the result of mouse actions. For example, if you select an option button or check an option box with the mouse while the re-corder is on, the result is precisely the same as if you had selected those op-tions with their keyboard shortcuts. In neither case is the method of selection recorded (the actual keystrokes or the position and number of mouse clicks). In both cases the result of the actions is recorded and placed into the macro.

Keystrokes that do not execute a command or specify an option, such as text typed directly into a document, will be recorded as typed.

A significant consequence of the fact that Word records results of actions rather than actions themselves is that you must execute a complete action. If, for instance, you attempt to record the calling of FileTemplate by pressing Alt+F-T, and then select Cancel, nothing will be recorded. You must make your selections in the displayed dialog box and confirm the results of those choices by selecting OK.

The fact that Word's macro recorder stores the result of keyboard and mouse actions rather than the actions themselves leads to one of the facility's limitations.

For instance, suppose you wanted a macro that would turn on revision marking. The check box to do this is under the Tools menu, on the Revision Marks dialog box. To turn on marking requires the key sequence Alt+O-K-M. If Word recorded the key sequence itself, then playing this macro back sev-eral times would alternately turn revision marking on and off, since the same key sequence performs a different action depending on the current state of the check box: If it is off, this key sequence turns it on; if on, off.

But if you record the above key sequence and play it back multiple times, you will find that what Word recorded was the state of the check box itself (the on state) not the steps to turn it on. In this sense the macro recorder is one-directional. Whatever it accomplishes at the time of the recording is what it will perform in all subsequent replays.

Well, if Word's macro recorder doesn't record key sequences, what does it record? The macro recorder doesn't actually record anything. It translates the key sequences and mouse clicks into the corresponding commands to per-form the recorded action. The macro recorder actually creates a macro that consists of the WordBasic *commands* that will result in the desired action.

To more clearly explain what it is that Word records when it records a macro, it is time to introduce the macro editor.

# Introducing the Macro Editor

To examine the result of a macro recording, create a macro named Revision-MarksOn by recording the key sequence necessary to turn revision marking on: Alt+O-K-M, Enter. Assign this macro to the temporary combination, Ctrl+Shift+Z. The steps to do this should be clear by now. (If you want to review the actual process of recording a macro, see either of the two examples contained in this book, or refer to Chapter 1 of *Using WordBasic*—this volume is free for the asking from Microsoft.)

After recording RevisionMarksOn, load it into the macro editor by following these steps:

1. Select Macro from the Tools menu (Alt+O-M).

2. Find RevisionMarksOn in the list of macros (it will be in either the global or template macros list depending upon where you were when you created it).

3. Press Alt+E to edit RevisionMarksOn.

You will see something similar to the screen displayed in Figure 5.2. If this is your first time entering the macro editor, don't be alarmed. It is a lot less forbidding than it seems at first glance. Each of the elements of this screen will be discussed in more detail in Chapter 8. For now we should focus on the macro itself to try and understand what, precisely, the macro recorder did when we recorded the key sequence Alt+O-K-M.

The first thing to note is the first and last line of the macro. The word "Sub" is an abbreviation, common in computer programming, for the word *subroutine*. A subroutine is a collection of instructions, stored together, and called by the controlling program. Sounds like computer-speak, no? Well, let's take it apart and render the concept harmless, with a plain English analogy.

Think of any activity that is routine. Making breakfast, for instance. This is something we do regularly; it is the general description of an action that consists of several parts. A subroutine contained by the routine of making breakfast might be making toast or frying eggs. Each of these subroutines could be further divided into other subroutines, such as spreading butter or cracking eggs. We don't think of the simple routine of making breakfast in such a modular fashion. Computer programs, however, which lack our ability for synthetic thinking, must think of every action as a collection of discrete components. Those discrete components are referred to, generally, as subroutines.

In the simplest computer program the main routine might be waiting for the user to press a key. When the main routine receives a key press it decides what to do with it and calls a subroutine to actually process the keystroke. For example, the main routine in our example is Word itself. Word waits for user input. If the input is a shortcut keystroke or a menu selection, Word passes control to the associated macro. If the input is text, Word passes the typed characters to the document. When Word received the key sequence Alt+O-K-M, it passed control to a subroutine named ToolsRevisionMarks. That passing of control is precisely what the macro recorder recorded.

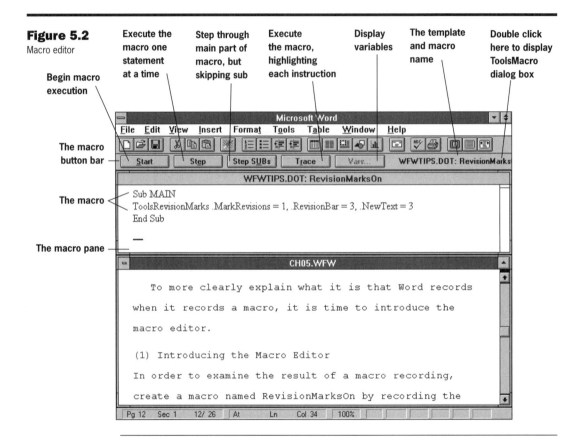

**Figure 5.2**
Macro editor

The fact that every macro begins with the phrase "Sub MAIN" and ends with the demarcation "End Sub" should be viewed in the light of the earlier discussion of translucence. Word, from this vantage, is simply a sophisticated macro processor, the main routine (like making breakfast) upon which are strung a series of smaller units that actually do the work. Those smaller units are called macros, "main subroutines" to the controlling "routine" known as Word. And each macro, each main subroutine, can itself contain yet smaller units called subroutines.

The macro itself consists of the text between the beginning Sub MAIN and ending End Sub. In our example, RevisionMarksOn is actually a single line macro; a single statement:

```
ToolsRevisionMarks .MarkRevisions = 1, .RevisionBar = 3, .NewText = 3
```

What precisely is this creature? The short form of the answer is this: a statement that calls a subroutine with three parameters. What? The goofy looking word "ToolsRevisionMarks" is the name of a built-in command macro (a subroutine to the main routine of Word using the paradigm discussed above). The three phrases that begin with periods and are separated by commas are the "parameters" passed to this internal macro by the user macro RevisionMarksOn.

"Parameter" is another of those terms appropriated by computer programmers from standard English. It is difficult, at first, to see what relation there could be between the colloquial meaning of the word "parameter" and its meaning in computerland. But, in fact, it isn't as farfetched as you might think. In common parlance the word "parameter" refers, generally, to the "boundary" of a given topic, idea, discussion. In mathematics, more precisely, a parameter is a constant in the case being considered, though variable in other cases. That is, for this task it has a specific value, but for other tasks that value might be different.

Let's render this concept harmless by returning to breakfast. We are going to execute the subroutine named MakeToast. But what kind of toast? If we thought like a computer, we would divide the act of making toast into several variable components: type of bread, buttered or not buttered, type of condiment. So, for instance, we could describe these specific (in this instance) but generally variable instructions as parameters. And if we wanted buttered raisin toast with strawberry jam, the instruction might look like:

```
MakeToast .Type=Raisin, .Butter=Yes, .Condiment=Strawberry Jam
```

Each of the parameters tells the computer breakfast cook a detail about the desired toast. Similarly, each of the parameters passed to ToolsRevision-Marks tells the subroutine precisely what to do. Let's take the parameters one by one and see what they are telling the subroutine.

- .MarkRevisions = 1

  This parameter simply informs ToolsRevisionMarks to check the box labeled Mark Revisions.

- .RevisionBar = 3

  Specifies the location of the revision bar.

■ .NewText = 3

Specifies the character formatting for text inserted while revision marks are on.

It is easier to see the correspondence between these parameters and actions taken by the subroutine if we place the macro next to its equivalent dialog box. See Figure 5.3.

**Figure 5.3**

Correspondence between ToolsRevisionMarks macro parameters and the dialog box options

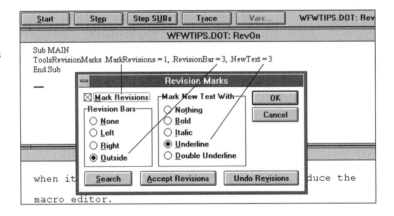

The second and third parameters, RevisionBar and NewText, both refer to choices among a group of buttons. Both are set, in our example, to 3. If you study the figure, however, you might wonder if there isn't a mistake in this since in both cases the fourth button choice is marked as active. Here we must recall a fundamental aspect of WordBasic: In virtually all cases, Word-Basic begins counting at zero. Therefore, the digit 3 actually does refer to the fourth choice.

The first parameter, MarkRevisions, is actually the one that interests us most in this example. By setting it equal to 1 you are, in effect, checking the box, turning revision marking on. This parameter can be only one of two values: 1 or 0. These digit values correspond, basically, to true and false, yes and no. Any parameter that is limited to yes and no is sometimes referred to as an *argument*. This is yet another example of a programming term that would appear to be appropriated from normal discourse. In fact, argument most likely entered programming from mathematics where it means "a value upon which a calculation depends." That makes sense. The "calculation" made by ToolsRevisionMarks depends upon the value of the argument .MarkRevisions. Even so, the sense of "debate," which is certainly the meaning most would assume, is also appropriate and might aid our understanding of argument as a subset of parameter. An argument has two sides, pro/con, for/against, yes/no. If a parameter can only be either yes or no, then it is an argument. In our MakeToast example, Butter=yes was such an argument. In actual use, the terms parameter and argument are often used interchangeably.

## A Frightening Intermission: A Glance at Debugging

Before moving on to actually editing our example macro, and introducing the smart part of WordBasic, let's take a breather. We just covered, believe it or not, some complicated stuff. It took me years to figure out what was sub about a subroutine, where the boundary lay in a parameter, and why programmers talked so much about arguments.

Now I'm gonna scare the beginners in the group. Assuming you've been following along with the example in this chapter, you should have a screen that looks something like Figure 5.2. (If you don't, and you'd like to catch up, do so.) Next:

1. Place the insertion point anywhere within the macro editing window.

2. Press Alt+Shift+S (or click on the Start button).

3. Stare blankly at the relatively uninformative error message:

4. Select OK to make the message go away.

What just happened? This message is one of the most frequent errors you will see when you program in WordBasic. So I figured I'd introduce it right at the top of our discussion. Get it over with. It isn't nearly as forbidding as it seems.

What we did was attempt to run RevisionMarksOn on itself. Word responded by informing us that it encountered a command which has no meaning while the focus is on the macro editing window. (To make this point a bit more graphically, pull down the Tools menu while in the macro. You will see that the Revision Marks menu item is grayed. It is unavailable.)

Notice that in addition to warning us that the command was unavailable, Word also, quite politely, changed the color of the offending macro statement to red. This might seem a small thing, but when you are testing a complex macro and allow a mistake to creep in, this ability of Word to highlight the location of the error will prove useful indeed.

To avoid the error message while running RevisionMarksOn, create a work document by doing the following:

1. Create a new document based on any template (pressing Alt+F-N, Enter would create a normal based template).

2. Select Arrange All from the Window menu to tile all the open documents. Notice that the focus has automatically moved from the macro editor to the document.

3. Press Alt+Shift+S (or click on the Start button) to execute the macro RevisionMarksOn while the focus is on the newly created document.

If the status bar is on screen, you can see that revision marking has been turned on by the presence of the MRK abbreviation in the third to last box. If you do not have the status bar showing, typing anything into the new document will display as underlined, with the revision marks vertical bar in the left margin.

The lesson in this is two-fold: After recording or editing a macro you have various tools at your disposal to test to see that the macro executes properly, including the Start button found on the macro editor button bar; if a macro is open it can be executed by selecting the Start button *even if the focus is on a document window other than the macro*. In fact, in most cases you will want to have the focus on a test document rather than on the macro itself. Many WordBasic commands have no meaning when executed on the macro itself.

Thus ends lesson one in what programmers call *debugging*. Historical note: The coinage of the term "bug" supposedly came in reaction to a moth fatally attracted by a vacuum tube in a 1940s behemoth protocomputer, causing it to fail. In fact, Thomas Edison used the word to refer to a mechanical problem in a phonograph as early as 1889, and it was a common term for defects in aeronautical engineering in the 1930s—long before the digital computer was invented. Debugging will be covered in more detail in Chapter 8.

Now back to the discussion of parameters.

## Fine-Tuning a Recorded Macro

Most of the statements that constitute WordBasic can be called with parameters that specify the nature of the action desired. However, a statement that takes, for instance, three parameters, does not require that all three parameters be present. For instance, in our example, the only parameter of interest is the first. Therefore, you could delete the second two parameters, resulting in the line:

```
ToolsRevisionMarks .MarkRevisions = 1
```

What this tells the macro ToolsRevisionMarks is: Change the MarkRevisions parameter and leave the other parameters alone. Whenever you record an action, *all the parameter options are inserted into the macro.* The first step in fine-tuning a macro is to remove those parameters you do not wish to affect.

The next logical question may have already occurred to you: How do I know what a given macro's parameters are? There are two ways to discover the specific parameters that are legal modifiers of a macro statement: You can consult the macro reference book, *Using WordBasic,* or you can consult the on-line help function. This second method is most convenient (and is new to version 2.0 of Word). To demonstrate this facility, place the insertion point anywhere within the word "ToolsRevisionMarks" and press F1. As you begin to write macros this context-sensitive help will prove invaluable.

The RevisionMarksOn macro in its current state will do one thing. It will turn on revision marking. We have removed the second and third parameters, so whatever the current document's settings are for those values, they will remain unchanged. Still, this macro is of limited utility. We would need a second macro to turn revision marking off. Such a macro would be simple to create. It would consist of the single line:

```
ToolsRevisionMarks .MarkRevisions = 0
```

However, having two macros to toggle between an on and off state is inelegant. And it would require two keyboard shortcuts for what is essentially a single function: toggling the current state of revision marks.

This kind of problem brings out the best in WordBasic. And despite the fact that we are getting a little ahead of ourselves (again), it is worth pursuing in order to demonstrate that recording a macro should in most cases be considered the first step in solving a problem, not the solution itself.

We have to make RevisionMarksOn smarter. And the key to doing so resides in this most interesting fact: Deep in the bowels of Word, stored somewhere in memory, is the current status for every possible variable in Word's environment. This means you can ask Word, if you know how to phrase the question, if revision marks are currently on or off, and change RevisionMarksOn to suit the answer Word gives.

In the discussion of parameters we spoke entirely of passing a parameter, an instruction, *to* a subroutine. The trick in querying Word about a particular option or state is this: Those same parameters *hold* the current state of a value. And when queried, a WordBasic statement can retrieve a value *from* a given parameter.

What follows will startle you if you've never explored WordBasic. The dialect spoken in the smarter version of RevisionMarksOn has not yet been described. Take it on faith for the moment, and know that you do not need to be fluent in WordBasic to make good use of it. All of the necessary statements can be discovered, either by using the macro recorder, the WordBasic reference *Using WordBasic*, or the help file.

We need to replace RevisionMarksOn, which was created by the recorder, with a series of WordBasic statements that could not be generated by the recorder. We must *write* this smarter macro. To do so, load the existing RevisionMarksOn into the macro editor (if you have been following along, it's already there); delete the entire macro by pressing Ctrl+Numpad5 and Del; and type in this series of macro statements:

```
Sub MAIN
Dim DialogRecord as ToolsRevisionMarks
GetCurValues DialogRecord
CurrentStatus = DialogRecord.MarkRevisions
If CurrentStatus = Ø Then
   ToolsRevisionMarks  .MarkRevisions = 1
Else
   ToolsRevisionMarks  .MarkRevisions = Ø
End If
End Sub
```

"Yikes! That looks like Greek to me," I hear the fainthearted saying. Don't close the book just yet. It looks a lot scarier than it is. Soon it'll seem truly trivial. For the moment don't worry about the details. Just follow the general explication of this odd group of lines.

```
Dim DialogRecord as ToolsRevisionMarks
```

This line translates into English as follows: create a temporary container named "DialogRecord" that has the same shape as the command macro ToolsRevisionMarks.

```
GetCurValues DialogRecord
```

This tells Word to store the current ToolsRevisionMarks settings into our temporary container. "GetCurValues" is an abbreviation for "Get Current Values."

```
CurrentStatus = DialogRecord.MarkRevisions
```

This statement creates a second container and assigns to it the current value of the parameter .MarkRevisions (remember, this is the parameter that tells ToolsRevisionMarks to check or uncheck the Mark Revisions check box).

```
If CurrentStatus = Ø Then
   ToolsRevisionMarks  .MarkRevisions = 1
Else
   ToolsRevisionMarks  .MarkRevisions = Ø
End If
```

These five lines should be considered as a unit. They mean just what they say (in pretty impoverished English, I admit): If revision marks are off, then turn them on, otherwise turn them off.

Close the macro editing window. You will be prompted to save the changes made to RevisionMarksOn. If you have followed the steps outlined in this chapter, you now have a macro named RevisionMarksOn, assigned to Ctrl+Shift+Z, which will toggle the state of revision marking. You could re-name this macro to ToggleRevisionMarks to more accurately reflect its smarter behavior.

To rename the macro:

1. Bring up the list of macros by selecting Tools, Macro (Alt+O-M).

2. Find RevisionMarksOn in the list of macros.

3. Press Alt+N and type the new name, **ToggleRevisionMarks**.

4. Press Enter to accept the new macro name.

5. Press Esc (or click on Close) to remove the ToolsMacro dialog box.

The ability to easily rename a user-macro will come in handy as you cre-ate more and more macros. Note that when you changed the name of the macro, the description was retained. However, if the macro has been assigned an access method (placed on a menu, given a keyboard shortcut, or assigned to the toolbar) with the old name, the access method(s) will be lost with the name change.

# Summary: Macro Basics

This chapter covered the following points.

■ The macro recorder does not record an action. It records the result of an action.

■ An action must be completed in order for it to register with the macro recorder.

■ Recorded macros act in one direction, duplicating the state of all options at the time of an action's completion during recording.

■ The macro recorder is often used as the starting point for a smarter, edited macro.

■ The macro recorder actually stores the name of the WordBasic command macro called by an action, including all the parameters for that command macro.

- A parameter modifies a WordBasic statement, specifying the details of its behavior.

- Superfluous parameters can be removed from a recorded macro.

- If a WordBasic statement is called with a single parameter, only that parameter is affected. All other options retain their current status.

- All macros are, in essence, subroutines called by the main control program known as Word.

- Certain WordBasic statements, or commands, only have meaning when the focus is on a document.

- Word stores the current state of all options within memory. These parameter states are accessible to WordBasic.

- WordBasic is more than the sum of the internal command macros.

This last item leads us directly to a discussion of why WordBasic is more like a programming language than a simple macro processor. The next chapter will explore the language aspects of WordBasic.

# CHAPTER 6

# Introducing WordBasic

**W**ORDBASIC IS MORE THAN A SIMPLE MACRO PROCESSOR, MORE THAN a means to record keystrokes. The previous chapter introduced several aspects of WordBasic's power. This chapter will detail the capabilities that make WordBasic a *language*.

All computer programs are constructed, composed if you will, in a programming language. Most of these languages are capable of producing "stand-alone" applications, full-fledged programs. Some programming languages, however, have no existence outside their specific application—the spreadsheet or database. WordBasic is such an application-specific programming language.

When Word was first introduced, many people thought it was odd to have a full-featured macro language such as WordBasic in a word processor. These same people had no difficulty visualizing the utility of application languages to control spreadsheets or to construct front-ends for databases. They simply didn't see the point. What could possibly be done with such a language in a text processor? This book will answer this puzzle. You will see how the inclusion of WordBasic radically changed the customization potential of Word. But before demonstrating the reason for WordBasic by building and describing some complex macros, we need to step lightly, for the non-programmer, through some necessary terms and concepts.

The easiest way to learn any language is to live in the country where it is spoken, to listen to native speakers. The best way to learn to write is to plagiarize other writers. The later chapters on WordBasic will contain many useful and instructive examples of my peculiar dialect of WordBasic. Those examples should be studied, not only for what they are, but for the solutions they imply. However, for the moment we must embark on an endeavor that is bound to infuriate the already fluent and bewilder the complete neophyte. It's always a drag to listen to someone talk about a language you can't yet speak (I recall this vividly from my Latin classes…). But, it's a necessary evil. Look upon the following discussion as groundwork, as a quick conceptual summary that will point to more interesting things to come. There will be a payoff.

## The Grammar of WordBasic

WordBasic, and any other programming language, has the following similarities to language as we commonly think of it:

- A vocabulary: A system of signs with specific significance.

- A specific and highly rigorous syntax: The combination of signs must obey a relational order in the same way a noun must come before its verb.

- A grammar: A program's code can be, like English, well or ill written. Programmers call well-written source code "elegant."

- An ability, on the most fundamental level, to communicate: A programming language communicates in three directions—with the user, with the computer, and with itself.

WordBasic takes its syntax and grammar from a pre-existing programming language called BASIC (Basic All-purpose Symbolic Instruction Code). (If you are familiar with BASIC, WordBasic will be a cinch.) Created as a teaching aid, BASIC is not the most powerful of computer languages, but is one of the easiest to learn. Its syntax and organization closely approximate normal English forms. For example, we might say:

```
If Jill is free, then I'll ask her to a movie, otherwise I'll ask Jack.
```

In BASIC, you might say:

```
If JillFree then
    AskJill
Else
    AskJack
End If
```

Oversimplifying greatly, you might say that a programming language has the following "parts of speech":

| | |
|---|---|
| Noun | Variables and constants |
| Active verb | Statements |
| Passive verb | Functions |
| Adverb | Parameters |

Although the analogy is imprecise, it provides a useful handle to grasp when first looking at the various elements of WordBasic's grammar.

## Parameters

We defined parameters in the previous chapter: values that are passed to an instruction that modify how that instruction is to be carried out. It should be obvious why a parameter has an adverbial thrust: A parameter alters the specific behavior of the verb-like statements and functions.

## Statements and Functions

The difference between a statement and a function is this: A statement performs an action, a function returns a result. The terminology is a little flaccid. "Statement" is sometimes used more generally to refer to any programming command, so it's like the old saw about all beagles being dogs but not all dogs being beagles: All functions are statements, but not all statements are functions. To make the distinction easier to follow, you will sometimes hear statements which perform a series of actions (and do not return a result) referred to as *procedures* or *procedural statements*. In what follows, I normally use "statement" to refer specifically to a procedural statement; "function" will always refer to a command that returns a result.

To make this abstract distinction concrete, take one of the simplest WordBasic statements: *Bold* (you may recall that this command was used in the SpecialBold macro recorded in Chapter 4). This statement can be called with an argument of 1 or 0, or with no argument at all. Unmodified, Bold toggles the state of the bold attribute of the currently selected text (or insertion point). Bold 1 boldfaces the current text. Bold 0 unboldfaces the current text. Simple.

There is also a function equivalent to this statement. It has the form **Bold( )**. Note the empty parenthesis after the function name. This function form, when executed, does not change the current insertion point's bold attribute. It performs no action. It is, itself, set to a value which can tell the running macro if the current selection is all bold, not bold, or partially bold. That's why I call functions "passive." They do not themselves do anything. Rather, they report. A function asks a question of Word and stores the answer in itself; a function becomes the answer it returns.

This sounds more complicated, perhaps, than it is. Here are two examples of WordBasic function calls:

```
CurrentState = Bold()
If CurrentState = 0 Then Bold 1
```

The first line creates a container (a variable) named CurrentState and assigns to it the result returned by the Bold( ) function. That is, Bold( ) is doing the work—asking Word if the current text is bold or not—becoming itself the answer, in the form of 1 or 0, and then assigning that value to CurrentState.

```
Sub Main
If UnderLine() Then
   UnderLine 0
Else
   UnderLine 1
End If
End Sub
```

This macro uses a slightly different tactic. It does not create a temporary variable to hold the value of the function. It evaluates the function UnderLine( ) itself. Remember, the function is equal to the answer it finds. This macro checks to see if the current text is underlined. If it is, it turns underlining off with the statement UnderLine 0; otherwise it turns underlining on with the statement UnderLine 1.

It is important to know that there are functions that return integers (Bold( ) is such an integer function) and functions that return strings. You can tell a function that returns a string because it always has a dollar sign between the function name and the open parenthesis. For example, the function Selection$( ) returns the currently selected text.

WordBasic consists of a group of statements and functions lifted wholesale from BASIC, and a group of functions that are specific to Word. So, in a sense, it is both a sub- and a super-set of BASIC.

There are 309 WordBasic commands (procedures and functions combined). Don't let this figure strike terror into your non-programmer's heart. You will not have to memorize the entire list. We are not learning Latin here. You will not have to resort to memory for two reasons: The help file contains an annotated list of all WordBasic commands, and the macro recorder can easily provide you with the syntax of most of the commands. Further, as stated in previous chapters, the format of the WordBasic commands consistently follows the function and menu location of each command's associated function. So, for instance, if you wish to execute the WordBasic statement to arrange all document windows, the equivalent of selecting Arrange All from the Window main menu, you will not be surprised to learn that the statement has the form: WindowArrangeAll.

You don't need to know the specific vocabulary of WordBasic. It is important, however, that you understand the grammar of WordBasic, and further, the possible arrangement of the commands—the syntax.

## Variables

In several of the examples given thus far in this book, I have spoken of "creating a container" to hold a value. I have avoided, until now, naming this element of WordBasic: Such a container for a value is more rightly called a *variable*. A variable is just what it sounds like, just what it was back in sixth grade algebra: a symbol that holds an assigned value, with the ability to change and be changed.

A variable comes in two basic flavors:

- A variable that retains the same value throughout the execution of the macro. In most programming languages this type of container is more accurately called a *constant*.

- A variable that begins with one value, usually assigned by the programmer, that is changed during the execution of the macro, either by the macro itself or by user input.

As we explore the various example macros presented in the next chapters this distinction will become clear. For now, hold onto this basic concept: A variable provides an easy way for a macro to store a value, to increment or alter that value according to either a programmed equation or through user input.

### String Variables

Unlike variables in algebra, programming variables are not limited to numeric values. When you create a macro, you can assign a character, word, phrase, or sentence to an easily accessed (and easily altered) *string variable*.

For example, suppose you have a program that repeatedly displays the message "Now is the time for all good folk to come to the aid of their country." Without a string variable you would have to type the above phrase at every location in the macro where the message is to be displayed. With a string variable you would make the following assignment at the beginning of the macro:

```
Message$ = "Now is the time for all good folk to come to the aid of their
country."
```

and then call that variable in all subsequent instances where that message will be displayed.

A string variable always ends with a dollar sign ($). The actual text assigned to a string variable, the *string literal*, is always enclosed in quotation marks. For example:

```
NameBoy$ = "Jack"
```

assigns the string literal "Jack" to the variable NameBoy$. Note that the name of the variable can be of any length, and should be chosen for its descriptive value, following the same conventions and considerations used in naming a macro.

One of the simplest operations you can perform on a string or a string variable is concatenation: adding strings together. For example:

```
NameBoy$ = "Jack"
NameGirl$ = "Jill"
NameCouple$ = NameBoy$+" and "+NameGirl$
```

The last example concatenates, that is, combines, two string variables with a string literal. Note that the string literal—space, "and," space—is surrounded by quotation marks.

To create a null string variable, that is, a string that is completely empty, you would make the following assignment:

```
Null$ = ""
```

Notice the string literal is literally nothing. The assignment value is just two quotation marks with nothing in between. If you have never programmed, this may seem an odd variable. Nothing will come of nothing. But if you want to test if a variable has any value at all, it is quite common to ask a question such as:

```
If AnyVariable$ <> "" Then Beep
```

meaning: "If the variable named AnyVariable$ isn't empty, then do this or that (in this case, beep the internal speaker)."

There are 12 string functions in WordBasic, which allow you to perform various manipulations on text strings or request certain information about the string.

For example, there are string functions to determine the length of a string, to discover if a string contains a specified character or substring, and to return a portion of a string. We will use each of these functions within macros in the course of later examples. Table 6.1 describes each of the string functions available in WordBasic.

### Numeric Variables

A numeric variable name can be any combination of alphanumeric characters with the single limitation that the first character cannot be a digit. For example:

```
JackAge = 35
JillAge = 24
ItemsSold = 260
Days = 24
JackAge1 = 35
JillAge1 = 24
```

are all legal numeric variable assignments. Note that the numeric literals are not enclosed in quotation marks. A string literal, whether being passed as a parameter or being assigned to a variable, must be enclosed in quotation marks. A numeric literal, again, whether a parameter or an assignment, must not be enclosed in parentheses. If a number is enclosed in quotation marks, then it is viewed as the string representation of the value, not as the value itself. For instance:

```
JillAge$ = "24"
```

and

```
JillAge = 24
```

are most definitely not equivalent. The first assigns the string literal "24" to a string variable; the second assigns the numeric literal, the value 24, to a numeric variable. Also note, if you mix a numeric integer with a string variable, you will elicit a none-too-informative error message. The line:

```
JillAge$ = 24
```

will fail every time.

**Table 6.1**    **Table of String Functions**

| Function | Description | Example | Result |
|---|---|---|---|
| Asc() | Returns the ANSI character code of the first character in a string. | Asc("Jill") | 74 |
| Chr$() | Returns a one-character string based on the specified ANSI code. | Chr$(74) | J |
| InStr() | Searches for one text string in another. Returns the location. | Instr("Jack","c") | 3 |
| LCase$() | Returns Source$ converted to lowercase. | LCase$("BOGUS") | bogus |
| Left$() | Returns the leftmost n characters of Source$. | Left$("Bogus",3) | Bog |
| Len() | Returns the number of characters in Source$. | Len("Exciting") | 8 |
| Mid$() | Returns a requested number of characters from a specified string, starting at a specified index. If no number is specified in the third parameter position, the rest of the string is returned. | Mid$("Exciting",5,3)<br>Mid$("Exciting",5) | tin<br>ting |
| Right$() | Returns the rightmost n characters of Source$. | Right$("Exciting",5) | Excit |
| Str$() | Returns the string representation of a value. | Str$(101) | "101" |
| String$() | Returns a string composed of a specified character repeated a specified number of times. | String$("!",4) | !!!! |
| UCase$() | Returns a string $ converted to uppercase. | UCase$("bogus") | BOGUS |
| Val() | Returns the numeric value of a string. | Val("101") | 101 |
| | Strings that begin with characters other than a digit return 0 (zero). | Val("Bogus") | 0 |

It is sometimes confusing to people who are familiar with BASIC why a string must terminate with a dollar sign ($), yet an integer need not terminate with a number sign (#). It does help with ease of reading to adopt this convention and end all numeric variables with a number sign. However, if you adopt this convention, be consistent. If you create a variable named JackAge and another named JackAge#, WordBasic can get terribly confused.

**Arithmetic on Numeric Variables**  In the same way that you can combine strings to form larger strings, you can perform various operations upon numeric variables.

The most basic numeric operations are arithmetic: addition, subtraction, multiplication, and division. For example:

```
AgeDifference = JackAge - JillAge
```

subtracts Jill's age from Jack's age and assigns the difference to a variable named AgeDifference. And

```
AverageItemsSold = ItemsSold / Days
```

divides the number of items sold by the number of selling days, and assigns the result to the numeric variable AverageItemsSold.

Table 6.2 lists the arithmetic operations supported by WordBasic.

**Table 6.2**  **Arithmetic Operations**

| Operator | Description | Example |
|---|---|---|
| – | Subtraction or negation | x–y |
|  |  | 7–2 |
|  |  | –4 |
| + | Addition | x+y |
|  |  | 7+2 |
| / | Divides first number by second | x/y |
|  |  | 7/2 |
| * | Multiplication | x*y |
| Mod | Rounds operands to integers, divides the first by the second, and returns the remainder | 7 Mod 2 |

Word will perform multiplication and division before addition and subtraction. So, the following two lines:

```
6 * 7-6
6 * (7-6)
```

are not equivalent. The best idea is to always group discrete operations in parentheses.

WordBasic includes the arithmetic functions listed in Table 6.3.

**Logical Comparison**   Variables, both string and numeric, can be compared "logically." Such a relational comparison is called a Boolean expression and returns a value of true or false.

The logical operators and their functions are shown in the following table.

| Operator | Function |
|---|---|
| = | Tests if two variables are equal |
| <> | Tests if two variables are not equal |
| > | Tests if the first variable is greater than the second |
| < | Tests if the first variable is less than the second |
| <= | Tests if the first variable is equal to or less than the second |
| => | Tests if the first variable is equal to or greater than the second |

**Table 6.3**   **Arithmetic Functions**

| Function | Description | Example | Result |
|---|---|---|---|
| Abs() | Returns the absolute, unsigned, value of a number. | Abs(−12) | 12 |
| Int() | Returns the integer portion of a decimal number. | Int(1.5) | 1 |
|  |  | Int(−1.5) | −1 |
| Sgn() | Returns the sign of a number. | Sgn(15) | 1 |
|  |  | Sgn(−16) | −1 |
|  |  | Sgn(0) | 0 |
| Rnd() | Generates a random number between 0 and 1. | Rnd() | 0.9729491532 |
| Val() | Returns the numeric value of a string. | Val("101") | 101 |
|  | Strings that begin with characters other than a digit return 0 (zero). | Val("Bogus") | 0 |
|  | Notice this function is in both the string and arithmetic tables. |  |  |

Logical relations between numeric values are self-evident. However, WordBasic also allows comparison between strings. For example:

```
"A" < "B"
```

evaluates to true, and

```
"Any" > "Another"
```

also evaluates to true.

In these examples string literals are compared logically. The first example is obvious: We have no trouble understanding that the letter "A" is less than the letter "B." Think alphabetically: "A" is 1 and "B" is 2. The second example is a little less obvious. The word "Another" is physically larger than "Any." It has more characters. However, the alphabetical comparison done by WordBasic proceeds one character at a time and stops when it reaches the end of either of the words being compared. So, in this case, the first two characters in each word are identical; it is in the third character that there is a difference: "y" is greater than "o." The comparison stops there and the logical evaluation returns true: "Any" is greater than "Ano."

You can also compare string variables:

```
NameBoy$ = "Jack"
NameGirl$ = "Jill"
If NameBoy$ < NameGirl$ Then Beep
```

In this case "Jack" is less than "Jill," so the internal speaker beeps.

A further note on how WordBasic makes string comparisons. A lowercase letter is different from the uppercase of that same letter. "A" does not have the same value as "a." Paradoxically, lowercase letters are "larger" than uppercase counterparts. The reason is this: The value being compared is not simply an alphabetical index, the value of each character ranging from 1 to 26. Rather, the value of each possible letter, 26 lowercase and 26 uppercase, corresponds to a number known as its *ANSI value*. It seems obvious, once you think about it, that a computer must distinguish case; to the computer an uppercase "A" and a lowercase "a" must be unique objects. The way in which Windows, and all Windows applications, make this distinction has been codified in a standard table of *character codes* called the American National Standard Institute character set or ANSI set for short. In this chart, included in the Windows manual and in Appendix XX, "A–Z" corresponds to values 65-90; "a–z" corresponds to 97–122.

So, to be more precise, WordBasic translates the comparison:

```
"A" > "B"
```

into

```
65 > 66
```

and the comparison

```
"a" < "A"
```

into

```
97 < 65
```

which, of course, is false. Because of this difference in the value of case, you should always force strings into the same case before or during the comparison. For example:

```
NameBoy$ = "Jack"
NameGirl$ = "Jill"
If LCase$(NameBoy$) < LCase$(NameGirl$) Then Beep
```

The addition of the **LCase$( )** function transforms both of the string variables to lowercase while making the string comparison.

A logical evaluation of two variables, or the current state of a single variable (that is, for instance, is it 1 or 0, on or off, true or false), provides an easy way to test a condition and branch to different parts of a macro dependent on the status of that condition. Logical evaluations are sometimes referred to as *expressions*. In the statement:

```
If X > Y Then Beep
```

the expression is "X > Y"; this expression is evaluated logically, returning an answer of true or false. The statement proceeds according to the result of the evaluation of the expression.

This brings up an interesting and sometimes confusing issue: What constitutes truth? When a check box is checked, that is, its associated function is on, the value associated with that parameter is the integer 1. If it is off, the value is 0. This was demonstrated in the example macro RevisionMarksOn. Similarly, if you execute the macro function

```
x=Bold()
```

on bold text, the value of x would be 1, that is, Bold( ) returns the integer 1 when the queried text is, in fact, boldface.

You would be justified in extrapolating from this fact that if you wanted to create a variable, named True, to represent the Boolean state true in a macro, you would assign a variable the integer value of 1 with the statement

```
True=1
```

Not so. In a macro, truth is represented by –1:

```
True=-1
```

and false by 0:

```
False=0
```

In fact, for most WordBasic statements any non-zero value will tell the statement to behave as if –1 were the parameter. Or to put it another way, zero always means false; anything that is not zero means true to a WordBasic statement.

So, for example:

```
Bold 1
Bold 1992
Bold -1
```

all mean: "Make the current text bold," but only

```
Bold 0
```

means: "Make the current text not bold."

If you are creating a variable to be manipulated within a macro, a variable that will be tested as true or false for conditional purposes, set that value to –1, not to just any old non-zero value.

# Communicating—To and From the Macro

The preceding section described variables in some detail. If you are completely new to programming, the question must have arisen, how do I get at a variable? How do I set it? How do I change it? How do I see its current value? This points us directly to a discussion of the fundamental definition of a language: communication. There are several WordBasic statements and functions designed for the purpose of displaying information to the user and eliciting information from the user.

## Displaying a Value or a Variable

There are two ways for a macro to display a value. You are already familiar with both methods. You have seen messages flash across the bottom of Word's application screen, on the status bar, when a file is being saved, or when a menu item is selected. You have also seen, both in Word and in many other Windows applications, what are known as message boxes. What you may not have realized is that WordBasic provides ways to display custom messages in either of these formats.

### On the Status Bar—The Print Statement

In BASIC, the Print command directs information, that is "prints," to various destinations: the printer, a file, or the screen. In WordBasic, the default Print destination is the status line.

The syntax for Print, as a method of displaying information on the status line, is

```
Print VariableName[$]
```

Let's create a completely useless, but demonstrative, macro called JackAndJill.

```
Sub Main
Print "Jack"
End Sub
```

When you run this macro, the name "Jack" will be displayed on the status bar.

To exemplify string concatenation, modify JackAndJill to read

```
Sub Main
BoyName$ = "Jack"
GirlName$ = "Jill"
Print BoyName$+ " and " +GirlName$ +" went up to the Odeon."
End Sub
```

When you execute the macro JackAndJill, you will see the following on the status line:

```
Jack and Jill went up to the Odeon.
```

One of the most convenient aspects of the Print statement is that you can easily mix strings, string variables, numbers, and numeric variables. A numeric value is separated from a string literal by a semicolon. To exemplify the ability to print both string variables and numeric variables, create a macro named JackJillAge:

```
Sub Main
BoyName$ = "Jack"
GirlName$ = "Jill"
bAge = 35
gAge = 25
Print BoyName$+ " is"; bAge;" and "+GirlName$+ " is";gAge
End Sub
```

To exemplify the ability to print the results of an arithmetic operation:

```
Sub Main
BoyName$ = "Jack"
GirlName$ = "Jill"
bAge = 35
gAge = 18
Print BoyName$ + " is ";bAge-gAge; " older than "+ GirlName$
End Sub
```

The Print statement is useful as a way of keeping a user informed about the progress of a macro. It is also a good means of testing whether a macro is functioning as expected. More will be said on that use of Print in Chapter 8.

The advantage of the Print statement is that the message remains on the status bar until a subsequent message, generated by another Print statement or by Word, replaces it. The disadvantage is that the user can easily overlook the message flashed on the bottom of the screen.

### In a Box—The MsgBox Statement

A message displayed in a message box is hard to ignore, especially since the user must select OK before the macro will continue executing.

The syntax for MsgBox is

```
MsgBox Message$, [Title$],[Type]
```

**NOTE.** *Both in this book and in* Using WordBasic, *if a parameter is bracketed, as are Title$ and Type above, then that parameter is optional. If an optional parameter is not given when a statement is called, WordBasic will use the default value. In the case of MsgBox the default title is "Microsoft Word" and the default type is 0.*

For example, we can modify JackAndJill to use MsgBox instead of Print:

```
Sub Main
BoyName$ = "Jack"
GirlName$ = "Jill"
MsgBox BoyName$+ " and " +GirlName$ + " went up to the Odeon."
End Sub
```

The result of running this macro would be

The MsgBox statement requires that the message be either a string literal or a string variable. Unlike the Print statement, MsgBox cannot display numeric values directly. If you wish to display the value of a numeric variable in a message box, you must first convert the numeric variable to a string using the built-in Str$( ) function. For example, if

```
Number = 35
```

then

```
Str$(Number)
```

would return the string "35". The statement

```
MsgBox Number
```

would display an error message; but the statement

```
MsgBox Str$(Number)
```

would display the number as a text string. So, we could alter the macro Jack-JillAge to use MsgBox as follows:

```
Sub Main
BoyName$ = "Jack"
GirlName$ = "Jill"
bAge = 35
gAge = 25
MsgBox BoyName$ + " is" + Str$(bAge) + " and "+GirlName$+" is " + Str$(gAge)
End Sub
```

Notice the use of the Str$( ) function to convert bAge and gAge to strings.

Unlike the Print statement, MsgBox requires confirmation before the macro continues execution. For example, the following macro

```
Sub Main
MsgBox "This is message one"
MsgBox "This is message two"
MsgBox "This is message three"
MsgBox "This is message four"
End Sub
```

would display four messages, pausing at each for the user to press OK.

There are two optional parameters that can be sent to MsgBox along with the message. The first optional parameter is a text string. If there is a second string passed to MsgBox, then that string will be printed as the title of the message box.

```
MsgBox "This is message one", "Message One Title"
```

There is an optional third parameter that determines which icon will be displayed to the left of the message. By default, MsgBox displays no icon. Below is a table of the possible Type values and the corresponding icon description:

| 16 | Stop sign |
| 32 | Question mark |
| 48 | Attention (exclamation point) |
| 64 | Information (the letter "i") |

For example:

```
MsgBox "This is message one", "Message One Title", 64
```

displays the message, with a title, accompanied by the Information icon.
Here's a macro that will demonstrate all of the icons in order:

```
Sub Main
MsgBox "This is message one","Stop sign",16
MsgBox "This is message two","Question mark",32
MsgBox "This is message three","Attention", 48
MsgBox "This is message four","Information",64
End Sub
```

The message displayed by MsgBox is limited to 255 characters.

## User Input

So much for a macro communicating information to the user. Now we must explore the reciprocal language attribute of WordBasic: communicating information from the user to the macro.

### From the Status Bar—The Input Statement

The simplest way to allow a user to modify a variable, either string or numeric, is the Input statement.
Like Print, this function uses the status bar. The syntax for Input is

```
Input [Prompt$], Variable[$]
```

Since this function can be used to modify either string or numeric variables, the variable parameter can be either a number or a string, which is why the ending "$" is in brackets.

The statement

```
Input "How old is Jill", JillAge
```

would place the user's numeric response in the variable JillAge. Yet the statement

```
Input "Open which directory", OpenDir$
```

would place the string entered by the user into the string variable OpenDir$.

We could make a macro that prompted the user for the name of an existing directory and then changed to that directory:

```
Sub Main
Input "Start in what directory", OpenDir$
ChDir(OpenDir$)
End Sub
```

The limitations of Input as a way to get user input are twofold: Like the Print function, messages on the status bar can be easily overlooked, and Input allows only limited editing capabilities.

### Response in a Box—The InputBox$() Function

A second WordBasic command, specifically designed for allowing the user to change a string variable, is InputBox$.

The syntax for InputBox$ is

```
Response$ = InputBox$(Prompt$,[Title$],[Default$])
```

A couple of things to note: This is a string function and therefore ends with a dollar sign. That is, it returns a string as its result. The returned result can either be manipulated directly or assigned to a variable. So, for instance:

```
Sub Main
A$ = InputBox$("Insert what string")
Insert A$
End Sub
```

and

```
Sub Main
Insert InputBox$("Insert what string")
End Sub
```

are equivalent macros.

Note that this function has two optional parameters. The first, as with MsgBox, displays a title; the second presents a default value to the user.

Using InputBox$( ) we can now make our example macro smarter:

```
Sub Main
OpenDir$ = "C:\WINWORD\DATA"
OpenDir$ = InputBox$("Type in the directory to open", "Open Dir", OpenDir$)
ChDir OpenDir$
End Sub
```

This macro demonstrates a fundamental programming concept: *variable substitution.* At the start of the macro the variable OpenDir$ is hard-coded, that is, directly defined, as C:\WINWORD\DATA. After the user answers the InputBox$( ) query, the contents of the variable OpenDir$ are altered; one value is substituted for another. The ability of a variable to change, and for macros to make judgments based upon this dynamic variable, is precisely what allows a macro to respond flexibly to various circumstances.

### Asking a Yes or No Question—The MsgBox() Function

Earlier we discussed using the MsgBox statement to pause a macro and display a message, with or without an icon. Such a message box has limited utility since all it can do is display the message and wait for the user to press OK to cancel the message box. However, there is another form of MsgBox which in addition to displaying a message asks the user to choose one button out of either two or three choices, and set a variable that enables the macro to proceed according to which button is pressed.

The syntax of the function MsgBox( ) is

```
x=MsgBox(Prompt$, [Title$], [Type]):
```

Notice that while InputBox$( ) returns a string variable, this function returns an integer. You can tell this by two signals: The function name does not end with a dollar sign, and the variable created to contain its result is a numeric variable.

The following line would display a message, with a title, without an icon; but instead of only an OK button, it also displays a Cancel button.

```
Response = MsgBox("Continue?","Get an OK/Cancel",1)
```

The Cancel button is displayed because the third parameter, the Type, has been set to 1 rather than the default value of 0.

In the above example, if the user selects OK, the MsgBox( ) function will return –1 (which, recall, is the value WordBasic reads as true). If the user selects Cancel, the MsgBox( ) function will return 0. A subsequent evaluation of the variable Response, which contains the return result of the MsgBox( ), can determine the further action of the macro. For instance:

```
Sub Main
True = -1
False = 0
Response = MsgBox("Continue?","Get an OK/Cancel",1)
If Response = True Then
    MsgBox "I'm going to continue"
Else
    MsgBox "I'm going to stop."
End If
End Sub
```

If, instead of OK and Cancel, you wanted to display buttons labeled Yes and No, simply change the Type parameter from 1 to 4.

```
Response = MsgBox("Should I continue?","Get a Yes/No",4)
```

In the previous section the optional parameter Type was described as a way to display icons in message boxes. This parameter also controls the number and type of the buttons displayed by the function MsgBox( ). Here follows a table describing the button type values:

| | |
|---|---|
| 1 | OK and Cancel |
| 2 | Abort, Retry, Ignore |
| 3 | Yes, No, Cancel |
| 4 | Yes and No |
| 5 | Retry and Cancel |

But, you might ask, what if I want to display both an icon and a button group other than the default OK? The answer is to add the two type values together, that is, add the icon value and the button value:

```
Response = MsgBox("Continue?","Get a Yes/No",4+32)
```

The 4 changes the button from OK to Yes/No; the 32 displays the question mark icon. As with OK and Cancel, if the user selects Yes, the function returns –1; if the user selects No, the function returns 0.

Notice that there are two button type values that will display three buttons. In the following example, where type is 3 (Yes/No/Cancel) + 32 (Question Mark)

```
Answer = MsgBox("Continue?","Get a Yes/No/Cancel",3+32)
```

the variable Response will be set to –1 for Yes, to 0 for No, and to 1 for Cancel.

It is this ability to set a variable according to which button is selected that allows MsgBox( ) to control the flow of a macro's execution.

# Control Structures

We have been gathering and reviewing some of the basic concepts of Word-Basic programming. We have introduced the notion of variable substitution, demonstrated how to manipulate variables (arithmetic and string), and provided a way to pause a macro and display variables and messages. Now we will show how to combine these ideas to perform more intricate tasks, primarily by adding a single concept to our arsenal: *conditional branching*.

The most frequent use of a variable is as a container that tells the macro, as it executes, about a specific condition. A variable is used by the macro to determine the current landscape. A variable allows a macro to make a judgment about a given value—such as true or false—and alter its own behavior accordingly.

A macro's ability to modify its own actions is called conditional branching. This is the aspect of WordBasic that raises it above a simple macro processor to a macro language. Think of the five conditional branching facilities, or *control structures*, in light of the definition of language given above: It must communicate. Print and MsgBox allow a macro to communicate with the user. Input, InputBox$( ), and MsgBox( ) allow the user to communicate with the macro. Control structures allow a macro to communicate with itself.

A control structure is a syntactical unit that evaluates a specific condition, usually represented by a variable, and then points the macro in a specific direction. It passes control to, that is, "branches off to," an appropriate group of statements.

## Goto

The Goto statement is an extremely powerful aspect of WordBasic. It allows you to jump to another part of a macro if a specific condition is met. A Goto statement takes the form:

```
Goto LabelMarker
```

where LabelMarker references a single-word line, ending in a colon, that marks the destination of the Goto statement.

A label must be on a line by itself; it must begin in the first column of that line; and it cannot be more than 40 characters long. As with naming macros and variables, I would highly recommend choosing informative labels. (Actually, an argument can be made for humorous as well as descriptive naming. Keep it goofy, if possible.) For example:

```
If BooleanExpression Then Goto RemainingStuffLabel
    ...DoLotsOfStuff
RemainingStuffLabel:
    ...DoRemainingStuff
```

The above lines are what programmers call *pseudocode*. That is, it represents an idea of a piece of code without being code itself. There is no built-in constant or variable named BooleanExpression. There is no WordBasic statement named DoLotsOfStuff or DoRemainingStuff. I use these terms to represent the general format of the code.

What this pseudocode represents is the following logic: If a certain expression is true, then skip to a label; in this case the label is named "RemainingStuffLabel." The consequence of this jump is that the code represented by DoLotsOfStuff will not be executed at all and DoRemainingStuff will be executed immediately. If the expression is evaluated as false, then both DoLotsOfStuff and DoRemainingStuff will be executed.

Let's take an example macro from the previous section and demonstrate how Goto makes it more meaningful.

```
Sub Main
True = -1
False = 0
Response = MsgBox("Continue?","Get an OK/Cancel",1)
If Response = True Then
    MsgBox "I'm going to continue"
    DoLotsOfUsefulStuff
Else
    Goto EndOfMacro
End If
EndOfMacro:
End Sub
```

One of the pitfalls inherent in creating complex macros is that they become susceptible to user input error. For example, what happens, in a macro that asks the user to input a path specification, if the user types an invalid path, either because of a typing error or because the path specified doesn't exist? What happens when you try to cancel the command? A complex macro, especially one that asks for user input, must check to see that user input is in the proper form. And the macro must have an alternative to perform when the input is incorrect or irrelevant. This is called *error checking* or *error trapping.* One tool often used when checking if an error has occurred is the Goto statement.

To demonstrate error trapping and the Goto statement, let's create a macro named OpenDir.

```
Sub Main
OpenDir$ = "C:\WINWORD\DATA"    'define a variable and assign it a value

Again:                          'start of main part of macro

On Error Goto Bye               'if Escape is pressed, jump to end
OpenDir$ = InputBox$("Type in the directory to open", "OpenDir", OpenDir$)

On Error Goto ErrorMsg          'if there's a problem changing to OpenDir$,
                                'jump to ErrorMsg

ChDir (OpenDir$)                     'change directory

On Error Goto Bye               'prepare for the next error
ToolsMacro "FileOpen", .Run      'call the command macro FileOpen
Goto Bye                        'everything went well, so exit

ErrorMsg:                           'there was an error in changing directory,
MsgBox "You typed the path incorrectly"  'so display a message
Err = 0                             'reset the error variable for the next try
Goto Again:                         'jump back to the top and try again

Bye:                                'label marking the end of the macro
End Sub
```

This macro is the first we've created that is fully *commented*. A comment is a line or a part of a line in a macro that is disregarded by Word when the macro is executed. A comment is preceded by either an apostrophe or the letters REM (an abbreviation for remark). OpenDir combines several of the pieces discussed in previous sections into a single, useful macro. Here's an analysis of the logic:

- Create a string variable and assign a default path to it.

- Allow the user to edit this path using InputBox$( ).

- Check for cancellation of the InputBox( ).

- Jump to the end of the macro if the InputBox( ) call is canceled.

- Change to the specified directory.

- If the directory change fails, jump to the label named Again, which marks the beginning of the macro.

- Execute the built-in command macro FileOpen.

- Check for cancellation of the FileOpen dialog box.

- Jump to the end if found.

The program logic of the macro OpenDir can be graphically represented by the flowchart found in Figure 6.1. Using a flowchart to outline the structure of a macro, like using pseudocode, is a good programming practice.

**Figure 6.1**
Program flow of
OpenDir

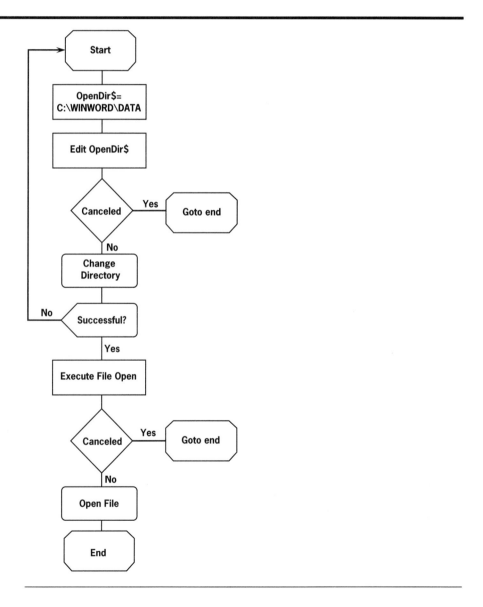

Note that the statement On Error appears on the line before both the

```
InputBox$()
```

and the

```
ToolsMacro "FileOpen", .Run
```

statements. Essentially, On Error is saying: "If an error occurs on the next statement, then jump to the named label."

Goto allows a macro to pass control to another portion of the macro. The other control structures allow you to do more complex evaluations and perform more complex branching.

## If...ElseIf...Else...End If

The most frequently used control structure is called, in shortened form, If...Then. This control structure has the following basic syntax:

```
If BooleanExpression Then DoSomething
```

You can complicate the evaluation made by an If...Then control structure:

```
If BooleanExpression Then
    DoOneThing
Else
    DoAnotherThing
End If
```

Note that in this case the control structure has two choices. The two choices are separated by the word Else, and the entire unit ends with the phrase End If. For example:

```
Sub Main
JackAge = 35
JillAge = 25
AgeDifference = JackAge - JillAge
If AgeDifference < 10 Then
    Print "Not such a problem"
Else
    Print "Time to think a bit."
    Beep
End If
End Sub
```

You can add any number of conditions, branching to an equal number of choices, by using the ElseIf construction:

```
If BooleanExpression Then
    DoOneThing
```

```
ElseIf SecondBooleanExpression Then
   DoSecondThing
ElseIf ThirdBooleanExpression Then
   DoThirdThing
Else
   DoFourthThing
End If
```

Note: ElseIf is a single word; End If, the terminating statement to an If…Then control structure, is two words. (Oddly enough, EndIf works as well as End If; Else If, however, causes a syntax error.)

When the number of conditions to test is more than three or four, The Select Case…End Select control structure is more convenient and easier to read than an extended If…Then structure. However, according to various comments made by Word's developers, it seems that If…Then requires less memory and executes marginally faster than other control structures.

## Select Case…End Select

The Select Case control structure has the following syntax:

```
Select Case Expression
    Case CaseExpression1
        FirstCaseStatementsToExecute
    Case CaseExpression2
        SecondCaseStatementsToExecute
    Case Else
End Select
```

The Select Case control structure tests the value of a variable against a "list" of possible values. When it hits a match (that is, when the comparison evaluates to true), a series of statements is executed. When a match is made, the case structure ends, and the macro continues on to the next statement.

For example:

```
Sub Main
TryAgain:
Input "Pick a number between 1 and 10)", PickedNumber        'Get a number
Select Case PickedNumber      'the expression checked is the variable
PickedNumber
    Case 1                    'a single value
        MsgBox "You selected 1"
    Case 2, 3, 4              'a group of values separated by commas
        MsgBox "Less than 5"
    Case 5 To 10              'a range of values
        MsgBox "Between 5 and 10"
```

```
      Case Else              'all other "cases"
           MsgBox "I said between 1 and 10", 16
           Goto TryAgain
End Select
Beep
End Sub
```

The Case Select control structure is particularly useful when a macro uses a custom dialog box (which will be covered in Chapter 8). MsgBox( ) returns at most three values (Yes, No, Cancel), and therefore an If...Then clause is usually sufficient to manage macro flow according to the results. A custom dialog box can return as many values as you like; therefore a control structure that can evaluate many possible values, such as Case Select, is required.

**NOTE.** *In the above example there is a Goto statement that is executed if the number entered is not between 1 and 10. The label jumped to in this call is located prior to the Select Case statement. It is an idiosyncrasy that if the label jumped to with a Goto statement is below the Select Case statement, an error message is generated. You cannot Goto a label from within a Select Case...End Select if that label is located beneath the control structure. To get around this, simply set a temporary variable, a* flag, *to a specific value, and then evaluate the* flag *once the control structure ends. For instance:*

```
Sub Main
TryAgain:
Input "Pick a number between 1 and 10", PickedNumber        'get a number
Select Case PickedNumber           'the expression checked is the variable
PickedNumber
      Case 0                        'if 0 or nothing is entered
           TempFlag = -1            'set the TempFlag variable to -1
      Case 1                        'a single value
         MsgBox "You selected 1"
      Case 2, 3, 4                  'a group of values separated by commas
         MsgBox "Less than 5"
      Case 5 To 10                  'a range of values
         MsgBox "Between 5 and 10"
      Case Else                     'all other "cases"
         MsgBox "I said between 1 and 10", 16
         Goto TryAgain
End Select
If TempFlag = -1 Then Goto Bye     'jump to the label named Bye
Beep
Bye:
End Sub
```

Select...Case is particularly suited to evaluating multiple conditions.

## For...Next

The For...Next control structure has the following syntax:

```
For CounterVariable = Start to End
    Statement(s)
Next [CounterVariable]
```

This control structure is primarily used for repeating an action a finite number of times or for stepping through each of the elements in an array (arrays are a special form of variable which will be discussed in detail in the next section). For example:

```
Sub Main
CounterVariable = 1
For CounterVariable = 1 to 10
    Beep
Next CounterVariable
End Sub
```

would sound the speaker ten times.

Here is a more useful example that loops through all the currently available fonts and inserts the font number, the font name, and a string of text properly formatted:

```
Sub Main
For Count = 1 To CountFonts() 'loop through all the fonts and
    Font Font$(Count)          'apply the font
REM the next line inserts a concatenated string
REM composed of the count variable, the font name,
REM and a text string.
    Insert Str$(Count) + ":  " + Font$(Count) + "—Every good boy deserves fun"
    InsertPara                 'insert a paragraph
    Print Font$(Count)         'print a message
Next Count                     'loop to next font
End Sub
```

This macro determines the number of fonts currently available with the built-in function CountFonts( ). It uses a loop to format the current paragraph with each of those fonts, inserting an index number, the font name, and a string.

For...Next is particularly suited to stepping through all the elements in a predefined list of variables.

## While...Wend

The syntax for While...Wend is

```
While BooleanExpression
    Statement(s)
Wend
```

Like the For…Next loop, While…Wend allows a macro to repeat a series of statements. But instead of using an incremented counter variable, it uses a true or false condition as the controlling test. As long as the test condition is true, the statements contained between the While and the Wend will be executed. When the Boolean expression is evaluated to false, the loop stops. Note: If the condition is false at the outset of the loop, the statements will not be executed at all.

For example, we could rewrite the beeping macro as follows:

```
Sub Main
Count = 1                'declare a count variable
While Count < 11         'a relational comparison that returns true or false
    Beep                 'the statement to execute
    Count = Count+1      'increment the count variable
Wend                     'end of the loop
End Sub
```

This macro would sound the speaker ten times. Then, when the count has been incremented to 11, and the condition is no longer true, the loop is exited.

The While…Wend loop is particularly useful if you need to perform an action at every occurrence of a word, or for every paragraph in a document. For instance, the following would boldface every instance of the abbreviation "QED":

```
Sub Main
StartOfDocument
FindString$ = "QED"
EditFind .Find = FindString$, .Direction = 2, .MatchCase = 1
While EditFindFound()
Print "Working…"
    Bold 1
    EditFind .Find = FindString$, .Direction = 2, .MatchCase = 1
Wend
End Sub
```

The following example would count the number of paragraphs in the current document:

```
Sub Main
StartOfDocument
While ParaDown()
    Count = Count + 1
Wend
Print "There are" ;Count;" paragraphs in this document "
End Sub
```

# Getting at a Dialog Box—Introducing Arrays

A dialog box is a structured presentation of a number of related options, navigated by clicking the mouse, or by a combination of Tab, spacebar, and arrow keys. One of the virtues of the Windows interface is that a single dialog box can present as much information, and provide for changing as many options, as several option screens in character-based applications.

But beyond this presentational virtue, dialog boxes in Word have a much more fundamental utility. They are groupings of values and options of a macro. We've already discussed how virtually every editing function in Word can be seen as a built-in command macro. Now, as we delve into the nature of dialog boxes, the power of this paradigm will become clear.

In Chapter 5 we created an example macro, RevisionMarksOnOff, which toggled revision marks on and off:

```
Sub Main
Dim DialogRecord As ToolsRevisionMarks
GetCurValues DialogRecord
CurrentStatus = DialogRecord.MarkRevisions
If CurrentStatus = 0 Then
   ToolsRevisionMarks .MarkRevisions = 1
Else
   ToolsRevisionMarks .MarkRevisions = 0
End If
End Sub
```

We have now covered sufficient WordBasic fundamentals to take a second look at this macro, and explain how, precisely, it managed to look under the hood and see the current status of revision marking.

The statement

```
Dim DialogRecord As ToolsRevisionMarks
```

was described in Chapter 5 with the sentence: "create a temporary container named 'DialogRecord' that has the same shape as the command macro ToolsRevisionMarks." Now it's time to be more precise. The word "dim" is an abbreviation for "dimension." This is another case of computer programming appropriating an English word, and putting a unique spin on it. In this case a noun is turned into a verb. So, our new translation might be: "Dimension a variable with the same shape as ToolsRevisionMarks." The implication of the use of this word, dimension, is that the variable so created has an expansive nature. That is, it is not, like normal string or numeric variables, unitary. This kind of variable is called an *array*.

An array variable allows for easy access to and manipulation of a group of related variables. The difference between an array variable and a unitary variable is that an array can hold more than one value. You should think of an array as a single variable divided into a specific number of slots or cubby-holes, each of which can contain a value.

In WordBasic there are two basic types of array variables: *internal command arrays* and *user arrays*. In the current section we are concerned exclusively with internal command arrays.

In the example above, the statement

```
Dim DialogRecord As ToolsRevisionMarks
```

creates an array that has the same "dimensions" as ToolsRevisionMarks. This particular command macro possesses three related variables (corresponding, not coincidentally, to the three parameters that can be passed to the command when executed): MarkRevisions, RevisionBar, and NewText. So, to get more specific, our Dim statement creates an array with a dimension of three: three positions, or *fields*, to hold the integer values associated with each of the three options associated with ToolsRevisionMarks.

The statement

```
GetCurValues DialogRecord
```

is much simpler to explain: having defined the array variable, this statement fills it, and queries Word about the current state of each of the array's fields.

The next statement

```
CurrentStatus = DialogRecord.MarkRevisions
```

assigns the value of one of the array's fields to an integer variable named CurrentStatus. Notice how this field is accessed: the name of the array variable, a period, the name of the field. Or to state this example as a generalized syntax:

```
ArrayVariableName.FieldName
```

This syntax is used to get a value from any field contained in an internal command array (or what I like to call a *dialog box array* since it invariably possesses a dialog box equivalent).

## A Macro, a Dialog Box, and a Command Array

To demonstrate the correspondences among a macro, the dialog box it displays, and the internal command array that underlies them both, let's record a macro that makes a change to a frequently used dialog box, and then compare the resulting macro to the dialog box.

1. Select Tools, Macro. The ToolsMacro dialog box appears.

2. Name the macro ArrayExample.

3. Select Format, Paragraph. the FormatParagraph dialog box appears.

**4.** Set the Alignment to Right.

**5.** Set the left indent to 1.5".

**6.** Set the right indent to .25".

**7.** Set the first line indent to 0".

**8.** Set Line Spacing to 1.5 Lines.

**9.** Check Keep With Next. The dialog box, after editing, should look like this:

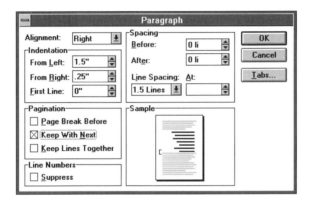

**10.** Click on OK.

**11.** Select Macro Stop Recorder.

If you were to load the macro just recorded, ArrayExample, into the macro editor, you would see:

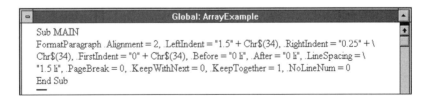

```
Sub MAIN
FormatParagraph .Alignment = 2, .LeftIndent = "1.5" + Chr$(34), .RightIndent = "0.25" + \
Chr$(34), .FirstIndent = "0" + Chr$(34), .Before = "0 li", .After = "0 li", .LineSpacing = \
"1.5 li", .PageBreak = 0, .KeepWithNext = 0, .KeepTogether = 1, .NoLineNum = 0
End Sub
```

Note the syntax of this type of WordBasic statement:

`MacroName .Field1=Value, .Field2=Value,... .Fieldn=Value`

There are several things to note about this general syntax:

■ The various fields correspond, precisely, to options in the dialog box.

■ Fields are always prefaced by a period.

■ The values assigned to these fields can either be strings (in which case they are included in quotation marks) or numbers (in which case they are not).

■ Numeric values are either on/off switches (in which case the numbers are either 0 (off) or 1 (on); or the numbers correspond to an item in a list (where the first item of the list is 0; computers usually begin a sequential count at 0, not at 1).

■ String values are always enclosed in quotation marks. Numbers enclosed in quotation marks should not be viewed as numeric variables, but as part of a measurement string, composed of the measurement—"1.5"— and the double quotation mark—Chr$(34). So, for instance, the value "1.5" + Chr$(34) actually represents the string "1.5"" (meaning one point five inches).

■ These three lines are actually a single command, and as far as WordBasic is concerned, are viewed as a single line. To make such a long command legible while editing, the macro recorder broke the lines, inserting a back-slash to indicate that the command is continued on the next line.

Figure 6.2 traces the connections between the parameters for the macro FormatParagraph and the dialog box this macro calls when executed with no parameters.

**Figure 6.2**

Correspondence between the FormatParagraph dialog box and the FormatParagraph macro parameters

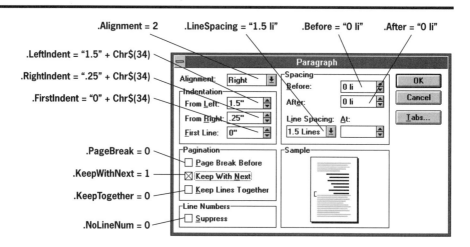

If we switch perspectives slightly, and look at the FormatParagraph not as a dialog box, but as a WordBasic statement that can be accessed via a command

array, we see that each of these 11 values can be queried. In the following macro, an array variable named fp is dimensioned to hold the 11 values of FormatParagraph. That variable is updated to hold the values of the current paragraph (that is, the paragraph which contains the insertion point when the macro is run), and then assigns each of the array fields to a variable:

```
Sub Main
Dim fp as FormatParagraph
GetCurValues fp
AlignmentIndex = fp.Alignment
LeftMeasure$ = fp.LeftIndent
RightMeasure$ = fp.RightIndent
FirstMeasure$ = fp.FirstIndent
BeforeMeasure$ = fp.Before
AfterMeasure$ = fp.After
SpacingMeasure$ = fp.LineSpacing
Break = fp.PageBreak
KeepNext = fp.KeepWithNext
Together = fp.KeepTogether
SuppressLine = fp.NoLineNum
Print "Alignment Index is : ";AlignmentIndex
MsgBox "Left Indent of the current paragraph is: " + LeftMeasure$
MsgBox "Right Indent of the current paragraph is: " + fp.RightIndent
End Sub
```

This macro illustrates a couple of interesting things. An internal command array can hold both integer and string values. In this case the values held by .Alignment, .KeepWithNext, .KeepTogether, and .NoLineNum are integers. The other fields all hold string values.

Figure 6.3 traces the connections between the parameters for the macro FormatParagraph, as represented by the dialog box, and the dialog array fields that can be queried by a macro to return specific information about the state of the current paragraph.

We can look at the internal macro FormatParagraph in two ways:

- From the point of view of a WordBasic statement that formats the current paragraph, it takes up to 11 parameters.

- From the point of view of an internal Word command array that describes the current paragraph, it holds 11 values, possesses 11 fields.

Every dialog box found in Word has precisely the same organization: a grouping of related parameters, stored in an internal command array, accessed via a corresponding WordBasic macro statement. If you record any dialog box action, you will see a similarly shaped macro. To access the fields of a given dialog box with a macro, you can create an array variable of the appropriate size, and query a specific field's value.

**Figure 6.3**

Correspondence between the FormatParagraph dialog box and the FormatParagraph internal command array

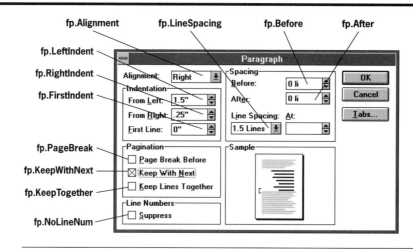

To define an internal command array variable, we use the Dim statement:

```
Dim ArrayVariable As MacroName
```

This statement means: create an array variable big enough to hold all the fields of MacroName. Note that MacroName always refers to a valid Word-Basic statement.

Any of the following would be legal:

```
Dim ParagraphArrayVariable As FormatParagraph
Dim ViewArray As ToolsOptionsView
Dim dlg As FileSummaryInfo
```

Once the array variable is declared, update the array variable with the current state of the named Word command macro by calling the statement GetCurValues with the array variable as parameter:

```
GetCurValues ParagraphArrayVariable
GetCurValues ViewArray
GetCurValues dlg
```

To query a specific value, examine the contents of a field by accessing the array field:

```
ParagraphArrayVariable.Alignment
ViewArray.Hidden
dlg.Subject
```

Notice the use of the period in the reference to a specific field. This field reference, consisting of the array variable name, a period, and the field name, should be thought of as a single unit.

## User Array Variables

The previous section described how to use Dim to create an array variable to hold the related values of a built-in macro/dialog box. We should now explore the creation and use of user array variables.

The unique thing about an array variable is that it has a magnitude or a size. The simplest syntax for Dim, as used to create a user array variable, is

```
Dim ArrayVariable(Size)
```

For instance, we could create an array variable to hold all the months of the year:

```
Dim Months$(11)
```

This would create an array variable with 12 "slots" (recall that computers start counting at 0).

However, it would be more accurate to describe the syntax of Dim as:

```
Dim ArrayVariable(Size,Depth)
```

What I mean is, the first parameter—Size—determines how many slots the array will have; the second parameter—Depth—specifies how many slots each slot has. Perhaps a good visual metaphor would be a spreadsheet. The array variable name would correspond to the name of the worksheet. The first parameter specifies the number of columns, the second parameter the number of rows. The array declaration statement:

```
Dim Words$(1,1)
```

would create a "two-dimensional" array with two slots, holding two items each; a total of four "cells."

Unlike internal command array values, which are accessed by specifying the field name (ArrayVariable.FieldName), a specific item in a user array is accessed with an *index*. For example, if you declare a user array of dimension 3 with the statement

```
Dim MyArray$(3)
```

then the possible slots are accessed with the index values 0–3. MyArray$(0) would return the value held by the first slot in the array. MyArray$(3) would return the last. You will recognize in this something that has been stated several times before: WordBasic starts counting at 0, not at 1.

Note that this example array has no second parameter. If no depth is specified, an array defaults to a single row. Therefore, the statement Dim MyArray$(3) is equivalent to Dim MyArray$(3,0).

To demonstrate how to define and use a string array variable, type in the following macro and then run it:

```
Sub Main
Dim Words$(1,1)                 'declare an array of two dimensions with two items
Words$(0,0) ="Microsoft "  'fill the array slots with text
Words$(0,1) = "Word"
Words$(1,0) = " is "
Words$(1,1) = "terrific."
Print Words$(0,0)+Words$(0,1)+Words$(1,0)+Words$(1,1)      'Print the string
End Sub
```

Figure 6.4 illustrates the creation of an array variable.

**Figure 6.4**

Defining string array variables

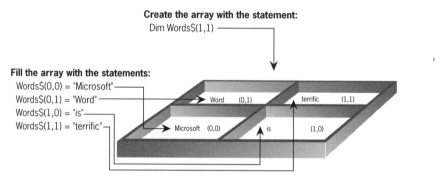

**Create the array with the statement:**
Dim Words$(1,1)

**Fill the array with the statements:**
Words$(0,0) = "Microsoft"
Words$(0,1) = "Word"
Words$(1,0) = "is"
Words$(1,1) = "terrific"

Here's a slightly more demonstrative example:

```
Sub Main
Dim Months$(11)                 'declare an array of one dimension with 12 items
Months$(0) = "January"       'assign the text of each month
Months$(1) = "February"      'to the array item slots
Months$(2) = "March"
Months$(3) = "April"
Months$(4) = "May"
Months$(5) = "June"
Months$(6) = "July"
Months$(7) = "August"
Months$(8) = "September"
Months$(9) = "October"
Months$(10) = "November"
Months$(11) = "December"
Input "Which month (1-12)", Month        'get the month digit
Print "You asked for "+ Months$(Month-1)     'display the month from the array
End Sub
```

A user array can hold either strings or numeric values, but not both (unlike an internal command array). That is, at the time of its declaration, an array is either a string array or a numeric array. If an array variable ends with a dollar sign, then it is limited to holding string values. If an array is declared and named without a terminating dollar sign, it is limited to holding numeric values.

There are several internal Word functions that store information in arrays. For instance, the names of the styles in the current document, the glossaries in a given context, and the fonts available are all accessible by calling a WordBasic function with an array index number:

```
Sub Main
For x = 1 To CountStyles()
    Print StyleName$(x)
Next x
End Sub
```

## Summary—The WordBasic Language

We have now covered most of the basic concepts necessary for creating macros in WordBasic.

To summarize:

- Print and MsgBox can be used to display information about the progress of the macro.

- Input and InputBox$( ) are used to get input from the user, allowing variables to be changed interactively.

- The function MsgBox( ) can be used to get simple yes/no and yes/no/cancel responses from the user, returning one of three values (–1, 0, 1).

- Flow control structures, in combination with the input procedures such as MsgBox( ) or UserDialog, can easily control the specifics of macro execution.

The five flow control structures are

- *If…Then…Else If…End If* uses relational comparison to determine which of several groups of statements to execute.

- *Goto* unconditionally branches to a Label if a given condition is true.

- *For…Next* uses a counter variable to execute a series of statements for a finite number of iterations.

- *While...Wend* uses a relational comparison to execute a series of statements while a given condition is true.

- *Select Case...End Select* compares a given variable to a list of possible values and executes the associated group of statements.

- Dialog boxes can be considered as arrays of associated values.

- Dialog box arrays can be addressed and evaluated using the Dim Array-Variable as DialogName and GetCurValues ArrayVariable statements. This allows for the easy addressing of Word functions found on dialog boxes (the toggles illustrated above).

- User arrays provide a convenient way to create and access a group of related variables.

In the following chapter we will build some macros that will demonstrate the power of WordBasic. It is time to recall that the best way to learn a language is to live with it. Many concepts, foreign to some readers, have been introduced. Seeing those concepts in action will greatly diminish whatever forbidding mystery may still adhere.

I would recommend arming yourself for the coming chapters. If you have never programmed before, it would prove useful, I am sure, to enter some of the following macros manually rather than loading them from the included disk. Like copying over a passage from Cicero, this will improve your ability to read WordBasic. I would also recommend that if you have not already done so, now would be a good time to flip through the alphabetic listing of WordBasic statements and functions found in *Using WordBasic*, the free-for-the-asking technical reference distributed by Microsoft.

C H A P T E R

7

# Building Macros— Introduction

T HIS CHAPTER WILL PRESENT A SERIES OF MACRO SOLUTIONS TO A RANGE of customization problems. I am not suggesting that these macros are necessary additions to your setup. In some cases they are not the best solution for the problem posed. I present them to demonstrate the kinds of modifications you can achieve with WordBasic. They should be seen as starting points. They are intended as food for thought. I hope they get you thinking about the specific needs you have of a word processor. At the very least, I intend for these examples to accustom you to reading WordBasic.

There are two ways to see these example macros in action. You can create a temporary work document based on NORMAL.DOT, create the individual macros, and type in the macro source code. This is perhaps a better idea for those who have done no programming. Nothing can substitute for actually typing, and mistyping, a macro to aid in learning the language. Alternatively, most of the macros in this chapter can be found in the file named CH07MACS.DOC on the example disk. That document allows you to list, demonstrate, or install the sample macros. You can also open and edit the macros while in CH07MACS.DOC.

## Some WordBasic Solutions

In Chapter 6 we covered the basic syntax and grammar of WordBasic. Now we can revise some of the sample macros presented in earlier chapters, making them smaller and smarter. And, though limited by the aspects of WordBasic covered thus far, we can pose some new problems and possible solutions.

Before I list and explain some sample macros, recall that many macros—those that perform editing functions such as Insert or FormatCharacter—cannot be executed on themselves. With such a macro you must place the focus—defined as the location of the blinking insertion point—on an open document rather than on the macro editing window. It is a good practice always to have a scratch document open when testing a macro.

### Toggle Macros

The simplest class of WordBasic macro is one you've already seen: the toggle macro. Word has many options that, essentially, can be in one of two states—on or off. A toggle macro simply automates the process of toggling any of these options from one state to the other, from the current state to its opposite. Any option that is controlled by a check box could be turned into a toggle.

### ToggleRevision

In Chapter 5 we created a macro to toggle the current state of revision marking. If you recall, that macro looked like:

```
Sub Main
Dim DialogRecord as ToolsRevisionMarks
GetCurValues DialogRecord
CurrentStatus = DialogRecord.MarkRevisions
If CurrentStatus = 0 Then
    ToolsRevisionMarks  .MarkRevisions = 1
Else
    ToolsRevisionMarks  .MarkRevisions = 0
End If
End Sub
```

The problem is, this particular piece of WordBasic code is not very *elegant*. Elegance is a quality virtually all programmers are taught to hold in high regard. We will discuss programming style, and elegance, in the next chapter. For now consider elegance in this context as a synonym for "gracefulness." That said, perhaps I can make the concept clear by quoting the Russian playwright Anton Chekhov. He defined graceful as "accomplishing the necessary in the fewest possible steps."

The above macro, written before we had discussed command arrays or functions, does not use the fewest possible steps. Its seven lines can be reduced to three:

**DISK**
ToggleRevisionMarks—
Toggle revision
marking on and off

```
Sub Main
Dim DialogRecord as ToolsRevisionMarks
GetCurValues DialogRecord
ToolsRevisionMarks  .MarkRevisions = DialogRecord.MarkRevisions - 1
End Sub
```

This revised version (which I would recommend naming ToggleRevision-Marks and assigning to Ctrl+Shift+R) does the following:

- Dimensions an array variable named "DialogRecord" of the same size and shape as the ToolsRevisionMarks command array

- Stores the current values in the array variable named DialogRecord

- Executes the WordBasic statement ToolsRevisionMarks with a single parameter, .MarkRevisions, assigning to this parameter the value of the current state (the array field stored in DialogRecord.MarkRevisions) minus one

To comprehend precisely how this macro works its magic so simply requires that we review two things: What are the two possible values stored in the array field named DialogRecord.MarkRevisions? And what are the two legal arguments of the ToolsRevisionMarks statement?

The array field DialogRecord.MarkRevisions is either equal to 1 (if revision marks are currently on) or equal to 0 (if revision marks are currently off). By subtracting 1 from the array field's value, we execute ToolsRevision-Marks with an argument opposite to that which had been returned: We send an argument that will be –1 (if the current value is 0) or 0 (if the current value is 1). Recall now that in WordBasic, –1 is the value associated with true, and 0 is the value associated with false. Remember that any non-zero value turns a toggle such as this on. A value of zero always forces such a toggle argument to off.

### ToggleHidden

This same principle of subtracting 1 from the value returned when the current state of a check box option is queried allows us to create toggle macros for many other Word settings. For instance, all of the options found on the Tools-OptionsView dialog box could be turned into a toggle macro using the paradigm of ToggleRevisionMarks.

For example, here is a macro (which I would recommend naming Toggle-Hidden and assigning to Ctrl+Shift+H) that toggles the display of hidden text:

**DISK**
ToggleHidden—
Toggle display of
hidden text

```
Sub Main
Dim dlg As ToolsOptionsView
GetCurValues dlg
ToolsOptionsView .Hidden = dlg.Hidden - 1
End Sub
```

This macro dimensions an array variable named "dlg" to hold the values of ToolsOptionsView; gets the current values; and executes ToolsOptionsView with the parameter .Hidden equal to the current state minus one.

### TogglePictures

Using precisely the same macro as ToggleHidden, but modifying a different array field, you can create a macro that toggles the display of picture placeholders.

**DISK**
TogglePictures—
Toggle display of
pictures and
picture placeholders

```
Sub Main
Dim dlg As ToolsOptionsView
GetCurValues dlg
ToolsOptionsView .PicturePlaceHolders = dlg.PicturePlaceHolders - 1
End Sub
```

This macro (which might be assigned to Ctrl+Shift+P) makes use of the fact that a document that contains graphics displays faster if you are not actually drawing the pictures to the screen. So, for rapid scrolling through a document during editing you might want to toggle picture placeholders on.

### ToggleStyleArea

All of the other check box options found on the ToolsOptionsView dialog box are susceptible to toggle macros using the same basic macro. One setting, however, is slightly different. The Style Area Width does not return a value of 1 or 0 (and so cannot be toggled with the simple equation of ArrayVariable-.FieldName-1). Rather, this option returns a string representing the width, in the currently active measurement, of the style area. As a result the logic of the macro must be altered a bit.

**DISK**
ToggleStyleArea—
Toggle the display
of style names at
the left of the
current document

```
Sub Main
Dim dlg As ToolsOptionsView
GetCurValues dlg
If Val(dlg.StyleAreaWidth) = 0  Then
    dlg.StyleAreaWidth = ".5" + Chr$(34)
Else
    dlg.StyleAreaWidth = "0"
End If
ToolsOptionsView dlg
End Sub
```

What this macro (which I have assigned to Ctrl+Shift+S) does is quite simple. Like the previous examples it creates an array variable and stores the current values. The line

```
If Val(dlg.StyleAreaWidth) = 0 Then
```

takes the string and converts it to an integer. No matter what the measurement units (Inches, Centimeters, Points, or Picas), if the current setting is zero, this string is converted to the integer 0. The If…Then statement evaluates this integer. If it is equal to 0, the style area width field is set to the string .5" (notice how this is done with the concatenation of ".5" and Chr$(34), Chr$(34) being computer-speak for the quotation mark/inch mark). If the value of the converted string is not 0, the array field is set to the string value "0".

The last line of the macro (not counting "End Sub," of course) executes ToolsOptionsView, not with a single field as the parameter, *but with the entire array variable.* This is a really neat trick, which will appear in other macro examples. It's such a neat trick it deserves generalizing: When executing a WordBasic statement that "covers" an array variable, you can send the array variable as the parameter.

The macro

```
Sub Main
Dim dlg As ToolsOptionsView
GetCurValues dlg
If Val(dlg.StyleAreaWidth) = 0  Then
    Temp$ = ".5" + Chr$(34)
Else
    Temp$ = "0"
```

```
End If
ToolsOptionsView .StyleAreaWidth = Temp$
End Sub
```

accomplishes precisely the same toggling of the style area, but uses a single field as the parameter. Instead of modifying the array variable field directly, and then sending the entire array variable as the parameter, it creates a temporary string variable to hold the new style area width measurement, and then calls ToolsOptionsView with the single field parameter .StyleAreaWidth = Temp$.

Be aware that you can only display the style area if you are in normal (or galley) view. If you are in page layout mode, ToggleStyleArea will do nothing.

### ToggleOutline

The outline facility in Word is quite powerful. It is relatively simple to select Outline from the View menu. However, it is even simpler to access this function, and allows for greater functionality, if you create a macro to toggle in and out of outline view (this might be assigned to Ctrl+Shift+O):

**DISK**
ToggleOutline—
Toggle in and out
of Outline View

```
Sub Main
If  ViewOutline() Then
    ViewNormal
Else
    ViewOutline
    ShowHeading5
End If
End Sub
```

What's remarkable in this toggle is that unlike the previous examples, which created a dialog array variable and then examined the value of a given field, this macro calls a built-in WordBasic function and examines its return value. The function ViewOutline( ) returns 1 if the current document is displayed as an outline; 0 if the current document is not displayed as an outline.

Therefore, the logic goes something like this: If this document is currently in outline view, change to normal view; if this document is not in outline view, turn on outline view and show headings 1 through 5.

This last functionality—collapsing the outline to show only headings 1 through 5—comes by adding the single statement ShowHeading5. You could change this to ShowHeading9, or ShowAllHeadings, or OutlineShowFirst-Line depending on your outline preferences.

### ToggleWindow

The last of the toggle macros I'll present provides easy access to a built-in function: splitting the current document window. Like the other toggle macros, the purpose of this macro is not to add a new functionality to Word, but to make access to a built-in function simpler, more convenient.

```
Sub Main
If DocSplit() Then        'If the current document is split
    ClosePane             'Close the split
Else                      'Otherwise
    DocSplit 50           'Split the window in half
End If
End Sub
```

The logic of this toggle also evaluates the return value of a WordBasic function, DocSplit( ), and branches accordingly, either closing the split or creating one.

We can accomplish the same task as the above five-line ToggleWindow macro in a way that is more graceful (if slightly more difficult to read). We can revise the If…Then evaluation to a single line:

**DISK**
ToggleWindow—
Toggle Window split

```
Sub Main
If(DocSplit() = 0) Then DocSplit 50 Else ClosePane
End Sub
```

Reading from left to right: Is the expression (DocSplit( )=0), meaning there is no split, true? If so, split at 50 percent of the current window's size; if not, close the split.

## SpecialBold

In Chapter 4 we created a macro to apply a specific character attribute. The problem with that macro, as recorded, was that it was one-directional.

**DISK**
SpecialBold—
Toggles special
boldface

```
Sub Main
'Variables; change to suit your preferences
    fName$ = "Arial"          'Font name
    pSize = FontSize()        'Point size; by default it simply accepts the
                              'current size
    F$ = Font$()              'Find out the current selection's font name
    If F$ <> fName$ Then      'If the font isn't already Arial
        Font fName$, pSize    'Turn Arial, and
        Bold 1                'Bold on (again, you could add other attributes)
        Else                  'Otherwise
        ResetChar             'Reset the insertion point to nothing special
    End If
End Sub
```

What does it do? This improved version of SpecialBold is actually a toggle. If the current selection (whether a block of text or an insertion point) is already formatted as Arial, the selection is reset to its default value (as defined in the current style). If the current selection is not already Arial, it is formatted as Arial bold.

As delivered, this macro has only one hard-coded variable: fName$, which holds the name of the font you wish to apply, in this case Arial. By hard-coded, I mean a value that is entered when you create the macro and is not thereafter altered by the macro. In this case, we are specifying that SpecialBold will *always* use Arial as the font to apply. Such a variable as fName$ is more properly called a *constant*. The programmer gives it a value. That value remains unchanged.

The other possible hard-coded value would be pSize, an integer variable that by default is assigned the current FontSize( ). But, for instance, you could change this line to:

```
pSize=10
```

to force the selection to be formatted as 10 point as well as Arial and bold.

To make SpecialBold more functional, you could add other character attributes, such as Italic, within the portion of the If…Then control structure that is executed if F$ <> fName$ (that is, when the current font is not equal to the hard-coded special font).

## EditTemplate

In Chapter 2, I pointed out that some modifications must be made directly on a template. Loading a template in order to modify boilerplate, margin settings, or style definitions is such a frequent necessity that I have created a macro to automate the task.

The following macro examines the FileSummaryInfo data, pulls out the name of the current document's template, and then loads it.

**DISK**
EditTemplate—
Loads the current
template

```
Sub Main
Dim dlg As FileSummaryInfo
GetCurValues dlg
FileOpen dlg.Template
End Sub
```

There is one limitation with this macro. If you are editing a template disguised as a document (and perhaps you've forgotten that fact), this macro will not warn you. It will simply open a copy of NORMAL.DOT.

## FileCloseAll

If you're like me, you sometimes get totally fed up with the various projects under construction. You want to start from scratch. You'd like a simple way to close all of the currently active documents with a single command. Here it is:

**DISK**
FileCloseAll—
Close all open files

```
Sub Main
y = CountWindows()
For x = 1 To y
    NextWindow
    FileClose
    y = CountWindows()
Next x
End Sub
```

This macro

■ Counts the number of open documents, including macro editing windows, and assigns this value to the variable y.

■ Creates a loop that executes from 1 to y. The inside of the loop consists of three statements: move to the next document window; close that window; recount the number of open documents.

## AssignKey

In Chapter 5, I suggested that there are more powerful ways to assign a keyboard shortcut to a macro than the method supplied by the built-in Tools-OptionsKeyboard macro. You can use the macro language itself to directly assign a shortcut. And by using the WordBasic statement to do the assigning, you can access many more keyboard combinations.

The following macro allows you to assign a macro to virtually any combination of keystrokes. It is not for the faint of heart. It requires that you know the precise name of the macro as well as the numeric value of the key to be assigned. Determining the name of the macro is a simple matter. You are either working on a macro of your own creation, and therefore know the name, or you are working with an internal command macro and can find the name in the list of commands displayed by ToolsMacro. Determining the numeric code for the *base key* is a little trickier. By "base key" I mean the unmodified key. For instance, if the desired combination is Ctrl+Shift+Z, the base key would be the letter Z. There is a table of key codes in the reference section of *Using WordBasic*. The same chart is found in the help file, which can be easily accessed by pressing F1 with the insertion point within the WordBasic statement ToolsOptionsKeyboard. A more complete table of key codes can be found in Appendix D.

To use AssignKey you must manually edit the macro to supply the macro name, the base key code, the context, and the modifier keys.

AssignKey is unique among the examples given so far because it actually requires that you have the macro open before you can use it. That is, you must load the macro into the macro editor and run the macro.

I present AssignKey to you not because it is the best way to assign a shortcut to a macro (the application macro named MacroKey, found on the example disk is much friendlier), but because it illustrates many useful aspects of WordBasic (as well as being a quick and dirty, as programmers say, way to accomplish the task).

**DISK**
AssignKey—
Assign virtually any
key combination to
a macro

```
Sub Main
'*********************************************************************
REM USAGE:
REM    1) Place this macro in NORMAL.DOT
REM    2) Open the macro
REM    3) Edit the variables section, providing the macro name, the context,
REM       the base key, the modifier combination, the Assign value
REM    4) Either Click on Start or press Alt+Shift+S to run the macro
'*********************************************************************
'Constants
'These values should not be changed
     Global = 0
     Template = 1
     Ctrl = 256
     Shift = 512
     Alt = 1024
     True = - 1
     False = 0

'Variables
'These values should be changed each time you execute the macro.
     Macro$ = "FileCloseAll"   'What's the macro to assign this to?
     Context = Global          'Where to make the changes, Global or Template?
     Key = 115                 'What's the base key code? In this case F4
                               'A listing of valid key codes can be easily found
                               'by placing the insertion point on
                               '"ToolsOptionsKeyboard" below and pressing F1.
                               'A more complete list is found in
                               'the Appendix of PCM Customizing Word for Windows
     Modifier = Alt + Ctrl     'Which shift keys to use?
     Assign = True             'Change this to zero to unassign the above-defined
                               'key/macro

     'If the value of Assign is 0, jump to the unassign loop
If Not Assign Then Goto Unassign

'Do the assignment:
ToolsOptionsKeyboard .Context = Context, .Name = Macro$,\
     .KeyCode = Modifier + Key, .Add
```

```
Goto Bye                          'Jump to the end of the macro

Unassign:                         'The unassign loop
For x = 1 To 2                    'This loop executes the command twice
    ToolsOptionsKeyboard .Context = Context, .Name = Macro$, \
        .KeyCode = Modifier + Key, .Delete
Next x

Bye:                              'The End of the macro

End Sub
```

The first thing to notice is that this macro is fully commented. Styles of commenting macro code in order to explain the macro to another user or to maintain it more easily will be discussed in the next chapter. Here, notice that the usage instructions are included in the macro itself, prefaced by the abbreviation REM, and that virtually every line has an in-line comment, prefaced by an apostrophe.

The default values assigned to the variables in AssignKey will assign the example macro, FileCloseAll, to Alt+Ctrl+F4 (see Figure 7.1). If you are going to use this macro to assign a keyboard shortcut to any other macro, you must manually change the variables.

Here's what AssignKey does:

- Defines a series of seven constants to be used later in the macro.

- Declares five variables to determine the macro, key, context, modifier combination, and task (to assign or unassign).

- Tests whether the variable Assign is true or false. If false, jumps to the unassign section of the macro.

- To unassign a keyboard shortcut you must execute the ToolsOptionsKeyboard statement twice: once to remove the custom assignment, once to reset the macro to its default shortcut (if there is a default). The unassign statement is executed twice by a For…Next loop.

- If Assign is true, the macro executes the ToolsOptionsKeyboard statement and then jumps to the end of the macro.

Note the use of backslashes in this macro to break up the long lines. If you place a backslash between two lines, WordBasic reads the two lines as a single command. So, for instance:

```
ToolsOptionsKeyboard .Context = 0, .Name = Macro$,\
        .KeyCode = Key, .Add
```

and

```
ToolsOptionsKeyboard .Context = 0, .Name = Macro$, .KeyCode = Key, .Add
```

are functionally identical. Using a backslash to break up long lines allows you to write much more legible code.

**Figure 7.1**

Anatomy of the AssignKey macro

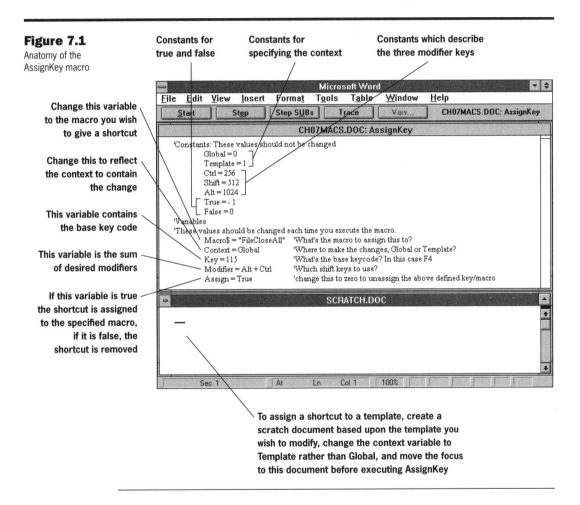

Constants for true and false

Constants for specifying the context

Constants which describe the three modifier keys

Change this variable to the macro you wish to give a shortcut

Change this to reflect the context to contain the change

This variable contains the base key code

This variable is the sum of desired modifiers

If this variable is true the shortcut is assigned to the specified macro, if it is false, the shortcut is removed

To assign a shortcut to a template, create a scratch document based upon the template you wish to modify, change the context variable to Template rather than Global, and move the focus to this document before executing AssignKey

You can use AssignKey to create a template-specific keyboard shortcut assignment. Load AssignKey into the editor (as you would to create a global keyboard shortcut assignment). Create (or open) a document based on the template you wish to hold the new shortcut assignment. Edit the variables, setting them to the macro name, the key, and the modifier combination you wish to add to the template. Set the Context variable equal to Template rather than Global. Now place the focus on the template based document (selecting Arrange All from the Window menu makes this easier). Execute the macro by either clicking on the Start button on the macro editor button bar, or pressing Alt+Shift+S (see Figure 7.1).

## StripCarriageReturns

Documents created by text editors or captured from on-line services have a carriage return at the end of each line. Paragraphs are usually delineated by a carriage return pair. A simple macro can convert such documents into Word format. In Word each paragraph, not each line, is terminated by a carriage return.

**DISK**

StripCarriageReturns—
Reformat ASCII files
containing carriage
returns at each line
end into paragraphs

```
Sub Main
Marker$ = "@"                       'Create a temporary marker
StartOfDocument                     'Go to start of document
EditFindClearFormatting             'Clear the find field of formatting
EditReplaceClearFormatting          'Clear the replace field of formatting

'Replace all carriage returns with marker character
EditReplace .Find = "^p", .Replace = Marker$, .WholeWord = 0, \
    .MatchCase = 0, .Format = 0, .ReplaceAll

'Replace marker pairs with a single carriage return
EditReplace .Find = Marker$ + Marker$, .Replace = "^p", \
    .WholeWord = 0, .MatchCase = 0, .Format = 0, .ReplaceAll

'Replace each remaining marker with a space
EditReplace .Find = Marker$, .Replace = " ", \
    .WholeWord = 0, .MatchCase = 0, .Format = 0, .ReplaceAll
End Sub
```

The logic of StripCarriageReturns is straightforward:

- Create a unique marker. It is important that this marker not appear anywhere in the document to be converted. In the above code this marker is set to the @ sign.

- Move to the start of the document.

- Clear any formatting instructions from the EditReplace command.

- Replace all carriage returns with the marker.

- Replace all marker pairs with a single carriage return.

- Replace all remaining markers with a space.

# The AutoMacros

Every user of Word has a completely unique set of requirements and habits. But all users have the following in common: They launch Word, they open previously edited documents, and they create new documents.

These are the most basic (and repetitious) actions associated with working in Word. And the designers of Word have provided a convenient way to control what happens when any of these actions is taken. They have given special properties to five specifically named macros:

- *AutoExec*    determines what happens when you first load Word.

- *AutoOpen*    specifies what happens each time you open a previously edited document.

- *AutoNew*    specifies what happens when you create a new document.

- *AutoClose*    specifies what happens when you close a document.

- *AutoExit*    specifies what happens when you close Word.

These macros are completely optional. By default there are no auto macros. But, when combined with custom templates, they are extremely powerful, enabling you to customize and standardize the features, look, and behavior of Word.

To create an auto macro requires nothing more than naming the macro properly. That is, the magic resides in the name itself. If Word finds a macro named AutoExec, that macro is executed when Word first loads; if there is a macro named AutoOpen, Word will execute that macro whenever a document is opened. No additional steps are required to create an auto macro beyond following this naming convention. The names themselves generate the special functionality of "auto-ness."

## AutoExec

If there is a macro named AutoExec stored in NORMAL.DOT, it will be executed every time you start Word. This is an extremely tricky macro to construct. There are several limitations. For one thing, this macro is executed before any document is loaded, and therefore any command you might wish to include in this macro has to be a command that is valid whether a document is loaded or not. There aren't that many such commands.

I have not found an AutoExec macro that fits my peculiar needs. However, here are some possibilities that might get you thinking.

### Back Up NORMAL.DOT

WordBasic contains a statement that will copy a file. So, you could ensure that you never lose any of your customizations by saving the current state of NORMAL.DOT every time you start Word.

```
Sub Main
CopyFile "C:\WINWORD\DOT\NORMAL.DOT", "C:\"
End Sub
```

This one-line macro, which isn't very smart, would copy NORMAL.DOT from C:\WINWORD\DOT to C:\. The directories are provided to the Copy-File command as "hard-coded" string literals. That is, the macro above assumes that you have your templates stored in C:\WINWORD\DOT and you are copying it to C:\.

We could make it a little smarter by using a WordBasic function which reads the DOT-Path setting from WIN.INI (if you're not familiar with the various Word settings contained in WIN.INI, look up WIN.INI in the index to the Word manual, or jump to Chapter 13):

```
Sub Main
NormalDot$ = GetProfileString$("Dot-Path") + "\NORMAL.DOT"
CopyFile NormalDot$, "C:\"
End Sub
```

In this slightly improved version, the destination for the copy operation, C:\, is still hard coded, while the location of NORMAL.DOT has now been connected, not with a string literal in the macro, but with a value stored in WIN.INI.

GetProfileString$( ) and its corresponding SetProfileString( ) are extremely powerful WordBasic functions that we will see again in future examples.

Unfortunately, CopyFile cannot be told whether you want to automatically copy over a file that already exists. As a result, after you run this macro once (that is, load Word once with this as AutoExec), you will be prompted if you want to overwrite the existing file named NORMAL.DOT found in C:\. You can either leave this prompt enabled, or make the macro a little smarter still by changing it to:

**DISK**
AutoExecBackup—
Possible AutoExec
macro to backup
NORMAL.DOT

```
Sub Main
NormalDot$ = GetProfileString$("Dot-Path") + "\NORMAL.DOT"
SendKeys " "
CopyFile NormalDot$, "C:\"
End Sub
```

What we've added is the SendKeys statement with a space as argument:

```
SendKeys " "
```

What this command does is stuff a space into the keyboard buffer in anticipation of the confirmation message box. That space executes the OK button and confirms that, yes, you want to overwrite the existing file. The message box never appears, but you will notice a slight flicker as WordBasic starts to display the confirmation box, realizes there's a space in the keyboard buffer, and goes on its way copying the file.

Note that the SendKeys statement appears *before* the statement to which it is addressing keystrokes.

### Specify How Word Loads

Here is another idea for an AutoExec macro. Word saves the state of the application window when you quit. If Word is maximized (that is, full screen) when you quit, the next time you load Word it will load maximized. If Word is a "windowed" application when you quit, it will load windowed. What follows are two macros to force Word to load either maximized or restored no matter what the state at the time of the last exit.

To ensure that Word always starts maximized, create this AutoExec macro:

**DISK**
AutoExecMaximize—
Possible AutoExec
macro to maximize
Word

```
Sub Main
If Not AppMaximize() Then AppMaximize
End Sub
```

This macro queries the current state of Word's application space with the function AppMaximize( ). This returns either a 1 (maximized) or a 0 (windowed). The second half of the If…Then control structure, the statement AppMaximize, is only executed if AppMaximize( ) returns zero, or false.

To ensure that Word loads as a sized window rather than full screen, create this AutoExec macro:

**DISK**
AutoExecRestore—
Possible AutoExec
macro to restore
Word

```
Sub Main
If AppMaximize() Then AppRestore
AppMove 15, 10
AppSize 480, 350
End Sub
```

This macro reverses the test. If the Word application space is maximized to full screen, then execute the WordBasic statement AppRestore to restore Word to a window. The last two statements move and size the Word application space. Of course, the parameters passed to AppMove and AppSize could be modified to suit your own preferences.

## AutoOpen

The global AutoOpen macro will execute upon the opening of any document unless that document is based on a template that also has an AutoOpen macro.

As with AutoNew (or any other macro for that matter), if there is a template-specific version of that macro, it will take precedence over a global version.

I will present one of each—a useful global AutoOpen and a possible template AutoOpen.

### Return to Last Edit Location

When you open an existing document, Word places the insertion point at the first line. If you frequently work with the same document (like that novel that never ends), you might find it more useful if Word returned to precisely the same place where you were last working when you closed the file.

There's a simple solution: Record the action of Shift+F5 into a global macro named AutoOpen.

The resulting macro will be

```
Sub Main
GoBack
End Sub
```

But, sadly, this doesn't work in all possible instances. For example, if you open a template directly, you will be popped out of the template and back to the previously active document. Since I tend to edit templates quite often, I had to come up with a better solution. The key lies in one of several built-in *bookmarks*. The complete list of built-in bookmarks will be presented in Chapter 9. For now it will suffice to realize that every time you save a document you also save a bookmark named "\PrevSel1." This is an abbreviation for "previous selection one." In fact, when you press Shift+F5 (and execute GoBack), what you are telling Word to do is to return to \PrevSel1. When you press Shift+F5 a second time, you are telling Word to return to \PrevSel2. But once you realize that this command uses a bookmark, we can make our AutoOpen macro smarter by testing if there is a bookmark named "PrevSel1" before jumping to it:

**DISK**
AutoOpenLastEdit—
Possible AutoOpen
macro to return to
last edit location

```
Sub Main
If ExistingBookmark("\PrevSel1") Then EditGoTo "\PrevSel1"
End Sub
```

The essential difference between these two macros is that in the first, GoBack looks across all open documents for a last edit location. If it doesn't find one in the current document, as when you open a template, it will return to the last edit location in some other open document. The second, smarter macro checks for the existence of a last edit location in the current document or template. If it doesn't find one, it does nothing.

### Insert Date and Time

Another possible AutoOpen macro, best suited to a template specifically designed to keep a journal, would move to the end of the document and insert Date and Time fields, properly spaced and formatted.

```
Sub Main
EndOfDocument            'Goto end of document
InsertPara               'Insert a new paragraph
InsertDateField          'Insert a date field {Date}
PrevField                'Select the date field
UnlinkFields             'Replace the field with its latest result
EndOfLine                'Goto end of line
Insert " "               'Insert a space
InsertTimeField          'Insert a time field {Time}
PrevField                'Select the time field
UnlinkFields             'Replace the field with its latest result
OutlinePromote           'Make this line heading 1
EndOfLine                'Goto end of line
InsertPara               'Insert a paragraph
End Sub
```

Notice the following points of interest. There are WordBasic commands to insert time and date fields: InsertDateField and InsertTimeField. Notice that after inserting each of these fields the macro selects the field by moving to it with PrevField, and then replaces the field with its result, by executing UnlinkFields. This command is worth some note. Once unlinked a field is no longer dynamic. It becomes plain old text, same as if you typed the result manually.

This macro is okay, but what if you have a blank paragraph at the end of your last journal entry? The above macro will add another paragraph before inserting the date. Here's how to make the macro a little smarter:

**DISK**
AutoOpenInsert-
DateTime—
Possible AutoOpen
macro to date-
stamp last line of
document

```
Sub Main
EndOfDocument
EditGoTo "\Line"
If Asc(Selection$()) <> 13 Then
    EndOfLine
    InsertPara
End If
FormatStyle .Name = "heading 1"
InsertField .Field = "date \@dddd MMMM d, yyyy h:mm AM/PM"
PrevField
LockFields
EndOfLine
InsertPara
End Sub
```

The improved macro goes to the end of the document, selects the last sentence, using the built-in bookmark "\Line", and examines the numeric

---

character value of the first letter of the line. If this value is anything but character 13 (which is the numeric value for a carriage return), it goes to the end of the line and inserts another carriage return. If, on the other hand, the line is itself just a carriage return, that is, a blank line, the macro proceeds without inserting another carriage return.

Note a couple of other improvements. The new paragraph is formatted as heading 1. You could change this to suit your own preferences. Instead of inserting the date field and unlinking, then inserting the time field and unlinking, this macro uses the InsertField command with a parameter named .Field. This allows you to insert a field that will return the date and time in precisely the format you want. For instance, you could change the line

```
InsertField .Field = "date \@dddd MMMM d, yyyy h:mm AM/PM"
```

to

```
InsertField .Field = "date \@d MMMM yyyy HH:mm"
```

to insert the date in standard European format. The instructions for date format, which here follow the @ sign, are called the *date-picture*. The Word help file contains a detailed listing of legal date-picture information. Search for "Date-Time Picture switch."

Lastly, instead of using UnlinkFields to freeze the inserted date field with its current result, this macro uses LockFields. This command has the same effect. The field will not change if you subsequently update all the fields in the file. However, it is still a field and can be unlocked if desired.

## AutoNew

This type of auto macro is perhaps the most useful of the lot. It allows you to create a default action for all new documents by defining an AutoNew macro in the global context, and to override that default action by creating any number of template based AutoNew macros.

The most frequent use of an AutoNew macro is to set up a specific class of document, for instance, the AutoNew macro created in Chapter 3, which updated all the fields of a new document based on NEWMEMO.DOT. Another, much more complex, example would be the AutoNew macro found in the LETBLOCK.DOT template that ships with Word. Such complex Auto-New macros allow you to completely automate and standardize the initial steps in creating a document.

### Getting File Information for a New Document

Word has a setting, found on the ToolsOptionsSave dialog box, which determines if you are prompted for summary information when you save a new document for the first time. Some people might prefer to be prompted at the time the document is created rather than when it is saved. You could do this in an AutoNew macro.

```
Sub Main
On Error Resume Next
ToolsMacro "FileSummaryInfo", .Run, .Show = 0
End Sub
```

This macro contains two WordBasic statements worth examining further. The first line

```
On Error Resume Next
```

is a special form of error trapping. What it means is simply this: If the next statement generates an error condition, continue to the next line rather than displaying an error message. This error check watches the line

```
ToolsMacro "FileSummaryInfo", .Run, .Show = 0
```

This statement is incredibly important, and goes to the heart of WordBasic's power. It demonstrates how to run an internal command macro, in this case the macro named FileSummaryInfo, from within a user-macro. Note that the parameter named .Run is not assigned a value. A parameter whose existence alone tells a command to perform in a specific way is called a *switch*. Notice that the parameter named .Show is assigned a value of zero. What this means is "The macro being run is contained within Word, that is, it is a command macro." A value of 1 for this parameter would tell ToolsMacro to look in the global context for the specified macro; a value of 2 would tell the ToolsMacro statement to look in the template context.

### Setting View Options for a New Document

A possible use for a template-specific AutoNew macro would be to set the document view preferences. For instance, the macro

```
Sub Main
ToolsOptionsView .ShowAll = 1
End Sub
```

would set the view preferences for the newly opened document to show all the various marks: paragraph marks, hidden text, spaces, tabs, and so on.

Or, if the class of documents based on the template containing this AutoNew macro makes use of fields, you might want to force ViewFieldCodes to on:

```
Sub Main
ViewFieldCodes 1
End Sub
```

Such an AutoNew macro could manipulate any number of view preferences. The following example

```
Sub Main
ViewFieldCodes 1
ViewPage 1
ViewZoomWholePage
ToolsOptionsView .Paras = 1, .Tabs = 1
End Sub
```

would force ViewFieldCodes to on, toggle into page layout mode, zoom the view to fit a whole page on the display, and turn on paragraph and tab marks.

## AutoClose

An excellent use for the AutoClose macro would be to make a backup copy of the current document.

Here's a macro that will ask if you want to back up the current document. If this AutoClose is stored in the global context (in NORMAL.DOT), you will be prompted every time you close a document.

```
Sub Main
If ViewOutline() Then ViewNormal
Dim dlg As FileSummaryInfo
GetCurValues dlg
Name$ = dlg.FileName
Dir$ = dlg.Directory
FullName$ = Dir$ + "\" + Name$
If MsgBox("Back up: " + FullName$ + " to A:\ ? ", "AutoClose", 4 + 32) Then
    CopyFile FullName$, "a:\"
End If
End Sub
```

Here's how this macro works:

- Check to see if the current document is in outline view; if so, change to normal view. This is because the next statement, accessing FileSummary-Info, is not valid while in outline view.

- Define an array variable to hold the information stored in FileSummaryInfo.

- Store the current values of FileSummaryInfo into the array variable dlg.

- Assign the file-name field, dlg.FileName, to the variable Name$.

- Assign the directory field, dlg.Directory, to the variable Dir$.

- Create a full path designation by concatenating Dir$, a backslash, and Name$.

■ Use the function form of MsgBox( ) to ask the user to confirm backing up the current file to drive A. Note that the destination of the backup is hard coded in this example. On a network you might change this to a directory designation.

■ If the user selects Yes, the macro executes the file copy.

As stated above in the discussion of the AutoExec macro that copied NORMAL.DOT to another directory, the WordBasic command CopyFile cannot be told to automatically overwrite an existing file. By default it will prompt you a second time to confirm replacing an existing file with the new copy.

You can, however, test to see if the file already exists, and if it does use SendKeys to bypass the second prompt. Here's a smarter version of AutoClose:

```
Sub Main
If ViewOutline() Then ViewNormal
Dim dlg As FileSummaryInfo
GetCurValues dlg
Name$  = dlg.FileName
Dir$ = dlg.Directory
FullName$ = Dir$ + "\" + Name$
If  MsgBox("Back up: " + FullName$ + " to A:\ ? ", "AutoClose", 4 + 32) Then
    If Files$("A:\" + Name$) <> "" Then SendKeys Chr$(32)
    CopyFile FullName$, "a:\"
End If
End Sub
```

We have added the line:

```
If Files$("A:\" + Name$) <> "" Then SendKeys Chr$(32)
```

This line uses the WordBasic function Files$( ), which searches for the file specification passed to it within the parentheses, in this case "A:\" + name$; if Files$( ) does not find a match, it returns a null string. So this If…Then expression basically means: If Files$( ) does not return a null string, which means the file already exists, then place a space into the keyboard buffer; that space will be received by the confirmation prompt.

There is one more improvement we should make to this AutoClose macro. When you close a document that has not been saved, Word prompts you to save it. However, Word executes the AutoClose macro (if there is one) before it checks if the document being closed contains unsaved changes. As a result, if you close a document that contains unsaved changes, the above macro would copy the most recently saved version—the current disk version—

of the file. We can compensate for this fact with a single-line addition to the macro:

```
Sub Main
If ViewOutline() Then ViewNormal
Dim dlg As FileSummaryInfo
GetCurValues dlg
Name$  = dlg.FileName
Dir$ = dlg.Directory
FullName$ = Dir$ + "\" + Name$
If  MsgBox("Back up: " + FullName$ + " to A:\ ? ", "AutoClose", 4 + 32) Then
    If IsDirty() Then FileSave
    If Files$("A:\" + Name$) <> "" Then SendKeys Chr$(32)
    CopyFile FullName$, "a:\"
End If
End Sub
```

What has been added is the line:

```
If IsDirty() Then FileSave
```

The WordBasic function IsDirty( )—colorful name, no?—returns true if the current document contains changes that have not been saved. So, this line means: If there are unsaved changes, save the file.

But what about those times when you don't want to save the most recent changes? We can make the line a little smarter:

```
If IsDirty() Then If MsgBox("Save before backing up?", 4 + 32) Then FileSave
```

This adds an additional prompt to confirm saving the most recent changes before proceeding to the actual copying of the file.

If this macro is named AutoClose, and is stored in the global context, it will be executed on every file that is closed. It will also be executed if instead of closing each open file you choose Exit from the File menu. Exiting Word will execute the Global AutoClose on each open file.

If you don't want every document to be automatically copied in this fashion, you can create a version of this AutoClose macro for each template controlling a class of document you do want backed up. For instance, you might not want to back up every letter or memo, but you might want to back up the Great American Novel with each close, and would therefore create a template version of this macro for your NOVEL.DOT.

## AutoExit

This macro is executed when you exit Word. It differs from AutoClose in this: It is executed after all open documents are closed.

There are several possibilities. You could use this macro to automatically activate another application. For instance, if Program Manager is your shell, you could ensure that after exiting Word, Program Manager would gain the focus:

```
Sub Main
SendKeys "% R"
AppActivate "Program Manager", Ø
End Sub
```

The first line of this macro places the key sequence Alt+spacebar+R into the keyboard buffer. The reason for the SendKeys statement is to accommodate the instances when Program Manager is on the desktop as an icon. The second line activates Program Manager. The key sequence, which executes the command to restore the application, is sent once the focus settles on Program Manager.

Another possible use for the AutoExit macro would be to reset any (or all) of the various view settings to your preference.

```
Sub Main
FileNewDefault         'Create an empty document to work on
ViewNormal             'Turn on normal view
ViewDraft Ø            'Turn off draft view
ViewRuler Ø            'Turn off ruler
ViewRibbon 1           'Turn on ribbon
ViewToolbar 1          'Turn on toolbar
ToolsOptionsView \
    .HScroll = Ø, \
    .VScroll = 1,\
    .StatusBar = 1, \
    .ShowAll = Ø
End Sub
```

# Extending the Functionality of a Command Macro

Previous chapters have referenced a unique ability in Word: You can alter virtually any of the built-in command macros. It is time to show how this is done.

## FileOpen—Show All Files

By default Word displays a listing of all DOC files when you execute the File-Open command. It is possible to change the default extension to something other than DOC by changing the WIN.INI setting Doc-Extension (see Chapter 13). However, you cannot change the default file extension to the wildcard file extension (the asterisk). To display a list of all files in a directory, no matter what their extension, you must modify the FileOpen macro itself.

If you edit FileOpen (by selecting Macro from the Tools menu, pressing Alt+C to display the list of commands, selecting FileOpen, and pressing Alt+E to edit), you will see the following macro code:

```
Sub Main
Dim dlg As FileOpen
GetCurValues dlg
Dialog dlg
Super FileOpen dlg
End Sub
```

There are several interesting things about this built-in macro. First, notice that an array variable is created of the same shape as the command FileOpen—just as it would be if a user-macro were going to query FileOpen. The FileOpen dialog box is displayed, with the statement Dialog dlg, so the user can select a file. And finally FileOpen is executed with the updated array variable as the parameter. Note, however, that the final line that calls FileOpen looks a little different than you might have expected. Notice the use of the prefix *Super* before the actual macro name.

Every built-in macro uses the Super prefix to call an internal command of the same name. FileOpen calls Super FileOpen, FileNew calls Super FileNew, and so on. If you look up this command in the Word help file, you will see the following definition: "If two macros have the same name, Word runs the template macro before a global macro, and a global macro before a built-in command. Super was originally intended to override this order, running the named macro at the next higher context level, but has no effect in the current release of Microsoft Word." In essence, the existence of this prefix in the built-in macros is a vestige of a design that was abandoned or left incomplete. Originally, Super in a template macro would mean "run the global macro;" Super in a global macro would mean "run the built-in command;" and Super in a built-in macro would mean "run the hidden, internal command of this name." Currently, Super should be viewed as a sort of marker. It has no meaning in a user-macro. Removing Super from a command macro, such as FileOpen, signals Word that the command macro has been modified, changed into a user-macro.

You can change the default file extension by changing the array field associated with the Name edit box before displaying the dialog.

**DISK**
FileOpenShowAll—
A possible FileOpen
replacement which
displays all files

```
Sub Main
Dim dlg As FileOpen
GetCurValues dlg
dlg.Name = "*.*"          'Changes the default
On Error Goto Bye         'Error checking in the event that the dialog is
                          'canceled
```

```
Dialog dlg                     'Display the FileOpen dialog box
FileOpen dlg                   'Open the selected file if OK is pressed
Bye:                           'Label marking jump point if cancel is pressed
End Sub
```

You could change the default extension to any extension or wildcard by customizing the string literal assigned to dlg.Name. For instance, to display both DOC and DOT files, you would change the third line to:

```
dlg.Name = "*.DO?"
```

Note that one of the additions to the macro is the line of error trapping:

```
On Error Goto Bye
```

This line anticipates the cancellation of the FileOpen dialog box. If you press Cancel, the macro jumps to the last line. Whenever you alter a built-in command macro—even if the addition is only a space or a comment—you transform that command macro into a user-macro; and consequently its error checking must follow the conventions required in a user-macro.

## FilePrint—Update All Fields

Another good candidate for modification is the built-in FilePrint macro. For instance, suppose you have a class of documents that make extensive use of fields. One of the options in the ToolsOptionsPrint dialog box determines whether all fields in a document are updated before printing. Having this option checked may not be necessary for most of your documents. The solution is to create a template-specific version of FilePrint which will automatically be used when you print a document ruled by that template.

**DISK**
FilePrintUpdate—
Possible FilePrint
replacement which
forces an update of
all fields

```
Sub Main
Dim dlg As ToolsOptionsPrint
GetCurValues dlg
Current = dlg.UpdateFields
ToolsOptionsPrint .UpdateFields = 1
Redim dlg As FilePrint
GetCurValues dlg
On Error Goto Bye
Dialog dlg
Super FilePrint dlg
Bye:
ToolsOptionsPrint .UpdateFields = Current
End Sub
```

This macro queries ToolsOptionsPrint to discover the current state of the check box Update Fields. It stores that state in the integer variable Current and calls ToolsOptionsPrint, setting Update Fields on. The macro then continues, displaying the FilePrint dialog and executing FilePrint.

Notice that the same array variable, dlg, is used both for the query to ToolsOptionsPrint in lines 1–4, and again in lines 5–9 to execute the FilePrint. This could be two different array variables, but there is no need, since once the array field dlg.UpdateFields is stored in the variable Current you no longer need to keep dlg defined as ToolsOptionsPrint. The fifth line uses a variation of the Dim statement, Redim, which does just what you'd guess: Re-Dimensions an existing array variable.

The last line of the macro calls ToolsOptionsPrint a second time, setting the field .UpdateFields to the value stored in the integer variable Current.

## FilePrint—Change Active Printer

Another possible modification that could be made to a template-specific version of FilePrint would be to automatically change the printer before printing.

Take this circumstance: You have a template designed specifically for writing electronic-mail messages. These messages are never printed on your standard printer. Instead, you would like to print them to a disk file for later distribution, either by disk or by modem.

The following macro, stored in a template dedicated to composing such messages, would store the current printer in a variable, change the active printer to "Generic / Text Only on FILE:", call the FilePrint dialog box, allow you to print the document to a disk file, and then, when complete, reset the active printer to the original device.

This macro assumes only one thing: You have installed the generic printer driver, named TTY.DRV, from the Windows control panel.

**DISK**
FilePrintGeneric—
Change active
printer to
Generic/TTY before
printing

```
Sub Main
NewPrinter$ = "Generic / Text Only on FILE:"
Dim dlg As FilePrintSetup
GetCurValues dlg
Current$ = dlg.Printer
FilePrintSetup NewPrinter$
Redim dlg As FilePrint
GetCurValues dlg
On Error Goto Bye
Dialog dlg
FilePrint dlg
Bye:
FilePrintSetup Current$
End Sub
```

Note that the variable NewPrinter$, which holds the necessary description of the printer to change to, is hard coded. This string literal is precisely the same string as is listed in the FilePrintSetup dialog box.

## Notes on Customized Command Macros

Recall that when you alter a built-in command macro, that macro becomes a user-macro. It must use proper error checking to trap for cancellation of dialog boxes, for example.

Another way in which a modified command macro behaves like a user-macro is the appearance of availability. When unmodified, the command macros, as displayed on the various menus, know when they are valid commands. That is to say, a command that has no meaning in a particular circumstance is grayed. Take, for instance, the top-level table menu. All but two of the submenu items are unavailable unless the insertion point is located in a table when the menu is accessed.

A user-macro assigned to a menu is never grayed. Word cannot know if a user-macro is only valid in a specific circumstance. A modified command macro, like other user-macros, always appears as valid on the menus.

## Hierarchy—Which Macro Has Control When

To properly organize the use of macros, either strict user-macros or modified command macros, we must review the concept of context as it applies to macro execution.

When you ask Word to perform a command, by selecting an access method associated with a macro, Word searches for that macro in the following order:

- If the insertion point is located in a document based upon a template, Word first searches the associated template for the named macro.

- If Word does not find the named macro in the template context (or the insertion point is in a normal based document), Word searches for the named macro in the global context, that is, in NORMAL.DOT.

- If Word cannot find the named macro in either the associated template or the global context, it searches the internal command macros.

This order of searching for a macro is a strict hierarchy. It is the same hierarchy established among access methods. If you press Ctrl+Shift+Z, Word first looks to see if there is a template-specific definition of which macro this combination executes; if there is none, Word looks to the global context for instruction; if there is none in the global context, Word looks to see if there is a default assignment for the key combination.

This hierarchy applies to modified command macros as well as user-macros and access methods. For instance, if you are working on a document which has a modified FilePrint macro installed in the document's associated template, that modified version of FilePrint will always have rule when in the template context, even if you also have a globally defined modified FilePrint. When Word finds the macro, in this case after the first step of the hierarchical search, it stops looking.

If you have a modified FilePrint stored in the global context, all documents that do not themselves have a modified FilePrint in their associated templates will use that global FilePrint. Once you define a global version of a command macro, you cannot access the default, built-in version of that macro. You have, essentially, blocked Word's view of the internal command.

Another way of looking at the question of which version of a macro has control when, is by considering the idea of scope. The scope of a macro refers to the range of influence that macro has. A template-specific macro's scope is the most limited. It has control, or rule, only while the insertion point is located in a document based on the template containing the macro. A global macro's scope is wider, extending to any document—any document, that is, not associated with a template that contains an identically named macro. The internal command macros, like global macros, have scope covering every document unless there is a contravening, identically named macro in either the global or template context.

So, in summary, you can think of a macro's availability from either of two vantages. From the point of view of Word searching for the macro to execute, think of a hierarchical search, starting with the template, moving to the global context, and ending with the internal command macros. The search stops as soon as there is a match. From the point of view of the macro, think of the range of influence: Template macros possess scope limited to the document based on the template holding those macros. Global macros have a wider range, extending to any open document that does not possess a template-specific contravening macro. The internal command macros have a similarly wide range, also extending to all documents. However, whereas a global macro can only be contravened by a template macro, an internal command macro can be contravened by either a global macro or a template macro. A contravening macro, quite simply, is a macro of the same name higher up in the hierarchy.

## Resetting a Command Macro

Changing a built-in macro seems much scarier than it is. You have not actually deleted the built-in command macro. You have only blocked Word's using that command macro by placing a macro of the same name within the search hierarchy. It is impossible to delete an internal command macro.

When you run ToolsMacro, and display the list of macros, you will notice that if you have Commands as the active button in the Show group, selecting any of the internal command macros will gray both the Delete and the Rename buttons. If you select Global Macros or Template Macros in the Show group, any macro, including a macro that has the same name as an internal command macro (such as FileOpen or FilePrint), will leave the Delete and Rename buttons active. The rule is this: If it can be deleted or renamed, then it is a user-macro, even if it *seems*, because of a coincidence of name, to be a command macro.

To remove a modified version of a command macro, and thereby reactivate access to the unmodified built-in command macro, you can do one of two things: You can delete the user-macro that is blocking Word's access to the internal command, or you can rename the user-macro to any other name.

For instance, suppose you have created a modified FilePrint macro using either of the examples in the previous section and then decide that you wish to activate the default version of the FilePrint command macro. Simply run ToolsMacro, find FilePrint (in the Global or Template list), and press either Alt+D to Delete or Alt+N to rename the macro. Unless you are certain that you will never wish to reactivate this modified version, I would recommend renaming rather than deleting. You should choose a descriptive name when renaming. For instance, the modified FilePrint macro, which forces an update to all fields before printing, might be renamed FilePrintUpdateFields.

## Building Summary

This chapter demonstrated the kinds of problems WordBasic can solve. The particular power of macros specially named with any of the five auto macro designations was detailed and possible uses explored. We also illustrated the ability to extend the functionality of a built-in command macro, and explained the hierarchy Word follows when looking for a macro.

I hope that the macro listings and explanations in this chapter have made you more comfortable reading macro source code. Perhaps you have even begun thinking in WordBasic.

The next chapter will discuss various advanced topics in WordBasic programming, adding to your arsenal, providing the tools necessary to construct more complex application macros.

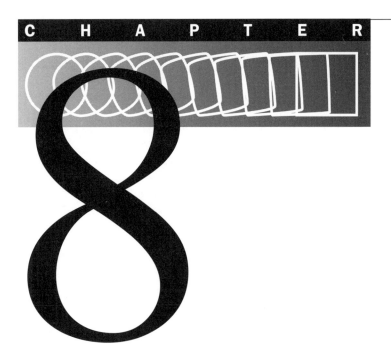

# Program Structure,
# the Macro Editor, and
# Debugging

I
N THIS CHAPTER WE SHALL DELVE DEEPER INTO WORDBASIC, LOOKING AT
the macro editor in more detail, discussing error messages and debugging, as well as looking at individual WordBasic commands and capabilities. The tools and tips presented in this chapter will provide the
groundwork for the creation of more complex application macros.

# Modular Programming

All of the macros presented thus far consisted of a single subroutine, a continuous sequence of WordBasic statements delineated by Sub Main and End
Sub. But, just as we suggested that a macro is a subroutine of Word, so a
macro itself can have subroutines of its own.

Breaking a complex macro down into a series of subroutines called by a
main subroutine is known as *modular programming*. It allows you to create
longer macros that are easier to read and maintain. And it allows you to write
more economical code.

For instance, if a specific group of WordBasic statements is used in several places in your macro, gathering the statements together under a subroutine name will save space typing as well as make your macro smaller. (Smaller
is always better.)

## User Subroutines

The pseudocode syntax for a user-defined subroutine would look something
like:

```
Sub Main
...Any Series of WordBasic Statements
Call TheUserSub
...More WordBasic Statements
End Sub

Sub TheUserSub
...The Sub's WordBasic Statements
End Sub
```

Realize that the macro consists of both the Sub Main and any user-defined
subroutines. So, in the above syntax example, the macro is not one or the
other of the "subs," but the combination of both.

### Do Something

A user-subroutine should be thought of as a relative to the WordBasic statement. In essence it gathers together a series of WordBasic commands to accomplish an action that may consist of several parts. This should sound

familiar. It sounds like the definition of a macro. A user-subroutine, in a sense, is a macro's macro.

Recall that we characterized a programming statement as the (semi) equivalent of an active verb. At its simplest level a subroutine is used to do something, to perform an action. Such a subroutine is often referred to as a *procedure* or a *procedural statement*. For example, here's a macro that consists of a main subroutine and a single user-defined subroutine:

```
Sub Main
Call DisplayMessageAndBeep
End Sub

Sub DisplayMessageAndBeep
Beep
MsgBox "This is the message","DisplayMessageAndBeep"
End Sub
```

The main sub (hereafter "sub" will be used as an abbreviation for "subroutine") consists of a single statement: Call the user-sub named DisplayMessage-AndBeep. The user-sub consists of two statements: Beep and MsgBox.

Incidentally, the use of the Call statement before the name of the user-sub is entirely optional. The code

```
Sub Main
DisplayMessageAndBeep
End Sub
```

is equivalent to

```
Sub Main
Call DisplayMessageAndBeep
End Sub
```

The reason for using the Call "prefix" is clarity. It ensures that you can distinguish a user-defined subroutine from the built-in WordBasic statements.

### Do Something with a Parameter

Just as most WordBasic statements allow you to pass a modifying (adverbial) parameter, so a user-sub can accept a parameter.

The next level of complexity in a user-sub is to take a user-supplied parameter and do something *with* it. For example:

```
Sub Main
Call DisplayMessageAndBeep "This is the message"
End Sub

Sub DisplayMessageAndBeep Message$
Beep
MsgBox Message$,"DisplayMessageAndBeep"
End Sub
```

In this instance the string literal "This is the message" is passed to the user-sub parameter named Message$. When you call this user-sub, a temporary variable (a string variable because Message$ ends in a dollar sign) is created. The user-sub then displays that string variable in the message box.

You can have multiple parameters, and you can mix string and integer variable names in the parameter list:

```
Sub Main
Call DisplayMessageAndBeep "This is the message","Title",4
End Sub

Sub DisplayMessageAndBeep Message$,Title$,Icon
Beep
MsgBox Message$,Title$,Icon
End Sub
```

In this example the main subroutine calls DisplayMessageAndBeep with three parameters: the message, the title, and the icon. Notice that the last parameter requires an integer value.

Know that if you have defined a subroutine as having three parameters, the calling statement must provide all three parameters, in the proper order, and of the proper type. That is, passing an integer to a subroutine that expects a string will result in an error; passing two parameters to a user-sub that expects three parameters will result in an error.

### Do Something to a Parameter
The third type of action performed by a user-sub is to do something *to* one or more of the passed parameters. This type of subroutine is extremely useful. For instance:

```
Sub Main
FullName$ = "Gallo,Guy"
Marker$ = ","
Call SplitTheString(FullName$,One$,Two$,Marker$)
MsgBox One$
MsgBox Two$
End Sub

Sub SplitTheString(S$,One$,Two$,Marker$)
Index = Instr(S$,Marker$)        'Find the location of the comma in the FullName$
                                 'string
One$ = Left$(S$,Index-1)         'Assign left of the comma to the variable One$
Two$ = Mid$(S$,Index+1)          'Assign right of the comma to the variable Two$
End Sub
```

If any of you have tried to manipulate an address database in Word, you can see immediately the utility of this subroutine. Notice that the name of the parameter can be different in the calling statement than it is in the user-sub parameter list. In this case FullName$ and S$ refer to the same value.

## User Functions

In the earlier discussion of the language elements of WordBasic, I suggested that statements are similar to active verbs and functions are similar to passive verbs. Statements do something. Functions tell something.

Just as you can create user-subroutines to perform a series of actions, so you can define a user-function to evaluate a condition or an expression and return a value.

The pseudocode syntax for a user-defined function would look something like:

```
Sub Main
x = UserFunction
End Sub
```

```
Function UserFunction
If EvaluatedExpression Then UserFunction = Value
End Function
```

### Is Something True

The simplest form of WordBasic function is Boolean: Is something true. We've seen several examples of this, such as Bold( ) and ViewOutline( ). The simplest form of a user-function is one that returns a true or false value depending upon a condition.

```
Sub Main
x = BlankLine
If x = -1 Then MsgBox "This is a blank line"
End Sub
```

```
Function BlankLine
StartOfLine
t = Asc(Selection$())
If t = 13 Then BlankLine = -1
GoBack
End Function
```

The main sub assigns the value of the user-function BlankLine to the variable *x*. The user-function BlankLine moves to the start of the current line and assigns the ASCII value of the selection (the first letter of the line) to the variable *t;* if *t* equals 13 (the ASCII value of a carriage return), then the function is set to –1 (true); otherwise it retains the default value of 0 (false). Finally, BlankLine returns the insertion point to its previous location.

A slightly smarter version of this user-function (but one that cannot be run with the focus in a macro window), would be

```
Sub Main
If BlankLine Then MsgBox "This is a blank line"
End Sub
```

```
Function BlankLine
EditGoTo "\Line"
t = Asc(Selection$())
If t = 13 Then BlankLine = - 1
GoBack
End Function
```

This cannot be run on a macro window because the macro editor does not support bookmarks. Notice in this version the main routine's single statement has been changed to an evaluation of the value of BlankLine. When WordBasic reaches the evaluation "If BlankLine," the function is immediately queried, and the result stored in the name of the user-function itself.

### Is Something True about a Parameter
Just as built-in functions sometimes accept parameters when queried, such as ExistingBookmark$(BookmarkName$), so too user-functions can accept parameters. A slightly contrived example of this would be

```
Sub Main
TryAgain:
Input "Type a number from one to ten", x
If NotLegal(x) Then Goto TryAgain
Print "You picked "; x
End Sub

Function NotLegal(x)
If x > 1, Or x < 1 Then NotLegal = -1
End Function
```

This function, like the previous example, evaluates a condition and returns, in itself, a true or false value. The additional functionality in this example lies in the fact that the evaluation itself depends upon the passed parameter.

### Return the Parameter Altered
A function can return more than true or false. Here's another slightly contrived example:

```
Sub Main
S$ = "This is a string full of spaces"
MsgBox S$
MsgBox StripSpaces$(S$)
MsgBox S$
End Sub

Function StripSpaces$(S$)
Temp$ = S$
Index = Instr(Temp$,Chr$(32))
While Index <> 0
    Temp$ = Left$(Temp$,Index-1) + Mid$(Temp$,Index+1)
    Index = Instr(Temp$,Chr$(32))
```

```
Wend
StripSpaces$ = Temp$
End Function
```

This example macro assigns a string literal to the variable S$; displays the variable; displays the result of passing that string variable to the user-function StripSpaces( ), which removes all spaces from the string variable; and displays the variable again.

Notice that the first and third calls to MsgBox display the same string: the original variable that contains spaces. This is because the variable is left unchanged by the user-function. It is left unchanged because the string parameter is assigned by the function to a temporary variable, Temp$, on which the actual string manipulation is performed.

Notice that in the main routines the function itself is a parameter for the MsgBox statement. This quality of a function has been shown several times, but still bears repeating: The name of a function itself is equivalent to the answer found when the function is executed.

Notice as well that the parameter passed to the function is assigned to a temporary variable, Temp$, on which the actual string manipulation is performed. This points to a subtle limitation in Word: If a variable is passed to a subroutine or function and altered by that function, it is passed back to the main routine, *even if the names of the passed variable and the receiving variable are different*. That seems really convoluted. The best way to demonstrate this idea is to modify the above macro slightly, and run it:

```
Sub Main
S$ = "This is a string full of spaces"
MsgBox S$
MsgBox StripSpaces$(S$)
MsgBox S$
End Sub
Function StripSpaces$(Temp$)
Index = Instr(Temp$,Chr$(32))
While Index <> 0
    Temp$ = Left$(Temp$,Index-1) + Mid$(Temp$,Index+1)
    Index = Instr(Temp$,Chr$(32))
Wend
StripSpaces$ = Temp$
End Function
```

In this example, instead of passing S$ to the function and assigning S$ to the variable Temp$ within the function, S$ is passed directly to the variable Temp$. In addition to assigning the stripped variable to the function name, the passed variable itself, S$, is stripped of spaces. That is, after the function executes, the variable S$ of the main routine has also been altered. Notice that in this example only the variable displayed by the first MsgBox contains any spaces. In the second MsgBox instance, the result of StripSpaces( ) is displayed. The third MsgBox statement displays the modified string variable, which now contains no spaces. To avoid altering a main routine variable, have the function or subroutine assign it to a new, temporary, discardable variable.

This fact, that a sub or function will *pass back* the altered parameter, can be useful. It allows you to have a function that returns more than one value. Here is an example that returns a value in the function name and alters the passed variable:

```
Sub Main
Name$ = "temp string"
If IsMacroPane(Name$) Then
    MsgBox "The macro is named: " + Name$
Else
    MsgBox Name$
End If
End Sub

Function IsMacroPane(Name$)
If SelInfo(27) Then
    IsMacroPane = -1
    Name$ = WindowName$()
    Name$ = Mid$(Name$, Instr(Name$, ":") + 2)
Else
    IsMacroPane = 0
    Name$ = "Not a macro"
End If
End Function
```

The user-function IsMacroPane is an integer function. That is, the value stored in the function name itself is either 0 or -1. However, in addition to testing if the insertion point is currently located in a macro editing window, the function modifies the variable named Name$. If the built-in function SelInfo(27) returns a true value, meaning the insertion point is located in a macro editing window, then Name$ is assigned the macro name portion of the current WindowName$( ); otherwise it is assigned the string literal "Not a macro."

## Thinking in Pieces

Knowing what a user-sub or a user-function looks like may not help at all in knowing when to use one. Here are some general thoughts about designing macros to take advantage of user-defined subroutines and functions.

The best time to think modularly is at the beginning. After you have discovered a need that might be met by a macro, approach the problem of designing the solution with this concept of modularity in mind. Break down the problem into parts (without defining the constituents so finely as to lose all structure). Think of the main body of the macro, the Sub Main/End Sub portion, as the controlling routine from which the necessary subroutines and functions (both internal WordBasic commands and user-defined subs/functions) will be called like so many messengers from a centralized dispatcher.

Any group of statements that is used repeatedly in the course of a macro's normal execution is a good candidate for a simple user-subroutine. It is apparent that if seven lines, say, of code are used five times in a non-modular program, revising that macro to use a seven-line subroutine called five times will save 23 lines of code. (This figure is arrived at through the following calculation: If no user-sub is used, 7 statements repeated in 5 places equals 35 lines of code; a user-sub containing 7 statements called 5 times equals 12 lines of code. The difference between the two is 23.) You should be parsimonious when coding a macro. Most programmers don't like to type more than they have to (who does?). And in addition to the economy of using a subroutine to provide access to a repeated sequence of statements, the subroutine will make the macro much easier to read, both by other users and by yourself when you want to improve the macro at some future date.

In addition to simply grouping repetitive tasks into a single unit, a subroutine/function can be used to create new "commands." An example of this is the StripSpaces( ) function used above. Later in this chapter we will examine several such user-functions that expand the arsenal of tools available to examine and alter strings.

Another good candidate for a user-function is any operation that would test a condition and return a true or false value. Possible examples of such Boolean user-functions would be confirming the validity of a path or checking to see if a macro exists in a given context.

One additional value in writing your macros in small units, or modules, is *reusability*. If you write a user-function to perform a specific action or evaluation, chances are that same function will prove useful in a future macro. By creating a user-sub/function the code is automatically independent of the specific context of the original macro. It will prove much easier to transport a sub/function to a subsequent macro project if the code has been generalized and written as a module than it would be if you had to remove the relevant statements from within the main portion of the macro. Writing modularly encourages generalization.

## Shared Variables

Modular programming brings with it a limitation: Variables defined in one subroutine are not accessible by another. A variable defined in one subroutine has scope only in that subroutine. Although variables can be passed as parameters from one subroutine to another, it is impossible (and sloppy) to define a parameter list to accommodate every conceivable variable. For one thing, variables tend to sprout like wildflowers as a macro gets more complex.

WordBasic provides a solution by way of *shared variables.* A variable can be declared, or created, as shared by the entire macro, no matter how many subs or functions it contains. A shared variable has scope over the entire macro.

The pseudocode syntax for a shared variable is as follows:

```
Dim Shared SharedString$, SharedNumber
Sub Main
...Main sub statements
End Sub
```

Notice that to declare a shared variable you use the same WordBasic statement used to dimension an array: Dim. Notice as well that you can define multiple shared variables in a single line by separating the individual variable names by commas. Also notice that you can mix string and integer variables on the same line.

In addition to string and integer variables you can also dimension an array variable to be shared among all the subroutines and functions in a macro. This is an important ability since WordBasic does not support passing an entire array as a parameter to a subroutine or function. This is such an important limitation and equally important work-around that it bears detailed illustration:

```
Dim Shared MyArr$(0)
Sub Main
Redim MyArr$(1)
MyArr$(0) = "First word"
MyArr$(1) = "Second word"
Call ManipulateArray
End Sub

Sub ManipulateArray
Print MyArr$(1)
End Sub
```

Notice that when first defined MyArr$( ) is dimensioned with size 0 (which means 1, recall: Computers start counting at 0). When, in the body of the main subroutine, the array is given its actual size, the Redim statement is used. When you Redim the array, you can change both the size and the depth of the array. For instance, the following code is also legal:

```
Dim Shared MyArr$(0)
Sub Main
Redim MyArr$(0,1)
MyArr$(0,0) = "First word"
MyArr$(0,1) = "Second word"
Call ManipulateArray
End Sub
```

```
Sub ManipulateArray
Print MyArr$(0,1)
End Sub
```

Note, however, that all references to the array have been altered to reflect that it is now a "two-dimensional" array.

You can also declare a command array variable as shared. That allows us to perform a pretty neat trick.

```
Dim Shared ViewState As ToolsOptionsView
Sub Main
Call SetViewState
MsgBox "View Settings Changed"
Call RestoreViewState
End Sub

Sub SetViewState
GetCurValues ViewState
ToolsOptionsView .ShowAll = 1, .HScroll = 1
End Sub

Sub RestoreViewState
ToolsOptionsView ViewState
End Sub
```

This macro declares a shared command array variable to hold the various options controlled by the ToolsOptionsView command. The user-sub SetViewState then executes a GetCurValues to update the variable ViewState with the current settings. The user-sub RestoreViewState passes the entire command array variable to the ToolsOptionsView statement. This short example provides a basis for you to control the way your application macros look to a user, and then restore the various view settings to the user's preferences when done. That's a good practice. It's rude for a macro to change any preference without changing it back after exiting.

## The Macro Editor

Word's macro editor provides a fairly complete macro development environment. The macro editor is integrated into the program itself. You do not have to run a special editor or macro facility. In some macro facilities each macro is saved to a separate disk file. In Word macros are not saved individually. Rather, they are saved within a template, either the global NORMAL.DOT or a specific, local template. Every Word document is based upon a template, either global or local, and therefore every document is linked to a list of macros as well as to the list of internal command macros.

The integrated editor is always available. You can write and test macros while other, standard Word documents are open (and usable as test documents).

When you invoke the macro editor to create a new macro, Word automatically provides the first and last line, the Sub Main/End Sub pair. The editing functions are limited. You cannot use any of Word's advanced formatting functions, bookmarks, or outlines (sadly). But you can select blocks of text for easy copying, cutting, and moving. The font used in the macro editor is limited to either Times New Roman (if Word is in normal view) or the default system font, usually MS Sans Serif (if Word is in draft view). The only "word processing" type function available in the macro editor is the ChangeCase command (by default assigned to Shift+F3). If you examine the main menu while in a macro window, you will see that virtually all the menu items except those on the Macro and the Window menus are grayed.

The real power of Word's macro editor resides in its development and debugging tools. The two most significant aspects of the WordBasic development environment are the ease with which the programmer can control and query the macro being tested and Word's ability to detect and explain errors.

## The Macro Bar

Even if all the macro editor did was allow you to write and run an open macro on an open document, and was smart enough to tag your errors, Word would be a leg up on many macro facilities in terms of ease of use. But in addition to these abilities there are others that allow you to watch the macro execute and examine the individual actions and results of each line.

Much of this development capacity is accessed through the macro button bar. This bar was first described in Chapter 5 (see Figure 5.2). At that time we limited our use to the Start button. Now it is time for a closer look.

When you open a macro for editing, the macro button bar appears beneath the top menu, or beneath the toolbar if you have it showing. If you have the ribbon bar displayed, the macro bar replaces it. That is, the ribbon and the macro bar can never co-exist. The macro bar, unlike the ruler, is not context specific. That is, as long as you have even one macro open on the desktop the macro button bar will display even if the focus switches to a document. This is what allows you to execute an open macro on a scratch document, as was the case with AssignKey in Chapter 7. If you have more than one macro open at a time, the macro controlled by the macro bar is the last macro that had the focus. This macro is displayed, along with its template's name, to the right of the buttons. Think of it this way: The macro bar remembers the last macro that held the insertion point.

There is no way to remove the macro bar from the display (other than closing all macros). The fact that the macro bar remains available even when the focus moves to a document allows you to execute a macro interactively.

**TIP.** *Here's a capability many people overlook. Several of the special bars displayed on Word's screen have "hot-spots." If you place the pointer anywhere on the right side of the macro bar (where the macro name is displayed), and double-click the left mouse button, the ToolsMacro dialog box is displayed. This comes in handy when testing several macros at once. Double-clicking on the formatting Ribbon will bring up the FormatCharacter dialog box. Double-clicking on the toolbar will display the ToolsOptionsToolbar dialog box. The Ruler has several hot-spots: Clicking once at the far left toggles between indent and margin scale; double-clicking at the bottom of the ruler brings up the FormatSection dialog box in margin scale and FormatTabs dialog box in indent scale; double-clicking to the right brings up the FormatParagraph dialog box.*

### Start

We have already used the Start button in several examples in previous chapters. Its function is obvious: When you select this button, either by clicking or by pressing Alt+Shift+S, the macro referenced on the bar executes.

The first thing to note about this button is the accelerator key combination. In most cases, such as menus and dialog boxes, the underscored character is used in combination with the Alt key to access the named function. A button bar such as the macro bar (or the bar created when editing headers and footers, or footnotes and annotations) requires that you use Alt+Shift in combination with the underscored accelerator key. This fact is documented in the Word manual but in somewhat obscure fashion.

Executing the macro with the Start button has the same effect as running the macro from ToolsMacro, or from the assigned shortcut key (if there is one).

### Step

The Step button, accessed with Alt+Shift+E, is the most useful of the macro bar buttons. It allows you to execute the macro one statement, or line, at a time. Each time you select the Step button the current macro will advance by a single statement. By "stepping" through a macro you can easily see the flow of the program logic.

When you step through a macro, the macro bar changes in two ways: The Start button changes to Continue and the Vars button (discussed later in this section) becomes available, that is, it is no longer grayed.

The Step command does have one limitation. If your macro contains a SendKeys statement, Step will, at best, disable the command or, at worst, send the keys to the wrong place. A step execution of a SendKeys statement will not produce an error message. (This can be completely confusing if you don't know about it.) The following macro will fail:

```
Sub Main
ChDir "C:\WINWORD"
```

```
SendKeys "%TA%N"    'Send Alt+T-A, Alt+N
On Error Resume Next
ToolsMacro "FileOpen", .Run
End Sub
```

Of course, this example is so simple you wouldn't need to step through it; but for the sake of the example, if you step through this macro, you will see the Format menu (brought down by the Alt+T) followed by two beeps as the T and Alt+A are sent to the format menu (where they have no meaning). Basically, stepping through a SendKeys sends the keys immediately rather than stuffing them into the keyboard buffer to await the next dialog box.

WordBasic does, however, provide a way around this limitation. As in other implementations of BASIC, you can place multiple statements on the same line, separated by a colon. For example, the above macro can be revised in the following manner:

```
Sub Main
ChDir "C:\WINWORD"
On Error Resume Next
SendKeys "%TA%N" : ToolsMacro "FileOpen", .Run
End Sub
```

By placing the SendKeys statement on the same line, separated by a colon, as the statement that generates the dialog box meant to receive the sent keys, you can ensure that the macro can be stepped through successfully. The Send-Keys and ToolsMacro statements are treated as a single "step" by the Step command.

**NOTE.** *Marcos which make too frequent use of the ability to place multiple statements on a single line can become difficult to read. I would advise limiting this trick to those statements, such as a SendKeys and its destination, that are obviously and inextricably linked.*

## Step SUBs

The Step SUBs button, like Step, executes one line of code at a time. However, it treats any user-subroutine or user-function as a single statement.

Since Step SUBS treat all statements contained within a user-sub/function as if they were a single statement, it allows a second method to work around the SendKeys limitation mentioned above. If your macro contains a SendKeys statement, you can still step through the main part of the macro and have it execute as expected (sending the keys) by placing the SendKeys command and the command to which the keys are directed into a separate subroutine. The above example that failed when stepped through will succeed if changed to:

```
Sub Main
ChDir "C:\WINWORD"
```

```
Call MySendKeys
End Sub

Sub MySendKeys
SendKeys "%TA%N"     'Send Alt+T-A, Alt+N
On Error Resume Next
ToolsMacro "FileOpen", .Run
End Sub
```

and then stepped through using Step SUBs.

Using Step SUBs allows you to more speedily step through a modular macro by skipping subroutines or functions that you know are not the problem (and therefore don't need to be tested). Realize that you can combine the use of Step and Step SUBs. That is, you can start out skipping subs until you get to a sub that needs stepping and then use Step.

### Continue

When either the Step or the Step SUBs button is selected, the Step button changes to Continue. If you select Continue, the macro exits step mode and executes to completion as if you had selected Start.

### Trace

I have always found the Trace button relatively useless. It executes the macro, highlighting each line as it executes, but without pausing. All this really accomplishes is a visual display of the flow of the macro. Even though the macro executes more slowly than normal, it is still too fast for the eye to follow with any real insight.

### Vars

The Vars button is only available when a macro is paused, either because you have begun execution using Step or Step SUBs, you have pressed Esc to interrupt the macro, or the macro has encountered the Stop statement. When you select the Vars button (or press Alt+Shift+V), you will see the following list box:

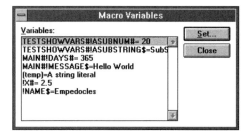

Used in conjunction with either the Step or Step SUBs button, Vars allows you to view and change the current state of all the variables in a macro.

This enables you both to check that things are working as planned and to test alternate variable values.

There is, however, the following limitation: Vars does not display the contents of array variables. To display an array variable you must assign it to a named variable.

## A Bug Warning

There is a bug in version 2.0a of Word for Windows which can result in the loss of a template's customized menu structure. This bug may bite if you have multiple macros open from different templates and select FileSaveAll.

Here are two detailed scenarios which will result in the loss of custom menu assignments from a template.

Case One involves an unsaved template macro in combination with an unsaved global macro:

- Template A contains customized menu assignments.

- A document based upon Template A is open on the desktop.

- A macro from Template A is open on the desktop. This macro has not been saved (which means that Template A is "dirty").

- A global macro is also on the desktop, and also dirty.

- With the focus on the dirty global macro, select FileSaveAll and answer yes to all save prompts (in this sequence there would be two: one for Template A and one for Global changes).

- The menu assignments in Template A will be lost (interestingly, any separator assignments will remain, but all menu text assignments associated with macros will be nuked).

Case Two involves two unsaved macros from different templates:

- Template A contains customized menu assignments.

- A document based upon Template A is open on the desktop.

- A macro from Template A is open on the desktop. This macro has not been saved. Template A is dirty.

- A document based upon Template B is open on the desktop.

- A macro from Template B is open on the desktop. This macro has not been saved. Template B is dirty.

- With the focus on Template B's macro, select FileSaveAll and answer yes to all save prompts (in this sequence there would be two: one for Template A and one for Global changes).

- The menu assignments in Template A will be lost.

These circumstances may seem baroque. They are, but that doesn't prevent them from being relatively common once you get involved in macro programming. To avoid losing menu changes when working on a template macro, follow these precautions:

- The simplest solution is to always work with a single template while developing. However, that may not be practical.

- Call FileSaveAll with the focus on the modified template macro, not on an open global macro.

- If you have multiple templates open, place the focus on the one that possesses menu assignments when calling FileSaveAll.

- If both templates hold menu customizations, you should close the macros associated with one of the templates, and then execute FileSave on the associated document. This will save both the document and the template.

It's ironic, isn't it, that the act of saving your work can, in some circumstances, result in the loss of customizations. There is a macro on the samples disk, in UTILITY.DOC, named BackupTemplateMenus, which will protect against the loss of your menu customizations. See Appendix G.

# Debugging Macros

Designing a macro, figuring out its structure, and finding the pieces—the individual WordBasic commands available and appropriate to the task—are just the beginning. No matter how carefully conceived, the chances of a macro working as expected on the first try are slim to none. That's one of the reasons the macro environment is so useful for both the beginner and the advanced macro programmer. It allows you to write, test, fail, write some more, test some more, and fail again without very much effort at all.

Finding where a macro fails, and figuring out why, is half, if not all, the fun of writing complex macros. Compulsive personalities will love debugging (the general term used to describe the testing of a computer program). Half brainteaser, half video game, creating and debugging macros provides a ready-made distraction from the frequently arduous task of writing. But this fact shouldn't inspire guilt. At the end of the procrastination, unlike shooting pool or watching the tube, you will have an object of value, a tool that will save time on future projects. I often think of hacking away at custom macros as a productive form of procrastination, an odd combination of doodling and carpentry. What I like most about programming, especially when it is in the service of making my primary tool, my word processor, more productive, is that when all the creative fiddling, the problem-solving logic bashing, and the sometimes tedious testing is complete, I have a product, a machine, an object that *does* something. It works.

## WordBasic Statements to Aid Macro Testing

There are several WordBasic statements that have meaning only while you are developing a macro, that is, when the macro is open. Understanding these statements is crucial to fluid macro testing.

### Stop

The WordBasic statement Stop interrupts macro execution. When encountered, a message box is displayed and the macro ribbon changes: Start becomes Continue and the Vars button is available. This allows you to stop macro execution at a particular point and examine the current contents of the macro's variables.

Using the Stop command helps isolate a problem. One of the problems with the Step button is that it starts from the top every time. This means that even if you're certain the first 50 lines of code are solid (no bugs), you have to step through them all before getting to the section of the macro that needs a second look. Instead of stepping through a long macro from the top, place a Stop statement at the place you know you need to examine more closely.

Usually Stop is simply placed on its own line at approximately the location you need to start stepping. However, it is possible to combine Stop with an If…Then statement to conditionally stop a macro according to a variable value. In this case, where you know the problem is being caused by a faulty variable, the trick is to figure out what variable to check, what value would be illegal, and to stick an evaluation in the appropriate place, for instance:

```
If TestVariable > 10 Then Stop
```

### ShowVars

This statement, like Stop, allows you to examine the current state of the macro's variables. The main difference—a big one—is that ShowVars does not allow you to continue with the Step button. Once the ShowVars dialog box is removed, the macro continues until it completes, or hits another ShowVars or Stop statement.

Here is an example macro that will illustrate some of the features of ShowVars:

```
Dim Shared x, Name$
Sub Main
days = 365
Message$ = "Hello World"
Name$ = "Empedocles"
x = 2.5
Call TestShowVars(x,Name$,"A string literal")
End Sub

Sub TestShowVars(x,one$,two$)
ShowVars
End Sub
```

This macro contains several types of variables: shared, Main-specific, user-sub specific, variables passed to the user-sub, and a string literal passed to the user-sub. Notice how the manner of presentation tells you something about the variable: Numeric variables have a number sign appended to their names; the variables defined in the main subroutine are prefaced by the marker MAIN#!; those defined in a user-subroutine are prefaced by the name of the subroutine (plus a number sign and an exclamation point); variables declared as shared have no subroutine name, only the exclamation point, as prefix; and the string literal that is passed to the subroutine is designated as a temporary variable by "(temp)." See Figure 8.1.

ShowVars also allows you to change the value of a variable before continuing with macro execution. This can be extremely useful in locating which variable is causing an error condition.

### MsgBox and Print

The MsgBox and Print statements are normally used to communicate with the user, displaying status messages, warnings, or instructions. However, they are also useful tools during the debugging stage. They can be used effectively to communicate to the programmer (rather than the user) the progress of the macro's execution.

For instance, one of the limitations of the ShowVars statement is that its list of variables will not include any user-defined arrays. One way around this limitation is to use a MsgBox statement when interested in the contents of an array variable.

```
Sub Main
Dim MyArr$(0)
MyArr$(0) = "This is an array variable"
MsgBox MyArr$(0)
End Sub
```

MsgBox can also be used to display a specific grouping of variables.

**Figure 8.1**

ShowVars dialog box

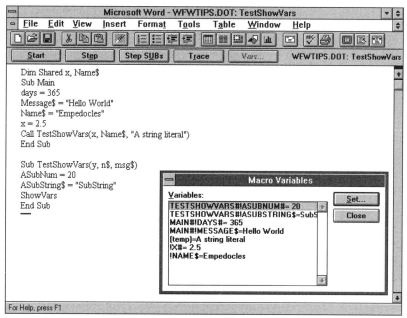

The Print command can also be used to display the value of a group of variables. The difference, of course, is that the macro is not paused. A status bar message will be replaced by a subsequent message (generated by either a Print statement or an internal command macro). Print is most useful in displaying the current value of variables within a control structure such as While…Wend or For…Next.

Print can also be used in place of a command you know works but does not need to be executed during the testing phase of macro development. For instance, if you are writing a macro that prints a document, you don't need (or want) the document to actually print. For example:

```
Sub Main
REM FilePrint .Name = TestDoc$
Print "Printing " + TestDoc$
End Sub
```

Notice that the actual command, the FilePrint statement, has been disabled with the REM prefix.

### Using Comments While Testing

Comments can be used to disable commands you know will work when the macro is complete. Comments can also be used to locate the cause of a macro's failure. When you are not sure which line is generating an error condition, one way to track down the problem is to "comment out" all related, suspect lines by inserting the REM prefix or an apostrophe, and then run the macro repeatedly, activating the suspect statements one at a time until the error condition occurs.

### RecordNextCommand

In earlier chapters we examined how to use the recorder to create the outlines of a macro. Using the macro recorder is a great way to find the proper syntax for a WordBasic command (since the recorder inserts all parameters, even those that are not changed during recording). Although using the macro recorder as a starting point is straightforward, what happens if you are in the middle of writing and testing a complex macro? You have two options: You can use the macro recorder to create a temporary macro that holds the commands of interest, or you can use the WordBasic statement RecordNextCommand.

The first method requires that you record a new macro containing the desired commands, open that macro, and copy the commands into the active macro (the one you're testing). The RecordNextCommand statement makes this process much easier.

RecordNextCommand requires that a macro be open in the workspace. When Word encounters RecordNextCommand, it waits for the user to execute a built-in command macro and inserts that command, in its WordBasic form, into the active macro at the insertion point. It's hard to describe, easy to demonstrate.

1. Open a new document (based on any template…this example will not be saved, so it doesn't matter whether this is a global or a template document).

2. Create a macro named TestRecordNext that consists of:

```
Sub Main
RecordNextCommand
Stop
End Sub
```

3. Place the focus on TestRecordNext; place the insertion point at the beginning of the Stop statement.

4. Press Alt+Shift+S to execute TestRecordNext.

5. Press OK to remove the Macro Interrupted message box.

6. Select Arrange All from the Window menu (Alt+W-A).

Pretty neat, huh? The WindowArrangeAll statement is added to the macro TestRecordNext at the insertion point. In this case, the focus was on the macro at the time of execution (and so the number of commands available was limited). To continue the example:

**7.** Place the focus on the blank document.

**8.** Press Alt+Shift+S to execute TestRecordNext.

**9.** Press OK to remove the Macro Interrupted message box.

**10.** Select Paragraph from the Format menu.

**11.** Make any number of changes to the paragraph format, and press OK.

The complete FormatParagraph statement, with all parameters, magically appears on the line before the stop.

There is a second way to execute the RecordNextCommand. Instead of placing the statement (followed by Stop) into the macro under development, simply place the insertion point where you want the recorded command inserted and execute RecordNextCommand. By default, RecordNextCommand does not have a shortcut access method, therefore you would run the command from the ToolsMacro dialog box:

**1.** Select Macro from the Tools menu (Alt+O-M).

**2.** Type RecordNextCommand. Note that the Run button becomes active.

**3.** Press Enter (or Alt+R) to run the macro.

**4.** Execute the command you wish to record.

RecordNextCommand can be extremely useful. You might want to consider assigning it a shortcut key or a toolbar button (remember that microphone icon?). Just remember to place the focus on the test document before accessing this command, otherwise the number of commands available will be limited; and if you switch focus after accessing RecordNextCommand, the switch itself (a command) will be recorded.

## Common Error Messages

Word's macro environment is interactive. That is to say, not only do you talk to Word—by composing and running a macro—but Word talks back: telling you where an error occurred, and in most cases, what kind of error you have made.

Part 4 of *Using WordBasic* contains a complete listing of Word's macro error messages, with short descriptions of the probable causes. In addition, every error message dialog box has two buttons: OK, which removes the message box and stops the macro execution; and Help, which loads WINWORD.HLP and displays a screen explaining the error messages.

The majority of errors flagged by Word when testing a macro will turn out to be typographical errors. In most cases, after examining the offending line (marked as red and boldfaced by Word), you will find one of these conditions to be true:

- There's a simple misspelling of a statement or a parameter.

- You have forgotten to place an apostrophe or REM at the beginning of a line intended as a comment.

- You have left off a quotation mark on either end of a string literal.

- There is an extraneous or omitted parenthesis.

- You have omitted the dollar sign at the end of a string variable or function.

- There's a missing (or extra) comma between multiple parameters.

- There's a missing (or extra) period prefix in front of a keyword parameter.

In this section I'll describe a handful of the most frequent messages you'll encounter when programming in WordBasic.

### Command Is Unavailable (509)

As described in Chapter 5, this error message is caused when WordBasic encounters a command that has no meaning in the context defined by the location of the insertion point.

Some commands are unavailable when you are in a macro. To avoid this error, simply open a scratch document while testing the macro, emulating the normal circumstances that would obtain during macro execution.

Other commands will generate this error if the insertion point is in a header, footer, footnote, or annotation. For instance, the command Insert-Bookmark will generate an error if executed in any place but the body of a document.

### Command Failed (102)

The most common cause of this error is a failure to trap for an error condition before displaying a dialog box.

Whenever a dialog box is displayed—whether by calling a built-in command macro that uses a dialog box, or the InputBox$( ) function, or a custom dialog box—canceling the dialog box (by selecting Cancel or pressing Esc) generates an error message.

For instance, if you run the following macro:

```
Sub Main
Test$ = InputBox$("Cancel Me")
End Sub
```

and click on Cancel, you will see the Command Failed message. Revising this macro to include an On Error statement and a corresponding Label will avoid the error on cancellation:

```
Sub Main
On Error Goto Bye
Test$ = InputBox$("Cancel Me")
Bye:
End Sub
```

Similarly, if a user-macro executes one of the built-in command macros using the ToolsMacro command, you must trap for a cancellation error:

```
Sub Main
On Error Goto Bye
ToolsMacro "FileOpen", .Run
Bye:
End Sub
```

### Syntax Error (100)

This is probably the most frequently seen error message. *Using WordBasic* describes this error condition as follows: "The macro contains a line with an incorrect sequence of characters." Put more simply: There's a typo.

A syntax error can also be caused by a missing comma in a list of parameters, such as the following:

```
Text 10 20, 45, 13, "No comma between 10 and 20"
```

### Undefined Sub or Function (124)

This is another error which can be generated by a simple misspelling. If you type any random sequence of characters and try to execute it as a macro, you will see this error. It can also be caused if you forget to preface a comment with an apostrophe or REM.

Other typos that can cause this error are more subtle. For instance, if you forget the dollar sign at the end of a string function, as in:

```
z$ = Selection()
```

### Type Mismatch (122)

There are, in WordBasic, two basic types of variables: string and numeric. The Type Mismatch error is generated when you assign a value of one type to a variable of the other type.

For instance, either of the following lines will cause this error:

```
StringVar$ = 1
NumVar = "1"
```

Passing an incorrectly typed parameter will also cause a type mismatch; for instance, if a statement or function expects a string and you send an integer.

When you encounter this error, Word will highlight the offending line. It is simple to figure out which variable assignment has caused the problem. Most frequently, it's a missing quotation mark or dollar sign.

### Label Not Found (114)

Label Not Found is an error condition that is easily fixed. It means that Word has encountered a Goto statement whose destination can't be found.

The most frequent cause of this is forgetting to terminate the label designation at the destination of the jump (not the location of the Goto statement) with a colon. For example:

```
Sub Main
On Error Goto Bye
a$ - InputBox$("Enter anything")
Bye
End Sub
```

### Argument-count Mismatch (116)

This error is generated when you call a subroutine or a function, either internal or user-defined, with an incorrect number of parameters. For example:

```
Sub Main
x = 1
y = 2
Call TestSub(x,y)
End Sub

Sub TestSub(x,y,z)
Print x+y+z
End Sub
```

will generate an Argument-count Mismatch error. Here is an example of a call to a built-in function that has the incorrect number of arguments:

```
Sub Main
AppSize 200
AppMove 10,20,30
End Sub
```

The first command has one too few arguments; the second command has one too many.

### Out of Memory (7)

The Out of Memory error message has very little to do with the amount of memory installed on your system. It reflects the state of memory within Word. Word reserves a specific amount of memory for macro execution (64k). It is possible, when doing extensive testing of complex macros, that you will eat up this space and that Word will fail to clean up after itself. Word can also think it is out of memory when in fact the problem is too many levels of subroutines. I have heard that WordBasic only supports seven levels of subroutine nesting. However, I believe this depends on how much memory each subroutine requires.

There are two circumstances that can generate this message that you should know. If your macro does a great many EditReplace operations, Word will run out of memory (which memory? I don't know). I'm not sure of the actual number of operations required to generate the error. The work-around (inelegant at best) is only available if the failure happens in a macro that does EditReplace on multiple strings. You can place a FileSave between the EditReplace commands. In a macro that encounters this error during a single EditReplace operation, there is no fix. You could probably cause this failure by replacing every instance of the letter e (with anything) in a very large document.

The second circumstance I know of that can cause an Out of Memory error is a macro that does a great many string manipulations, such as Left$( ), Right$( ), and Mid$( ). The only work-around I know of is to redesign the string manipulation to be as efficient as possible.

### No Such Macro (511)

This error is generated when you attempt to manipulate a macro that doesn't exist in the specified context. WordBasic statements that can generate this error are ToolsMacro, IsExecuteOnly, MacroCopy, and MacroDesc$( ).

## Catching and Avoiding Errors

Not all errors are caused by bugs. Some error conditions are generated by normal usage. For instance, selecting Cancel on an InputBox( ) will be interpreted by Word as an error. Other errors are caused by simple mistyping or mistakes (known generically as *user error*). The term "error" in programming does not refer specifically to a bug, or to a mistake made by the user. Rather, an error is the state, the condition generated by the bug or mistake. In a sense an error in programming (unlike the real world) is neutral. It just is. What caused the error is secondary to figuring out what to do with it once it's there.

After you have found and eradicated as many bugs as possible (as any programmer will admit, it's virtually impossible to get them all), you must also try and anticipate the myriad error conditions that can be generated by users and circumstances.

## Trapping for Error Conditions

When an error condition is detected, Word displays a message box describing the error and providing an error number. However, it is possible to disable the display of the standard error message boxes. You can test for an error condition, evaluate the specific error, and guide the macro in an alternate direction. When Word's built-in error handling is disabled, it becomes the responsibility of the programmer to detect and respond to error conditions. This task is called *error trapping*.

Using customized error trapping allows for a much greater flexibility, an ability to respond to a wider range of contingencies, to bypass Word's built-in error handling (which usually aborts the macro entirely) and provide alternate pathways for the macro to follow. There are four WordBasic statements, and one built-in variable, used to detect, trap, and respond to errors.

**On Error Goto LabelName**   The most frequently used form of error trapping was described earlier, in Chapter 6, in the discussion of the Goto statement. Before executing a WordBasic statement that is error-prone, you warn Word to look for an error, and if one does in fact occur, you use the Goto statement to jump to another section of the macro.

The simplest form of this error trap is to accommodate the user canceling an operation. For instance, if you use the InputBox( ) function, you must precede it with an error trap, as canceling the box will be read by Word as an error. For example:

```
Sub Main
On Error Goto Bye
A$ = InputBox("Type anything")
MsgBox A$
Bye:
End Sub
```

Another example we have seen in previous examples is the error trap used before a ToolsMacro statement. When you use ToolsMacro to execute another macro (either built-in or user-defined), the current macro passes control to the called macro. If the called macro is canceled, an error condition is returned to the calling macro. For instance, if you have a macro that calls File-Open, and you cancel FileOpen without opening a file, the cancel/error condition is returned to the calling macro, and so the calling macro must anticipate and provide a response:

```
Sub Main
On Error Goto Bye
ToolsMacro .Name = "FileOpen", .Run
MsgBox "You opened the file successfully"
Bye:
End Sub
```

Anytime you transform a built-in command macro into a user-macro, by adding even the slightest modification, you must also add error trapping.

In all of the above examples the On Error statement is simply jumping to the end of the macro. Realize that you could jump to a portion of code that performs an alternative action. For instance:

```
Sub Main
StartOfThings:
On Error Goto ErrorTrap
ToolsMacro .Name = "FileOpen", .Run
Goto Bye
ErrorTrap:
MsgBox "You really ought to open a file"
Goto StartOfThings
Bye:
MsgBox "You opened the file successfully"
End Sub
```

In this macro, if you cancel the FileOpen command, the macro jumps to the label ErrorTrap which, after an admonitory message, jumps back to the label StartOfThings. If you open a file, the macro jumps to the label Bye, displays a congratulatory message, and ends.

The interesting thing about this macro is that it doesn't work. The error trap is not complete. It will trap the first cancellation. But if you cancel the FileOpen command a second time, a Command Failed error message box will display. Why? Because after the first cancellation Word continues to evaluate the error landscape and still thinks there's an error in the air. The macro never *resets the error state*. This brings us to the next error trapping statement.

**On Error Goto 0**    On Error Goto 0. What? This is a special form of the On Error statement. There isn't, shouldn't be, and cannot be, a label named with the digit 0. When Word encounters this On Error statement, it basically wipes clear the current error state. If we change the above macro by adding this statement:

```
Sub Main
StartOfThings:
On Error Goto ErrorTrap
ToolsMacro .Name = "FileOpen", .Run
Goto Bye
ErrorTrap:
MsgBox "You really ought to open a file"
On Error Goto 0
Goto StartOfThings
Bye:
MsgBox "You opened the file successfully"
End Sub
```

you can cancel indefinitely. Basically, when Word gets the error from the canceled FileOpen, it does three things: displays the admonition, clears out the error state, and jumps to the start of the macro.

Clearing away the last error is a critical part of error trapping. Failing to do so brings chaos. So, be sure to think in three steps when setting an error trap:

- Where is an error possible?

- What do I want the macro to do (where to jump) if an error does occur?

- Does the error slate need to be wiped clean?

Some error traps, such as those that simply jump to the end of the macro, do not require resetting the error state.

**On Error Resume Next**    The third flavor of On Error is called On Error Resume Next, and it does just what it says: If an error is encountered, ignore it completely and proceed to the next statement in the macro. This error trap, you might say, is the flimsiest. It should only be used when a non-critical error is anticipated.

```
Sub Main
On Error Resume Next
a$ = InputBox$("Type something")
b$ = InputBox$("Type something else")
c$ = InputBox$("Type anything")
End Sub
```

In this example, canceling an input box simply moves to the next one.

On Error Resume Next is particularly useful in user-defined string functions where a call to a built-in function that would normally return an error should instead return a default string (such as a null, or empty, string). We shall see examples of this use later in this chapter.

**Creating an ErrorHandler**    Every error message has two parts: a description and an error number. There is a built-in variable named Err, which contains the number of the last error encountered by a macro. So, for instance, the value of Err after encountering an Undefined SUB or FUNCTION error would be 124. The value of Err after canceling a dialog box is 102. Every time an error condition is encountered this variable is updated.

The On Error Goto 0 statement discussed above has the same effect as directly setting the value of Err to 0. So, for instance:

```
On Error Goto 0
```

and:

```
Err = 0
```

are equivalent statements and can be used interchangeably to clear the Err variable.

Knowing the various integer values associated with individual errors allows you to use the Err value to trap some errors more effectively. For instance, in the next example, there are two On Error statements: The first traps for a cancellation, the second traps for an error that changes directories.

```
Sub Main
Again:                          'Label marking the start of things
On Error Goto Bye               'If the input box is canceled, quit
A$ = InputBox$("Enter Path")    'Assign a string to the variable A$
On Error Goto ErrorHandler      'Set a trap for the ChDir command
ChDir A$                        'Change to the path stored in A$
Print Files$(".")               'Display the current path
Goto Bye                        'Jump to the end of the macro
ErrorHandler:                   'Label for the ChDir error trap
If Err = 76 Then                'Error 76 corresponds to Path not found
    MsgBox "Error changing to " + A$ + ". Try again."
    Err = 0                     'Reset the Err variable using assignment
    Goto Again                  'Jump to the beginning of the macro
End If
Bye:                            'Label marking the end of things
End Sub
```

Notice that when there is an error changing to the path designation stored in A$, the macro jumps to the label ErrorHandler and evaluates the contents of the Err variable. If it is 76, which is the error number for the Path Not Found error, it displays a message box (more informative than the default error message), resets the Err variable to 0, and returns to the top of the macro. This example should point in interesting directions. You can see how this could prove extremely useful in avoiding some errors and allowing others their natural course. As long as you know the numbers of the errors you wish to disable (and what the macro should do about them), you can create a general-purpose error handler.

WordBasic has a built-in statement named (confusingly enough) Error, which does nothing but display the standard error message for a given error number. It has the syntax:

```
Error ErrorNumber
```

The Error statement allows you to trap for all errors, evaluate the Err variable, handle some errors yourself, and pass the remaining errors to Word to handle.

The generalized syntax for such an error handler would look like:

```
Sub Main
On Error Goto ErrorHandler
...WordBasic statements that might generate errors
```

```
ErrorHandler:
Select Case Err
    Case x
        ...Handle Error x
    Case y
        ...Handle Error y
    Case Else
        Error Err
End Select
```

Using the Select...Case control structure makes it easy to trap multiple error conditions. Notice that the Case Else portion of the control, which is modified if none of the previous cases is true, simply displays the standard error message by executing Error Err.

To modify the previous example, in which we were only interested in one error (Path Not Found), we can use an If...Then evaluation:

```
Sub Main
Again:                              'Label marking the start of things
On Error Goto Bye                   'If the input box is canceled, quit
A$ = InputBox$("Enter Path")        'Assign a string to the variable A$
On Error Goto ErrorHandler          'Set a trap for the ChDir command
ChDir A$                            'Change to the path stored in A$
Print Files$(".")                   'Display the current path
Goto Bye                            'Jump to the end of the macro
ErrorHandler:                       'Label for the ChDir error trap
If Err = 76 Then                    'Err 76 corresponds to Path not found
    MsgBox "Error changing to " + A$ + ". Try again."
    Err = 0                         'Reset the Err variable using assignment
    Goto Again                      'Jump to the beginning of the macro
Else
    Error Err                       'Display the standard error message for the rest
End If
Bye:                                'Label marking the end of things
End Sub
```

This type of error handling could also prove invaluable while debugging and testing a macro. For instance, you could trap all errors and jump to a ShowVars or Stop statement:

```
Sub Main
Again:                              'Label marking the start of things
On Error Goto Bye                   'If the input box is canceled, quit
A$ = InputBox$("Enter Path")        'Assign a string to the variable A$
On Error Goto ErrorHandle           'Set a trap for the ChDir command
ChDir A$                            'Change to the path stored in A$
Print Files$(".")                   'Display the current path
Goto Bye                            'Jump to the end of the macro
ErrorHandler:                       'Label for the ChDir error trap
ShowVars                            'Display the current variables
```

```
Err = 0                              'Reset the Err variable
Goto Again
Bye:                                 'Label marking the end of things
End Sub
```

This would allow you to examine the contents of all variables and figure which might be causing the error condition.

### CommandValid()

Error 509, Command is Unavailable, is caused when a macro attempts to execute a WordBasic command that has no meaning in the insertion point's current location. When a macro attempts to edit itself, for instance, you will see this error. When you attempt to insert a bookmark into a header or a footer, you will see this error. One way to avoid such location-related errors is to use the built-in function CommandValid( ) to check whether a command will execute properly in the current geography. The syntax for CommandValid( ) is

```
x = CommandValid(CommandName$)
```

The function returns −1 (true) if the command specified by the string variable parameter is meaningful. It returns 0 if the command is meaningless. Note: CommandValid( ) does not actually execute anything. It simply tells you if you *could* execute the command in question successfully.

```
Sub Main
If CommandValid("InsertBookmark") Then
    InsertBookmark "A_BOOKMARK"
Else
      MsgBox "Bookmarks not supported here."
End If
End Sub
```

The above example is actually more useful than it might seem. Bookmarks are not supported in headers, footers, footnotes, or annotations. Used in combination with the SelInfo( ) function, CommandValid( ) would allow you to check where the insertion point is located and perform the necessary action before inserting a bookmark. For instance:

```
Sub Main
If Not CommandValid("InsertBookmark") Then       'Bookmarks aren't valid
    If SelInfo(25) Or SelInfo(26) Or SelInfo(28) Then  'If in a footnote, an
        ClosePane                                    'annotation, or a
        InsertBookmark "A_BOOKMARK"                  'header/footer, close
    ElseIf SelInfo(27) Then                          'Insert the bookmark
        Print "Bookmarks illegal in macro pane..."   'If in a macro window
    End If                                            'No bookmarks allowed
```

```
    Else
        InsertBookmark "A_BOOKMARK"              'Legal to begin with, so
    End If                                       'insert
End Sub
```

Most curiously, if the command name passed to CommandValid( ) is entirely bogus—that is, doesn't exist at all—CommandValid( ) will return true. So, for instance:

```
Sub Main
If CommandValid("BogusCommand") Then MsgBox "BogusCommand is valid"
End Sub
```

Very strange. Perhaps in the next version of WordBasic, CommandValid() will get a little smarter.

### DisableAutoMacros
Any macro that opens or creates files must be aware that some files are associated with AutoNew and AutoOpen macros. It can wreak havoc on an application macro if it opens or creates a document and that document takes control and runs its associated auto macro.

The DisableAutoMacros statement can be used to avoid this situation. The syntax for DisableAutoMacros is

```
DisableAutoMacros OnOff
```

where OnOff is either 1 (auto macros disabled) or 0 (auto macros not disabled).

```
Sub Main
DisableAutoMacros 1
FileOpen "MYDOC.DOC"
DisableAutoMacros 0
End Sub
```

The default setting for DisableAutoMacros is 0, not disabled. If you disable auto macro execution, be sure to re-enable it before the macro ends, otherwise auto macros will not execute until Word is started again.

### DisableInput
When a macro begins execution, you can interrupt it by pressing the Escape key. If the macro is open, the effect is the same as if a Stop statement had been encountered: The message Macro Interrupted is displayed; Start becomes Continue; Vars becomes available; and the line executing at the time of the interruption will be highlighted in red. If the macro isn't open, you will simply see the Macro Interrupted message box.

This is useful when developing a macro. It allows you to examine the variables, for instance. It also allows you to break out of the dreaded infinite loop, a series of endlessly repeated actions caused by certain types of programming errors. If the hourglass doesn't go away, press Esc.

However, once a macro is completely tested and debugged, you may want to disable the ability to cancel the macro's execution. The WordBasic statement DisableInput does precisely that; the syntax is

```
DisableInput OnOff
```

where the parameter OnOff is either 0 (Escape is not disabled) or 1 (Escape is disabled). The default for DisableInput is off (0).

# Programming Style

When writing a macro there is a constant tension between economy and clarity. Purists will suggest that all user-created names (for variables, subs, or functions) should be kept as small as possible. My own feeling, as you may have surmised from the principles outlined previously regarding the naming of macros and variables, is that a macro that contains extremely economical parts but cannot be understood is a failed macro. For this reason I always err on the side of the verbose. A WordBasic macro is not a professional program. Usually it is not for consumption by anyone but the creator. There are speed and size limitations built into WordBasic. You should regard coding in WordBasic as an exercise in architecture rather than an exercise in symbolic mathematics. You are creating an object that needs to be livable, not theoretically perfect.

## Some Comments on Naming

I have already suggested that when naming a macro, or a subroutine, you should attempt to convey as much information as possible, using the convention of mixed-capitalization to evince the action and function of the macro: ToggleHidden, AssignKey, and so on. When naming a variable or subs/functions there are several conventions, in addition to this one, that might prove useful.

## Naming Variables

I would argue that variable names should be descriptive at the expense of economy. However, there is no need for a 50-character variable identifier. A string variable *must* terminate with a dollar sign. It is legal to terminate a numeric variable with a number sign. If you follow this convention, while losing nothing in descriptiveness, you gain in clarity:

```
Message$ = "Hello World"
Num# = 22
```

In addition, if you follow this convention strictly, that will leave non-terminated variable names free for numeric constants, that is, for numeric variables that never change value in the course of a macro.

```
Message$ = "Hello World"
Num# = 22
Pi = 3.1415927
```

This leaves only a convention for string constants. Curiously, WordBasic distinguishes between one and two terminating dollar signs. So, we could have

```
Message$ = "Hello World"
Num# = 22
Pi = 3.1415927
Message$$ = "String Constant"
```

Another way to distinguish variables would be to settle upon a single character prefix. For instance c for constants, n for numerics:

```
nNum = 22
cPi = 3.1415927
cMessage$ = "String Constant"
```

This convention would use a non-prefixed variable name for Boolean variables:

```
nNum = 22
cPi = 3.1415927
cMessage$ = "String Constant"
Toggle = -1
```

It is a good practice to group all constants and variables at the top of your macro, labeled with comments:

```
'Constants
Pi = 3.1415927
Message$$ = "String Constant"

'Variables
Message$ = "Hello World"
Num# = 22
```

This allows you to easily locate and change any value while testing the macro. It is also a good idea to segregate shared variables by type:

```
Dim Shared OneString$, AnotherString$, Message$      'Shared strings
Dim Shared x,y,Num,Pi                                'Shared numbers
```

Like any set of rules these are easy to bend, if not ignore, while preoccupied with coding. I certainly cannot contend that I am completely consistent in my own adherence to these conventions. However, they are offered to point out ways of thinking about coding. They are not intended as a hindrance, and should be adapted to suit your own way of conceptualizing.

## Naming Subroutines and Functions

The one possible problem with modular programming is distinguishing user-subs/functions from built-in WordBasic commands.

When executing a user-subroutine you can preface the sub's name with the Call statement. For instance:

```
Call MySub
```

This makes it clear that MySub is a user-sub and not a built-in command. However, you cannot use Call when executing a user-function.

One solution is offered by a naming convention. You could preface every subroutine name with lowercase s, and every function with lowercase f:

```
sMySub
x = fMyFunction(y)
```

## Comments

Comment liberally. It is much easier to maintain and revise a macro if you have left informative explanations, definitions, notes, even puzzles, throughout your macro while you are writing it.

There are, as stated previously, two ways to comment: by prefacing a line with either the keyword REM, or an apostrophe. There is no particular reason to use one over the other. My own habit is this: If I am commenting a line *on the same line*, usually a short annotation, I use an apostrophe. If I am inserting a longer remark, perhaps over several lines, I use REM. Generally, REM draws more attention, so I would reserve it for comments that need to be located easily.

Comments should be used to distinguish the major portions of a macro. For instance, it is a good idea to explain the purpose of a label, or the condition under which a particular loop will be executed.

Another good habit to develop is to place a comment line before the beginning of a user-sub or function, optionally including a description of the function and its syntax:

```
REM ********************fFileCount********************
REM        Count files in a specified directory
REM        FileSpec$ is a full path designation:
REM        e.g. C:\WINWORD\*.DOT
REM ****************************************************
Function fFileCount(FileSpec$)
A$ = Files$(FileSpec$)
Count = 0
While A$ <> ""
    Count = Count + 1
```

```
    A$ = Files$()
Wend
fFileCount = Count
End Function
```

This is, I admit, a time-consuming practice. However, it makes the use of sub-routines and functions much easier if you fully document them at the time of their creation.

Another good practice regarding subroutines and functions is to place all user-functions together immediately after the end of the Main subroutine, place all utility subroutines next, and place all large, application subroutines last. Of course, if outlining were supported in the macro editor, this would be trivial to accomplish. As is, it requires a fair amount of cutting and pasting.

## Logic Level Indentations

It is infinitely easier to follow the logic of a program if you follow a simple rule when entering or editing the source code: Indent according to the control level. In several of the example macros you have seen instances of two-deep logic. All this means is that you should indent when you arrive at a line that is conditional on the previous line assuming control. The easiest way to illustrate this is with an If...Then structure:

```
Sub Main
If x > 3 Then                               'The base level is unindented.
    y = x*2                                 'This is the second level
    If y > 10 Then
        Beep                                'This is the third level
    Else                                    'back to second level
        Print "Not big enough to beep"      'back to third
    End If
Else                                        'back to first
    Print "x is less than or equal to 3"
End If
End Sub
```

Contrast the above example with the unindented version of the same control structure:

```
Sub Main
If x > 3 Then
y = x*2
If y > 10 Then
Beep
Else
Print "Not big enough to beep"
End If
```

```
Else
Print "x is less than or equal to 3"
End If
End Sub
```

Clearly, the indented version is easier to read. It doesn't matter whether you use tabs or spaces to indent a logic level. A tab is much the easier (fewer keystrokes); however, the macro editor does not allow for variable-length tabs, and therefore it is possible that a fifth or sixth logic level will become illegible because of wrapping.

## Summary: Programming Notes

This chapter covered some of the conceptual underpinnings to macro design, creation, and testing. The next chapter will move to more practical considerations, namely the creation of custom dialog boxes and the use of libraries to organize subroutines.

Take a breath. It's going to get deep.

# WordBasic:
# Advanced Topics

THE MACRO EXAMPLES PRESENTED IN THE PREVIOUS CHAPTERS HINT AT the types of solutions WordBasic can provide; however, they barely scratch the surface. The more familiar you become with WordBasic the greater will be the range of problems you consider solvable through macros. The very way you conceive of solutions will change as you become more comfortable with the tools available. This chapter will present several advanced aspects of WordBasic. By combining what you already know of basic macro recording and editing with tools such as custom dialog boxes, utility libraries, and parameter passing, you will be far along on your way to creating complex application macros.

## Custom Dialog Boxes

The feature of WordBasic that enables the creation of truly integrated mini-applications, macros that take on the status of new features grafted onto Word, is the custom dialog box.

Often you will want your macro to communicate more information than is possible with a simple message box; you will want your macro to gather more information or offer more options than are available with InputBox( ) or MsgBox( ). The solution is to create a custom dialog box.

Custom dialog boxes possess most (though not all) of the features you have become accustomed to by using Windows:

- Text

- Text editing boxes

- Option buttons

- Check boxes

- List boxes and combo boxes

- Push buttons

Sadly, WordBasic's dialog box capability does not extend to *triggers*. Whether you realize it or not, you've seen dialog box triggers in action umpteen times. When a normal dialog box action, such as selecting an item or clicking a check box, *also* produces an immediate change to the dialog box, you have a trigger—for instance: when clicking on a check box changes the rest of the dialog box, or when making multiple selections in a list box, opening a secondary dialog box when a button is selected, or disabling (graying) an option entirely. WordBasic has none of these advanced dialog box features (yet). That is to say, you can check a box, but doing so cannot automatically change another feature on the dialog. Still, what we have is pretty powerful. And there's always version 3.0, right?

## The Dialog Box Editor

When you installed Word, a second application, MACRODE.EXE, was installed on your disk, and an icon to launch it placed in the Word group of Program Manager. This program, which is run independently from Word, automates the process of creating dialog boxes in WordBasic. If you ever tried creating complex dialog boxes in Word version 1.x, you know what a boon was there in this dedicated dialog box editor.

If this is old news, you might want to skip the next section, skim "Dialog Box Statements," and land on the "Managing Dialog Boxes" section. For those who are unfamiliar with the dialog editor, read on.

There is a section of Chapter 42, "Using Macros," in the *Microsoft Word User's Guide* which discusses the dialog box editor. It can be consulted, along with *Using WordBasic*, to explain details about creating dialog boxes. However, the best way to learn about the dialog editor is to step through an example.

### A Step By Step Example

Take it on faith: You will learn quite a lot about what the dialog editor can do, and how best to do it, if you follow along with this example at the computer.

1. Create a macro and name it DialogExample.

2. The insertion point is positioned between Sub Main and End Sub. Copy the following lines of code:

```
Dim MyArray$(10)
For x = 0 To 10
MyArray$(x) = Str$(x) + ": List Option"
Next x
DefaultText$ = "Edit Box Example"
ButtonDefault = 2
```

3. Load the dialog box editor (by activating Program Manager and clicking on the Dialog Editor icon).

4. Double-click anywhere on the blank dialog box (or press Alt+E-I).

5. Press Alt+W, to change the width; type **335**.

6. Press Alt+H, to change the height; type **220**.

7. Press Alt+T, to change the title; type **Dialog Box Example**.

8. Make sure that Auto Quote is checked (press Alt+Q if it isn't); press Enter.

We have titled and sized the dialog box itself. By checking the Auto Quote option you ensure that all strings, such as the title entered in the Text$: edit box, will be stored as string literals.

Now let's begin defining the elements of the dialog box with two text-related items, one which displays a text message, the other which allows you to enter or edit a text string:

**9.** Press Alt+I-T to insert a text field.

**10.** Type **Edit text here:**.

**11.** Press Enter.

**12.** Press Alt+I-E to insert a text edit box.

**13.** Double-click anywhere on the newly inserted edit box (or press Alt+E-I).

**14.** Press Alt+F to change the variable to hold the result of the edit box; type **.Text**.

**15.** Press Enter.

A text edit box provides the same functionality, in a custom dialog box, as the InputBox$( ) function. The user is optionally presented with a default string value which can be accepted or edited.

Now let's create a list box:

**16.** Press Alt+I-L, Enter to insert a standard list box.

**17.** Double-click on the newly inserted list box (or press Alt+E-I).

**18.** Press Alt+A to change the name of the array that will fill the list; type **MyArray$( )**.

**19.** Press Alt+F to change the name of the variable to hold the choice returned by a list box selection; type **.Selected**.

**20.** Press Enter.

A standard list box allows selection from a predefined list of choices. A second type of list box combines the text edit box and list box (called a combo box), which allows the user to either type an item directly into an edit box field at the top of the list or select an item from the list. Deciding which type of list box to use depends upon the range of variables controlled by the list: If the list should be confined to specific string choices, a list box is preferable; if any string is legal, a combo box allows more flexibility.

The next item to explore is the option button:

**21.** Press Alt+I-G to insert a group box.

**22.** Type **Choose:** to change the box title.

**23.** Press Enter. This automatically inserts an option button.

**24.** Type **Option One**.

**25.** Press Enter.

**26.** Type **Option Two**.

**27.** Press Enter.

**28.** Type **Option Three**.

**29.** Press Alt+E-A to select all items in the dialog box.

**30.** Press Alt+E-R to resize the dialog box elements.

Option buttons are useful when the user must choose one option among several choices. That is, within a group of buttons only one can be selected. Notice that because these buttons have all been defined within a single group box you can select and resize them without affecting the rest of the dialog box.

If the user must select more than one option at a time, we can create a series of check boxes:

**31.** Press Alt+I-B-B, Enter to insert a check box.

**32.** Using the cursor keys (or by clicking on the check box field and holding down the left button and dragging) move the check box to the right and up until it is positioned parallel to the edit box.

**33.** Press Enter.

**34.** Type **Check &1**. Note: By typing the ampersand symbol before the 1 you are specifying that the dialog box should display the 1 character as an underlined speedkey for this item. The result is that Alt+1 will activate this option.

**35.** Press Enter. A second check box will be inserted automatically.

**36.** Type **Check &2**.

The last thing to do to complete this example is to insert a series of buttons to accept or cancel the dialog box.

**37.** Press Alt+I-B, Enter. This inserts the default button: OK.

**38.** Press Enter. This inserts the Cancel button.

**39.** Press Enter. This inserts a text push button.

**40.** Type **&Help**.

**41.** Press Alt+E-S to select the entire dialog.

**42.** Press Alt+E-R to resize the dialog.

The dialog box definition is complete. We now must move the definition to Word. This is done using the Windows clipboard:

**43.** Press Alt+E-C to copy the dialog to the clipboard.

**44.** Return to Word for Windows, making sure the insertion point is in the macro DialogExample, positioned on a blank line above the End Sub that marks the end of the macro.

**45.** Press Shift+Ins to paste the dialog box from the clipboard into the macro.

**46.** After the inserted text, copy the following lines of code:

```
Dim dlg As UserDialog
dlg.Text = DefaultText$
dlg.OptionGroup1 = ButtonDefault
dlg.CheckBox1 = 1
Choice = Dialog(dlg)
CheckOne =(dlg.CheckBox1 = 1)
If Choice = 0 Then Goto Bye
Print Choice
If Choice = 1 Then
    MsgBox "Help on the way"
Else
    MsgBox dlg.DefaultText
    MsgBox MyArray$(dlg.Selected)
End If
If CheckOne Then MsgBox "Check Box One is checked"
Bye:
```

**47.** Press Alt+Shift+S to run the macro. See Figure 9.1 for an illustration of the resulting dialog box.

Play with this example macro. Select different options from the list box, edit the text in the edit box, select the Help button. And after seeing what the macro can do, study how it's done.

**NOTE.** *You can copy a dialog box definition back to the dialog editor for re-finements. This is done via the clipboard. Simply select the dialog box definition (from Begin Dialog UserDialog to End Dialog), copy it to the clipboard, activate the dialog editor, and copy the definition from the clipboard.*

**Figure 9.1**

Dialog box
displayed by the
ExampleDialog
macro

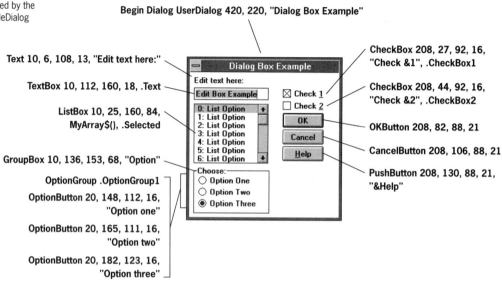

Begin Dialog UserDialog 420, 220, "Dialog Box Example"

Text 10, 6, 108, 13, "Edit text here:"

TextBox 10, 112, 160, 18, .Text

ListBox 10, 25, 160, 84,
MyArray$(), .Selected

GroupBox 10, 136, 153, 68, "Option"

OptionGroup .OptionGroup1

OptionButton 20, 148, 112, 16,
"Option one"

OptionButton 20, 165, 111, 16,
"Option two"

OptionButton 20, 182, 123, 16,
"Option three"

CheckBox 208, 27, 92, 16,
"Check &1", .CheckBox1

CheckBox 208, 44, 92, 16,
"Check &2", .CheckBox2

OKButton 208, 82, 88, 21

CancelButton 208, 106, 88, 21

PushButton 208, 130, 88, 21,
"&Help"

You have just exercised all of the fundamental operations of creating a custom dialog box. You may have noticed some similarities to the internal dialog boxes we've discussed previously. For example, the contents of various options in this custom dialog box are stored in variables of the "dot-keyword" format (.Selected, .CheckBox1, .DefaultText, and so on); and those fields are addressed (or accessed) by the ArrayVariable.FieldName convention (dlg-.Selected, dlg.CheckBox1, dlg.DefaultText, and so on). Let's go through the relevant WordBasic statements and see what's doing what.

### Dialog Box Statements Explored

The statements that produce a custom dialog box are always grouped together between the statements Begin Dialog UserDialog…End Dialog. The individual component statements have no meaning outside this dialog-sandwich.

Here is the code that was generated by the dialog box editor (and inserted into DialogExample if you followed along):

```
Begin Dialog UserDialog 322, 210, "Dialog Box Example"
    Text 10, 6, 108, 13, "Edit text here:"
    TextBox 10, 22, 160, 18, .Text
    ListBox 10, 46, 160, 84, MyArray$(), .Selected
```

```
    GroupBox 10, 136, 163, 68, "Choose:"
    OptionGroup .OptionGroup1
        OptionButton 20, 148, 112, 16, "Option One"
        OptionButton 20, 165, 111, 16, "Option Two"
        OptionButton 20, 182, 123, 16, "Option Three"
    CheckBox 200, 23, 111, 16, "Check &1", .CheckBox1
    CheckBox 200, 40, 111, 16, "Check &2", .CheckBox2
    OKButton 200, 59, 88, 21
    CancelButton 200, 83, 88, 21
    PushButton 200, 107, 88, 21, "&Help"
End Dialog
```

(If you didn't trudge through the above example, you can find a copy of the complete macro DialogExample in the disk file CH09MACS.DOC. If you did trudge, pat yourself on the back.)

**Begin Dialog...End Dialog**   This statement, actually more like a structure since you can't have one without the other, contains the definition of the dialog box. In our example, the first line:

```
Begin Dialog UserDialog 322, 210, "Dialog Box Example"
```

accomplishes two things: It determines the size of the dialog box (height and width), and it provides a caption to be displayed in the title bar at the top of the dialog box. If you do not supply a caption, the default "Microsoft Word" will be displayed.

You could also specify the location of the dialog box with an additional two integer values. For instance:

```
Begin Dialog UserDialog 10, 10, 322, 210, "Dialog Box Example"
```

would position the dialog box 10 units from the left edge of the document workspace and 10 units down from the top of the document workspace. The actual screen position (relative to your entire screen) is determined by whether Word is maximized, and which bars (Ribbon, Ruler, Toolbar) you have active. If you specify only two integer parameters to UserDialog, Word assumes that you want to center the dialog box within the document workspace, and processes the two passed values as width and height.

What precisely are these units? Thankfully, since the dialog box editor takes care of generating these numbers, and all you have to do is grab and drag the units using the mouse, it isn't really important to know how Word calculates these units. But for the incorrigibly curious: All x-values (that is, horizontal positioning) are measured in increments of $1/8$ of the system font; all y-values (vertical positioning) are measured in increments of $1/12$ of the system font.

The reason for such an arcane way of calculating screen position actually makes sense when you consider how Windows works. It is capable of running on different systems with very different video capabilities, varying degrees of video resolution. So the method of calculating screen position cannot be as simple as a text-mode application (which calculates according to a fixed number of columns and rows, say 80 columns by 25 lines). It must be flexible enough to handle EGA, VGA, SVGA, and 8514/A resolutions. Each of these resolutions uses a specific system font, which has a specific size (measured in wonderfully colorful units such as *twips* and *pixels*). So, Windows (and Word as a Windows application) can determine placement as a fraction of the system font size. The system font is what you see when you activate draft mode.

However, if you must think in terms of characters and lines, you can approximate what the dialog editor does automatically by thinking of an object's width with the following equation:

```
Number of Characters * 8
```

and an object's vertical placement or height as:

```
Number of Lines * 12
```

Glad you asked?

All of the dialog box generation statements, with the single exception of OptionGroup, have this same format:

```
StatementName x-position, y-position, width, height
```

The OptionGroup statement is the only dialog box statement that does not use these four position/size parameters (since it does not display anything). The ListBox, ComboBox, GroupBox, OptionButton, CheckBox, and PushButton statements take a fourth parameter specifying the text or variable to display. The ListBox, ComboBox, CheckBox, and TextBox statements require an array variable field (a dot-keyword) to hold the results of user choices after the dialog finishes.

**Text**   The Text statement does not have a dot-keyword. All it does is display text. So, in our example:

```
Text 10, 6, 108, 13, "Edit text here:"
```

simply displays the string literal 10 x-units ($1/8$ * System Font size) from the left edge, not of the document workspace, but of the dialog box as defined in the UserDialog statement; and 6 y-units ($1/12$ * System Font size) from the top of the dialog box. The third and fourth integer parameters, as with UserDialog, specify the width and height of the item in question.

You can create a text item that will wrap a text line. This would allow you to create a single multiline text item rather than multiple single-line items. To do this you simply increase the fourth parameter (which determines height) with the equation 13*Number of Lines. For instance, we could change the text item in our example to read:

```
Text 10, 1, 70, 26, "Edit text here:"
```

**TextBox**   The TextBox statement draws a text edit box on the dialog, allowing the user to enter and edit a string. From the example dialog, the line:

```
TextBox 10, 112, 160, 18, .DefaultText
```

places a box 160 x-units wide, 18 y-units high, at 10 x-units from the left and 112 y-units from the top of the dialog. The result of the edit is returned in the array variable .DefaultText.

**ListBox**   The ListBox statement presents a list of choices to the user. From our example, the statement:

```
ListBox 10, 25, 160, 84, MyArray$(), .Selected
```

creates a list box, positioned at 10x, 25y, of width 160x and height 84y. Notice that in addition to the field variable named .Selected, an array parameter is passed to the statement (in this case MyArray$( )). The passed array contains the individual items listed in the box. The array field .Selected contains the index of the item selected when the dialog box terminates. For example, if the user highlights the first choice, the array variable named dlg.Selected will be equal to 0 (recall arrays are numbered from 0, not 1).

**ComboBox**   There is a related dialog box statement (which does not appear in our example) called ComboBox. This is a special form of ListBox which, essentially, combines the capability of a TextBox with that of a ListBox. You can type a string directly into the edit box portion of the combo box, or you can choose, as you would from an ordinary list box.

The creation of a ComboBox uses precisely the same syntax as that of ListBox. So, you could change the ListBox statement in our example to:

```
ComboBox 10, 25, 160, 84, MyArray$(), .Selected
```

to demonstrate this dialog item.

The only difference between a ListBox and a ComboBox is the nature of the returned result. The ListBox variable contains an integer which points to the array item: A ComboBox field variable contains not the index to an array item, but the contents of the array itself (if a selection is made from the list portion) or the string typed in the edit box. That is, dlg.Selected (in our example) is an integer in the ListBox statement, and a string in the ComboBox statement.

Limitation: The items of the array passed to the ListBox and ComboBox statements are displayed in the order they are listed; that is, you cannot automatically sort the items in a list box. They must be sorted before they are passed to the ListBox statement. It is one of the major inconveniences of array handling in WordBasic that there is no command to automatically sort an array. To sort an array you must write a routine to do so manually on a large array, and that always takes more time than it is worth.

**GroupBox**    The GroupBox statement draws a box, positioned using the same measurement system, with an optional title.

```
GroupBox 10, 136, 153, 68, "Option"
```

If the fifth parameter is a null string, no title will be displayed at all:

```
GroupBox 10, 136, 153, 68, ""
```

Any dialog box item can be placed within a group box. Normally, however, it is used to delimit related option buttons or check boxes.

**OptionGroup and OptionButton**    These two statements, OptionGroup and OptionButton, are inextricably related. You cannot have one without the other. The reason is simple: The OptionGroup statement defines the dialog field variable that will contain the integer index of the button selected from a group of option buttons. The buttons presenting the related options must immediately follow the OptionGroup statement, and they must be contiguous (that is, no other dialog box statement can be placed between two related OptionButton statements).

```
OptionGroup  .OptionGroup1
OptionButton 20, 148, 112, 16, "Option one"
OptionButton 20, 165, 111, 16, "Option two"
OptionButton 20, 182, 123, 16, "Option three"
```

The fifth variable (after the location/size integer parameters) passed to OptionButton is the text that will be displayed to the right of the circular button.

The function of a group of option buttons is to allow the user to select one (and only one) option from a group of choices. The index for the first button is 0; the index for the last button in a group is $n-1$, where $n$ is the total number of buttons. In the above example, the dialog variable dlg.OptionGroup1 will contain either 0, 1, or 2 (not, as you might expect, 1, 2, or 3).

**CheckBox**    If you want a user to be able to select more than one option at a time, you can use the CheckBox dialog statement. Each check box returns a value of 0 (unchecked) or 1 (checked) in the dialog field variable.

```
CheckBox 208, 27, 92, 16, "Check &1", .CheckBox1
CheckBox 208, 44, 92, 16, "Check &2", .CheckBox2
```

The fifth parameter passed to CheckBox is the string that will be displayed to the right of the box. The sixth parameter is the unique field name.

**OKButton**  The OKButton creates one of the two default buttons. It takes no parameters other than those that determine placement and size:

```
OKButton 208, 82, 88, 21
```

When this button is selected, the dialog box is removed from the screen and the macro continued.

**CancelButton**  The CancelButton statement creates the other default button:

```
CancelButton 208, 106, 88, 21
```

When this button is selected, the Err variable is set to 102 (Command Failed). Properly trapped the macro can then exit gracefully (or at least continue without processing the contents of the dialog box fields).

**PushButton**  The PushButton statement allows you to define custom buttons.

```
PushButton 208, 130, 88, 21, "&Help"
```

Multiple buttons can make for easy to use and professional looking dialog boxes. To determine which custom button has been selected is relatively simple: The value returned by a custom button's selection corresponds to the button's position in the dialog definition. The first PushButton statement returns 1, the second returns 2, and so on. Where this value is stored is the subject of the next section.

## Managing Dialog Boxes

Once the dialog box editor has been used to design the dialog box, and the resulting statements have been inserted into the macro, there are several steps necessary to ready, display, and process the dialog box and its information.

### Loading Variables into the Dialog Box

The first step after defining the look of a dialog box by using the editor is to examine the various dialog field variables and alter any you wish to have more informative names than the ones supplied by the dialog editor. In the above example, we modified the field variable for the ListBox and TextBox statements at the time of their creation, naming them .Selection and .DefaultText, respectively. However, the OptionGroup and CheckBox variables were left to the dialog editor to define. You will see that the OptionGroup variable is named OptionGroup1 and the CheckBox variables are named CheckBox1 and CheckBox2. These default names are good enough for a first draft. However, in practice you will want to change these variables to reflect the purpose of the particular dialog item.

Before anything else can happen you must dimension an array variable to hold the fields of the dialog. This is done, in this example, with the line:

```
Dim dlg As UserDialog
```

UserDialog is the reserved WordBasic statement that holds the dialog box definition generated in the preceding series of dialog-related statements. The array variable named "dlg" is a user-specified name. This name can be any word that has meaning to you. The abbreviation "dlg" (short for "dialog"), is often used by convention. One reason to stick to this name is ease of use. You will often have to recall the name of the last array variable holding a user-dialog.

Before actually displaying the dialog box, you can alter any of the default values held by any of the dialog box fields. For instance, in our example, the lines:

```
dlg.DefaultText = DefaultText$
dlg.OptionGroup1 = ButtonDefault
dlg.CheckBox1 = 1
```

assign these defaults: the variable DefaultText$ (which is the string "Edit Box Example") to the field variable of the TextBox statement; the variable ButtonDefault (which is the integer 2) to the field variable of the Option-Group statement; and the value 1 to the field variable of the first CheckBox statement.

Notice that in each of these assignments the dialog field was "addressed" in the same manner as an internal command array's field:

```
ArrayVariableName.FieldName
```

The array variable name in this example was dlg.

### Displaying the Dialog Box

Now that an array variable, dlg, has been dimensioned to hold the contents of UserDialog, and the individual fields have been assigned the desired defaults, all that remains is to display the dialog box. This is done with the WordBasic statement Dialog.

Dialog has two forms. It can be executed as a statement *or* as a function. For instance, in our example the line:

```
Choice = Dialog(dlg)
```

uses the function method of displaying the dialog box. But the dialog could have been displayed (more simply, but with less power) using a statement format:

```
Dialog dlg
```

The reasons to use the function format are twofold: It allows for very simple detection of a cancellation, and it allows you to evaluate whether a custom PushButton was selected. That's where the number of the button selected is stored: in the function Dialog( ) itself. In the above line the value of the function Dialog( ) is assigned to the integer variable Choice.

### Processing Dialog Box Results

The first thing that should happen after a dialog box has been displayed is determining whether it has been canceled, and therefore the point of the dialog box can be ignored (and perhaps the macro aborted).

If you use the Dialog statement, this is done with an On Error Goto statement. For instance, you might have the following two lines to display and test for cancellation:

```
On Error Goto Bye
Dialog dlg
```

If, as I would recommend, you use the Dialog( ) function, you simply need to look at the contents of the variable holding the return value. For instance, if you have defined a variable, Choice, to hold the result of Dialog(dlg), the following pseudocode would cover all bases:

```
If Choice = -1 Then
    OkWasPressed
ElseIf Choice = 0 Then
    CancelWasPressed
Else
    Select Case Choice
        Case N
            NthPushButtonPressed
        Case Else
    End Select
End If
```

Restated in pseudo-English: If Dialog( ) returned –1 (notice this is the normal value of true), then the OK button was selected; if Dialog( ) returned 0 (notice this is the normal value of false), then the Cancel button was selected; if Dialog( ) returned a value greater than 0, then the corresponding PushButton was selected (if 1, the first; if 2, the second; and so on). This last possibility—that a custom PushButton was selected—is the real reason to use the function Dialog( ) rather than the statement. If you use the statement format, there is no way to manage multiple PushButton statements.

The Dialog( ) function accepts a second, optional, parameter. You can specify which button should be the default (that is, which one will be selected by pressing Enter). So, in the above example, the line:

```
Choice = Dialog(dlg,1)
```

would present the dialog box with the Help button as the default and

```
Choice = Dialog(dlg,-1)
```

would make the Cancel button the default.

Tip: It is possible to define a dialog box that has no OK or Cancel button, as long as you do have at least one PushButton statement. This would disable the Escape key (you could still close the dialog box with Alt+F4). Similarly, you can have only a CancelButton or only an OKButton.

Immediately after the dialog box has been displayed and modified by the user, you should gather the significant array fields and store them into variables. This isn't strictly necessary, but it is a good habit to develop for two reasons: It is possible that you will want a second dialog box using the same array variable name (another dlg, for instance), and it is much simpler to create Boolean variables (variables that can be evaluated as true or false). This second capability is quite useful. For instance, in the example the line:

```
CheckOne = (dlg.CheckBox1=1)
```

creates a Boolean variable named CheckOne. CheckOne is true if CheckBox one is checked. This allows for the subsequent evaluation:

```
If CheckOne Then MsgBox "Check Box One is checked"
```

which is easier to read and remember, and more fluid, than:

```
If dlg.CheckBox1 = 1 Then MsgBox "Check Box One is checked"
```

## Notes on the Dialog Editor

Here are some tips about using the dialog editor:

- The Information dialog box allows modification of the position, size, text, and variable of a dialog box item. This dialog box is accessed by double-clicking the left mouse button on an item or by selecting Alt+E-I.

- You can alter the dot-keyword (the field) which the item controls as well as the displayed text from the Information dialog box.

- You can optionally add a comment to any item. This is a good idea for complicated dialog boxes.

- The Auto Quote check box on the Information dialog box will automatically place quotation marks around text entered in the Text$ edit box when the dialog is copied to Word. This is necessary if you are supplying a string literal as the text to display. However, if you are specifying a string variable, such as DefaultText$, as the value of the Text$ edit box, turn Auto Quote off.

- The dialog editor places each new item beneath the last item created. The order of creation is the order in which the focus (which item is "active") will change when you press Tab. You can alter this focus order simply by rearranging the dialog box statements.

- To select multiple items, hold down the Shift key while clicking on each item. The last item selected will be outlined in a broken-dash box, the previously selected items will be displayed in reverse video.

- To select related items, such as option buttons or check boxes in a group box, press Alt+E-G.

- Holding down the Shift key while dragging an item (or group of items) limits the movement vertically or horizontally (whichever direction you initiate first). This helps in the alignment of items.

- If an item seems stuck—you can't get it to change position or size—check the information dialog and turn off Auto settings controlling the relevant setting.

# Development Tips and Tools

Now we're getting into esoterica. You already have everything that is required to write extensive WordBasic macros (everything except some practice, perhaps). What follows are some tips about macro organization, the use of libraries, parameter passing, and some hard-won insights that will save you some time as you get deeper into macro programming.

## Calling One Macro's Sub/Functions from Another

A macro can call another macro. There have been several examples illustrating the use of ToolsMacro to run both internal command macros and other user-macros. A portion of a macro can call a subroutine. There have been several examples where the main subroutine called a user-sub or function. Now it is time to combine the two: It is possible for a macro to execute a subroutine from another macro. The syntax for calling a subroutine or a function contained in another macro is

```
MacroName$.SubName[$] [parameterlist]
MacroName$.FunctionName[$] [parameterlist]
```

Why would you want to use a subroutine contained in a macro other than the one being executed? Simple: for the same reasons you use modular programming at all. You save a lot of space by not duplicating a subroutine in every macro; the subroutine becomes easier to alter and maintain since you only have to revise a single copy. The ability to call a subroutine from within another macro allows you to create a *library* of frequently used routines. This can significantly speed program development.

## Creating a Library of Utility Routines

A macro can be said to add a command (like SpecialBold or FileCloseAll) or even a feature (like AssignKey or AutoClose-FileBackup). A library of subroutines and functions should be seen as adding commands to WordBasic. For instance, you could create a library macro named zLib to gather in one place what you might call utility subs/functions that add to the built-in string manipulating routines. (I chose the name "zLib" for a mnemonic reason: z for "Ziff," the publisher of this book. The prefix z also has the advantage of placing the library at the bottom of the list of macros.)

A library macro does nothing when you execute it directly. Therefore the Sub Main portion of the macro should either do nothing, or simply beep, or print a message saying it does nothing:

```
Sub Main
Print "This macro cannot be executed directly."
Beep
End Sub
```

The user-subroutines or user-functions in this library macro would be the real meat of the matter:

**DISK**
zLib—A collection of string handling routines

```
Sub Main
Print "This macro cannot be executed directly."
Beep
End Sub

' String manipulation routines
Function Trim$(S$, ZapChar$)
Source$ = S$
While Left$(Source$, Len(ZapChar$)) = ZapChar$
    Source$ = Mid$(Source$, Len(ZapChar$) + 1)
Wend
While Left$(Mid$(Source$, Len(Source$) -(Len(ZapChar$) - 1), Len(ZapChar$)),
```

```
Len(ZapChar$)) = ZapChar$
    Source$ = Left$(Source$, Len(Source$) - Len(ZapChar$))
Wend
Trim$ = Source$
End Function


Function Replace$(S$, Old$, New$)
Source$ = S$
While Instr(Source$, Old$) <> 0
    A$ = Left$(Source$, Instr(Source$, Old$) - 1)
    B$ = Right$(Source$, Len(Source$) -(Len(a$) + Len(old$)))
    Source$ =  A$ + New$ + B$
Wend
Replace$ = Source$
End Function


Function CountChar(s$, c$)
Count = 0
Index = 1
While Instr(Index, s$, c$)
    Count = count + 1
    Index = Instr(Index, s$, c$) + 1
Wend
CountChar = Count
End Function
```

Notice that the three functions contained in this library macro perform extensive manipulation on a string. These are precisely the kinds of operations that
are candidates for sequestering into a library. You do not want to duplicate
this code in every macro you create. One criterion for a library routine is this:
Do you wish it was built into WordBasic by the developers? Another way of
posing the question is this: Is a subroutine or function specific to a given
macro, or can it be generalized to work in any macro? If the former is the
case, then it should remain within the macro under development. If the latter,
it should be copied to a library where it will be available to any macro.

Once this macro has been created, you could then write a second macro,
named zLibDemo, that showed off its stuff:

**DISK**
zLibDemo—
Demonstration of
the string routines
found in zLib

```
Sub Main
LongString$ = ".....This is a long String....."
MsgBox LongString$
LongString$ = zLib.Trim$(LongString$, ".")
MsgBox "This is the String after trimming the periods from Left And Right: " +
LongString$
LongString$ = zLib.Replace$(LongString$, " ", "|")
MsgBox "This is the String after replacing all spaces with vertical bar: " +
LongString$
x = zLib.CountChar(LongString$, "|")
MsgBox "There are " + Str$(x) + " vertical bars in the String: " + LongString$
End Sub
```

**NOTE.** *If you change the name of a library macro, all of the macros that call its routines will fail. The library created in this chapter, and included on disk in CH09MACS.DOC, was for demonstration purposes only. A more comprehensive library, named gLib for purposes of compatibility with existing macros I have written and distributed, can be found in UTILITY.DOC. This is the library of routines you should install and modify. See Appendix G.*

The template containing the library must be open and in the current context when a macro makes a call to one of its subroutines or functions. This is a significant limitation. Word cannot load a macro from disk. Word cannot scour all of the active templates to locate the called macro library. The macro library must be in one of two places: the active local context (that is, in the same template as the calling macro) or in the global context (NORMAL.DOT).

If you have created a specialized template which contains a suite of macros, some of which share a common set of task-specific subroutines, then it makes sense to create a template-specific library of routines that the template macros can call. So, for instance, I have created a complex template for formatting screenplays named GSCRIPT.DOT. It contains 32 macros. One of these is a template library named gsLib which gathers several subroutines shared by the other 31 GScript macros. Since these macros will never be executed outside the context controlled by GSCRIPT.DOT, the routines held in the template-specific library will always be available.

In contrast, LETBLOCK.DOT and some of the other shipped templates, take a slightly different tack: Instead of storing commonly accessed subroutines in a dedicated library, macros simply borrow subroutines from one another—AutoNew calls a sub in Configure, for example. The LETBLOCK macros, in a sense, make cross-references to subroutines in other LETBLOCK macros rather than to a single library. This makes following the logic of the template macros more difficult than need be (I should know: I had a hand in revising some of those templates…).

A dedicated library for shared routines is more "user-friendly." However, it is important to know that a subroutine does not have to be in a dedicated library to be borrowed. There are times when such a cross-reference makes sense. For instance, if a subroutine is used by only two macros, you can justify leaving it in one macro and simply referencing it by the second macro. Otherwise, you would be creating a third macro to hold the common routine (thereby violating one of the cardinal rules of programming parsimony).

However, if a routine is shared by more than two macros, or if there is already a library of routines, I would recommend storing any shared subs or functions in the library rather than using the cross-referencing solution.

For general use, a macro library should be installed into the global context, saved into NORMAL.DOT. Macros stored in NORMAL.DOT are always available, and therefore the routines stored in a Global zLib will be available to any macro, global or local, no matter what the underlying template.

## Passing Parameters to Sub Main

It is possible to call another macro and pass parameters to the Main subroutine. For example, if you had a macro named ParamMac:

```
Sub Main(msg$)
MsgBox msg$
End Sub
```

you could call this macro with a parameter from a second macro, named CallMac:

```
Sub Main
Param$ = "Hello World"
ParamMac.Main Param$
End Sub
```

However, this ability has a drawback. You cannot execute ParamMac by itself, from the ToolsMacro list for example, without generating an error condition. It can only be called from another macro. However, suppose we modify ParamMac so that it has a subroutine which, when called, does two things—sets a shared variable to contain the passed parameter and calls the Main section of the macro:

**DISK**
ParamMac—Demo of how to call a macro with a parameter

```
Dim Shared msg$
Sub Main
If msg$ = "" Then
    MsgBox "Called directly with no parameter."
Else
    MsgBox "Called with the parameter: " + msg$
End If
End Sub

Sub StartUp(m$)
msg$ = m$
Call Main
End Sub
```

We can then have a calling macro that calls, not Main, but the subroutine named Startup:

**DISK**
CallMac—Calls the Startup subroutine of ParamMac with a parameter

```
Sub Main
Param$ = "Hello World"
ParamMac.Startup Param$
End Sub
```

Essentially, this method does not pass a parameter directly to the Main routine; rather it passes the parameter to the subroutine Startup; Startup stores the parameter in a Shared variable and then calls the Main routine; the Main routine then evaluates the shared variable to determine what to do. It's not the most elegant work-around, but it's effective.

## Passing Parameters from a MacroButton

It is not possible, even if Sub Main accepts parameters, to pass a parameter to a macro from the ToolsMacro dialog box. Similarly, you cannot pass a parameter to a macro from a MacroButton field. Only a macro can pass a parameter to another macro; human agency cannot.

There is a rather baroque work-around for the MacroButton limitation. The following field would create a MacroButton that executes the macro named ButtonMac:

```
{macrobutton ButtonMac <Click Here to run ButtonMac>}
```

When the field is updated, you will see only "Click here to run ButtonMac." Suppose you add an additional field to set a bookmark to a text value:

```
{macrobutton ButtonMac <Click Here to run ButtonMac>{set message Hello}}
```

Then you create a macro named ButtonMac, which updates the current field, looks for the bookmark named message, and stores it in a variable. You have, in essence, started ButtonMac with the parameter stored in the bookmark created by the set field:

**DISK**
ButtonMac—
Example of how to
pass a paramter to
a macro that is
launched with a
MACROBUTTON
field

```
Sub Main
UpdateFields
msg$ = GetBookmark$("message")
MsgBox msg$
End Sub
```

The passing of a string parameter to a macro via a MacroButton/set field combination is demonstrated in CH09MACS.DOC.

Similarly, you could pass an integer value in this way:

```
{macrobutton ButtonMac <Click Here to run ButtonMac>{set number 1}}
```

would set the bookmark "number" to the string "1." The following macro:

```
Sub Main
UpdateFields
ParamNum = Val(GetBookmark$("number"))
Print ParamNum
End Sub
```

would update the current field and convert the bookmark value to an integer.

## Using External DLLs—The Declare Statement

A library of subroutines and functions extends the capabilities of WordBasic by writing complex routines that can be thereafter accessed by all macros. But these utility routines are themselves written in WordBasic. There is another way to extend the capabilities of WordBasic, and that is to use the Declare statement to borrow a functionality from another program.

The Declare statement is an extremely complex and often dangerous command. It should be approached with some apprehension. What it does is allow you to create a subroutine or a function that uses an external library of subroutines and functions as if they were in WordBasic.

Some background before moving to an example. You may have heard the term "DLL." This is an abbreviation for *Dynamic Link Library*. In fact this is a program—some DLLs are stored on disk as EXE files, others as DLL files—that contains subroutines and functions used by other, controlling programs. Windows itself is composed of a series of Dynamic Link Libraries. The functionality contained in a DLL is only loaded into memory when it is called by the controlling program (which is why it's dynamic: The link to a DLL only happens when demanded).

If you know the syntax of a routine contained in a DLL—whether that DLL was written in C or in Pascal—you can access it from WordBasic. This adds incredible power to our arsenal of macro tools. However, the Declare statement is the least friendly of all the WordBasic statements. It looks the most like computer programming gibberish. It requires either some knowledge of Windows programming or a great deal of faith in the person (me, in this case) telling you the proper syntax for the declare statement.

Though I would caution you again that this is a capability not for the fainthearted, there are some DLL declarable functions that are so useful, they warrant braving the complexity.

The generalized syntax for the Declare statement is

```
Declare Sub SubName Lib LibName[(Parameter[$] As String (or Integer, Double, or
Long))] [Alias ModuleName]

Declare Function FunctionName Lib LibName[(Parameter[$] As String (or Integer,
Double, or Long)] [Alias ModuleName] As String (or Integer, Double, or Long)
```

Double yikes! It's just as scary as it looks to the non-professional Windows programmer. Myself included. However, if you follow the cardinal rule of beginning programming—lift code from other programmers—the Declare statement can yield powerful results. That is, even if you are not familiar enough with Windows programming to originate the proper syntax for a declared DLL subroutine, you can still benefit from the work of others and use the Declare statement to great effect.

Here is a macro that will use a function contained in the Windows DLL named KERNEL to determine if an application is loaded on the Windows desktop.

```
Declare Function IsAppLoaded Lib "kernel"(Name$)\
Alias "GetModuleHandle" As Integer
Sub Main
App$ = "MACRODE.EXE"
Title$ = "Dialog Editor"
If IsAppLoaded(App$) = 0 Then
    SendKeys "% r"
    Shell App$, 0
Else
    AppActivate Title$
End If
End Sub
```

First off, notice that the Declare statement occurs *outside* of the Sub Main/End Sub pair. A declare always exists on its own, outside any subroutine, and usually at the top of the macro (more for convenience than for necessity).

Now to a parsing of this Declare statement:

```
Declare Function IsAppLoaded
```

Declare a function named IsAppLoaded. This name is user-specified. This could just as legally be "IsItThere."

```
Lib "kernel"(Name$)
```

IsAppLoaded will use the library named Kernel and take a string variable as its single parameter.

```
Alias "GetModuleHandle"
```

The function IsAppLoaded is an alias for the Kernel function named GetModuleHandle.

```
As Integer
```

The function IsAppLoaded will return an integer.

The macro GotoDialogEditor simply passes this declared function, in the much more legible line

```
If IsAppLoaded(App$) = 0 Then
```

the full name of the application we're looking for. This is the file name of the executable disk file, including the EXE extension, excluding the path designation. Notice that the "name" of the dialog editor is not the same as the title of the application as displayed on the title bar.

If the dialog editor is not loaded, that is, if IsAppLoaded returns 0, the
macro stuffs the keyboard buffer with Alt+spacebar+R, and loads it with the
statements:

```
SendKeys "% r"
Shell App$, 0
```

Notice that this macro assumes that MACRODE.EXE is located in your DOS
path. In most cases this will be true, since this executable file is located in the
same directory as WINWORD.EXE and the Word installation procedure puts
the Word program directory into the path specified by AUTOEXEC.BAT.
However, if you have modified your path, renamed your Word directory, or
moved MACRODE.EXE, this macro will fail. We can make the macro
smarter and have it determine the directory that contains WINWORD.EXE
(and therefore MACRODE.EXE).

**DISK**
GotoDialogEditor—
Launches or
activates the dialog

```
Declare Function IsApploaded Lib "kernel"(Name$)\
Alias "GetModuleHandle" As Integer
Sub Main
App$ = "MACRODE.EXE"
Title$ = "Dialog Editor"
Path$ = GetProfileString$("programdir") + "\"
If IsAppLoaded(App$) = 0 Then
    SendKeys "% r"
    Shell Path$ + App$, 0
Else
    AppActivate Title$
End If
End Sub
```

This version of GotoDialogEditor uses the GetProfileString$( ) function
to retrieve the value of the keyword "programdir" under the Microsoft Word
2.0 section of WIN.INI. This keyword, created by the Word installation program, points to the directory that contains WINWORD.EXE. Notice that a
backslash is appended to the directory returned by this function. If, for some
reason, GotoDialogEditor still fails, then either MACRODE.EXE has been
removed from your hard disk, or there is no programdir keyword in WIN.INI.
In the latter case you could simply change the path$ variable to point to a spe-
cific, hard-coded directory:

```
Path$ = "C:\MYSTUFF\"
```

or copy MACRODE.EXE to your Windows directory (which is always on the
DOS path).

If IsAppLoaded returns something other than 0 (like –1), then the existing instance of MACRODE.EXE is activated by sending the string "Dialog
Editor" to the WordBasic statement AppActivate.

You cannot simply store the Declare statement within a library. However, you could create a library that contained the Declare statement *and* a user-function that called it. For instance, here is a library macro that contains only the IsAppLoaded user-function, which in turn calls the Declared function IsLoaded:

```
Sub Main
Print "This library contains several useful Declare statements..."
End Sub

Declare Function IsLoaded Lib "kernel"(Name$) Alias "GetModuleHandle" As Integer
Function IsAppLoaded(app$)
    IsAppLoaded = IsLoaded(app$)
End Function
```

This would allow you to call IsAppLoaded from any macro:

**DISK**
GotoDialogEditorTwo—
Launches or loads the
dialog editor, using
zDeclare library

```
Sub Main
App$ = "MACRODE.EXE"
Title$ = "Dialog Editor"
Path$ = GetProfileString$("programdir") + "\"
If zDeclare.IsAppLoaded(App$) = 0 Then
    SendKeys "% r"
    Shell Path$ + App$, 0
Else
    AppActivate Title$
End If
End Sub
```

We will expand on the zDeclare library in the coming pages.

## Undocumented Commands

Virtually every computer program possesses some hidden features—commands that the programmers know about but have not documented (perhaps because they are unfinished or because they are considered dangerous). One of the pleasures of hacking away at a particular application is the chance to discover one of these hidden and often useful features.

### CommandName$

This discovery is my pride and joy. One of my reasons for documenting it in this book is the hope that once documented, the programmers of Word for Windows will resist any temptation to remove it. It is an extremely obscure capability; so obscure, I'm not even sure it was intentional on the part of the Word development team. I have not spoken to a single programmer who knew of its existence. What's the big secret?

You can call virtually any internal command macro, retaining the built-in error correcting ability, by appending a dollar sign to the statement name.

In an earlier example we modified the built-in FileOpen macro so that it would display all files in a directory. That macro was

```
Sub Main
Dim dlg As FileOpen
GetCurValues dlg
dlg.Name = "*.*"
On Error Goto Bye
Dialog dlg
FileOpen dlg
Bye:
End Sub
```

With what I call "The dollar sign trick" we can reduce this macro to two lines:

**DISK**
FileOpenShowAll—
The second version
of a modified
FileOpen
command; this
version uses the
dollar sign trick

```
Sub Main
SendKeys "*.*{Enter}"
FileOpen$
End Sub
```

The first macro creates an array variable, stuffs it with the current field values, changes the .Name field to "*.*", activates an On Error Goto trap in the event the dialog box is canceled, displays the dialog box, and then executes the FileOpen command with the array variable as the single parameter. This revised macro takes a very different tack to solve the same problem. It stuffs the keyboard with the wildcard string "*.*" and a carriage return. It then calls FileOpen with a dollar sign appended to the name. The key fact here is that when you call a command macro with the appended dollar sign *you do not have to insert any error trap.* If the displayed dialog box is canceled, the macro continues on its way rather than displaying "Command Failed."

FileOpen$ has precisely the same effect as the statement ToolsMacro .Name = "FileOpen", .Run. However, the latter requires an error trap, the former does not.

There are obvious limitations to this mode of calling a macro. You cannot pass any parameters. You cannot read results (which you can do if you are using the array variable route to display a dialog box). However, if all you need to do is execute a command macro, this is most convenient.

In case you're wondering how I stumbled upon this, and just for the record, here's the story. I was fiddling late one night trying to take some screen shots of various error messages. Why I didn't use the Error statement and the manual is a mystery. Just goes to show everyone forgets. In any case, I knew I could create various error conditions by mistyping statements. One of the typos I tried, expecting a "Syntax Error" message, was FileOpen$.

### ExitWindows

Here is a WordBasic statement that falls into the category of "Too dangerous to let the user know about it." However, if your application requires the functionality of this command, there is no simple way to accomplish its effect without it. So, here goes.

ExitWindows will immediately shut down Windows and drop to DOS. If you have any unsaved work, either in Word or in any other application, it will be discarded, lost, obliterated. For this reason you should *never* use this statement when other applications may have valuable unsaved active data, and you should make sure that any macro which calls this command saves any unsaved data currently active in Word.

The possible uses for this command are pretty arcane. The simplest would be to create an AutoExit macro that saved all files and then closed Windows:

```
Sub Main
FileSaveAll 1
ExitWindows
End Sub
```

But it is equally possible that you could develop a system that uses a batch file and two macros to: automatically exit Windows, run your DOS tape backup program, and reload Windows.

For instance, if the above macro was named ShutDown, you could have a batch file named WINDOWS.BAT which looked like:

```
WIN WINWORD.EXE /mStartOnTime
TAPEBACK
WIN WINWORD.EXE
```

This would load Windows, automatically load Word, and run the macro named StartOnTime. The StartOnTime macro, in turn, would look like:

```
Sub Main
OnTime "Ø6:3Ø:ØØ", "ShutDown"
End Sub
```

What this macro does is simply wait for 6:30 a.m. and execute the macro named ShutDown. ShutDown, remember, saves all open files and then returns to DOS. Since, in this example, Windows was launched with a batch file, control is returned to the batch file, which executes the command TAPEBACK. When TAPEBACK is complete, control returns to the WINDOWS.BAT file, and the last line reloads Windows and Word for Windows.

I told you it was arcane, but for those who recognize this as a possible solution, it will point in interesting and powerful directions.

## A Colossal Coupla Kludges

A "kludge," pronounced to rhyme with "huge," is a neologism coined to represent a solution that works but is ugly. It refers to a programming solution that might be called, colloquially, a "jimmy-rig."

A great deal of programming is stretching the boundaries of what is possible. Some of the most interesting solutions I've seen (or created) are essentially kludges. In fact, some people would argue that Windows, in attempting to breathe life into DOS and break various memory boundaries, is itself nothing but an enormous and extremely clever kludge.

There are two deficiencies in the WordBasic programming language that can only be corrected with kludges of one sort or another. WordBasic does not allow for either "global" variables or "document-specific" variables.

### Faking Global Variables

A variable created by a macro dies when the macro ends. This means there is no built-in way to execute one macro, and then run a second macro later during your Word session and use the values generated by the first. Another way of stating this is *a WordBasic variable does not persist past the execution of the macro that defined it.*

At minimum, it would be nice to have a variable persist as long as you don't exit Word. That may come in the next version. However, the kludges described here all write a variable to disk, and therefore variables created in any of the following ways not only persist during the current session, but can be retrieved and used in subsequent sessions as well.

**Using Glossaries**   The simplest way to store a variable for later use is to place it into a unique glossary name stored in NORMAL.DOT.

This uses two WordBasic commands:

```
SetGlossary Name$, Value$, [Context]
```

and

```
GetGlossary(Name$,[Context])
```

where Name$ is the name of the glossary entry; Value$ is the text string to assign to that name; and Context is an optional integer parameter that specifies where to store the glossary (0=global, 1=template).

Here is an example macro that uses a subroutine and a function to set and get a global glossary entry:

```
Sub Main
SetGlossVar("Num","1")
MsgBox GetGlossVar$("Num")
SetGlossVar("String", "Hello World")
```

**DISK**
GlossaryVar—
Example of using
SetGlossVar and
GetGlossVar$ to
create persistent
variables

```
MsgBox GetGlossVar$("String")
MsgBox GetGlossVar$("Bogus")
End Sub

Sub SetGlossVar(Name$, Value$)
    SetGlossary Name$, Value$, 0
End Sub

Function GetGlossVar$(Name$)
    GetGlossVar$ = GetGlossary$(Name$,0)
End Function
```

In this example, writing and reading a "glossary variable" happens within the same macro. You could just as easily run one macro to write:

```
Sub Main
SetGlossVar("Num","1")
SetGlossVar("String", "Hello World")
End Sub
```

and a second to read:

```
Sub Main
MsgBox GetGlossVar$("Num")
MsgBox GetGlossVar$("String")
MsgBox GetGlossVar$("Bogus")
End Sub
```

Notice that if you try to GetGlossVar$( ) from a glossary that does not exist (as is the case with GetGlossVar$("Bogus"), the function returns a null string. Also notice that the GetGlossVar$ user-function returns a string. So if you are interested in storing numeric variables, you must convert after retrieving using the Val( ) function.

```
N$ = GetGlossVar$("Num")
```

stores the string "1" in the string variable N$.

```
N = Val(N$)
```

converts this string variable to the integer 1. You can combine the two functions to do the conversion at the same time as the retrieval:

```
N = Val(GetGlossVar$("Num"))
```

The severe limitation inherent in storing variables this way is that the global template, NORMAL.DOT, is irrevocably set to "dirty." That is to say, running SetGlossVar will always cause you to be presented with the prompt "Do you want to save the global glossary and command changes?" when you exit Word or execute a FileSaveAll. This is so even if you immediately remove the just-created glossary.

If a user does not save the changes to the global landscape, the variables stored in the glossary will not persist, and running the subsequent macro that assumes their existence will fail. So, although it works, it isn't perfect.

**Using WIN.INI**   A more reliable place to store a "global" variable is in WIN-.INI. Before I give an example, some general comments are in order on the structure of WIN.INI for those who have never examined it closely.

WIN.INI is a configuration file that stores gobs and gobs of information used by Windows when it first loads, as well as by other Windows applications (like Word). WIN.INI is a plain ASCII text file that can be easily edited using NOTEPAD.EXE. Information is stored in WIN.INI in the following way:

```
[section name]
Keyword=value
```

For instance:

```
[Microsoft Word 2.0]
doc-path=C:\WINWORD
dot-path=C:\WINWORD\DOT
```

The "values" associated with a keyword are stored as simple text strings.

WordBasic allows you to read and write values in WIN.INI with two related commands—one statement and one function:

```
SetProfileString [App$,] Key$, Value$
```

and

```
GetProfileString$([App$,]Key$)
```

Notice that the parameter App$ is bracketed. This is because by default both of these statements assume you want to look in the "Microsoft Word 2.0" section of WIN.INI. Therefore, the two expressions:

```
DotPath$ = GetProfileString$("Microsoft Word 2.0", "Dot-Path")
```

and

```
DotPath$ = GetProfileString$("Dot-Path")
```

are functionally identical. Notice, incidentally, that the case of the keyword sent by GetProfileString does not matter; "Dot-Path" and "DOT-PATH" are both legal and will all return the value associated with the keyword "dot-path."

**DISK**
WinINI1—Example of how to use GetProfileString and SetProfileString to create persistent variables

```
Sub Main
SetVar("Num", "1")
MsgBox GetVar$("Num")
SetVar("String", "Hello World")
MsgBox GetVar$("String")
```

```
MsgBox GetVar$("Bogus")
End Sub

Sub SetVar(Name$, Value$)
    SetProfileString(Name$, Value$)
End Sub

Function GetVar$(Name$)
    GetVar$ = GetProfileString$(Name$)
End Function
```

This uses the built-in WordBasic commands SetProfileString and GetProfileString$( ). In this example they are placed in a user-sub and a user-function solely for convenience and parallelism to the previous example.

By default SetProfileString( ) and GetProfileString$( ) assume that the section of WIN.INI to use for storage and retrieval is "[Microsoft Word 2.0]." However, we could revise the macro to write values under their own section of WIN.INI:

**DISK**

WinINI2—Example of how to use GetProfileString and SetProfileString to write to private section

```
Sub Main
Section$ = "Word Variables"
SetVar("Num", "1", Section$)
MsgBox GetVar$("Num", Section$)
SetVar("String", "Hello World", Section$)
MsgBox GetVar$("String", Section$)
MsgBox GetVar$("Bogus", Section$)
End Sub

Sub SetVar(Name$, Value$, Section$)
    SetProfileString(Section$,Name$, Value$)
End Sub

Function GetVar$(Name$, Section$)
    GetVar$ = GetProfileString$(Section$,Name$)
End Function
```

When this macro executes SetVar, it creates the new section (in this case "Word Variables") if it doesn't already exist, and then writes the keyword/value pair.

Notice that GetProfileString$( ) always returns (as the name implies) a string. If the value stored is a number, it is retrieved as a numeric string (such as "1"), and must be converted using the Val( ) function.

```
N = Val(GetVar$("Num", Section$))
```

Tip: You can examine the contents of WIN.INI while still in Word (rather than using NOTEPAD.EXE). This is done by selecting WIN.INI from the Options dialog box (accessed by pressing Alt+O-O-W). By default, the list of Startup Options shows those values stored in the "Microsoft Word 2.0" section. However, you can change the active section by selecting a different keyword under the Application drop-down menu. You can also type a new application section (such as "Word Variables") directly into the Application edit box. Once entered, this section will be added to the drop-down list. The list of available sections is stored in its own section of WIN.INI, under "MSWord Editable Sections."

**Private INI Settings**   Many people would argue that WIN.INI is large enough. They contend that polite programming requires that you store any program-specific variables in a "private" INI file. I think this can be argued both ways. It is no more difficult to clear WIN.INI of obsolete sections than it is to delete obsolete private INI files. And a proliferation of small INI files has a cost: They can take up more disk space (every file, even if it only contains ten characters, takes up a minimum of 2,048 bytes of disk space; on some systems this number grows to 4,096 or 8,192).

In any case, there is a way to write a WordBasic variable to a private INI file. It requires using the Declare statement (so be forewarned) to borrow a couple of functions from the Windows "kernel."

Here is a sample macro that creates an INI file named BOGUS.INI, creates a section named "Word Variables," and writes two keywords ("Num" and "String") and two values ("1" and "Hello World"):

**DISK**

PrivateINI1—
Demonstration of
how to write values
to a private INI file

```
Sub Main
ININame$ = "BOGUS.INI"
Section$ = "Word Variables"
WritePrivateINI(Section$, "Num", "1", ININame$)
WritePrivateINI(Section$, "String", "Hello World", ININame$)
MsgBox GetPrivateINI$(Section$, "Num", ININame$)
MsgBox GetPrivateINI$(Section$, "String", ININame$)
MsgBox GetPrivateINI$(Section$, "Bogus", ININame$)
End Sub

Declare Function GetPrivateProfileString Lib "kernel"(Section$, Key$, Default$,
ReturnedValue$, MaxChars As Integer, FName$)   As Integer
Declare Function WritePrivateProfileString Lib "kernel"(Section$, Key$, Value$,
FName$)   As Integer

Sub WritePrivateINI(Section$, Key$, Value$, ININame$)
    n = WritePrivateProfileString(Section$, Key$, Value$, ININame$)
End Sub

Function GetPrivateINI$(Section$, Key$, ININame$)
    n = GetPrivateProfileString(Section$, Key$, "", Temp$, 255, ININame$)
GetPrivateINI$ = Temp$
End Function
```

The ININame$ variable can provide a full path designation. If you do not provide a full path, WritePrivateProfileString (the declared sub) will assume your

Windows directory as the destination. Notice as well that when you attempt to GetPrivateINI on a keyword that doesn't exist ("Bogus" in this case), the function returns a null string.

Most Windows applications now create application-specific INI files rather than storing settings in WIN.INI. If your macro requires many stored settings, it is advisable to use a private INI file. No matter how you feel about the disk space question, it is true that a dedicated INI file is easier for the user to find and modify manually if need be.

Writing a value to a private INI file has one clear advantage over using the SetProfileString command to store a new keyword/value pair in WIN.INI: You can delete not only the value but the keyword as well. This allows a macro to create temporary keyword/value pairs that the user need never even know about. Your macro can set a value, use it, and then remove it from the INI file completely.

To delete a keyword you use the same Declare statement used for WritePrivateINI with a single parameter altered.

For example:

**DISK**
PrivateINI2—
Writes, reads, and
deletes private INI
file keyword/value

```
Sub Main
ININame$ = "BOGUS.INI"
Section$ = "Word Variables"
WritePrivateINI(Section$, "Num", "1", ININame$)        'Write the value
MsgBox GetPrivateINI$(Section$, "Num", ININame$)       'Display the value
DeletePrivateINIKey(Section$, "Num", ININame$)
MsgBox GetPrivateINI$(Section$, "Num", ININame$)       'Try and read it; returns
                                                       'nothing

End Sub

Declare Function GetPrivateProfileString Lib "kernel"(Section$, Key$, Default$,
ReturnedValue$, MaxChars As Integer, FName$)   As Integer

Declare Function WritePrivateProfileString Lib "kernel"(Section$, Key$, Value$,
FName$)   As Integer

Declare Function DeletePrivateProfileString Lib "kernel"(Section$, Key$, Value$
As Long, FName$) As Integer Alias "WritePrivateProfileString"

Sub DeletePrivateINIKey(Section$, Key$, ININame$)
    n = DeletePrivateProfileString(Section$, Key$, 0, ININame$)
End Sub

Sub WritePrivateINI(Section$, Key$, Value$, ININame$)
    n = WritePrivateProfileString(Section$, Key$, Value$, ININame$)
End Sub

Function GetPrivateINI$(Section$, Key$, ININame$)
    n = GetPrivateProfileString(Section$, Key$, "", Temp$, 255, ININame$)
GetPrivateINI$ = Temp$
End Function
```

You can also "blank-out" a value without removing the keyword from the INI file. That is, you can send a null string to a keyword:

```
Null$ = ""
WritePrivateINI(Section$, "Num", Null$, ININame$)
```

would blank the value associated with the keyword "Num":

```
[Word Variables]
Num=
```

**WARNING!** *The above procedure to blank a keyword value will not work with Word version 1.x. Sending a null to WritePrivateINI will invariably cause a crash in versions of Word prior to 2.0.*

We could now modify the macro library named zDeclare to include the functions to set and get from a private INI file:

**DISK**
zDeclare—Example
library of useful
Declare statements

```
Sub Main
Print "This library contains several useful Declare statements..."
End Sub

Declare Function GetPrivateProfileString Lib "kernel"(Section$, Key$, Default$,
ReturnedValue$, MaxChars As Integer, FName$) As Integer

Declare Function WritePrivateProfileString Lib "kernel"(Section$, Key$, Value$,
FName$)   As Integer

Declare Function DeletePrivateProfileString Lib "kernel"(Section$, Key$, Value$
As Long, FName$) As Integer Alias "WritePrivateProfileString"

Sub DeletePrivateINIKey(Section$, Key$, ININame$)
    n = DeletePrivateProfileString(Section$, Key$, 0, ININame$)
End Sub

Sub WritePrivateINI(Section$, Key$, Value$, ININame$)
    n = WritePrivateProfileString(Section$, Key$, Value$, ININame$)
End Sub

Function GetPrivateINI$(Section$, Key$, ININame$)
    n = GetPrivateProfileString(Section$, Key$, "", Temp$, 255, ININame$)
GetPrivateINI$ = Temp$
End Function
```

The on-disk sample template for this chapter (CH09MACS.DOC) contains both zLib and zDeclare, but in fact you could combine them (along with any other utility functions you may have gathered or created) into a single library. Be aware, however, that the global library cannot be named "Lib." This word is reserved for use in the Declare statement. Also, if you create a custom library, be sure that all macros are edited to reflect the new name. For instance, if you combine zLib and zDeclare into a library macro named MyLib, you must be sure to replace any instance of "zLib" and "zDeclare" in the sample macros with "MyLib." Any reference to a library that doesn't exist will produce an error message 124, Undefined SUB or FUNCTION.

### Faking Template and Document Variables

Every document created in Word does possess some significant "document variables." These are accessible via the FileSummaryInfo command. Below is a macro that accesses and displays each of the fields stored in FileSummaryInfo:

**DISK**
FileInfo—
Demonstrates the
retrieval of the
contents of
FileSummaryInfo

```
Sub Main
Dim dlg As FileSummaryInfo
GetCurValues dlg
MsgBox "Author is: "+ dlg.Author
MsgBox "Title is: " + dlg.Title
MsgBox "Subject is: " + dlg.Subject
MsgBox "Keywords: " + dlg.Keywords
MsgBox "Comments: " + dlg.Comments
MsgBox "FileName: " + dlg.FileName
MsgBox "Directory: " + dlg.Directory
MsgBox "Based on: " + dlg.Template
MsgBox "Created: " + dlg.CreateDate
MsgBox "Last saved: " + dlg.LastSavedDate
MsgBox "Last saved by: " + dlg.LastSavedBy
MsgBox "Revision number: " + dlg.RevisionNumber
MsgBox "Minutes open: " + dlg.EditTime
MsgBox "Last printed: " + dlg.LastPrintedDate
MsgBox "Total pages: " + dlg.NumPages
MsgBox "Total words: " + dlg.NumWords
MsgBox "Total characters: " + dlg.NumChars
End Sub
```

This macro can only be run with the focus on a document (that is, it will generate an error if executed on a macro editing window).

Note: Both the Help file and *Using WordBasic* describe the fields .RevisionNumber, .LastPrintedDate, .NumPages, .NumWords, and .NumChars as numbers. They are all returned as strings.

However, there may be occasions when you would like to store an additional piece of information with the document.

**Template Variables Using the Glossary**   If you have created a disguised template (that is, your document is actually a template with a DOC extension), then you can use a variation of the GlossVar method described above.

Simply change the context parameter in the set/get routines from 0 to 1. This will write and read the template glossary rather than the global glossary:

```
Sub SetTemplateGlossVar(Name$, Value$)
    SetGlossary Name$, Value$, 1
End Sub

Function GetTemplateGlossVar$(Name$)
    GetGlossVar$ = GetGlossary$(Name$, 1)
End Function
```

The same limitation applies: Once you set a template glossary, the template is set to dirty.

Even if you haven't created a disguised template, this method could be used to create a "template-wide" variable (that is, it would not be global and it would not be available only in a specific document; rather it would be available to any document based on the template in question).

**Document Variables Using Bookmarks**   There's another way to insert information into a document: bookmarks. Bookmarks are used to specify a location in a document. When you press F5 twice, you see a list of bookmarks in a document. Normally a bookmark covers an area of text, and in addition to specifying a location (where the covered text is in the document), you can retrieve the covered text itself with the following function:

```
GetBookmark$(Name$)
```

where Name$ is the name of a bookmark.

A bookmark can also be an insertion point (that is, it "covers" no text). However, one of the most obscure features in Word is the fact that even an insertion point bookmark can be assigned a text string *as if the bookmark covered the assigned text.*

Here's the kludge that uses bookmarks as a way to store document-specific variables:

**DISK**

BookmarkVar—
Demonstrates how
to use Bookmarks
as document-
specific variables

```
Sub Main
StartOfDocument
SetBookmarkVar("Num", "1")
MsgBox GetBookmarkVar$("Num")
SetBookmarkVar("String", "Hello World")
MsgBox GetBookmarkVar$("String")
MsgBox GetBookmarkVar$("Bogus")
Bye:
ClearBookmarkVar("Num")
ClearBookmarkVar("String")
End Sub

Function GetBookmarkVar$(Bookmark$)
    GetBookmarkVar$ = GetBookmark$(Bookmark$)
```

```
End Function

Sub ClearBookmarkVar(Bookmark$)
    If ExistingBookmark(Bookmark$) Then EditGoTo Bookmark$ : EditClear
End Sub

Sub SetBookmarkVar(Bookmark$, Value$)
    If Value$ <> "" Then \
    InsertField .Field = "Set " + BookMark$ + " " + Chr$(34) + Value$ + Chr$(34)
End Sub
```

This macro inserts a {set} field into your document in the form:

```
{Set BookmarkName "Text associated with BookmarkName"}
```

When such a field is updated, an interesting thing happens: It vanishes (unless you have ViewFieldCodes set to on). It does not print. The {set} field is intended to facilitate the creation of form letters in which a specific string occurs in several locations. You would normally use it in conjunction with the {ref} field in the following manner:

```
{Set name "John Doe"}
Dear {ref Name},
```

When these two lines are updated, what you see in the document (and what will print) is

```
Dear John Doe,
```

Our BookmarkVar macro uses this ability to create an insertion point bookmark and assign it a text string as well as a location, without using a {ref} field to reference and insert the string into the document. The GetBookmark-Var$( ) function simply looks for the named bookmark and returns the text associated with it. This macro must be run with the focus on a document. To most clearly see how it works and what it does, I would recommend using the Step button to execute one instruction at a time.

This method of creating and reading a bookmark makes it possible to create document variables because the actual text assigned to a bookmark *isn't in the document.* It is hidden in the internals of the document, next to the bookmark name. Subsequent calls to GetBookmarkVar will be able to "read" this text string even if the user never sees it.

The one danger associated with this method of creating bookmarks to hold text strings is that the user will inadvertently delete the {set} field inserted by SetBookmarkVar( ). There is no way to lock, or protect, a portion of a document. For this reason, I would suggest always moving to the top line of the current document before inserting the {set} field. We could change the

SetBookmarkVar to ensure that all such fields are inserted at the top of the document:

```
Sub SetBookmarkVar(Bookmark$, Value$)
  If Value$ <> "" Then
    StartOfDocument
    InsertField .Field = "Set " + Bookmark$ + " " + Chr$(34) + Value$ + Chr$(34)
    GoBack
  End If
End Sub
```

# Miscellany

Before leaving the more or less theoretical discussions of this chapter (and moving on to annotated macro examples), I'd like to describe a handful of the more interesting and powerful (and sometimes overlooked) capabilities accessible through WordBasic.

## SelInfo()

*SelInfo*( ) is an extremely useful function. The name betrays the purpose: Selection Information. Once you know how to use this function, your macros learn more than you'll ever need to know about the current selection. The selection is defined as either the current insertion point (the blinking vertical bar) or the highlighted block covering a range of text.

The syntax for SelInfo( ) is a little different from other functions we have examined. Most WordBasic numeric functions are called without a parameter:

```
Bold()
Underline()
ViewOutline()
```

and return either –1 or 0 as their result.

SelInfo( ) has the following syntax:

```
n = SelInfo(x)
```

Notice that the SelInfo( ) takes an integer parameter (x in the above syntax description). Depending on the value of this integer argument, SelInfo( ) will ask a different question of the selection, and return a result. Here, the strict mathematical definition of an argument is appropriate: the value upon which a calculation depends.

Below is a table of the 30 possible argument values that can be passed to SelInfo( ).

| Argument | Returns |
|---|---|
| 1 | Number of the page containing the selection. Returns –1 if in header or footer; returns page of previous footnote or annotation if in a footnote or annotation pane. |
| 2 | Number of the section containing the selection. |
| 3 | Number of current page, disregarding section numbering. |
| 4 | Number of pages in the selection. |
| 5 | Only available in page layout view. Returns the horizontal position of start of selection, relative to the left edge of the page; measured in twips (1/20 of a point or 1/1440 of an inch). Returns –1 if the selection is not visible. |
| 6 | Returns the vertical position of start of selection, relative to the top edge of the page; measured in twips (1/20 of a point or 1/1440 of an inch). Returns –1 if the selection is not visible. |
| 7 | Returns horizontal position of start of selection, relative to enclosing display rectangle. |
| 8 | Returns vertical position of start of selection, relative to enclosing display rectangle. |
| 9 | Location of the insertion point measured in columns (characters) from the start of the current line. (Same as the Col value displayed on status bar.) |
| 10 | Line number of the first character in the selection. Requires Background Pagination and Line Breaks And Fonts as Printed to be set to on. |
| 11 | Returns –1 if the selection is an entire frame. |
| 12 | Returns –1 if the selection is in a table. |
| 13 | The row containing the beginning of the selection (only available in a table). |
| 14 | The row containing the end of the selection (only available in a table). |

| Argument | Returns |
|---|---|
| 15 | The total number of rows in a table (only available in a table). |
| 16 | The column containing the beginning of the selection. |
| 17 | The column containing the end of the selection. |
| 18 | The maximum number of columns within any row in the selection. |
| 19 | The current zoom factor. |
| 20 | The selection type (corresponds to the box on the status bar EXT/COL): |

    0 for normal (insertion point)
    1 for extended mode
    2 for block selection

| Argument | Returns |
|---|---|
| 21 | Returns –1 if Caps Lock is on. |
| 22 | Returns –1 if Num Lock is on. |
| 23 | Returns –1 if Word is in overtype mode. |
| 24 | Returns –1 if revision marking is on. |
| 25 | Returns –1 if the selection is in a footnote. |
| 26 | Returns –1 if the selection is in an annotation. |
| 27 | Returns –1 if the selection is in a macro-editing window. |
| 28 | Returns –1 if the selection is in a header or footer. |
| 29 | The number of the bookmark enclosing the start of the selection; 0 if none or invalid. |
| 30 | The number of the last bookmark that starts before the selection; 0 if none or invalid. |

The most frequent use I have made of this function is to query whether the selection is currently located in a macro-editing window. I do this so often that I have created a user-function, stored in my global library, named IsMacroPane:

**DISK**
IsMacroPane—A
user-function
located in zLib

```
Function IsMacroPane
If SelInfo(27) Then
    Macro$ = Mid$(WindowName$(), Instr(WindowName$(), ":") + 2)
    MsgBox("You cannot execute [" + Macro$ + "] when the focus is a macro
```

```
        editing window.  Try WindowArrangeAll and place the focus on a document.",
        "Warning", 48)
        IsMacroPane = - 1
Else
        IsMacroPane = Ø
End If
End Function
```

Another frequently useful test, which was very difficult to make before SelInfo( ), is to check if the insertion point is in a footnote or annotation pane and if so, move back to the body of the document:

```
Sub Main
If SelInfo(25) Or SelInfo(26) Or SelInfo(28)  Then
        If ViewPage() Then
                Print "Moving to body of next page..."
                EditGoTo
                EditGoTo "\PrevSel"
        Else
                Print "Closing pane..."
                ClosePane
        End If
End If
End Sub
```

SelInfo( ) is a complicated function. However, it is worth some study. It can make complex maneuvering in a document much, much easier.

## Special Bookmarks and CmpBookmarks()

Word has a number of predefined/reserved bookmarks. They all have the same format:

```
\BookmarkName
```

| Bookmark Name | Definition |
| --- | --- |
| \Sel | Current selection. |
| \PrevSel1 | Most recent editing location. |
| \PrevSel2 | Second most recent editing location. |
| \StartOfSel | Start of the current selection. |
| \EndOfSel | End of the current selection. |
| \Line | Current line (if the selection is an insertion point) or the first line of the current selection (if the selection is a block). |

| Bookmark Name | Definition |
|---|---|
| \Char | Current character; the character following the insertion point if there is no selection or the first character of the selection. |
| \Para | Current paragraph. If more than one paragraph is selected, the first paragraph. |
| \Section | Current section. If more than one section is selected, the first section in the selection. |
| \Doc | The entire document. |
| \Page | Current page. If more than one page is selected, the first page of the selection. |
| \StartOfDoc | Beginning of the document. |
| \EndOfDoc | End of the document. |
| \Table | Current table. If more than one table is selected, the entire first table covered by the selection. |
| \HeadingLevel | Current heading, plus any subordinate headings and text. |

These bookmarks can be used in one of two ways from within a macro: as navigation and for comparison purposes.

For instance, you could have a macro that moved the selection to the current line:

```
Sub Main
EditGoTo "\Line"
End Sub
```

This is more convenient than the alternative:

```
Sub Main
StartOfLine
EndOfLine 1
CharLeft 1,1
End Sub
```

It's always better to do in one statement what would otherwise take three.

You can also use the WordBasic function that compares bookmarks:

```
n = CmpBookmarks(Bookmark1$, Bookmark2$)
```

to do some neat things. For instance, assume there is a user-bookmark named "StartOfThings." You could then have a macro determine where the current insertion point is in relation to this bookmark with the statement:

```
n = CmpBookmarks("\Sel","StartOfThings")
```

Below is a table of the possible values returned by CmpBookmarks( ).

| Value | Means |
|---|---|
| 0 | Bookmark1$ and Bookmark2$ are equivalent. |
| 1 | Bookmark1$ is entirely below Bookmark2$. |
| 2 | Bookmark1$ is entirely above Bookmark2$. |
| 3 | Bookmark1$ is below and inside Bookmark2$. |
| 4 | Bookmark1$ is inside and above Bookmark2$. |
| 5 | Bookmark1$ encloses Bookmark2$. |
| 6 | Bookmark2$ encloses Bookmark1$. |
| 7 | Bookmark1$ and Bookmark2$ begin at the same point, but Bookmark1$ is longer. |
| 8 | Bookmark1$ and Bookmark2$ begin at the same point, but Bookmark2$ is longer. |
| 9 | Bookmark1$ and Bookmark2$ end at the same place, but Bookmark1$ is longer. |
| 10 | Bookmark1$ and Bookmark2$ end at the same place, but Bookmark2$ is longer. |
| 11 | Bookmark1$ is below and adjacent to Bookmark2$. |
| 12 | Bookmark1$ is above and adjacent to Bookmark2$. |
| 13 | One or more of the bookmarks do not exist. |

It can be really dizzying to try and keep track of all the possible permutations. One of the simplest, and most useful, comparisons has the form:

```
While CmpBookmarks(First$, Second$)
    ...DoLotsOfStuff
Wend
```

This basically means "as long as the two bookmarks aren't identical, Do-LotsOfStuff." The reason is that, as you might recall, any non-zero value is interpreted as true. So, the above loop is really saying:

```
While CmpBookmarks(First$, Second$) <> 0
    ...DoLotsOfStuff
Wend
```

Like SelInfo( ), CmpBookmarks( ) is not simple to use. But, also like SelInfo( ), there are some things it can accomplish that cannot be done otherwise.

## Summary: Advanced Topics

The examples presented in this chapter demonstrated a wide range of powerful features available in WordBasic. In the next chapter we will examine these features, and many others, in action by presenting specific macro solutions to various problems and examining how these macros accomplish their minor magic.

**Macro Examples**

**Fields**

**Putting It All Together: Sample Templates**

**Miscellaneous Tips, Bugs and Secrets**

# An Encyclopedia
# of Tips

C H A P T E R

# 10

## Macro Examples

YOU NOW HAVE, AT MINIMUM, A STUTTERING FAMILIARITY WITH MY PARticular dialect of WordBasic. I repeat that the way to learn a language is to live in the neighborhood, to listen to it spoken, to read its literature. Theoretical discussions of syntax and grammar can only take the foreigner so far. With a programming language, of course, the neighborhood, the conversations, and the literature exist only in the source code written by other programmers. Every self-taught programmer follows the same basic path (which, essentially, is what this book facilitates): studying and adapting preexisting source code. The trick is learning enough of the basics to be able to follow the logic of a macro, no matter the particular programming style of the author; to recognize when a section of code solves a problem elegantly; to know when another programmer's code can be adapted to solve your problem. There is nothing dishonorable in borrowing from source code written by others (assuming, of course, they have not forbidden such borrowing). Most of the WordBasic code available for examination is presented with the understanding that users can (and will) adapt the macros for their own use.

Much, if not all, of what I have learned about WordBasic I gleaned by studying source code written by other programmers. In addition to the macros contained in the predefined templates, there are several sources you should know:

- In Word version 1.x there was a template (disguised as a document) of sample macros named EXAMPLES.DOC.

- The reference *Using WordBasic* comes with an accompanying disk full of macros.

- In Word version 2.x there are two templates which contain useful macros that can be studied: NEWMACRO.DOC and PSS.DOC. The former improves and expands upon EXAMPLES.DOC; the latter is a collection of macros created by the Microsoft Product Support Services. If you have not examined these utilities, I'd advise doing so.

- One of the largest resources for information on WordBasic can be tapped only if you are equipped with a modem and an account on CompuServe. Microsoft sponsors a forum dedicated to the discussion of Word where you will find many knowledgeable people, including representatives from Microsoft, who will be glad to help with virtually any aspect of Word.

This chapter will present a selection of my favorite macro solutions. I will step through the nature of the problem and the specific points of interest in the WordBasic macro I devised to provide a solution. You will, at the end of it all, have a group of potentially useful utilities as well as a better understanding of WordBasic and the flexibility and power it provides in customizing Word.

# Window Arrangement

Word allows you to have up to nine documents open at any one time. This is a great boon. It allows you to work on several projects or a set of related documents at once. However, Word provides only one command for arranging multiple document windows within the Word document workspace: Window-ArrangeAll. This command *tiles* the open documents, resizing each so that all fit within the workspace without any overlap. This command loses utility in proportion to the number of documents you have open. With each additional document, each individual document window gets smaller (and less usable). There are at least three additional window arrangement options I would like to have in Word. So, I wrote some macros.

## WinCascadeAll

Most Windows applications have a command to cascade all open "child" windows. Rather than tiling all open document windows, the windows are stacked one atop the other, leaving sufficient overlap to see all the title bars. Here is a macro named WinCascadeAll that adds just such a cascade window arrangement command to Word.

**DISK**
WinCascadeAll—
Arranges open
documents in a
stack

```
Sub Main
ZoomPercent = SelInfo(19)           'get the current zoom percentage
If DocMaximize() Then DocRestore    'make sure the current document is not
                                    'maximized

ViewZoom .ZoomPercent = 100         'set zoom to 100%
Count = CountWindows() - 1          'count the number of windows overlapped
VShift = 14 'The shift constants. These two numbers specify how many screen
HShift = 7  'units to shift each document window vertically and horizontally
px = 0           'the starting x and y positions are at the top Left
py = 0
x = Val(AppInfo$(6)) -(Count * HShift)    'the document workspace minus the
y = Val(AppInfo$(7)) -(Count * VShift)    'number of windows overlapped times the
                                          'shift constants.
For i = 1 To Count + 1              'loop through all Open documents
   NextWindow                       'move to the Next window
   DocMove px, py                   'move to the current x and y position
   DocSize x, y                     'size to the dimensions figured above
   px = px + HShift                 'increment the x and y position
   py = py + VShift                 'using the shift constants
Next i
ViewZoom .ZoomPercent = ZoomPercent 'reset the zoom percentage
End Sub
```

Let's step through and take a closer look at what this macro does and how it does it. The macro starts by determining the current zoom factor with the line:

```
ZoomPercent = SelInfo(19)
```

This is necessary because of a *glitch* (not quite a bug, but a weirdness) in the way Word calculates the document workspace. If the zoom factor of the focus document is greater than 100 percent Word thinks (quite contrarily) that the document workspace is smaller by precisely the percent over 100. The solution is to grab the current zoom factor and force the current document to 100 percent zoom with the line:

```
ViewZoom .ZoomPercent = 100
```

Before the macro can proceed, the current document must be in a "restored" state. That is, if the focus document is maximized, the statements that rearrange the windows will fail. This is taken care of with the line:

```
If DocMaximize() Then DocRestore
```

The logic is quite simple: If the internal function DocMaximize() returns true, meaning that the focus document is taking up the entire document workspace, execute the DocRestore command, toggling the focus document into a window.

Seven variables are then defined and assigned values. Count stores the number of open documents minus 1. This constant will be used to do two things: to determine the dimensions of each window, and to act as a counter variable in the For…Next loop. VShift and HShift hold the constant number of screen units to shift each document window when they are cascaded. PX and PY are the position values that will be passed to DocMove. X and Y are the dimensions of the individual document windows. This brings us to another interesting WordBasic statement not seen thus far. The lines

```
x = Val(AppInfo$(6)) -  (Count * HShift)
y = Val(AppInfo$(7)) -  (Count * VShift)
```

call a WordBasic function worthy of further comment. AppInfo$(), like SelInfo(), is a function that takes an integer argument and returns information on a specific aspect of the Word application. Table 10.1 describes the 15 arguments that can be passed to AppInfo$() and the corresponding information returned.

---

**Table 10.1**  **The AppInfo$() Function**

| Argument | Tells AppInfo$() to Return Information About |
|---|---|
| 1 | The Windows environment string; for example, "Windows 3.1" |
| 2 | The version number of Word |

**Table 10.1** **The AppInfo$() Function (Continued)**

| Argument | Tells AppInfo$() to Return Information About |
| --- | --- |
| 3 | Returns -1 if Word is in a special mode such as CopyText or MoveText mode |
| 4 | X position of the Word window, measured in points from the left of the screen (returns -3 when maximized, due to the window's borders) |
| 5 | Y position of the Word window, measured in points from the top of the screen (returns -3 when maximized, due to the window's borders) |
| 6 | Width of the active document workspace, in points ($1/72$ inch) |
| 7 | Height of the active document workspace, in points ($1/72$ inch) |
| 8 | Returns -1 if the application is maximized or 0 if the application is restored |
| 9 | Total conventional memory |
| 10 | Amount of conventional memory available |
| 11 | Total expanded memory |
| 12 | Amount of expanded memory available |
| 13 | Returns -1 if a math coprocessor is installed, 0 if not |
| 14 | Returns -1 if a mouse is present, 0 if not |
| 15 | Amount of disk space available |

In WinCascadeAll, AppInfo$() is used to get the dimensions of the current document workspace. These x and y measurements, which are returned as strings, are then converted into integers. The dimensions used later to size the stacked documents are calculated by multiplying the number of documents to be overlapped (the total number of windows minus 1) by the shift constants, and subtracting that total from the document workspace width/height dimensions gathered by AppInfo$(6) and AppInfo$(7).

The remainder of WinCascadeAll introduces no new commands or concepts. However, I would like to point out the utility of defining a constant such as HShift and VShift. These numbers are used in two locations (calculating both the x/y dimensions and the x/y starting positions). By placing these values in an easily accessible location at the top of the macro you can easily try other values by changing each once. This becomes even more important in longer macros.

## WinArrangeTwo

Although cascading all open documents is useful to show at a glance everything in your workspace, often you will want to work simultaneously on two documents. This is particularly true during macro development when you want to step through a macro while also watching its actions on an open document.

When you have only two documents open and select WindowArrangeAll, the two documents are positioned one atop the other. But what if you have more than one document open and still only want to arrange two out of the total documents stacked one atop the other?

Here's a macro named WinArrangeTwo. It assumes that the current document is one of the two documents you wish to arrange one atop the other. If there are more than two documents open, it presents a dialog box listing all of the other available documents, such as:

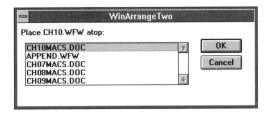

When you select the second document from the list, WinArrangeTwo positions the current document atop the selected document.

**DISK**
WinArrangeTwo—
Arranges two open
documents
vertically

```
Sub Main
ZoomPercent = SelInfo(19)
ViewZoom .ZoomPercent = 100
Count = CountWindows()
If Count < 2 Then Goto Bye
x = Val(AppInfo$(6))         'width of document workspace
y = Val(AppInfo$(7)) / 2     'height of document workspace divided by two
CurDoc$ = WindowName$()
If Count > 2 Then
  Dim Names$(Count - 2)
  For i = 0 To Count - 2
    Names$(i) = WindowName$(((Window() + i) Mod Count) + 1)
  Next i
  Begin Dialog UserDialog 510, 50 + 12 * Count, "WinArrangeTwo"
    Text 8, 8, 338, 13, WindowName$() + " atop:"
    ListBox 18, 30, 350, 12 * Count - 8, Names$(), .Window
    OKButton 393, 24, 88, 21
    CancelButton 393, 48, 88, 21
  End Dialog
  Dim dlg As UserDialog
  On Error Goto Bye
  Dialog dlg
```

```
   On Error Goto 0
   Activate Names$(dlg.Window)
Else
   NextWindow
End If
If DocMaximize() Then DocMaximize
DocMove  0, y
DocSize x, y
Activate CurDoc$
DocMove 0, 0        'move active window
DocSize x, y
Bye:
ViewZoom .ZoomPercent = ZoomPercent
End Sub
```

This macro uses essentially the same logic as WinCascadeAll. It stores
the current zoom percent, counts the number of active documents, and
asks AppInfo$( ) for the current document workspace. Notice that with the
statement

```
y = Val(AppInfo$(7)) / 2
```

the macro determines the y dimension of the sized windows to be half the
total document workspace height (since we are sizing two documents vertically). Also note the use of WindowName$( ) to store the current document's
title bar name into the string variable CurDoc$.

Three other elements of this macro deserve comment. The array variable
name is dimensioned with the statement

```
Dim Names$(Count - 2)
```

This array is two less than the total number of windows because one window
is left out of the list (the current document) and because the first element of
an array is 0, not 1. The loop

```
For i = 0 To Count - 2
    Names$(i) = WindowName$(((Window() + i) Mod Count) + 1)
Next i
```

uses a clever equation to return the window index (the number as listed
under the Window menu) to all open documents *besides* the current one. It
does so by combining two features: Window( ) returns the window number
(from 1 to 9) of the current document; if the first number in a Mod operation
is greater than the second, the first number is returned. So, for instance, if
there are three documents open, and the focus is on the second document,
the equation will be executed twice. Filling in the variables we can see how
the array is filled. The first time through the loop the values are

```
Window() = 2                        'The current window index
i = 0                               'The loop counter starts at 0
```

```
Count = 3                           'The total number of document windows
((2 + 0) Mod 3) + 1 =               'The equation adds window index to counter
    2      Mod 3  + 1 =             'Mod Count + 1
    2             + 1 = 3           'Mod result in this case is the first integer
Names$(0) = WindowName$(Window(3))
```

The second time, i is incremented to 1:

```
Window() = 2                        'The current window index
i = 1                               'The loop counter number at 1
Count = 3                           'The total number of document windows
((2 + 1) Mod 3) + 1 =               'The equation adds window index to counter
    3      Mod 3  + 1 =             'Mod Count + 1
    0             + 1 = 1           'Mod result in this case returns 0
Names$(1) = WindowName$(Window(1))
```

This trick allows us to create a list of all open documents *except* the current one.

The other interesting trick employed in WinArrangeTwo is within the dialog definition. The line

```
ListBox 18, 30, 350, 12 * Count - 8, Names$(), .Window
```

contains an equation as the fourth parameter, the parameter that controls the height of the list box. This equation—12 * Count - 8—dynamically sizes the list box to precisely match the number of items in the list. If you run this macro while nine documents are open, you will notice that the list box sizes to accommodate eight items.

The end of WinArrangeTwo ensures that the focus document is restored, positions and sizes the document selected from the list, then switches to the original document window with the statement

```
Activate CurDoc$
```

and ends by positioning and sizing it, and restoring the zoom factor stored in the first line of the macro.

## WinSideBySide

Arranging two documents one atop the other is useful if you are switching from one to the other, or stepping through a macro. However, to compare two documents line by line it would be preferable to position two document windows side by side. Here is a macro named WinSideBySide.

**DISK**
WinSideBySide—
Arranges two
documents side by
side

```
Sub Main
ZoomPercent = SelInfo(19)
ViewZoom .ZoomPercent = 100
Count = CountWindows()
If Count < 2 Then Goto Bye
x = Val(AppInfo$(6)) / 2     'width of document workspace divided by two
```

```
y = Val(AppInfo$(7))           'height of document workspace
CurDoc$ = WindowName$()
If Count > 2 Then
   Dim Names$(Count - 2)
   For i = 0 To Count - 2
      Names$(i) = WindowName$(((Window() + i) Mod Count) + 1)
   Next i
   Begin Dialog UserDialog 510, 50 + 12 * Count, "WinSideBySide"
      Text 8, 8, 338, 13, WindowName$() + " next to:"
      ListBox 18, 30, 350, 12 * Count - 8, Names$(), .Window
      OKButton 393, 24, 88, 21
      CancelButton 393, 48, 88, 21
   End Dialog
   Dim dlg As UserDialog
   dlg.Window = 0
   On Error Goto Bye
   Dialog dlg
   On Error Goto 0
   Activate Names$(dlg.Window)
Else
   NextWindow
End If
If DocMaximize() Then DocMaximize
DocMove  x, 0
DocSize x, y
Activate CurDoc$
DocMove 0, 0      'move active window
DocSize x, y
Bye:
ViewZoom .ZoomPercent = ZoomPercent
End Sub
```

The only difference between WinSideBySide and WinArrangeTwo lies in the calculation of the x and y dimension parameters. In WinArrangeTwo the height of the document workspace was halved. In WinSideBySide the width of the document workspace is halved.

## Style Utilities

Styles can get complicated.

As described in Chapter 3, styles actually reside in two locations: in the underlying template and in the document itself. Because the whole point of a template is to create a consistent model for a class of documents, it is important to be able to easily control the template styles. There are ways in Word to ensure that a template's styles are defined as you would wish. One way is always to create and modify styles directly on the template in question. However, most style manipulation happens within a document.

I have created three macros that aid in management of styles.

## SyncStyles

Styles begin in a template and are "copied" into a document at the time of the document's creation. Subsequently, you change an existing style or create a new style within the document, and must explicitly instruct Word if you would like the updated or new style to also be saved into the underlying template (see Chapter 3). This is done by checking the Add to Template check box at the bottom of the FormatStyle, Define dialog box.

Because you can easily forget to consistently save new or altered styles, it is often the case that a document and its template get out of synch. You might create a style in a document (and forget to save it to the template) that you subsequently want to make available to all documents ruled by that template.

One facility to move styles from one document to another, or from a template to a document, is found on the FormatStyle, Define dialog box:

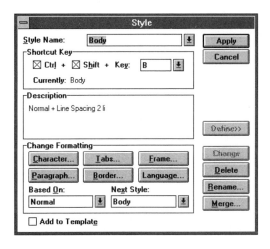

Notice the Merge button at the lower right. If you select this button you will see the dialog box shown in Figure 10.1.

There are several things to note about this facility. The list automatically displays the templates contained in the current DOT-Path. This makes sense, as you will normally be merging styles from a template to a document. But realize that you can also merge styles from another document. Also notice that the To Template button is grayed (unavailable) unless you select the template upon which the current document is based. I think this is a limitation. You should be able to copy styles to any template or document, but then they didn't ask me. The final thing to notice is how well hidden this feature is: You must go through four levels, make four selections, to access it. Because it is so deep in the menu structure, and because its use is not completely clear, most people ignore the power it provides.

**Figure 10.1**
Merge Styles
dialog box

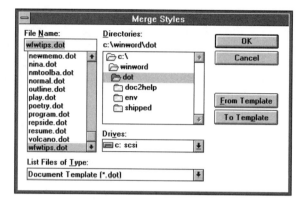

So, I present the following macro which takes a subset of the Format-Style, Define, Merge function and makes it easy to understand and use. SyncStyles presents you with two choices: to copy all styles in the current document to the underlying template or to copy all styles in the underlying template into the current document.

SyncStyles displays a dialog box (the specific document and template, of course, will vary) such as:

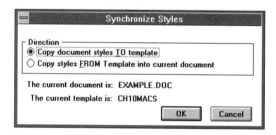

Here is a listing of SyncStyles.

**DISK**
SyncStyles—
Synchronizes styles
between a
document and its
template

```
Sub Main
If SelInfo(27) Then \
    Print "You are in a macro pane.  Cannot get template information." : Beep :
Goto Bye
If FilePrintPreview() Then \
    Print "You are in Print preview.  Cannot get template information." : Beep
: Goto Bye
If SelInfo(25) Or SelInfo(26) Or SelInfo(28)  Then
    If ViewPage() Then
        Print "Moving To body of document..."
        EditGoTo
```

```
        EditGoTo "\PrevSel1"
    Else
        Print "Closing pane…"
        ClosePane
    End If
End If
Dim dlg As FileTemplate
GetCurValues dlg
t$ = dlg.Template
If t$ = "" Then Beep : MsgBox("This is a template.") : Goto Bye
d$ = fFileName$(FileName$(0))
Begin Dialog UserDialog 528, 146, "Synchronize Styles"
    GroupBox 10, 19, 502, 52, " Direction "
    OptionGroup .Direction
        OptionButton 20, 31, 293, 16, "Copy document styles &TO template"
        OptionButton 20, 48, 412, 16, "Copy styles &FROM Template into current
        document"
    Text 20, 81, 499, 13, "The current document is:  " + d$
    Text 28, 100, 499, 13, "The current template is:  " + t$
    OKButton 314, 117, 88, 21
    CancelButton 420, 117, 88, 21
End Dialog
Redim dlg As UserDialog
On Error Goto Bye
Dialog dlg
FormatStyle .FileName = t$, .Merge, .Source = dlg.Direction
Bye:
End Sub

Function fFileName$(b$)
While Instr(b$, "\") <> 0
    b$ = Right$(b$, Len(b$) - Instr(b$, "\"))
Wend
fFileName$ = b$
End Function
```

There are several circumstances in which the FileTemplate command is unavailable. Since this macro must access FileTemplate to determine the name of the underlying template, the first thing the macro must do is a series of tests to find out where the insertion point is located.

The first test is

```
If SelInfo(27) Then
```

This checks to see if the insertion point is in a macro editing window. If so, a message appears on the status bar, a beep sounds, and the macro exits. Similarly,

```
If FilePrintPreview() Then
```

checks to see if we are in print preview mode (where FileTemplate is unavailable). The third test may seem familiar. It appeared in Chapter 7:

```
If SelInfo(25) Or SelInfo(26) Or SelInfo(28) Then
```

This line makes three calls to SelInfo to see if the insertion point is in a footnote, an annotation, or a header/footer pane. The code that follows responds to true in any of these three tests by taking action appropriate to either page or normal view.

You may wonder why I don't replace these tests with the single line:

```
If Not CommandValid("FileTemplate") Then Beep : Goto Bye
```

The answer: This call to CommandValid( ) will return an accurate answer *only* if you have not modified the built-in FileTemplate. Recall, CommandValid( ) always returns true on a user-macro (or on a bogus command name, for that matter). Since the next example macro is a modified version of FileTemplate, it is necessary to make SyncStyles smarter than CommandValid( ) would allow.

Back to the macro. The next section of code retrieves the template name and the document name:

```
Dim dlg As FileTemplate
GetCurValues dlg
t$ = dlg.Template
```

by defining an array variable the size and shape of the internal FileTemplate command. It then assigns the .Template array field to the string variable t$. The next line is interesting.

```
If t$ = "" Then Beep : MsgBox("This is a template.") : Goto Bye
```

Remember that I suggested you can disguise a template as a document (that is, you can save it with the extension DOC). This line is an example of error checking that anticipates the failure of memory. If the current "document" is actually a template, the string returned by the call to FileTemplate will be empty—in which case the macro pops up a reminder that this is a template (and so has no underlying template to merge styles to or from). Incidentally, the reason I don't gather both the template and document names by querying FileSummaryInfo is precisely because of the need to accommodate for disguised templates. If a template is disguised as a document, FileSummaryInfo mistakenly believes it is based on NORMAL.DOT.

The line

```
d$ = fFileName$(FileName$(0))
```

calls a user-function, fFileName$( ), passing to it the built-in function FileName$( ) as an argument. FileName$( ) with no argument or an argument of 0 returns the full path name of the current document. If the argument is an integer from 1 to 4, FileName$( ) returns the full path name of the corresponding document as displayed at the bottom of the File menu (the MRU, or Most Recently Used list of files). The user-function fFileName$ returns the file name portion of the full path name by locating the last backslash and returning the remainder of the string.

After all this preparation, SyncStyles displays the dialog box offering the two style copying options: to or from. The file name and template name are also listed.

The business end of SyncStyles is actually the single line:

```
FormatStyle  .FileName = t$, .Merge, .Source = dlg.Direction
```

This line passes FormatStyle the template name, the .Merge keyword, and the value returned from the option button selected on the dialog box (dlg.Direction is either 0 or 1) to specify the direction of the style merge.

## FileTemplate

Once a document is created based upon a template, both the styles and layout specifications are copied into the document. If you subsequently attach a different template, Word changes the various interface properties (macros, access methods, glossaries), but does not change the available styles or alter layout information. This is counter to what many expect. For instance, Word for DOS users are accustomed to changing style and layout definitions in a document by simply changing the underlying style sheet.

The following macro is proposed as a replacement for the built-in File-Template macro. In addition to presenting the normal FileTemplate dialog box, this custom FileTemplate allows you to check options to copy styles and/or margin settings from the template into the document.

**DISK**

FileTemplate—A version of FileTemplate that merges styles and layout information

```
Sub Main
If SelInfo(27) Then Print "You are in a macro pane. Cannot change templates." :
Beep : Goto Bye
If FilePrintPreview() Then Print "You are in print preview.  Cannot change
templates." : Beep : Goto Bye
If SelInfo(25) Or SelInfo(26) Or SelInfo(28)  Then
    If ViewPage() Then
        Print "Moving to body of document..."
        EditGoTo
        EditGoTo "\PrevSell"
    Else
        Print "Closing pane..."
        ClosePane
    End If
End If
```

```
Dim dlg As FileTemplate
GetCurValues dlg
If dlg.Template = "" Then \
    Beep : Print "This document is actually a template in disguise..." : Goto Bye
On Error Goto Bye
Dialog dlg
t$ = dlg.Template
FileTemplate dlg
Err = 0
Begin Dialog UserDialog 519, 114, "FileTemplate"
    GroupBox 10, 6, 497, 68, "Merge:"
    CheckBox 24, 23, 441, 16, "New template's &styles into the current
    document", .Style
    CheckBox 24, 50, 477, 16, "New template's &margin settings into the current
    document", .Margin
    OKButton 314, 87, 88, 21
    CancelButton 420, 87, 88, 21
End Dialog
Redim dlg As UserDialog
On Error Goto Bye
Dialog dlg
On Error Goto 0
Dim dlg_2 As FileSummaryInfo
GetCurValues dlg_2
t$ = dlg_2.Template
If dlg.Style Then FormatStyle    .FileName = t$, .Merge, .Source = 1
If dlg.Margin Then
    Print "Opening " + t$ + " to get the page and column setup..."
    DisableAutoMacros 1
    FileOpen  t$
    Redim dlg As FormatPageSetup
    GetCurValues dlg
    Redim dlg_2 As FormatColumns
    GetCurValues dlg_2
    DocClose 2
    DisableAutoMacros 0
    FormatPageSetup dlg
    FormatColumns dlg_2
End If
Bye:
End Sub
```

The beginning of this custom FileTemplate should look familiar. Like SyncStyles, this macro must determine the location of the insertion point and whether a call to the internal FileTemplate will result in an error. If all is well, the normal FileTemplate dialog box is displayed (so that you can select a new template to attach).

After attaching a template (either a new template or "reattaching" the current template), a second dialog box is displayed:

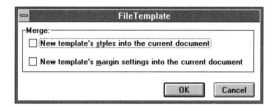

This allows you to select which further actions to perform. Note that these are check boxes, so you can select one, both, or none. The remainder of the macro examines the value returned by the user dialog box for the two check boxes and performs accordingly.

The lines

```
Dim dlg_2 As FileSummaryInfo
GetCurValues dlg_2
t$ = dlg_2.Template
```

retrieve the full path to the new template. By using FileSummaryInfo (rather than the variable created by calling the FileTemplate dialog box) we can handle various situations, such as attaching a template that is not in your DOT-Path, and systems on which there is no DOT-Path defined in the WIN.INI.

If the first check box is selected, the line

```
If dlg.Style Then FormatStyle .FileName = t$, .Merge, .Source = 1
```

merges styles from the template into the document.

If the second dialog box is selected, a more complex series of actions must be executed to copy the underlying template's margin and column settings into the current document.

If dlg.Margin is true (that is, checked), the template is opened. By using the DisableAutoMacros statement we circumvent execution of the template's AutoOpen macro (if there is one). Then comes a neat trick. Two array variables, dlg and dlg_2, are dimensioned to hold the current values of the FormatPageSetup and FormatColumns commands.

```
Redim dlg As FormatPageSetup
GetCurValues dlg
Redim dlg_2 As FormatColumns
GetCurValues dlg_2
```

By executing these commands on the open template we are storing the page and column setup information as defined in the template.

The template is then closed, auto macros are reenabled, and finally, with the focus on the orginal document, the FormatPageSetup and FormatColumns commands are executed with the array variables as the parameter:

```
FormatPageSetup dlg
FormatColumns dlg_2
```

copying the settings of FormatPageSetup and FormatColumns from the template to the document. This illustrates how to query an internal command macro, gathering *all* the values controlled by that command, and then passing the stored values to a subsequent call to the queried command, in this case getting the values on the template itself, and then passing the values to the document.

## DeleteIdleStyles

There are 36 built-in styles, each associated with a particular function of Word. These reserved style names are added to a document's list of styles as you implement functions that use a reserved style. As noted in Chapter 3, once these style names are added to a document there is no way to remove them.

However, you can delete user-defined styles. If you merge styles from several templates, the list of user styles may become cumbersome. It is also possible that a particular document does not require all the styles defined by the underlying template. In either of these cases, it would be nice to have a way to clean out the list of user styles, removing any that will not be used in the current document.

DeleteIdleStyles examines the list of available styles and searches the current document for each. If it finds the style, it does nothing. If it does not find the style, it removes it from the list. Sounds simple. Actually it requires a bit of programming gymnastics.

**DISK**
DeleteIdleStyles—
Removes idle user
styles from the
current document

```
Dim Shared TempString$
Sub Main
If SelInfo(27) Then Print "Cannot be run on a macro editing window…" : Beep :
Goto Bye
TempString$ = "This macro will permanently remove any user-defined styles that
are not active in the current document. This does not remove styles from the
underlying template.  Do you want to continue?"
If Not MsgBox(TempString$, "DeleteIdleStyles", 33) Then Goto Bye
'The standard styles
TempString$ = "annotation reference,annotation text,footer,footnote " + \
"reference,footnote text,header,heading 1,heading 2,heading 3,"+ \
"heading 4,heading 5,heading 6,heading 7,heading 8,heading 9,index 1,"+ \
"index 2,index 3,index 4,index 5,index 6,index 7,index heading," + \
"line number,Normal,Normal Indent,toc 1,toc 2,toc 3,toc 4,toc 5,toc 6,"+ \
"toc 7,toc 8,envelopeaddress,envelopereturn"
Dim s$(CountStyles(0) - 1)
```

```
Print "Gathering all styles in this document…"
For x = 1 To CountStyles(0)
   s$(x - 1) = StyleName$(x)
Next
For c = 0 To CountStyles() - 1
InsertBookmark "CurrentPosition"
StartOfDocument
If Not Check(s$(c))  Then'See if the style is built in
   EditFindStyle .Style = "" + s$(c)
   EditFind .Find = "", .WholeWord = 0, .MatchCase = 0, .Direction = 2, .Format
= 1
   Log = 2
   Log = EditFindFound()
   If Log = 0 Then                          'Didn't find it
      On Error Resume Next
      FormatStyle .Name = s$(c), .Delete       'So delete it
      Print "Deleting idle user style: " + s$(c)
   Else
      Print "Found user style: " + s$(c)         'Found it
   End If
Else
   Print "Can't delete built in style " + s$(c)
End If
Next c
Beep : Print "Done removing idle styles."
If ExistingBookmark("CurrentPosition") Then
   EditGoTo "CurrentPosition"
   InsertBookmark "CurrentPosition", .Delete
End If
EditFindClearFormatting
Bye:
End Sub

Function Check(Sty$)
   n = Instr(1, TempString$, Sty$)
   If n = 0 Then check = 0 Else check = - 1
End Function
```

The first thing DeleteIdleStyles does is warn the user what's about to happen:

```
TempString$ = "This macro will permanently remove any user-defined styles that
are not active in the current document. This does not remove styles from the
underlying template.  Do you want to continue?"
If Not MsgBox(TempString$, "DeleteIdleStyles", 33) Then Goto Bye
```

Since it is possible to delete more than you intend, this warning is very necessary. DeleteIdleStyles assumes that if you want to keep a style, there is a paragraph somewhere in the body of the document formatted in that style. So, make sure you are willing to lose all other styles. Actually, you won't be deleting styles from the template, just from this document. Therefore, no style that is also in a template is irrevocably deleted.

If the answer to the above posed warning is yes, the variable TempString$ is reused. It is assigned a very long string consisting of a comma-delimited list of all the reserved style names:

```
TempString$ = "annotation reference,annotation text,footer,footnote " + \
"reference,footnote text,header,heading 1,heading 2,heading 3,"+ \
"heading 4,heading 5,heading 6,heading 7,heading 8,heading 9,index 1,"+ \
"index 2,index 3,index 4,index 5,index 6,index 7,index heading," + \
"line number,Normal,Normal Indent,toc 1,toc 2,toc 3,toc 4,toc 5,toc 6,"+ \
"toc 7,toc 8,envelopeaddress,envelopereturn"
```

Note that TempString$ has been declared as a shared variable because this string variable will be examined in the user-function Check() to determine if a style is reserved.

DeleteIdleStyles uses the internal function CountStyles() to return the number of user styles in the document in conjunction with StyleName$() to create a user-array to hold each style name:

```
Dim s$(CountStyles(0) - 1)
Print "Gathering all styles in this document…"
For x = 1 To CountStyles(0)
   s$(x - 1) = StyleName$(x)
Next
```

Know that if a document has many styles, the creation of the s$() array can take what seems like an eternity.

DeleteIdleStyles then steps through the array with a For…Next loop:

```
For c = 0 To CountStyles() - 1
```

checking, with a user-function, if the style name held by the user-array s$(c) is contained in the TempString$ variable. If Check(s$(c)) returns true, the loop increments to the next array item. If this call to Check() is false, meaning that the named style is not reserved, the macro executes the following group of statements:

```
EditFindStyle .Style = "" + s$(c)
EditFind .Find = "", .WholeWord = 0, .MatchCase = 0, .Direction = 2, .Format = 1
Log = 2
Log = EditFindFound()
If Log = 0 Then                          'Didn't find it
   On Error Resume Next
   FormatStyle .Name = s$(c), .Delete    'So delete it
   Print "Deleting idle user style: " + s$(c)
Else
   Print "Found user style: " + s$(c)    'Found it
End If
```

First: Set the style to look for as s$(c), and then look for it. Notice that the Edit-Find statement has a parameter named .Direction. This is an important keyword. If .Direction is set to 2, the search proceeds to the end of the document without the message box asking if you want to continue searching from the beginning of the document when no further forward instance is encountered.

To know whether the style is found, the macro examines the built-in function EditFindFound( ). This is an extremely useful function. It is set to 0 when a search is not successful, to -1 when the search item is found.

If Log (the integer variable assigned the result of EditFindFound()) is 0, meaning the style was not found, remove it from the list of styles. If the named style was found, increment the loop and look for the next style in the list.

DeleteIdleStyles is polite. It returns the cursor to the current location when it is complete by creating a temporary bookmark. Note how the return to the bookmark CurrentPosition is accomplished:

```
If ExistingBookmark("CurrentPosition") Then
    EditGoTo "CurrentPosition"
    InsertBookmark "CurrentPosition", .Delete
End If
```

It is always a good idea to make sure a bookmark exists before calling Edit-GoTo. Notice also that the macro cleans up after itself, deleting the temporary bookmark before exiting.

## Making a Better Bookmark

A bookmark can be used in one of two ways: as a marker to a location or as a marker that references a text string. Here are a few rules for bookmarks: A bookmark name cannot be longer than 20 characters; a bookmark can range in size from an insertion point to an entire document; there is a limit of 450 bookmarks in a single document.

As markers for locations, bookmarks are connected to the EditGoTo command (accessed most easily with F5). As reference pointers to the marked text (rather than the location of the marked text), bookmarks are connected to the {ref} field. We saw a use of bookmarks and {ref} fields in Chapter 9 as a way to implement document-specific variables. Other uses of bookmarks as reference pointers include form letters (where a defined bookmark can be referenced in multiple places) and as cross-references from one document to another. When you insert one file into another file, you can specify that the link be formed specifically to a bookmark delineated section of the second file. (For more information on using bookmarks when creating links between files, see Chapters 36 and 40 in the *Word User's Guide.*)

There is, however, one major limitation with bookmarks. If you propose a bookmark name that already exists, you are not warned. The existing bookmark is replaced with the new one. This makes it very simple to inadvertently over-write a bookmark.

The macros that follow provide a way around this limitation.

## InsertSmartMark

InsertSmartMark prompts the user for a bookmark name using a custom dia-log box (this alone is an advance on the built-in InsertBookmark command, Ctrl+Shift+F5, which uses the status line for input) and then checks to see if the name entered by the user already exists as a bookmark name.

**DISK**
InsertSmartMark—
Creates a unique
bookmark

```
Sub Main
Again: Err = 0                          'label marking start; set Err To 0
Mark$ = GetMark$                        'Call the user Function
On Error Goto Invalid                   'set an Error trap For insertion Error
If Mark$ <> "" Then InsertBookmark Mark$        'Insert the bookmark If Mark$
                                                'isn't empty

Goto Bye                                 'jump To the End If successful
Invalid:
Goto Again                               'jump To beginning If not successful
Bye:
End Sub


Function GetMark$
Start:
Begin Dialog UserDialog 233, 70, "Edit Bookmark"
If Exists Then
    Text 10, 6, 212, 13, "Name in use; enter another:"
Else
    Text 10, 6, 185, 13, "Enter a bookmark Name:"
End If
    TextBox 10, 22, 160, 18, .Mark
    OKButton 10, 43, 88, 21
    CancelButton 114, 43, 88, 21
End Dialog
Dim dlg As UserDialog
On Error Goto fEnd
dlg.Mark = Mark$
Dialog dlg
Exists = 0                       'reset Exists variable
Mark$ = dlg.Mark
If Len(Mark$) > 20 Then
    MsgBox "Bookmark Name is" + Str$(Len(Mark$) - 20) + " characters too long."
    Goto Start
End If
If ExistingBookmark(Mark$) Then Exists = - 1 : Goto Start
GetMark$ = Mark$
fEnd:
End Function
```

InsertSmartMark displays the following dialog box:

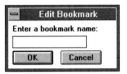

The part of InsertSmartMark that does most of the work is the user-function GetMark$. This function displays the dialog box and then checks if the name proposed by the user is longer than the legal limit of 20 characters. If it is, the dialog box is redisplayed. GetMark$ then determines if the proposed name already exists. It displays the dialog box until one of two things happens: either the user cancels, or the name proposed is unique and fewer than 20 characters long.

Notice one neat trick—the macro dynamically changes the prompt contained on the dialog box depending on the value of the variable Exists:

```
If Exists Then
    Text 10, 6, 264, 13, "Name in use; enter another:"
Else
    Text 10, 6, 264, 13, "Enter a bookmark Name:"
End If
```

This variable is set to true if the proposed bookmark name already exists with the line:

```
If ExistingBookmark(Mark$) Then Exists = - 1 : Goto Start
```

This is a useful trick. It allows you to create much more informative dialog boxes.

The main subroutine follows this logic: If the string variable Mark$ (which holds the results of the user-function GetMark$) is empty (which means the dialog box was canceled), quit; if Mark$ is not empty, insert a bookmark named Mark$. If an error occurs when inserting the bookmark—which would happen if the bookmark name contained an invalid character—return to the top of the macro and call GetMark$ again.

## InsertSmarterMark

Once you know that a proposed bookmark name exists, you can do several different things. In InsertSmartMark, all the macro does is prompt you again for a different name. You could jump to the existing bookmark and see if you wanted to use the name again anyway. Or, as in InsertSmarterMark, you could automatically alter the proposed bookmark name with a suffix.

**DISK**
InsertSmarterMark—
Automatically
increments an
existing bookmark
name

```
Sub Main
Again: Err = 0                          'label marking start; set Err To 0
Mark$ = GetMark$                        'Call the user Function
On Error Goto Invalid                   'set an Error trap For insertion Error
If Mark$ <> "" Then InsertBookmark Mark$          'Insert the bookmark If Mark$
                                                  'isn't empty
Goto Bye                                'jump To the End If successful
Invalid:
Goto Again                              'jump To beginning If not successful
Bye:
End Sub


Function GetMark$
Start:
Begin Dialog UserDialog 233, 70, "Edit Bookmark"
If Exists Then
   Text 10, 6, 212, 13, "Name in use; enter another:"
Else
   Text 10, 6, 185, 13, "Enter a bookmark Name:"
End If
   TextBox 10, 22, 160, 18, .Mark
   OKButton 10, 43, 88, 21
   CancelButton 114, 43, 88, 21
End Dialog
Dim dlg As UserDialog
On Error Goto fEnd
dlg.Mark = Mark$
Dialog dlg
Exists = 0
Mark$ = dlg.Mark
If Len(Mark$) > 20 Then
   MsgBox "Bookmark Name is" + Str$(Len(Mark$) - 20) + " characters too long."
   Goto Start
End If
If ExistingBookmark(Mark$) Then
   Exists = - 1
   Mark$ = Increment$(Mark$)
   Goto Start
End If
GetMark$ = Mark$
fEnd:
End Function


Function Increment$(T$)
   x = 2
   If x < 10 Then pad$ = "0" Else pad$ = ""
   While ExistingBookmark(T$ + pad$ + Mid$(Str$(x), 2))
      x = x + 1
```

```
   Wend
   If x < 10 Then x$ = "0" + Mid$(Str$(x), 2) Else x$ = Mid$(Str$(x), 2)
   t$ = t$ + x$
Increment$ = t$
End Function
```

The difference between InsertSmartMark and InsertSmarterMark lies in what happens if a bookmark already exists. In the former, the macro simply loops for reediting:

```
If ExistingBookmark(Mark$) Then Exists = - 1 : Goto Start
```

In the latter, a second user-function named Increment$( ) is called to add a suffix to the proposed name before redisplaying the dialog box:

```
If ExistingBookmark(Mark$) Then
   Exists = - 1
   Mark$ = Increment$(Mark$)
   Goto Start
End If
```

The incremented bookmark name consists of the base name plus a suffix representing the incidence of the bookmark name plus one. For instance, if the document already contains a bookmark named "Test", Increment$("Test") would return "Test02". If the document contains both "Test" and "Test02", Increment$("Test") would return "Test03", and so on. The best way to get a feel for this macro is to run it and propose the same name for a bookmark several times.

# The Missing Print Commands

Word's printing command is "brain-dead," a characterization often applied to a function that is not all it could, or should, be. This may seem harsh. After all, you can print the document (all, this page, the current selection, from one page to another), with or without annotations, file summary information, styles, glossaries, or key assignments. However, the built-in FilePrint command cannot handle two extremely useful tasks: There is no way to print either all odd or all even pages; there is no way to print a list of discrete page numbers (that is, though you can print from 3 to 7, you cannot print 3, 5, and 7 with one command).

The following two macros offer possible solutions for both of these inadequacies in FilePrint.

## PrintOddEven

Some printers allow for what is called *duplex* printing: printing on both sides of the page. The only way to accomplish this if you do not have a duplex-capable printer is to print the document in two passes: print all odd pages then, after reinserting the pages into the printer, all even.

The following macro, PrintOddEven, enables you to print either all odd or all even pages of the current document:

**DISK**

PrintOddEven—
Prints all odd or all
even pages of the
current document

```
Sub Main
If SelInfo(27) Then Beep : Goto bye
Macro$ = "PrintOddEven"
Ver$ = "2.3 (zd)"
MultiSection = (NumSections > 1)
vp = ViewPage()
InsertBookmark "CurrentPosition"
Again:
Begin Dialog UserDialog 283, 104, Macro$ + " " + ver$
    GroupBox 14, 6, 132, 71, "Print:"
    PushButton 24, 22, 111, 21, "O&dd pages"
    PushButton 24, 48, 111, 21, "&Even pages"
    CancelButton 184, 12, 88, 21
    PushButton 184, 38, 88, 21, "&Setup..."
    PushButton 183, 64, 88, 21, "&Options"
    If MultiSection Then CheckBox 10, 82, 161, 16, "Print &blank pages", .Blank
Dim Dlg As UserDialog
End Dialog
If MultiSection Then dlg.Blank = 1
Choice = Dialog(Dlg, 1)
If MultiSection Then Blank = (dlg.Blank = 1) Else Blank = 0
If Choice = 0 Then
    Goto bye
ElseIf Choice = 3 Then
    FilePrintSetup$
    Goto Again
ElseIf Choice = 4 Then
    ToolsOptionsPrint$
    Goto Again
Else
    If Blank = 0 And Not vp Then ViewPage
    If Blank = 1 And vp Then ViewNormal
    DoPrint(Choice, Blank)
    If vp Then ViewPage Else ViewNormal
End If
Print " " : Beep
Bye:
EditGoTo "CurrentPosition"
InsertBookmark "CurrentPosition", .Delete
End Sub
```

```
Sub DoPrint(Start, Blank)
StartOfDocument
ToolsRepaginateNow
Redim dlg As FileSummaryInfo
GetCurValues dlg
TotalPages = Val(Dlg.NumPages)
Count = 0
While pNum < TotalPages
    If  Flag Then EditGoTo "+"
    pPage = SelInfo(3)
    Page = SelInfo(1)
    s$ = Mid$(Str$(SelInfo(2)), 2)
    vPage$ = Mid$(Str$(Page), 2)
    If  (Count + 1 Mod 20) = 0 Then
        MsgBox "Twenty pages in queue for printing... Select OK after a bit."
        Count = 1
    End If
    If ((Start = 1) And IsEven(Page)) Or((Start = 2) And Not IsEven(Page)) Then
        Print "Skipping page " + vPage$ + " of Section " + s$
        Flag = - 1
        If Blank And(Page - lPage) = 2 Then
            f$ = "p" + Mid$(Str$(Page - 1), 2) + "s" + s$ : t$ = f$
            FilePrint  .From = f$, .To = t$, .Range = 3
            Print "Page " + vPage$ + " of Section " + s$ + " - " + f$+" - " + t$
            Count = Count + 1 : Flag = 0
        End If
    Else
        f$ = "p" + vPage$ + "s" + s$ : t$ = f$
        Print "Page " + vPage$ + " of Section " + s$ + " - " + f$ + " - " + t$
        FilePrint  .From = f$, .To = t$, .Range = 3
        Count = Count + 1 : Flag = - 1
    End If
    lPage = Page
    pNum = pPage
Wend
End Sub


Function IsEven(x)
    If x Mod 2 = 0 Then IsEven = - 1
End Function


Function NumSections
    EditSelectAll
    NumSections = SelInfo(2)
    EditGoTo "CurrentPosition"
End Function
```

PrintOddEven presents a dialog box with five buttons and a check box:

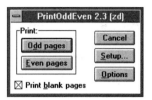

Before we examine how this macro works, some discussion of multisectioned documents is required. It is possible to specify that a section's page numbering be forced to the next odd or the next even page. For instance, when creating a manuscript that will be sent to a printer, a new chapter usually begins on an odd page. So, you might have a first section containing three pages and a second section formatted in FormatSectionLayout to begin on the next odd page, page 5. When you print such a document using the normal FilePrint command, what comes out of the printer will be pages 1–3, a blank page (meant as a "filler" for the skipped page 4), and page 5. The same effect is achieved in PrintOddEven by enabling the Print blank pages check box (the default). If you have a document with multiple sections, and those sections are formatted to be on either the next odd or next even page, you must print the blank pages.

In fact, the option to print blank pages only has meaning in a multisectioned document. Because of this, one of the first things PrintOddEven does is check to see if the current document contains more than one section. It does this with the line:

```
MultiSection =(NumSections > 1)
```

which calls the user-function:

```
Function NumSections
EditSelectAll
NumSections = SelInfo(2)
EditGoTo "CurrentPosition"
End Function
```

Notice that this user-function calls SelInfo(2), which normally returns the number of the section containing the insertion point. If, however, the selection covers the entire document, as it does after the call to EditSelectAll, SelInfo(2) will return the total number of sections in the document.

After determining if the document is multisectioned, and setting a Boolean variable accordingly, PrintOddEven can customize the dialog box. The check box asking if you want to print blank pages will only appear if it has relevance:

```
If MultiSection Then CheckBox 10, 82, 161, 16, "Print &blank pages", .Blank
```

Notice as well that before displaying the dialog box PrintOddEven does two bits of preparation—it sets a variable to hold the current state of ViewPage( ) and it drops a temporary bookmark:

```
vp = ViewPage( )
InsertBookmark "CurrentPosition"
```

Because of an oddity (which I could not fathom), printing blank pages only works if the document is *not* in page view; not printing blank pages works only if you *are* in page view. The value stored in the variable vp will be used to toggle to the necessary view mode before executing the print run and then to toggle back to the current state before the macro finishes.

After displaying the dialog box and storing the number of the button chosen in the variable Choice, PrintOddEven checks the Boolean MultiSection. If MultiSection is true, a new variable blank is set to true or false according to the state of the check box. If MultiSection is false, Blank is set to false:

```
If MultiSection Then Blank = (dlg.Blank = 1) Else Blank = 0
```

PrintOddEven then evaluates Choice to see which of the five possible values it contains:

```
If Choice = 0 Then
    Goto bye
ElseIf Choice = 3 Then
    FilePrintSetup$
    Goto Again
ElseIf Choice = 4 Then
    ToolsOptionsPrint$
    Goto Again
```

If Choice is equal to 0, the macro has been canceled. If Choice is equal to 3, PrintOddEven executes the built-in command macro FilePrinterSetup and then redisplays the dialog box. If Choice is equal to 4, PrintOddEven executes the built-in command macro ToolsOptionsPrinter and then redisplays the dialog box.

**NOTE.** *Although you can access the ToolsOptionsPrinter dialog box from PrintOddEven, enabling Reverse Print Order will have no effect.*

The If…Then control structure then handles the only remaining two possibilities. If Choice is equal to either 1 or 2, PrintOddEven prepares to execute a print run, and then calls the user-subroutine DoPrint, passing it the value of Choice (1 for odd, 2 for even), and the variable Blank:

```
Else
    If Blank = 0 And Not vp Then ViewPage
    If Blank = 1 And vp Then ViewNormal
    DoPrint(Choice, Blank)
    If vp Then ViewPage Else ViewNormal
    DoPrint(Choice, Blank)
    If Not vp Then ViewNormal
End If
```

The user-subroutine DoPrint actually does the work. And because of the complications possible in a multisectioned documents, the logic is somewhat complex:

```
Sub DoPrint(Start, Blank)
StartOfDocument
ToolsRepaginateNow
Redim dlg As FileSummaryInfo
GetCurValues dlg
TotalPages = Val(Dlg.NumPages)
Count = 0
While pNum < TotalPages
    If Flag Then EditGoTo "+"
    pPage = SelInfo(3)
    Page = SelInfo(1)
    s$ = Mid$(Str$(SelInfo(2)), 2)
    vPage$ = Mid$(Str$(Page), 2)
    If (Count + 1 Mod 20) = 0 Then
        MsgBox "Twenty pages in queue for printing... Select OK after a bit."
        Count = 1
    End If
    If ((Start = 1) And IsEven(Page)) Or((Start = 2) And Not IsEven(Page)) Then
        Print "Skipping page " + vPage$ + " of Section " + s$
        Flag = - 1
        If Blank And(Page - 1Page) = 2 Then
            f$ = "p" + Mid$(Str$(Page - 1), 2) + "s" + s$ : t$ = f$
            FilePrint .From = f$, .To = t$, .Range = 3
            Print "Page "+ vPage$ +" of Section "+ s$ +" - "+ f$ +" - "+ t$
            Count = Count + 1 : Flag = 0
        End If
    Else
        f$ = "p" + vPage$ + "s" + s$ : t$ = f$
        Print "Printing page "+vPage$+" of Section "+s$+" - "+f$+" - "+t$
        FilePrint .From = f$, .To = t$, .Range = 3
        Count = Count + 1 : Flag = - 1
    End If
```

```
       lPage = Page
       pNum = pPage
Wend
End Sub
```

The first thing DoPrint does is to repaginate the document. This is necessary to ensure that we know the document's current page count. The center of this subroutine is a While...Wend loop which steps through the document one page at a time. Within this loop there are three parts. First, a variable is checked to see if it is time to move to the next page and a series of variables is created to hold the physical page, the virtual page, and the section number:

```
If Flag Then EditGoTo "+"
pPage = SelInfo(3)
VirPage = SelInfo(1)
s$ = Mid$(Str$(SelInfo(2)), 2)
vPage$ = Mid$(Str$(Page), 2)
```

The physical page is the sequential page, disregarding the page number as specified in FormatSectionLayout. The virtual page is the page number. We need to know both in order to accommodate for multisectioned documents.

The second section of the loop calculates if twenty individual pages have been printed, and if so, presents a dialog box:

```
If (Count + 1 Mod 20) = 0 Then
    MsgBox "Twenty pages in queue for printing... Select OK after a bit."
    Count = 1
End If
```

The reason for this is simple: Every page sent to the printer constitutes a separate "print job." If your current printer is attached to the Windows Print Manager application, then every time you call FilePrint Windows generates a temporary file, a "spool file" on disk (in the directory specified by the environment variable Temp if one is defined). The Print Manager can only handle 20 discrete print jobs at a time. Since this macro steps through the entire document and prints each page (odd or even) as a separate print job, a document longer than 40 pages will exceed this limit. By displaying a dialog box, you can pause to allow the print queue to diminish before continuing.

The third portion of the loop is the most complicated. The ominous looking line:

```
If ((Start = 1) And IsEven(Page)) Or((Start = 2) And Not IsEven(Page)) Then
```

determines if the current page falls into the range being printed. The line could be rephrased in plain English as: "If the range to print is odd and the current page is even or if the range to print is even and the current page is odd...."

The user-function IsEven returns true if the number passed as its parameter is even:

```
Function IsEven(x)
    If x Mod 2 = 0 Then IsEven = - 1
End Function
```

If either case is true, the insertion point is in a page not to be printed. However, this is also the time to check and see if we need to print a blank page. This is done with the conditional loop:

```
If Blank  And(Page - lPage) = 2 Then
    f$ = "p" + Mid$(Str$(Page - 1), 2) + "s" + s$ : t$ = f$
    FilePrint  .From = f$, .To = t$, .Range = 3
    Print "Printing page "+vPage$+" of Section "+s$+" - "+f$+" - "+t$
    Count = Count + 1 : Flag = 0
End If
```

This loop first checks the Boolean variable Blank. If it is false, nothing happens. If it is true, the current last page printed is subtracted from the current page. If the result is precisely 2, meaning we skipped a page, then a print command is created that will print a blank page. For instance, if the current range is even, the current page is 5, and the last page printed was 3, it is safe to assume the insertion point is located in the first page of a section that has been formatted to start page numbering on the next odd page. If the Print blank pages check box is on, now is the time to print a blank page 4.

The remainder of the loop executes if the current page falls into the range to be printed:

```
Else
    f$ = "p" + vPage$ + "s" + s$ : t$ = f$
    Print "Printing page "+vPage$+" of Section "+s$+" - "+f$+" - "+t$
    FilePrint  .From = f$, .To = t$, .Range = 3
    Count = Count + 1 : Flag = - 1
End If
```

Notice that the print command specifies the page number and section number. The number of pages printed is incremented and the flag forcing the loop to move to the next page is set to true.

Before the loop moves to the next page, two variables are updated:

```
pNum = Page
lPage = pPage
```

The first variable is used to determine when the loop has reached the last page of the document. The second variable contains the page number just evaluated.

After DoPrint reaches the last page, control is returned to the main sub-routine. The view setting is reset:

```
If vp Then ViewPage Else ViewNormal
```

The insertion point is returned to the temporary bookmark set when the macro began:

```
EditGoTo "CurrentPosition"
InsertBookmark "CurrentPosition", .Delete
```

**NOTE.** *PrintOddEven is what I call a* tender macro. *It relies heavily on Word's way of thinking about page numbering, which in my experience can be some-what flaky. I have yet to figure out why, for instance, the macro behaves differ-ently in page view and normal view when you are not printing blank pages in a multisectioned document. I'm in the odd position of admitting the macro seems to work, but I'm not entirely sure* why *it works. And the concomitant admis-sion: I'm not entirely sure what can break it. Bear this general rule in mind: The more complicated the section divisions and the number format applied to these multiple sections, the higher the chances the macro will choke. Let's hope Microsoft builds in the ability to print all odd or even pages in the next release.*

Printing on both sides of the page can be somewhat confusing. There is no easy way to describe the process since every printer has a slightly different feed mechanism. In general, you want to print all the odd pages first, uncol-lated (that is, so that the top of the stack is the last page). You then reinsert the pages and print the even pages. If that sounds a little abstract, it is be-cause the physical layout of every printer is different. Once you figure out what's required by your printer, the above will seem obvious.

## PrintListOfPages

Although FilePrint allows you to print a single range of pages, it does not allow you to specify a list of single pages, or more than one range at a time. Here is a macro named PrintListOfPages that allows you to create a list of ranges to print.

**DISK**
PrintListOfPages—
Prints multiple page
ranges in a single
pass

```
Sub Main
Begin Dialog UserDialog 308, 149, "Print List"
    Text 10, 6, 240, 13, "Enter pages To Print, separating"
    Text 10, 21, 252, 13, "discrete pages with commas, and"
    Text 10, 36, 265, 13, "a consecutive range with hyphens:"
    Text 10, 55, 241, 13, "e.g. 3,10,11-15,20,p2s3-p10s3"
    TextBox 10, 71, 287, 18, .RangeString
    OKButton 105, 96, 88, 21
    CancelButton 202, 96, 88, 21
    PushButton 203, 122, 88, 21, "&Setup…"
```

```
End Dialog
Dim dlg As UserDialog
Again:
Choice = Dialog(dlg)
If Choice = 0 Then
    Goto Bye
ElseIf Choice = 1 Then
    FilePrintSetup$
    Goto Again
Else
    If dlg.RangeString = "" Then FilePrint$ : Goto Bye
    If Not PrintRange(dlg.RangeString) Then Goto Again
End If
Bye:
End Sub


Function PrintRange(RangeString$)
Comma$ = ","
Hyphen$ = "-"
On Error Goto ErrMsg
While Instr(RangeString$, Comma$)
    F$ = Left$(RangeString$, Instr(RangeString$, Comma$) - 1)
    RangeString$ = Mid$(RangeString$, Instr(RangeString$, Comma$) + 1)
    If Instr(F$, Hyphen$) Then
        From$ = Left$(f$, Instr(F$, Hyphen$) - 1)
        To$ = Mid$(F$, Instr(F$, Hyphen$) + 1)
    Else
        From$ = F$ : To$ = F$
    End If
        FilePrint .Type = 0, .Range = 3, \
         .From = From$, \
         .To = To$
Wend
f$ = RangeString$
    If Instr(F$, Hyphen$) Then
        From$ = Left$(f$, Instr(F$, Hyphen$) - 1)
        To$ = Mid$(F$, Instr(F$, Hyphen$) + 1)
    Else
        From$ = F$ : To$ = F$
    End If
FilePrint .Type = 0, .Range = 3, \
    .From = From$, \
    .To = To$
PrintRange = - 1   ' successful
Goto Bye
ErrMsg:
MsgBox "Something's wrong. Try again."
PrintRange = 0    'a problem
Bye:
End Function
```

When you execute PrintListOfPages, you will see the following dialog box:

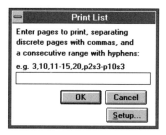

The list of pages to be printed must be entered in the following format: Single pages are separated by commas (for example: 1,6,10); consecutive ranges are entered with a hyphen between starting and ending pages (for example: 7-20); references to specific pages within a specific section are in the same format as that acceptable to FilePrint (for example: p2s3 or p1s3-p20s3). Like PrintOddEven, PrintListOfPages allows you to run the built-in FilePrintSetup.

The user-function PrintRange(RangeString$) uses a series of string functions to parse the comma-delimited list of pages and/or page ranges. The While...Wend loop examines the character or characters from the start of the variable RangeString$ to the first comma, then changes the variable Range-String$ to the portion of the string to the left of the first comma. This is done with the two lines:

```
F$ = Left$(RangeString$, Instr(RangeString$, Comma$) - 1)
RangeString$ = Mid$(RangeString$, Instr(RangeString$, Comma$) + 1)
```

F$ holds the portion of the string from the beginning to the first comma; RangeString$ is then assigned from the character after the first comma to the end.

The variable F$ is then examined to determine if it contains a hyphen, and if so is parsed into two strings:

```
If Instr(F$, Hyphen$) Then
   From$ = Left$(f$, Instr(F$, Hyphen$) - 1)
   To$ =  Mid$(F$, Instr(F$, Hyphen$) + 1)
Else
   From$ = F$ : To$ = F$
End If
```

If F$ does contain a hyphen, the variable From$ is assigned the portion to the left of the hyphen; the variable To$ is assigned the portion of the string to the right of the hyphen. If there is no hyphen within F$, then both From$ and To$ are assigned the value of F$.

Once the From$ and To$ variables are filled, FilePrint is called:

```
FilePrint .Type = 0, .Range = 3, \
    .From = From$, \
    .To = To$
```

with the .Range parameter set to 3 (a range of pages), .From set to From$, and .To set to To$.

The While...Wend structure then loops to handle the next portion of the list, that is, the next portion up to the first of the remaining commas. The While...Wend loop ends when RangeString$ no longer contains a comma. However, this leaves a single string still to parse and process, which is why after the While...Wend loop there is another call to the If...Then structure looking for a hyphen, and another call to FilePrint.

The most interesting thing about this macro is the use of a user-function rather than a user-subroutine to do the dirty work of parsing the list of pages entered by the user. This allows you to check if the actual printing was successful. The value of the function PrintRange is set to false if the various string manipulations used to parse the list of pages caused an error. It is set to true if all goes well. Because of this use of a function, the line:

```
If Not PrintRange(dlg.RangeString) Then Goto Again
```

returns to the dialog box when an error is encountered.

Also note that PrintListOfPages will execute the standard FilePrint if the edit box intended for the list of pages is left empty:

```
If dlg.RangeString = "" Then FilePrint$ : Goto Bye
```

## Start-up Directory Options

Windows allows you to launch a program in several different ways. By default Windows installs Program Manager as the shell. In this application you click on an icon and the associated program is loaded with an optional parameter in an optional start-up directory. A second way to launch an application is to double-click on a specific file listed within the File Manager.

When you install Word it does two things: it places the directory containing the Word program files into your DOS path, which allows you to launch Word from any directory; and it places a line in your WIN.INI file which associates WINWORD.EXE with the extensions DOC and DOT, which means double-clicking on a DOC file in File Manager would launch Word and load that file.

If you do not have the Word directory in your DOS path, you can still launch documents using File Manager if you associate the full path name pointing to WINWORD.EXE in the extensions section of WIN.INI. For example:

```
[Extensions]
doc=C:\WINWORD\WINWORD.EXE ^.doc
dot=C:\WINWORD\WINWORD.EXE ^.dot
rtf=C:\WINWORD\WINWORD.EXE ^.rtf
```

Word also allows you to create a default start-up directory by specifying the desired path next to the keyword DOC-Path under the Microsoft Word 2.0 section of WIN.INI. At first blush this might seem like a good idea. In fact, it is limiting. For example, if you have such a start-up DOC-Path directory specified in WIN.INI, any start-up directory specified in a Program Manager item will be ignored. I would recommend ignoring the DOC-Path option, and taking advantage of the various other ways to specify a start-up directory when you launch Word.

## LoadMRUList

In addition to being able to load Word with a specific document as the parameter, you can also load Word with a macro as the parameter. So, for instance, you could specify that Word be loaded and then execute the FileOpen macro:

```
WINWORD /mFileOpen
```

Note the parameter /m followed by the macro name. This often overlooked ability allows you to create several different load options for Word. One that is frequently useful is to load Word with the most recently edited file:

```
WINWORD /mFile1
```

The internal macro File1 loads the file stored under the File menu. Word stores the names of the four most recently used files (the MRU list). Here is a short macro that examines the MRU list and loads however many files, up to four, are listed under File:

**DISK**
LoadMRUList—
Loads the most
recently used files

```
Sub Main
For x = 1 To 4
  If FileName$(x) <> "" Then FileOpen FileName$(x)
Next
End Sub
```

To start Word with this macro you would specify a Program Manager item that contained the command line:

```
WINWORD /mLoadMRUList
```

This is useful if the last four documents you edited were all part of a "work group." It allows you to pick up where you left off (especially if you've installed the AutoOpen macro proposed in Chapter 7 that returns to the last edit location in every opened document).

## FileFindThisDir

One of the limitations of Word's built-in FileOpen command is that it does not allow you to select multiple files to open at a single stroke. Curiously, the FileFind command *does* allow you to mark multiple files. As a result of this I created a macro that first clears out the FileFind search specification, points the search path to the current directory, assigns the wildcard specification to the file name, and then calls FileFind.

```
Sub Main
FileFind .Title = "", .Subject = "", .Author = "", .Keywords = "", \
    SearchPath = Files$("."), .Text = "", .SavedBy = "", \
    DateCreatedFrom = "", .DateCreatedTo = "", .DateSavedFrom = "", \
    DateSavedTo = "", .Name = "*.*", .Location = "Path Only", \
    MatchCase = 0, .Options = 0, .SortBy = 4, .View = 3
FileFind$
End Sub
```

Note the parameters:

```
.SearchPath = Files$(".")
.Name = "*.*"
.Location = "Path Only"
```

The first uses the WordBasic function Files$( ) with a period as the file specification. This returns the current directory. The second specifies that FileFind should list all files in the directory. This could be changed to DO? to display only DOC and DOT files. The third forces FileFind to use only the search path just specified (the current directory).

Used in combination with the Program Manager (or any other shell that allows you to launch a program with a command line from a specified directory), this macro accomplishes three things: You can have separate launch items for different projects by specifying different directories for start-up. It allows you to customize the files to list. And it allows you to select multiple files for loading.

A Program Manager item that used this macro might have the following settings:

```
Description: Customizing Word for Windows
Command Line: WINWORD.EXE /mFileFindThisDir
Working Directory: C:\WFW\DATA\BOOK
```

When this icon is chosen from Program Manager, the directory is changed to C:\WFW\DATA\BOOK, Word is loaded, and the macro FileFindThisDir is executed. The result is a list of all files in C:\WFW\DATA\BOOK.

A further advantage of adapting this macro to your own purposes is that FileFind is more informative than FileOpen. You can change the format of the FileFind information to show titles, FileSummaryInfo, content, or statistics. You can change the sort order of the found files. All in all it's a great improvement over FileOpen.

One possible objection to the use of this macro as a start-up option might be that it changes the various settings in the FileFind command. That is, you might want to retain the settings as they were left the last time you used File-Find from within Word. This can be accomplished in the macro as well. Simply add two additional calls to FileFind, one to get the current values and one to restore them:

```
Sub Main
Dim dlg As FileFind
GetCurValues dlg
FileFind .Title = "", .Subject = "", .Author = "", .Keywords = "", \
    .SearchPath = Files$("."), .Text = "", .SavedBy = "", \
    .DateCreatedFrom = "", .DateCreatedTo = "", .DateSavedFrom = "", \
    .DateSavedTo = "", .Name = "*.*", .Location = "Path Only", \
    .MatchCase = 0, .Options = 0, .SortBy = 4, .View = 3
FileFind$
FileFind dlg
End Sub
```

For FileFindThisDir to work you must not have a DOC-Path defined in WIN.INI. Also note that any of the other FileFind parameters, such as .Author or .Keywords, could be customized to limit the list of files found.


## CreateIconThisDoc

Some advanced Windows applications support a powerful feature called Dynamic Data Exchange (DDE). Basically, this facility allows one application to talk to another. The application that starts the conversation is called the client; the other end of the conversation is called the server. A client can query the server, requesting or sending data; it can send commands to the server, in effect running one program from another.

DDE is extremely complicated (and could provide content for an entire book). One of the problems with discussing DDE is that every application supports a slightly different subset of the overall DDE command set. Every application implements DDE slightly differently. And every application accepts a different syntax when accepting commands for execution as a server.

Another problem in creating an illustrative example is quite obvious: Any example assumes that you possess both the client and server applications. It's safe to say you have a copy of Word (our client) on your computer. But any choice for a server would undoubtedly prove uninstructive for many readers.

Therefore, I will present a relatively simple DDE example that uses an application I know every Windows user has readily available: Program Manager.

The following macro, CreateIconThisDoc, first checks to see if Program Manager is loaded and loads it if it isn't. It then initiates a DDE conversation with the lines:

```
ChanNum = DDEInitiate("Progman", "Progman")
```

This command assigns a unique ID number to the variable ChanNum (which is representative of its purpose: It holds the *DDE Channel Number*).

The next command:

```
Groups$ = DDERequest$(ChanNum, "Groups")
```

asks Program Manager to return a list of all available groups. The list of group names is separated by carriage return/line feed pairs. CreateIconThis-Doc uses a user-function, CountChars, to determine how many groups are in the list. It then builds an array to hold the individual items by using a user-function named Chew, which steps through the string returned by Program Manager removing the carriage return/line feed characters and assigning the group titles to a user-array:

```
GroupNumber = CountChar(Groups$, CrLf$)
Redim GroupList$(GroupNumber - 1)
For x = 0 To GroupNumber - 1
   GroupList$(x) = Chew$(Groups$, CrLf$)
Next
```

All this string manipulation is necessary since we want to present the user with a list of all the available groups in Program Manager.

Next, CreateIconThisDoc examines the FileSummaryInfo for the current document and presents the user with the following dialog box:

The proposed Icon description is a combination of the document name and the title stored in FileSummaryInfo. When you select OK, CreateIconThis-Doc continues the DDE conversation with Program Manager and creates an

Icon in the specified group that can be used to load Word with the current
document.

**DISK**
CreateIconThisDoc—
Creates a Program
Manager icon for
the current
document

```
Declare Function IsAppLoaded Lib "kernel"(Name$)\
As Integer Alias "GetModuleHandle"
Sub Main
CrLf$ = Chr$(13) + Chr$(10)
Start:
If IsAppLoaded("PROGMAN.EXE") = 0 Then
    SendKeys("%{Tab}")
    Shell "progman.exe", 0
End If
ChanNum = DDEInitiate("Progman", "Progman")
Groups$ = DDERequest$(ChanNum, "Groups")
'If you are using Windows 3.0 send "" instead of "Groups"
GroupNumber = CountChar(Groups$, CrLf$)
Redim GroupList$(GroupNumber - 1)
For x = 0 To GroupNumber - 1
    GroupList$(x) = Chew$(Groups$, CrLf$)
Next
Redim dlg As FileSummaryInfo
GetCurValues dlg
t$ = dlg.Title : If t$ = "" Then FileSummaryInfo$ : Goto Start
N$ = dlg.FileName
dir$ = dlg.Directory
fName$ = dir$ + "\" + N$
Again:
Begin Dialog UserDialog 489, 186, "Create Program Manager Icon "
    Text 13, 6, 128, 13, "Icon description:"
    TextBox 10, 23, 468, 18, .Title
    Text 13, 42, 113, 13, "Full File Name:"
    TextBox 10, 56, 468, 18, .FName
    Text 17, 82, 119, 13, "Place in &Group:"
    ComboBox 17, 97, 300, 83, GroupList$(), .Group
    OKButton 345, 125, 88, 21
    CancelButton 345, 156, 88, 21
End Dialog
Redim dlg As UserDialog
dlg.Title = n$ + ":" + t$
dlg.Group = "Word for Windows 2.0"
dlg.FName =  fName$
On Error Goto Bye
Dialog Dlg
fName$ = dlg.FName
If(dlg.Title = "" Or dlg.Group = "") Then \
    MsgBox("Both an Icon Title and a Group must be entered", 48) : Goto Again
Print "Creating an icon in " + dlg.Group + " for the document " + fName$
ChanNum = DDEInitiate("Progman", "Progman")
DDEExecute ChanNum,("[CreateGroup(" + dlg.Group + ")]")
DDEExecute ChanNum,("[AddItem(" + fName$ +  "," + dlg.Title + ")]")
```

```
Bye:
DDETerminate ChanNum
End Sub

Function Chew$(Source$, Marker$)
Index = Instr(Source$, Marker$)
   If Index = 0 Then
      C$ = Source$
      Source$ = ""
   Else
      C$ = Mid$(Source$, 1, Index - 1)
      If Len(c$ + Marker$) < Len(Source$) Then
         Source$ = Mid$(Source$, Index + Len(Marker$))
      Else
         Source$ = ""
      End If
   End If
   Chew$ = C$
End Function

Function CountChar(s$, c$)
Count = 0
Index = 1
While Instr(Index, s$, c$)
   Count = count + 1
   Index = Instr(Index, s$, c$) + 1
Wend
CountChar = Count
End Function
```

Notice that the proposed group is hard-coded as "Word for Windows 2.0." This is the program group created when Word is installed. You could change this to suit your preferences. Also be aware that the list of groups is presented in the order in which they are stored in PROGRAM.INI. They are not sorted.

The DDE conversation which creates the icon is rather short. It consists of only two lines:

```
DDEExecute ChanNum,("[CreateGroup(" + dlg.Group + ")]")
DDEExecute ChanNum,("[AddItem(" + fName$ +  "," + dlg.Title + ")]")
```

**Note.** There is a second macro supplied on disk, named CreateIconSimple, which does not present a list of all available groups. It is marginally faster since it doesn't have to build the list of groups.

The first calls the WordBasic command to execute a command in the server application, DDEExecute, with the channel number as the first parameter and the execute string for the second. The execute strings vary from application to application. (Program Manager supports five commands: Create-Group, ShowGroup, AddItem, DeleteGroup, and ExitProgman.) This DDEExecute command tells Program Manager which group to use. If the group specified doesn't exist, it is created.

The second DDEExecute command specifies the command line and the title to display below the icon. The command line sent to Program Manager is the name of the document itself. This macro assumes that Word is either in your path or that its full path name has been associated with the document's file extension in WIN.INI. If neither of these cases obtain, the created icon will be blank, and won't work.

If you wanted to specify the Word program file as well as the document, you would change the line

```
DDEExecute ChanNum,("[AddItem(" + fName$ +  "," + dlg.Title + ")]")
```

to

```
DDEExecute ChanNum,("[AddItem(WINWORD.EXE " + fName$ +  "," + dlg.Title + ")]")
```

You could also specify a full path name to the Word executable file.

The DDE conversation is ended with the command:

```
DDETerminate ChanNum
```

Any open DDE channel must be closed. Word can have more than one conversation going at a time. When developing a DDE macro it is a good idea to place the command:

```
DDETerminateAll
```

at the top of the macro. This ensures that even if the macro aborts during testing that you will not run out of channel numbers.

For more information on DDE see Chapter 5 of *Using WordBasic*. Also, you might want to order the Macro Development Kit, which contains a collection of Word-related papers delivered at the Microsoft Developers' Tools Forum in 1991. This resource is available from Microsoft for the cost of shipping. See Appendix F for ordering information. Woody Leonhard's *Windows 3.1 Programming for Mere Mortals* demonstrates, quite thoroughly, how to use DDE between Word and Visual Basic.

## Making a Smarter SmartQuotes

SmartQuotes is a suite of four macros that Microsoft ships with Word. They are found in the package of utility macros in the file NEWMACROS.DOC. If you haven't installed this group of macros, don't bother. We're about to replace them.

What SmartQuotes does is simple. Ordinarily Word inserts what are known as typewriter quotation marks—what are actually the inch and foot marks. When you type a quotation mark, Word inserts Character #34:

```
"This is surrounded by normal quotation marks."
```

And, similarly, when you insert a "single quotation mark," Word for Windows inserts Character #39, the apostrophe:

```
"We're at the 'mercy' of our computers!" he said with chagrin.
```

The contraction apostrophe and the single quotation marks around 'mercy' are the same character. Similarly, the opening and closing double quotation marks around the exclamation are the same.

Well, that's all you need if you are using a fixed font such as Courier or Prestige Elite. Fixed fonts don't usually distinguish between opening and closing quotation marks. However, proportionally spaced fonts, such as Times Roman, do. Proportionally spaced fonts look better (more professional) if the quotation marks use the appropriate "Publishing" or typesetting characters. These marks are usually curved (for serif fonts) or slanted (for sans serif fonts).

The purpose of SmartQuotes is to replace the simple vertical single and double quotation marks with typeset-quality quotation marks.

The four macros which constitute the SmartQuotes facility are

- EnableSmartQuotes

- DisableSmartQuotes

- InsDoubleQuote

- InsSingleQuote

There are three major problems in SmartQuotes as shipped.

- The procedure for enabling and disabling SmartQuotes is not elegant. There are two macros when the same task can be accomplished with one, slightly smarter macro.

- If you have SmartQuotes enabled and you attempt to edit a macro, things can get really messed up: WordBasic requires the vertical apostrophe to mark comments and the vertical quotation marks to delimit string literals.

- SmartQuotes are not usually appropriate if a font is monospaced (such as Courier or Letter Gothic). The SmartQuotes supplied by Microsoft doesn't distinguish between fixed and proportionally spaced fonts.

The following suite of macros address all three of these problems.

## ToggleSmartQuotes

The first task is to make activating the SmartQuotes macros more elegant.

The following macro, named ToggleSmartQuotes, combines the functions of EnableSmartQuotes and DisableSmartQuotes.

**DISK**

ToggleSmartQuotes— Turns smart quotes on and off

```
Sub Main
DisableInput
If FilePrintPreview() Then \
    MsgBox("Cannot run While in Print Preview…", "Toggle Smart Quotes") :\
    Goto Bye
SmartOn = Val(GetProfileString$("SmartQuotes"))
If SmartOn Then
    On Error Goto Abort
    mName$ = "InsSingleQuote"
    'note first Unassign command unassigns, second resets To original key
    ToolsOptionsKeyboard .Name = mName$, .KeyCode = 222, .Context = 0, .Delete
    ToolsOptionsKeyboard .Name = mName$, .KeyCode = 222, .Context = 0, .Delete
    mName$ = "InsDoubleQuote"
    ToolsOptionsKeyboard .Name = mName$, .KeyCode = 222 + 512,\
    .Context = 0, .Delete
    ToolsOptionsKeyboard .Name = mName$, .KeyCode = 222 + 512,\
    .Context = 0, .Delete
    mName$ = "ToggleSmartQuotes"
    mText$ = "Smart &Quotes"
    ToolsOptionsMenus .Name = mName$, .Menu = "T&ools",\
        .MenuText = mText$, .Context = 0, .Add
    SetProfileString("SmartQuotes", "0")
Else
    mName$ = "InsSingleQuote"
    ToolsOptionsKeyboard .Name = mName$, .KeyCode = 222, .Context = 0
    mName$ = "InsDoubleQuote"
    ToolsOptionsKeyboard .Name = mName$, .KeyCode = 222 + 512, .Context = 0
    mName$ = "ToggleSmartQuotes"
    mText$ = "»Smart &Quotes"
    ToolsOptionsMenus .Name = mName$, .Menu = "T&ools",
        .MenuText = mText$, .Context = 0, .Add
    SetProfileString("SmartQuotes", "1")
End If
Goto Bye
Abort:
    MsgBox("To enable smart quotes the " + mName$ + " macro must be available.")
Bye:
End Sub
```

ToggleSmartQuotes first prevents interruption by the user with the DisableInput statement. It then checks to see if the current document is in print preview mode. Since the ToolsOptionsKeyboard command is unavailable if in print preview mode, if FilePrintPreview() is true, the macro presents a message box and then exits.

ToggleSmartQuotes uses a keyword named SmartQuotes stored in the Microsoft Word 2.0 section of WIN.INI to hold the current state of Smart-Quotes. This value is either 1 (on) or 0 (off).

ToggleSmartQuotes retrieves the current value of the WIN.INI keyword SmartQuotes and converts the returned string to an integer with the statement:

```
SmartOn = Val(GetProfileString$("SmartQuotes"))
```

If SmartOn is false (that is, equal to 0), ToggleSmartQuotes turns Smart-Quotes on by performing four actions (the second half of the If…Then structure). It

1. Creates or changes the menu item associated with ToggleSmartQuotes to: "»Smart &Quotes" (the chevron character indicates that Smart-Quotes are in effect)

2. Assigns the macro InsSingleQuote to the key #222, the apostrophe

3. Assigns the macro InsDoubleQuote to the key #734, the quotation mark

4. Writes the value 1 to the SmartQuotes keyword in WIN.INI

If SmartOn is true (meaning equal to 1), the first half of the If…Then control is executed, disabling smart quotes. ToggleSmartQuotes

1. Changes the menu item associated with the macro ToggleSmartQuotes to: "Smart &Quotes" (no chevron indicates that SmartQuotes are not in effect)

2. Unassigns the macro InsSingleQuote from the key #222, the apostrophe (note that both unassign calls are executed twice—this is always required when resetting a key to its default value)

3. Unassigns the macro InsDoubleQuote from the key #734, the quotation mark

4. Writes the value 0 to the SmartQuotes keyword in WIN.INI

The only circumstance that would generate an error when executing this macro is if one of the companion macros could not be found during the Tools-OptionsKeyboard assignments. This is handled by the statement:

```
On Error Goto Abort
```

If this error condition occurs, a message box will be displayed.

## InsSingleQuote

This is the first of the two macros that actually do the work. When smart quotes have been enabled, InsSingleQuote is executed when the apostrophe key is pressed.

**DISK**

InsSingleQuote—
Inserts smart single
quotation mark as
apostrophe

```
Sub Main
DisableInput
Exception$ = "COURIER NEW, LUCIDA SANS TYPEWRITER, PRESTIGE ELITE, LINEPRINTER"
If SelInfo(27) Or Instr(Exception$, UCase$(Font$())) <> 0 Then
    Insert Chr$(39)
Else
    stWhite$ = Chr$(34) + Chr$(147) + Chr$(146) + "({[-<>"
    SelType 1
    If(CharLeft(1, 0) = 0) Then
        Insert Chr$(145)    'Insert single Open quote
    Else
        chPrev$ = Selection$()
        CharRight 1
        If(Asc(chPrev$) <= 32) Or(Instr(stWhite$, chPrev$)) Then
            Insert Chr$(145)    'Insert single Open quote
        Else
            Insert Chr$(146)    'Insert single Close quote
        End If
    End If
End If
End Sub
```

InsSingleQuote first disables user interruptions. This is probably not necessary since the macro executes quickly. It then defines a string variable consisting of a comma-delimited list of all font names that *should not* use smart
quotes. As presented, this list contains some of the more popular monospaced
fonts. Obviously, if you wish to have either of the smart quote macros ignore
a particular font, you should add that font's name to this list (in all capitals).

The evaluation:

```
If SelInfo(27) Or Instr(Exception$, UCase$(Font$())) <> 0 Then
```

checks to see if either of two conditions is true: Is the insertion point in a
macro editing window; is the current font's name contained in the exception
list. If either of these conditions is met, the macro inserts the normal, typewriter apostrophe and exits.

If neither of these conditions is true, InsSingleQuote proceeds. It defines
a new string variable containing those characters that should be followed by
an open quotation mark:

```
stWhite$ = Chr$(34) + Chr$(147) + Chr$(146) + "({[-<>"
```

This is used later to determine which of the two single publishing quotes to insert. The selection is then forced to an insertion point:

```
SelType 1
```

The insertion point is moved one character to the left using the function
CharLeft( ) instead of the statement CharLeft. This allows you to test if in fact

the insertion point was successfully moved left one character. If it was not successful, assume we are at the top of the document and insert an open quote:

```
If(CharLeft(1, 0) = 0) Then
    Insert Chr$(145)    'Insert single Open quote
Else
```

If it was successful, assign the current character to a variable and move back to where we started:

```
chPrev$ = Selection$()
CharRight 1
```

and test if the previous character meets either of two criteria: Is its ASCII value less than or equal to 32 (meaning it is a space, a tab, a carriage return, a field character, or some other special character); is the previous character contained in the string variable stWhite$. If either of these conditions is true, insert the open quotation mark; otherwise insert the closing quotation mark:

```
If(Asc(chPrev$) <= 32) Or(Instr(stWhite$, chPrev$)) Then
    Insert Chr$(145)    'Insert single Open quote
Else
    Insert Chr$(146)    'Insert single Close quote
End If
```

## InsDoubleQuote

When smart quotes have been enabled, InsertDoubleQuote is executed when the quotation mark (Shift+Apostrophe) is pressed.

**DISK**
InsDoubleQuote—
Inserts a smart
double quotation
mark

```
Sub Main
DisableInput
Exception$ = "COURIER, PRESTIGE ELITE, LETTER GOTHIC, LINEPRINTER, PICA"
If SelInfo(27) Or Instr(Exception$, Left$(UCase$(Font$()), 6)) <> 0 Then
    Insert Chr$(34)
Else
    stWhite$ = Chr$(34) + Chr$(145) + Chr$(148) + "({[=<>"
    SelType 1
    If(CharLeft(1, 0) = 0) Then
        Insert Chr$(147)    'Insert double Open quote
    Else
        chPrev$ = Selection$()
        CharRight 1
        If(Asc(chPrev$) <= 32) Or(Instr(stWhite$, chPrev$)) Then
            Insert Chr$(147)    'Insert double Open quote
        Else
            Insert Chr$(148)    'Insert double Close quote
        End If
    End If
End If
End Sub
```

InsDoubleQuote is identical to InsSingleQuote except for the characters it inserts. Instead of Chr$(145) and Chr$(146), it inserts either Chr$(147) or Chr$(148).

If you change the exception list in one macro, be sure to change it in the other as well.

## Development Tools

One of Word's failings is the lack of a comprehensive template manager. It would make life a lot easier for macro developers, and Word a lot easier for everyone else, if there were a facility, either built into Word or a stand-alone application, that could copy macros, glossaries, styles, and access methods from one template to another. More wishful thinking.

As with many other small and medium failings, a partial solution can be created with the macro language.

Word does have a command to copy macros from one template to another. The command is called MacroCopy and has the following syntax:

```
MacroCopy [Template:]Macro1$, [Template:]Macro2$ [,ExecuteOnly]
```

Note that the first and second parameters allow you to specify the template holding the macro to copy. Legal examples of these parameters would be

```
MyMacro
Global:MyMacro
NORMAL.DOT:MyMacro
C:\WINWORD\DOT\LETTER.DOT:MyMacro
C:\WINWORD\FAKEDOT.DOC:MyMacro
```

One major limitation: *The template containing the macro must be loaded at the time of the execution of the MacroCopy command.* If the template (for instance, LETTER.DOT) is not loaded, Word will display an error message.

You can rename a macro during a copy:

```
MacroCopy "Global:MyMacro", "Global:YourMacro"
```

And finally, the third parameter, which is either 0 (false) or 1 (true), determines whether the macro should be encrypted during the copy. For example:

```
MacroCopy "Global:MyMacro", "Global:YourMacro", 1
```

would create an encrypted copy of MyMacro in NORMAL.DOT.

Encrypting a macro prevents it from being edited by the user. This is useful for two reasons: ensuring that the user doesn't change a delicately balanced macro and thereby wreak havoc, and preventing other developers from lifting your cleverest solutions. There is a danger, however: *Once encrypted a macro cannot be unencrypted.* Be sure you are encrypting a copy of a macro. Otherwise, I guarantee, and speak from experience, you will regret it.

As the above amply illustrates, the MacroCopy command isn't all that easy to use. It needs a front end. Here's the best solution I've come up with (to date).

## CopyMacros

There is a macro presented in *Using WordBasic* (and on that volume's companion disk) named MacroManager. I wrote the first version (contained in The Yellow Book of the *Macro Developer's Kit*). That macro allows you to choose a source and a destination template, select the macros to copy, copy all macros from one to another, and optionally encrypt during the copy.

It just goes to show you can grow. I no longer use MacroManager to meet my own (rather extensive) macro copying needs. The following macro, named CopyMacros, is the solution I use constantly.

**DISK**
CopyMacros—
Copies macros
from the current
template to an
open template

```
Sub Main
Magic = CountWindows()
If Magic < 2 Then Goto Bye
WindowArrangeAll
CurDoc$ = WindowName$()
If SelInfo(27) Then \
    Macro$ = Mid$(CurDoc$, Instr(CurDoc$, ": ") + 2) : Macro = - 1
CurTemplate$ = GetTemplate$(context)
cMacros = CountMacros(Context)
If CMacros = 0 Then \
    MsgBox "There are no macros in the current context/template", "Copy Macros",
48 : Goto Bye
Dim Macros$(cMacros - 1)
For i = 1 To cMacros
    Macros$(j) = MacroName$(i, Context)
    If Macro$ = Macros$(j) Then CurrentMac = j
    j = j + 1
Next
Temp$ =  CurTemplate$ + ","
If Magic > 2 Then
    Dim Temp$(Magic - 2)
    For i = 0 To Magic - 2
        NextWindow
        Temp$(i) = GetTemplate$(dummy)
        If Instr(Temp$, Temp$(i)+",") Then Temp$(i) = "duplicate" Else
Temp$=Temp$+Temp$(i)+","
    Next i
    For i = 0 To Magic - 2
        If Temp$(i) <> "duplicate" Then Count = Count + 1
    Next i
    Dim Dest$(Count - 1)
    j = 0
```

```
    For i = 0 To Magic - 2
        If Temp$(i) <> "duplicate" Then Dest$(j) = Temp$(i) : j = j + 1
    Next
Else
    Dim Dest$(0)
    NextWindow
    Dest$(0) = GetTemplate$(dummy)
End If
Activate CurDoc$
Again:
    Begin Dialog UserDialog 406, 270, "Copy Macros"
        Text 4, 7, 402, 13, "Macros in:  [" + CurTemplate$ + "]"
        ListBox 12, 27, 375, 88, Macros$(), .MacIndex
        Text 4, 124, 133, 13, "Copy macro(s) To:"
        ListBox 12, 141, 375, 55, Dest$(), .Window
        CancelButton 299, 207, 88, 21
        PushButton 21, 207, 146, 21, "Copy &Selected"
        PushButton 21, 234, 146, 21, "Copy &All"
        CheckBox 190, 224, 87, 16, "Encrypt", .Hide
    End Dialog
    Dim dlg As UserDialog
    dlg.MacIndex = Index
    If Macro Then dlg.MacIndex = CurrentMac
    dlg.Window = WinIndex
    Choice = Dialog(dlg, 1)
    On Error Resume Next
    WinIndex = dlg.Window
    Hide = dlg.Hide
    Macro$ = Macros$(dlg.MacIndex)
    Macro = 0
    If dlg.MacIndex = cMacros - 1 Then
        Index = 0
    Else
        Index = dlg.MacIndex + 1
    End If
    If Choice = 0 Then Goto Bye
    If Choice = 1 Then
        CopyMacro(CurTemplate$, Dest$(dlg.Window), Macro$, Hide)
        Goto Again
    Else
        CopyAll(CurTemplate$, Dest$(dlg.Window), Hide)
    End If
Activate CurDoc$
Bye:
End Sub


Sub CopyMacro(sName$, dName$, macro$, encrypt)
    source$ = sName$ + ":" + Macro$
    dest$ = dName$ + ":" + Macro$
    MacroCopy source$, dest$, Encrypt
    Print "Copied [" + Macro$ + "] from " + source$ + " To " + dest$
End Sub
```

```
Sub CopyAll(sName$, dName$, encrypt)
If  Instr(sName$, "NORMAL") Then Context = Ø Else Context = 1
Dim s$(CountMacros(Context) - 1)
z = CountMacros(Context)
    For x = 1 To CountMacros(Context)
        s$(x - 1) = MacroName$(x, Context)
        source$ = sName$ + ":" + MacroName$(x, Context)
        dest$ = dName$ + ":" + MacroName$(x, Context)
        MacroCopy source$, dest$, Encrypt
        Print x ; " of  " ; z ; " - " + source$
        source$ = ""
        dest$ = ""
    Next x
End Sub


Function GetTemplate$(Context)
Context = 1
If SelInfo(27) Then
   t$ = Left$(WindowName$(Ø), Instr(WindowName$(Ø), ":") - 1)
   If t$ = "Global" Then
      t$ = "NORMAL" : Context = Ø
   Else
      This$ = WindowName$()
      If Instr(t$, ".DOC") Then
         While Instr(WindowName$(), t$) = Ø Or  SelInfo(27)
            NextWindow
         Wend
      t$ = FileName$(Ø)
      Activate This$
      Else
         If Instr(T$, "DOT") Then
            T$ = Left$(WindowName$(Ø), Instr(WindowName$(Ø), ".") - 1)
         End If
      End If
   End If
Else
   Dim tlg As FileTemplate
   GetCurValues tlg
   t$ = Tlg.Template
   If t$ = "" Then
      t$ = FileName$(Ø)
   Else
      t$ = tlg.Template
      If t$ = "NORMAL" Then Context = Ø
   End If
End If
GetTemplate$ = t$
End Function
```

Unlike MacroManager, CopyMacros works on whatever templates are already loaded and active within Word. That is, you do not supply the source and destination templates to the macro. CopyMacros assumes that the template underlying the current document is the source document. It further assumes that one of the other templates currently loaded will be the destination.

Here's how it works. First, CopyMacros determines the name of the template associated with the current document by calling the user-function GetTemplate$():

```
CurTemplate$ = GetTemplate$(context)
```

This function is smart enough to recognize a disguised template. It can also gather the template name while in a macro editing window. Notice that GetTemplate$() returns a string (note the dollar sign): the name of the template. But it also takes, and alters, an integer parameter named Context. This variable is changed to reflect whether the underlying template is NORMAL-.DOT (in which case it is set to 0) or a custom template (in which case it is set to 1). The Context variable is used in several places throughout the remainder of the macro. When subsequent calls to GetTemplate$() are made, the variable passed is named "dummy"—because at those points CopyMacros doesn't care about the context, just about the template name.

After getting the current template and the Context integer, CopyMacros creates a list of all the macros contained in the current template by using the built-in WordBasic functions CountMacros() and MacroName$() to dimension and fill an array named Macros$():

```
cMacros = CountMacros(Context)
If cMacros = 0 Then \
   MsgBox "There are no macros in the current context/template", "Copy Macros",
48 : Goto Bye
Dim Macros$(cMacros - 1)
For i = 1 To cMacros
   Macros$(j) = MacroName$(i, Context)
   If Macro$ = Macros$(j) Then CurrentMac = j
   j = j + 1
Next
```

CopyMacros then steps through every open document gathering the template names and building a list of all available templates, removing any duplication.

```
Temp$ = CurTemplate$ + ","
If Magic > 2 Then
   Dim Temp$(Magic - 2)
   For i = 0 To Magic - 2
      NextWindow
      Temp$(i) = GetTemplate$(dummy)
      If Instr(Temp$, Temp$(i)+",") Then Temp$(i) = "duplicate" Else Temp$ =
Temp$ + Temp$(i)+","
   Next i
```

```
   For i = Ø To Magic - 2
      If Temp$(i) <> "duplicate" Then Count = Count + 1
   Next i
   Dim Dest$(Count - 1)
   j = Ø
   For i = Ø To Magic - 2
      If Temp$(i) <> "duplicate" Then Dest$(j) = Temp$(i) : j = j + 1
   Next
Else
   Dim Dest$(Ø)
   NextWindow
   Dest$(Ø) = GetTemplate$(dummy)
End If
Activate CurDoc$
```

The string Temp$ holds a comma-delimited list of all open templates. The
array variable Temp$( ) is filled with repeated calls to GetTemplate$(dummy).
If the retrieved template name already exists in the string Temp$, the Temp$( )
array item is set to "duplicate." The number of unique templates is counted to
determine the size of the user array Dest$( ). Then, finally, Dest$( ) is filled
with the contents of Temp$( ), skipping those items that are repeats of already
gathered template names.

The remainder of the main subroutine simply displays the dialog box:

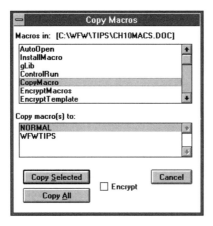

The current template and its macros are listed at the top. All of the other
available templates (that is, templates that are either loaded directly or associated with open documents) are listed in the second list box.

To use the macro you simply select the macro to copy and the destination
for the copy. Optionally you can check the Encrypt box to lock the macro
from editing during the copy process.

The dialog box redisplays until you press Cancel. Also note that the list of macros is not alphabetized. Rather, the macros are presented in the order in which they were created.

The code to this point constitutes the "interface" of CopyMacros. The actual work is done in two user-subroutines—CopyMacro and CopyAll:

```
Sub CopyMacro(sName$, dName$, macro$, encrypt)
   source$ = sName$ + ":" + Macro$
   dest$ = dName$ + ":" + Macro$
   MacroCopy source$, dest$, Encrypt
   Print "Copied [" + Macro$ + "] from " + source$ + " To " + dest$
End Sub


Sub CopyAll(sName$, dName$, encrypt)
If  Instr(sName$, "NORMAL") Then Context = 0 Else Context = 1
Dim s$(CountMacros(Context) - 1)
z = CountMacros(Context)
   For x = 1 To CountMacros(Context)
        s$(x - 1) = MacroName$(x, Context)
        source$ = sName$ + ":" + MacroName$(x, Context)
        dest$ = dName$ + ":" + MacroName$(x, Context)
        MacroCopy source$, dest$, Encrypt
        Print x ; " of  " ; z ; " - " + source$
        source$ = ""
        dest$ = ""
     Next x
End Sub
```

Which subroutine gets called depends upon which button the user selects. Note that both subroutines have a parameter to control the encryption.

CopyMacros is much more difficult to explain than it is to use. To test it out, simply load up a document based on NORMAL.DOT and a document based on any other template, say LETBLOCK.DOT. Then load CH10MACS-.DOC from this book's companion disk. Run CopyMacros from the installation menu. You will be able to copy any of the macros in CH10MACS.DOC (a disguised template, remember) to either NORMAL.DOT or LETBLOCK.DOT.

## EncryptMacros

EncryptMacros provides another useful macro development tool. It does a single thing: encrypt a macro. It does not make a copy of the macro. It simply locks it.

**DISK**
EncryptMacros—
Encrypts macros in
the current template

```
Sub Main
First = - 1
Index = 0
If SelInfo(27) Then
   MsgBox("Command not available in macro editor…", "EncryptMacros", 48)
```

```
    Goto Bye
End If
Dim dlg As FileTemplate
GetCurValues dlg
t$ = dlg.Template
If t$ = "NORMAL" Then SrcContext = 0 Else SrcContext = 1    '1=Template; 0=Global
If t$ = "" Then t$ = FileName$()
cMacros = CountMacros(SrcContext)
If cMacros = 0 Then MsgBox  "There are no macros available to encrypt." : Goto
Dim Macros$(cMacros - 1)
For i = 1 To cMacros
    Macros$(j) = MacroName$(i, SrcContext) : j = j + 1
Next
Again:
Begin Dialog UserDialog 334, 212, "Encrypt Macros"
    Text 18, 10, 135, 13, "&Macros available:"
    ListBox 10, 29, 297, 86, Macros$(), .Macro
    Text 10, 121, 76, 13, "Template:"
    Text 100, 121, 210, 16, t$
    CancelButton 207, 141, 88, 21
    PushButton 21, 141, 151, 21, "Encrypt &Selected"
    If First Then PushButton 23, 163, 149, 21, "Encrypt &All"
    CheckBox 21, 187, 148, 16, "Automatic Sav&e", .Save
End Dialog
Redim dlg As UserDialog
dlg.Macro = Index
Choice = Dialog(Dlg, 1)
If Choice = 0 Then Goto Bye
First = Not First
Index = dlg.Macro + 1        'increment the index
If Choice = 1 Then            'encrypt selected
    MacroCopy t$ + ":" + Macros$(dlg.Macro), t$ + ":" + Macros$(dlg.Macro), 1
    Goto Again
Else
    For x = 0 To cMacros - 1
        MacroCopy t$ + ":" + Macros$(x), t$ + ":" + Macros$(x), 1
        Print x + 1 ; " of  " ; cMacros
    Next x
End If
Bye:
On Error Resume Next
If dlg.Save Then FileSaveAll
End Sub
```

The logic is similar to CopyMacros. EncryptMacros determines the underlying template for the current document (if the current document is a template in disguise, it figures that out as well). It then presents a dialog box listing the macros in the current template:

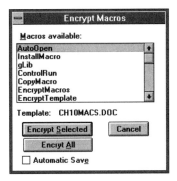

Like CopyMacros, you can act on one macro at a time or on all macros. If you check the Automatic Save box, FileSaveAll will be executed before EncryptMacros exits.

This macro should be used with extreme caution. As stated above, once encrypted a macro cannot be unencrypted. Be sure you are not encrypting the only copy of a macro.

# Miscellany

The following examples didn't fit into any of the above categories quite cleanly enough. Still, they are useful or instructive enough to warrant inclusion.

## BackupThisDoc

One of the examples presented in Chapter 7 was an AutoClose macro that prompted you to copy the current document to a backup directory. In that example the backup destination was hard-coded as A:\.

I have found this macro useful enough to give it a going-over to make it smarter and more flexible. Here's what I now dub BackupThisDoc.

**DISK**
BackupThisDoc—
Copies the current document to a backup directory

```
Sub Main
If ViewOutline() Then ViewNormal
BackupTo$ = GetProfileString$("Backup-Path")
If BackupTo$ = "" Then
    On Error Goto Bye
    BackupTo$ = NoSlash$(InputBox$("Enter backup destination:", "Configure"))
    SetProfileString("Backup-Path", UCase$(BackupTo$))
End If
Dim dlg As FileSummaryInfo
GetCurValues dlg
```

```
Name$  = dlg.FileName
Dir$ = dlg.Directory
FullName$ = Dir$ + "\" + Name$
On Error Goto ErrMsg
Again:
Begin Dialog UserDialog 271, 114, "Backup Document"
   PushButton 56, 87, 88, 21, "&Yes"
   CancelButton 172, 87, 88, 21
   PushButton 172, 87, 88, 21, "&No"
   Text 10, 6, 237, 12, "Backup: " + Name$
   Text 10, 25, 27, 13, "&To:"
   TextBox 45, 24, 160, 18, .Dest
   CheckBox 10, 44, 192, 16, "Warn of &overwrite", .Over
If IsDirty() Then \
   CheckBox 10, 61, 239, 16, "Save file before backing up", .Save
End Dialog
Redim dlg As UserDialog
If IsDirty() Then dlg.Save = 1
dlg.Over = 0
dlg.Dest = BackupTo$
Choice = Dialog(dlg)
If Choice = 2 Or Choice = 0 Then Goto Bye
On Error Goto 0
t$ = UCase$(NoSlash$(dlg.Dest))
If UCase$(BackupTo$) <> t$ Then SetProfileString("Backup-Path", t$)
If IsDirty() Then If dlg.Save Then FileSave
On Error Goto ErrMsg
If Files$(t$ + "\" + name$) <> "" Then \
   If dlg.Over = 0 Then  SendKeys Chr$(32)
MsgBox "Backing up " + Fullname$ + " to " + dlg.Dest, - 1
CopyFile FullName$, t$ + "\"
Goto Bye
ErrMsg:
MsgBox "Disk drive empty or invalid backup-path." : Goto Again
Bye:
End Sub

Function NoSlash$(S$)
   Source$ = S$
   While Left$(Mid$(Source$, Len(Source$)), 1) = "\"
      Source$ = Left$(Source$, Len(Source$) - 1)
   Wend
   NoSlash$ = Source$
End Function
```

BackupThisDoc is smarter than the previously proposed AutoClose macro for several reasons. It allows you to save, and later change, the destination for the backup copy. It dynamically alters its dialog box to suit the situation. It allows you to select all options from a single dialog box rather than answering separate message box prompts.

The first thing BackupThisDoc does is force the current document out of outline view (since FileSummaryInfo isn't available if ViewOutline( ) is true). It then checks to see if there is a keyword stored in the Microsoft Word 2.0 section of WIN.INI named Backup-Path. If there isn't (as there won't be the first time you run the macro) it prompts you to enter one:

```
If ViewOutline() Then ViewNormal
BackupTo$ = GetProfileString$("Backup-Path")
If BackupTo$ = "" Then
    On Error Goto Bye
    BackupTo$ = NoSlash$(InputBox$("Enter backup destination:", "Configure"))
    SetProfileString("Backup-Path", UCase$(BackupTo$))
End If
```

We then gather the document's name and directory using FileSummaryInfo and create a variable to hold the full path name:

```
Dim dlg As FileSummaryInfo
GetCurValues dlg
Name$  = dlg.FileName
Dir$ = dlg.Directory
FullName$ = Dir$ + "\" + Name$
```

BackupThisDoc then displays a dialog box such as the following:

Note that the "Save file before backing up" check box is only displayed if the current file is unsaved. This option is necessary because AutoClose executes before Word prompts you to save an unsaved document.

The other check box is always displayed, and by default is not checked. This controls whether you want Word to prompt you if the copy will over-write a file of the same name. Since this macro is most likely to be used to copy a document repeatedly, it makes sense to bypass this prompt. If, however, you want to be warned of an overwrite, change the line:

```
dlg.Over = 0
```

to

```
dlg.Over = 1
```

Before executing the copy, BackupThisDoc does a comparison of the original BackupTo$ variable and the most recently proposed destination as returned by the dialog box variable dlg.Dest. If the original destination doesn't match the current destination, we save the latter to the WIN.INI file:

```
t$ = UCase$(NoSlash$(dlg.Dest))
If UCase$(BackupTo$) <> t$ Then SetProfileString("Backup-Path", t$)
```

The most recently used backup destination is always proposed as the default.

The other neat trick used in BackupThisDoc lies in the dialog box definition. Notice that the push button declarations appear before the rest of the dialog definition. WordBasic determines the order of dialog box items by the order in which they appear in the definition. By placing the buttons first we can press Y or N to accept (without having to use the Alt key). Since the focus is set to the first item, the "Yes" button, you can press either Y or the spacebar to initiate the copy process.

If you look closer at the button definitions:

```
PushButton 56, 87, 88, 21, "&Yes"
CancelButton 172, 87, 88, 21
PushButton 172, 87, 88, 21, "&No"
```

you might be puzzled to see that there is a CancelButton definition with precisely the same placement and size as the "No" PushButton. There's a reason for this. If you do not have a CancelButton within a dialog definition, the Escape key is not available for canceling the dialog. In the above configuration I allow for both possibilities: You can press either N or the Escape key to cancel the operation.

If you want this macro to be run whenever a document is closed, install BackupThisDoc to NORMAL.DOT and create an AutoClose macro (global or template) that looks like:

```
Sub Main
ToolsMacro .Name = "BackupThisDoc", .Run, .Show = 1
End Sub
```

## ControlRun

There is a built-in command named ControlRun. It allows you to run either the clipboard or the control panel application. Here is a ControlRun replacement that adds several enhancements.

**DISK**

ControlRun—
Replaces built-in
ControlRun

```
Sub Main
Dim dlg As UserDialog
Begin Dialog UserDialog 200, 197, "Run Program"
    Text 10, 6, 40, 12, "R&un:"
    TextBox 10, 23, 181, 18, .Run
    GroupBox 10, 47, 181, 98, ""
```

```
    PushButton 20, 63, 160, 22, "Cli&pboard"
    PushButton 20, 87, 160, 22, "&Control Panel"
    PushButton 20, 113, 160, 22, "&Dialog Editor"
    CancelButton 20, 157, 160, 22
End Dialog
C = Dialog(dlg, 1)
If c = - 1 Then Goto Bye
If dlg.Run <> "" Then Shell dlg.Run : Goto Bye
Select Case c
Case 1
    Shell "clipbrd"
Case 2
    Shell "control"
Case 3
    Shell "c:\winword\macrode"
Case Else
    Beep
End Select
Bye:
End Sub
```

When executed, this replacement ControlRun presents the following dialog box:

Instead of using option buttons (as in the built-in ControlRun), this version uses PushButtons. This allows you to access an application with a single keystroke.

Another advantage is that you can easily add to the number of applications called by this macro. Simply add another PushButton and another test in the Select…Case control structure.

A third advantage is the Run edit box. This allows you to type in the name of any application.

## Searching for Formatting or Styles

One of the more powerful, and useful, commands in Word is EditFind. In addition to searching for normal text, EditFind can search for special characters (a listing of which can be found in Appendix E) and for text formatting or styles. This latter ability to search for formatting or styles can be combined with WordBasic to create macros that help reformat documents imported from other word processors.

What follows are three short example macros to search for all subsequent instances of the current character formatting, the current paragraph formatting, and the current style. The intention, in this case, is not to provide a finished macro, since the type of manipulation is different with every instance where such a macro would prove useful. Rather, these three macros provide a framework into which you might insert the text-altering commands called for to clean up an imported document.

These three examples make use of a little known, and often overlooked, fact: Certain WordBasic commands share the same parameter list. To express this in command array terminology: Certain commands have the same dimension. We have seen how an internal command can be queried and then passed the entire array variable in a subsequent call (see FileTemplate above). Now I would like to demonstrate how you can query one WordBasic command and pass the results to another.

The following WordBasic commands have precisely the same "shape":

- FormatCharacter, EditFindChar, and EditReplaceChar

- FormatParagraph, EditFindPara, and EditReplacePara

- FormatStyle, EditFindStyle, and EditReplaceStyle

This correspondence among WordBasic commands allows you to define an array variable and query the current text's formatting or style, and then search for all subsequent instances of the same type of text. To see the basic idea of this passing of an array variable in action, type in the following short macro:

```
Sub Main
Dim chardlg As FormatCharacter
GetCurValues chardlg
EditFindChar chardlg
EditFind$
End Sub
```

Notice that the Format description shown on the EditFind dialog box reflects the formatting of the current insertion point.

### EditFindThisChar
If you want to find every instance of a particular character formatting and reset the text to the attributes defined in the underlying style: Locate the first

instance of such text, place the insertion point at the start of the first instance, and execute the following.

**DISK**
EditFindThisChar—
Searches for
character
formatting

```
Sub Main
EditFindClearFormatting
Dim dlg As FormatCharacter
GetCurValues dlg
CharRight
EditFindChar dlg
Count = 1
'Do stuff To the current text, in this case simply ResetChar
ResetChar
CharRight
EditFind .Find = "", .Format = 1, .Direction = 2
While EditFindFound()
    Count = Count + 1
    Print "Finding similar paragraphs…"
    'Do stuff To the current text, in this case simply ResetChar
    ResetChar
    EditFind .Find = "", .Format = 1, .Direction = 2
Wend
Print "Found"; Count; " instances of this character formatting"
EditFindClearFormatting
End Sub
```

Such a macro could be used to massage text that was improperly imported from a foreign word processor (the conversion modules are not flawless). It could also be used to generate a list of all italicized words. You wouldn't need to use this simply to change a character formatting. You could use Edit-Replace more efficiently:

```
Sub Main
EditFindClearFormatting
EditReplaceClearFormatting
EditFindChar .Italic = 1
EditReplaceChar .Italic = 0, .Bold = 1
StartOfDocument
EditReplace .Find = "", .Replace = "", .Format = 1, .ReplaceAll
EditFindClearFormatting
EditReplaceClearFormatting
End Sub
```

would turn all italicized words into boldface.

### EditFindThisPara

If you want to find every instance of a particular paragraph formatting and perform some operation on that paragraph, place the insertion point in the first paragraph, the paradigm of what you want to manipulate, and execute the following.

**DISK**
EditFindThisPara—
Searches for
paragraph
formatting

```
Sub Main
EditFindClearFormatting
Dim dlg As FormatParagraph
GetCurValues dlg
ParaDown
EditFindPara dlg
Count = 1
'Do stuff to the current paragraph
EditFind .Find = "", .Format = 1, .Direction = 2
While EditFindFound()
    Count = Count + 1
    Print "Finding similar paragraphs…"
    Beep
    'Do stuff to the current paragraph
    EditFind .Find = "", .Format = 1, .Direction = 2
Wend
Print "Found"; Count; " instances of this paragraph formatting"
EditFindClearFormatting
End Sub
```

This is a potentially useful macro when importing text from another word processor. If, for instance, styles are not used during the import process (that is, everything seems to have *direct* paragraph formatting), you could use this macro to select a paragraph type and apply the associated style. For instance:

```
While EditFindFound()
    Count = Count + 1
    Print "Finding similar paragraphs…"
    FormatStyle "Quotation"
    EditFind .Find = "", .Format = 1, .Direction = 2
Wend
```

would apply the style Quotation to every paragraph with the same attributes as the insertion point.

## EditFindThisStyle

The last example is slightly different. Instead of creating an array to hold the current character or formatting attributes, it creates a string variable to hold the current style name.

It then loops through the document looking for every instance of the named style.

**DISK**
EditFindThisStyle—
Searches for styles

```
Sub Main
EditFindClearFormatting
ThisStyle$ = StyleName$(0)
StartOfDocument
```

```
EditFindStyle .Style = ThisStyle$
Count = 1
'Do stuff To the current paragraph
EditFind .Find = "", .Format = 1, .Direction = 2
ResetChar
While EditFindFound()
    Count = Count + 1
    Print "Finding similar paragraphs…"
    Beep
    ResetChar
    'Do stuff to the current paragraph
    EditFind .Find = "", .Format = 1, .Direction = 2
Wend
Print Count
EditFindClearFormatting
End Sub
```

This macro can be extremely useful because of a glitch in Word which some-times causes the formatting of text imported from another file or pasted from the clipboard to diverge from the underlying style. In such a case selecting the entire document and using ResetChar would also remove any direct format-ting such as underline or italics. You could use a macro such as this to find every style that you suspect has been corrupted and then test to see if it holds any special attributes before executing ResetChar:

```
Special = Bold() + Underline() + Italic()
If Special <> 0 Then ResetChar Else Beep : Goto Bye
```

This would stop the macro if the sum of the functions examining the charac-ter attributes of the selection were greater than 0.

A final couple of notes about searching for styles or text attributes. No-tice that these examples are careful to begin and end by calling EditFind-ClearFormatting. This is very important, otherwise the EditFind command will retain all the formatting for any subsequent search. If you are using Edit-Replace, be sure to finish with both EditFindClearFormatting and Edit-ReplaceClearFormatting.

There are two subtle bugs in the EditFind command. The following code:

```
EditFindChar .Bold = 1
EditFind .Find = "", .Format = 1, .Direction = 2
While EditFindFound()
    RepeatFind
Wend
```

should work fine. It doesn't. I have found that the safest thing is to repeat the entire EditFind instruction:

```
EditFindChar .Bold = 1
EditFind .Find = "", .Format = 1, .Direction = 2
```

```
While EditFindFound()
    EditFind .Find = "", .Format = 1, .Direction = 2
Wend
```

Even this sometimes fails. The solution is to always insert a print string within the While…Wend loop before the EditFind statement:

```
EditFindChar .Bold = 1
EditFind .Find = "", .Format = 1, .Direction = 2
While EditFindFound()
    Print "Looking For Bold…"
    EditFind .Find = "", .Format = 1, .Direction = 2
Wend
```

Don't ask me why, but it works.

One reason I leave this discussion of searching for styles or text formatting general is that no specific example will necessarily cover the individual need that may arise. Still, the ability to search and replace for text attributes can prove invaluable when it is necessary to make wholesale changes to a document, either because it was imported from another source or because Word's "phont phunnies" strike.

The essential ideas to recall when creating a macro to do extensive searching and/or replacing are

- You can gather the current text's attributes with FormatCharacter, FormatParagraph, or FormatStyle and pass the results to EditFindChar/EditReplaceChar, EditFindPara/EditReplacePara, or EditFindStyle/EditReplaceStyle.

- Use EditFindFound() to loop through a repeated search when EditReplace is not appropriate.

- Always include the entire EditFind command within a While…Wend loop rather than RepeatFind.

- Always include a Print statement as the first command within the While…Wend loop.

- Use .Format = 1, in either EditFind or EditReplace commands, to ensure that formatting will be used during the search.

- Use .Direction = 2 if the search is to proceed from the insertion point to the end of the document without the prompt asking if you wish to continue the search from the top of the document.

- Limit your search to character attributes with EditFindChar and alter the replacement text's character attributes with EditReplaceChar.

- Limit your search to paragraph attributes with EditFindPara and alter the replacement paragraph's attributes with EditReplacePara.

- Search and replace styles using EditFindStyle and EditReplaceStyle.

CHAPTER

11

# Fields

**B**EFORE CREATING A HANDFUL OF EXAMPLE TEMPLATES TO DEMONSTRATE the customization features of Word, I would like to return to a concept introduced briefly in Chapter 3: fields. This chapter will first present an overview of field usage and then examine some of the more common fields in detail.

A field is special code entered either automatically by Word when a function that uses fields is executed, or manually by the user. This code, when *updated*, displays a specific piece of information, creates a link between various functions, or performs an action.

A field code consists of three parts: the special *field characters*, represented on screen as a pair of curly braces ({}), the field name, and the field instructions. The special curly braces that delimit a field should not be confused with the curly braces that can be entered from the keyboard. Field characters are always paired and are entered by pressing Ctrl+F9. Normal curly braces can be entered individually from the keyboard. Fields are case insensitive. That is, {page}, {Page}, and {PAGE} are all equivalent. In the discussion that follows, text references to field names will be presented in uppercase for the sake of clarity.

There are 62 fields. The good news is that they all follow pretty much the same syntax, so understanding any gives you a fair idea of all. See Table 11.1 for a list, segregated by function, of all fields.

**Table 11.1    Fields by Function**

| Function | Field |
| --- | --- |
| Perform action | {ask} |
| | {fillin} |
| | {gotobutton} |
| | {macrobutton} |
| Manipulate bookmarks | {*BookMarkName*} |
| | {ref} |
| | {set} |
| Perform calculation | {=*expression*} |
| | {if} |
| Retrieve document information | {author} |
| | {comments} |

**Table 11.1    Fields by Function (Continued)**

| Function | Field |
|---|---|
| Retrieve document information (continued) | {createdate} |
| | {edittime} |
| | {filename} |
| | {info} |
| | {keywords} |
| | {lastsavedby} |
| | {numchars} |
| | {numpages} |
| | {numwords} |
| | {printdate} |
| | {revnum} |
| | {savedate} |
| | {subject} |
| | {template} |
| | {title} |
| Index generation | {index} |
| | {xe} |
| Link to other documents | {dde} |
| | {ddeauto} |
| | {embed} |
| | {import} |
| | {include} |
| | {link} |
| | {rd} |
| | {ref intern_link$n$} |

**Table 11.1    Fields by Function (Continued)**

| Function | Field |
| --- | --- |
| Numbering | {autonum} |
| | {autonumlgl} |
| | {autonumout} |
| | {seq} |
| Print merge | {data} |
| | {mergefield} |
| | {mergerec} |
| | {next} |
| | {nextif} |
| | {skipif} |
| Display special information | {date} |
| | {fntref} |
| | {eq} |
| | {glossary} |
| | {page} |
| | {pageref} |
| | {print} |
| | {quote} |
| | {styleref} |
| | {symbol} |
| | {time} |
| Table of contents | {tc} |
| | {toc} |
| User info | {useraddress} |
| | {userinitials} |
| | {username} |

The purpose of some fields is self-evident. For instance, the PAGE field displays the current page number; the TIME field displays the current time; the DATE field displays the current date. How and why to use other fields is not so clear. Fields such as SEQ, FTNREF, and GOTOBUTTON require a little study. To further complicate matters, a handful of fields are created and used internally by Word and do not display any result at all. By the end of this chapter, the various ways to use fields will be significantly clearer. As with all sophisticated tools, the hard part is the approach: learning how to think in fields, getting a handle on the paradigm, the concept.

## General Comments Concerning Fields

Although we have defined a field as a special code that displays a result in the current document, this definition, like any other we might come up with, falls short. Fields are used in so many ways that no single description of their purpose would cover all cases. It's almost as if the designers of Word fell back upon fields when all else failed.

### Field Uses

There are three broad categories which describe how fields are used: Result, Action, and Marker.

A *result field* displays information. This is the most common type of field. Result fields gather information from extremely disparate places: from File-SummaryInfo, from bookmarks contained in the document, from template or global glossaries, from the ToolsOptionsUserInfo dialog box, from the operating system, and from other files, such as Word documents, another application's files, or graphic files.

There are four *action fields*. ASK prompts the user for a text string and assigns it to a bookmark. FILLIN prompts the user for a text string and inserts it into the document (so it is part result field). GOTOBUTTON displays a text prompt and moves to a bookmark location when activated. MACRO-BUTTON displays a text prompt and executes a macro when activated.

*Marker fields* have no visible result. They are automatically inserted into the document, and formatted as hidden, by specific Word functions (such as index and table of contents generation).

What do these three field types have in common? If you examine a generalized list of the various actions performed by fields, a pattern emerges:

- Include in the document any of the information stored in FileSummaryInfo.

- Insert variable information into a document (such as date, time, page number).

- Create cross-references within a document using bookmarks to specify the text or footnote to reference.

- Display bookmark references in form or merge documents.

- Specify links to other Word documents, to documents from other applications, and to graphic files.

- Mark text within a document for inclusion in an index or table of contents.

- Perform math calculations, using values contained in the current document and referenced by bookmarks.

- Create equations or insert special symbols.

- Number outline levels.

- Number related sequences of paragraphs, illustrations, or figures.

The *Word Technical Reference* states that "Fields provide a common structure for performing dissimilar functions." At first glance this certainly seems true. However, from another angle, there does seem to be a common strain in the functions implemented by fields: All of these actions use, to some degree or another, the idea of a cross-reference, or a link. A field is used whenever a feature in Word utilizes a dynamic link—to variable information, a file, a location, or a bookmark. Fields, in a sense, might be viewed as the glue that binds together disparate functions.

## Notes on Inserting and Editing Fields

Some fields are automatically inserted by Word. In cases such as the insertion of a table of contents, an index or an index entry, the creation of a print merge document, or inserting a link to a document or graphic, Word will insert the necessary field codes automatically.

For instance, when you select Page Numbers from the Insert menu, Word automatically inserts the field {page} into the designated header or footer. When you select Index Entry from the Insert menu, Word inserts a special field to mark the text to be included in the index. And when you select either File or Picture from the Insert menu and activate the Link option, Word inserts a field pointing to the selected disk file.

In a sense, such fields are used by Word to keep track of links, storing information about references to other parts of the current document or to all or part of a second document.

The simplest way for a user to insert a field is through the InsertField command, executed by selecting Field from the Insert menu. You will be presented with the dialog box shown in Figure 11.1. This dialog box presents a list of field types; a list of instructions, if any, for each field; a short description of the field syntax; and an edit box containing the field as it will be inserted into the document. This dialog box is also the easiest way to get further details about individual fields. Select the field you want explained and press F1. The Word Help file will be loaded with the selected field's help entry active.

**Figure 11.1**
InsertField dialog box

List of instructions. This list changes with each field. In the current case it lists all bookmarks in the document

List of field types

Field syntax description

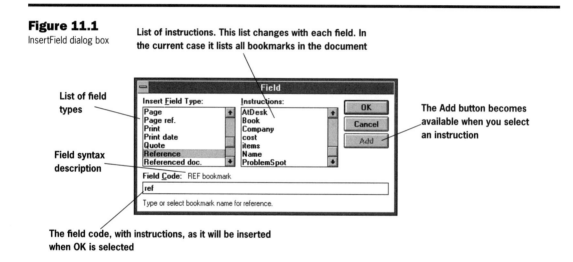

The Add button becomes available when you select an instruction

The field code, with instructions, as it will be inserted when OK is selected

You can also type a field directly into a document. This is done by pressing Ctrl+F9. This key combination inserts the *field characters*, a pair of curly braces. Note that these braces are *different* from those that can be inserted by typing the brace keys.

Once the field characters are inserted you can directly type a field name and any appropriate instructions or switches.

**TIP.** *You can also create a field by typing the field name first, selecting the field name, and pressing Ctrl+F9. The selected text will be enclosed in curly braces.*

Fields can also be inserted, as we have seen in Chapter 7, by the macro language. There are several dedicated WordBasic statements, such as Insert-DateField, InsertTimeField, and InsertPageField, which insert a specific field into the active document. You can also use the WordBasic statements Insert-Field or InsertFieldChars to build a custom field from a macro. For instance:

```
Sub Main
InsertField .Field = "author"
End Sub
```

and

```
Sub Main
InsertFieldChars
Insert "author"
End Sub
```

would both insert the field {author} at the current insertion point.

Here are some general notes about field usage:

- A document can contain up to 2,000 fields.

- An incorrect field, such as a field that references a bookmark that does not exist, will display a boldfaced error message in the document.

- Activating the All option on the ToolsOptionsView dialog box will not display field codes (as it did in Word 1.x).

- When editing a field it is advisable to split the active document into two panes, one of which has ViewFieldCodes on. This allows you to see the field code and its result at the same time.

## Field-Related Commands and Keys

Table 11.2 lists the 11 WordBasic commands which relate to the entry, display, or manipulation of fields.

**Table 11.2**    **Field-Related WordBasic Commands**

| WordBasic Command | Notes | Keyboard Shortcut |
| --- | --- | --- |
| InsertFieldChars | Inserts the field characters at the current insertion point. The field characters are always inserted as a pair (the opening and closing curly braces). Selecting either character will select the entire field. | Ctrl+F9 |
| NextField | Moves the insertion point to the next field and highlights the entire field. | F11 |

**Table 11.2**    **Field-Related WordBasic Commands (Continued)**

| WordBasic Command | Notes | Keyboard Shortcut |
|---|---|---|
| PrevField | Moves the insertion point to the previous field and highlights the entire field. | Shift+F11 |
| ToggleFieldDisplay | Toggles the display between field codes and field results, affecting only those fields covered by the current selection. If the insertion point is within a single field, only that field will be toggled. If the insertion point is not within a field, ToggleFieldDisplay will produce a beep. This command is useful when editing fields, allowing you to easily switch from viewing the field's codes to viewing the field's updated results. | Shift+F9 |
| ViewFieldCodes | Does not act directly on a field. Rather, it is a toggle that changes whether field codes or field results are displayed in the current document pane. Properly speaking this is a view toggle (similar to ViewDraft). When Field Codes on the View menu is on, a check mark will appear to the left of the menu text. In this state field codes will be displayed. When Field Code is off, the most recent result of the field code will be displayed. | The keyboard shortcut for ViewFieldCodes is the key combination used to access the menu item: Alt+V-C. |
| UpdateFields | Updates the result of all fields contained in the selection. This command has no effect on marker fields such as {XE IndexEntry} or fields that have been locked. On action fields (GOTOBUTTON and MACROBUTTON) UpdateFields updates the message instruction. Updating a field changes the field display to the current state of ViewFieldCodes. | F9 |
| UnlinkFields | Replaces a field with the result of the field. There is no way to reverse the effects of this command. | Ctrl+Shift+F9 |
| LockFields | Prevents the currently selected field (and any fields it may contain) from being updated. The field still exists. It simply cannot be updated until "unlocked." This is useful, for instance, if you want a particular field to retain its initial result. For instance, you might want to lock a {date} field. | Ctrl+F11 |
| UnlockFields | Unlocks a previously locked field. | Ctrl+Shift+F11 |

**Table 11.2     Field-Related WordBasic Commands (Continued)**

| WordBasic Command | Notes | Keyboard Shortcut |
|---|---|---|
| UpdateSource | If the current document contains a link to another Word document (represented by an INCLUDE field), selecting the field and executing this command will save any change made to the field result version of the document back to the source file. This command does not work with any other type of field or any file format other than Word's. | Ctrl+Shift+F7 |
| DoFieldClick | Executes an action field (GOTOBUTTON or MACRO-BUTTON). It is equivalent to doubleclicking on the field with the left mouse button. | Alt+Shift+F9 |

# Field Syntax

All fields employ a similar syntax: the field characters enclosing the name describing the field type, followed by any instructions. This general syntax can be represented as:

```
{FieldType Instructions [FieldSwitches] [GeneralSwitches]}
```

Though all fields possess this basic shape, there are many individual differences among the 62 fields. Fortunately, there is no need to memorize each field's particular syntax, since the InsertField command, used in conjunction with the Word Help function, can supply information about a field at the time of its creation.

To make the most of fields, however, you still need to understand the basic concepts of this syntax, and so here follow some basic definitions.

## Field Type

The *field type* is the reserved word, often referred to as the *field name,* that describes the specific field to insert. In the InsertField dialog box the names of all available fields are presented in the Insert Field Type list box.

## Instructions

Virtually every field takes a parameter which modifies the action or result of the field. This aspect of field syntax gets complicated because the instruction parameter can contain several different forms of required and optional modifying instructions.

There are six types of instruction: argument, bookmark, expression, identifier, text, and switch.

### Argument

An argument, as in WordBasic, provides the field with necessary information which specifies how the field will perform its action. For example, in the field

```
{include c:\\winword\\mydoc.doc}
```

the file specification is the argument which tells the include field the name of the disk file to link to the current document.

Notice that the backslashes within the path designation are doubled. This is because a single backslash signifies a "switch" (see below). Anytime you want to include a backslash as part of a field instruction, you must insert two backslashes.

The field:

```
{glossary "MyGloss"}
```

would display the contents of the glossary named MyGloss.

### Bookmark

Several fields use bookmarks to determine the text or numbers to manipulate. A bookmark might be viewed as a variable argument. That is, an argument must be typed accurately directly into the field. A bookmark name must be typed accurately into the field, but the contents of the bookmark can be altered outside the field, in the document itself, either automatically or by the user.

For instance, the field:

```
{pageref FieldExplanation}
```

would print the number of the page that contains the bookmark FieldExplanation. The actual value of this field would change dynamically as the page containing the bookmark changed with additions or deletions affecting pagination.

The field:

```
{=Cost*Items}
```

would display the result of multiplying the number referenced by the bookmark Cost by the number referenced by the bookmark Items. (The field name in this case is actually the equal sign. This signifies that the field is a mathematical expression.) If either of the bookmark references used as operators in the calculation is a bookmark covering a text string (rather than a numeric string), updating the field will fail.

## Expression

The expression or calculation field, represented by an equal sign, performs a mathematical calculation. The instructions for this field take the form of mathematical expressions. The operators and functions supported are: +, -, /, ^, =, <, >, <=, >=, Abs, Count, Int, Defined, Sign, Min, Max, Mod, Product, Round, And, Or, Not, and Sum. These functions, familiar to a spreadsheet user, must seem daunting to a user who doesn't crunch numbers. Still, the ability to do math calculations can come in handy even if all you need to do is add two digits. An invoice template in the next chapter will demonstrate the utility of this type of field.

The arguments in an expression can be number arguments, bookmark references to numbers in text, or references to specific cells or ranges of cells in a table.

With a little patience and ingenuity, Word's expression field allows you to create minispreadsheets within your document.

## Identifier

This type of instruction is used to pass a unique string to a field. For instance:

```
{seq Photos}
```

would generate an incremented number, specific to the identifier Photos, with every instance of this field.

An identifier allows you to distinguish between fields that perform the same action. That is, you can have multiple sets of sequence numbering, or multiple tables of contents, each with a unique identifier.

The difference between an identifier and a normal string argument is subtle. The argument provides the parameter on which an action is performed. An identifier defines and limits the range of a field's action.

## Text

Several fields take a string literal as part of the instruction. For instance:

```
{quote "Start here"}
```

when updated, simply displays the string "Start here."

Some fields use string literals as a prompt. For instance:

```
{fillin "Type your name"}
```

would display an input box with the string "Type your name" as the prompt.

## Switch

In addition to instructions that specify the general action of a field, many fields can take a further set of instructions in the form of *switches*. While other instructions determine the result, switches are used to alter the appearance or format of the field's result.

All switches are prefixed by a backslash, such as:

```
\d "Default Text"
\l
\@ "MMMM dd, yyyy"
\* mergeformat
\* dollartext
```

There are two kinds of switches: field-specific and general. Each field can contain up to ten field-specific and ten general switches. For detailed information about general switches search for "switches" in the Word Help file. For information about field-specific switches search the Help file for the name of the field in question.

# A Closer Look at Selected Fields

To discuss and demonstrate each of the 62 fields available in Word would require an entire book. As stated previously, fields are similar enough that understanding any field fully will point the way to understanding the rest. Now that we have a general grasp of field syntax, the best course is to examine in some detail a handful of fields. The remainder of this section will detail the use of the more common and useful fields.

Figure 11.2 presents a comparison of selected fields and their results.

## Getting at Document Information

When Word saves a document, it also saves 17 individual pieces of information about that document. The information, stored in a special corner of the disk file, is accessible from the FileSummaryInfo dialog box. We saw how to access each of these items using WordBasic in Chapter 9, by using the example macro FileInfo. You can also access all but one of these items using fields.

Table 11.3 lists the 17 items stored in FileSummaryInfo and the corresponding field name used to display that information in a document. Note that the directory information contained in FileSummaryInfo is not accessible via a field.

Four of these items must be entered by the user: Title, Subject, Keywords, and Comments. The Author field is taken from the ToolsOptionsUserInfo Name field. The remaining 12 items, which hold statistics about the document, are calculated and entered directly by Word.

The document information fields can be extremely useful in generating informative headers or footers, and provide an incentive for getting into the habit of filling out the FileSummaryInfo dialog box for all documents.

## Figure 11.2

Comparison of selected fields and their results

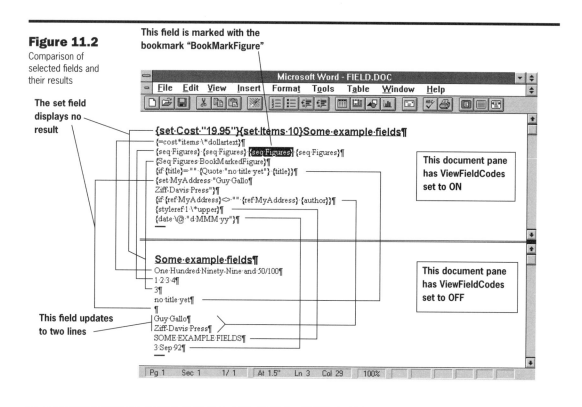

**This field is marked with the bookmark "BookMarkFigure"**

**The set field displays no result**

{set·Cost·"19.95"}{set·Items·10}Some·example·fields¶
{=cost*items·\*·dollartext}¶
{seq·Figures}·{seq·Figures}·{seq·Figures}·{seq·Figures}¶
{Seq·Figures·BookMarkedFigure}¶
{if·{title}=·""·{Quote·"no·title·yet"}·{title}}¶
{set·MyAddress·"Guy·Gallo¶
Ziff-Davis·Press"}¶
{if·{ref·MyAddress}◇·""·{ref·MyAddress}·{author}}¶
{styleref·1·\*upper}¶
{date·\@·"d·MMM·yy"}¶

Microsoft Word - FIELD.DOC

File   Edit   View   Insert   Format   Tools   Table   Window   Help

**This document pane has ViewFieldCodes set to ON**

**This field updates to two lines**

Some·example·fields¶
One·Hundred·Ninety-Nine·and·50/100¶
1·2·3·4¶
3¶
no·title·yet¶
¶
Guy·Gallo¶
Ziff-Davis·Press¶
SOME·EXAMPLE·FIELDS¶
3·Sep·92¶

**This document pane has ViewFieldCodes set to OFF**

Pg 1   Sec 1   1/ 1   At 1.5"   Ln 3   Col 29   100%

## Table 11.3   Document Information Fields

| FileSummaryInfo Item | Corresponding Field |
| --- | --- |
| Author name | {author} |
| Comments | {comments} |
| Creation date | {createdate} |
| Date of last printing | {printdate} |
| Date of last save | {savedate} |
| Directory | None |
| Filename | {filename} |
| Keywords | {keywords} |
| Name of person who last saved the document | {lastsavedby} |

**Table 11.3**     **Document Information Fields (Continued)**

| FileSummaryInfo Item | Corresponding Field |
|---|---|
| Number of characters | {numchars} |
| Number of pages | {numpages} |
| Number of words | {numwords} |
| Revision number | {revnum} |
| Subject | {subject} |
| Template name | {template} |
| Title | {title} |
| Total editing time | {edittime} |

For example, it is often desirable to include the document's title and author in the header in addition to the page number. You would do this, quite easily, by inserting the following combination of fields and text:

```
{author} - {title}                              page {page}.
```

These fields, inserted as I type this manuscript, would result in:

```
Guy J. Gallo - Take Word for Windows to the Edge   page 20.
```

Using the document information fields allows you to stamp your documents, either individually or classwide using templates, with statistics that can aid in tracking and identifying each document more easily.

## Referencing Text with the STYLEREF Field

The STYLEREF field displays the text of a paragraph formatted with a specified style. It uses the syntax:

```
{styleref "stylename"}
```

At first blush the utility of such a field may not be apparent. But I believe you'll find this one of the most useful fields in Word after a little experimentation.

There are three ways to use STYLEREF: in text, in a footnote or annotation, or in a header or footer. STYLEREF follows a different rule in searching for a style depending upon the location of the field.

If the STYLEREF field is in the body of your document, it first searches backward from the field toward the beginning of the document. If the named style is not found, it then searches forward from the field toward the end of the document.

If the STYLEREF field is in a footnote or annotation, the search follows the same logic, searching backward first, then forward, but it proceeds from the reference mark (which is in text).

The most frequent and powerful use of STYLEREF is in a header or footer. When encountered in a header or footer, the search for the named style follows a slightly different logic: from the beginning of the current page to the end of the current page; from the beginning of the page to the beginning of the document; from the end of the page to the end of the document.

By a careful use of styles you can automatically insert dynamic information in your header or footer. For instance, assume you are writing a long work of non-fiction which is divided into parts, chapters, and sections. The title for each part is formatted as heading 1, the chapter titles are formatted as heading 2, and the section titles are formatted as heading 3. You could insert three STYLEREF fields in your header:

```
{styleref "heading 1"}:  {styleref "heading 2"} - {styleref "heading 3"}
```

to automatically display part, chapter, and section titles on every page of your document. For instance, if I insert these fields into the header of this chapter's manuscript, I would see

```
Fields: A Closer Look at Selected Fields -  Referencing text with the STYLEREF
field
```

Note that in these examples, where the style name contains a space, you must enclose the name in quotation marks. This is not necessary when referencing other styles which do not have spaces in the name:

```
{styleref normal}
```

When referring to heading styles, you can use just the number of the heading level:

```
{styleref 4}
```

and

```
{styleref "heading 4"}
```

are equivalent.

The result of a STYLEREF field can be altered by an optional field-specific parameter: \l (lowercase "L"). This switch has meaning only when the field is in a header or footer. When appended to the field instruction, the \l switch changes the search rules. Instead of starting the search from the beginning of the current page the search begins at the end of the current page. Put more simply, {styleref "stylename"} displays the text of the *first* instance of a style on the current page (or on preceding pages if not found); {styleref "stylename" \l} displays the text of the *last* instance of a style on the current page. This allows you to create what is known as a *dictionary* header or footer. For example, if the current page contains four paragraphs formatted as heading 1, with the following text:

```
Aardvark
abase
abattoir
abecedarian
```

then a heading containing the fields:

```
{styleref 1} - {styleref 1 \l}
```

would result in the following header:

```
Aardvark - abecedarian
```

Neat, no?

## Sequence Numbering with the SEQ Field

The SEQ field allows you to easily number related items in a document. Because Word keeps track of a sequence by the unique identifier, you can have multiple sequence lists in the same document.

For example, if your document contains a series of figures that need to be numbered, you would simply insert the field:

```
{seq Figures}
```

into each paragraph used to describe the individual figures, at the point where you want the number to display.

If you insert a new SEQ field, or move a SEQ field, the sequence is automatically renumbered when you update the fields or print the document.

The SEQ field can accept a bookmark instruction. This allows you to make a cross-reference to a specific item in the sequence. To enable this feature you must insert a unique bookmark identifier within (or over) the field to be referenced. For instance, if you have a sequence of illustrations numbered with a series of {seq illus} fields, you could insert a bookmark describing each at the time of the SEQ field creation, and then easily refer to a specific illustration in text using a SEQ field with a bookmark identifier as part of the instruction: {seq illus BookmarkName}. It sounds more complicated than it is. The easiest way to explain is through an example:

1. Open a scratch document.

2. Insert the following SEQ field: **{seq illus}**.

3. Press Ctrl+Shift+F5 to insert a bookmark.

4. Name the bookmark **"IllOne"** and press Enter.

5. Move the insertion point to a new paragraph.

6. Insert the following field: **{seq illus IllOne}**.

7. Select both fields and press F9 to update.

8. Make sure ViewFieldCodes is off so that you can see the results.

No matter how much text intervenes between the {seq illus} and {seq illus IllOne} fields, no matter how many additional {seq illus} fields are inserted, no matter if the order (and therefore number results) of the {seq illus} fields is changed, the number referenced by {seq illus IllOne} will always reflect the sequence number result of the {seq illus} field that is associated with bookmark IllOne. (Incidentally, the FTNREF field uses the same idea to allow in-text cross-references to specific footnote reference marks.)

Note: When you use the InsertField command to insert a SEQ field, the instructions list will display all the bookmarks in the current document. This can cause terrible confusion. There is no indication, from this list, which bookmarks refer to SEQ fields. There is no list of sequence identifiers. Adding a listed bookmark to the field code, even a bookmark that in fact does refer to an existing SEQ field, will start a new sequence. If you want to make a cross-reference by selecting a bookmark from this list, you must be sure that you first add the sequence identifier to the Field Code edit box, and you must know which of the listed bookmarks refer to existing SEQ fields (which will be fairly obvious if you settled on an informative naming convention at the time of the bookmarks' creation).

The SEQ field has four optional switches, none of which appears in the Instructions list of the InsertField dialog box. These switches allow you to manipulate the result of a SEQ field:

| Switch | Meaning |
| --- | --- |
| \c | Display the result of the most recent sequence number above the insertion point. |
| \n | Display the next number in the sequence. This is the default action. |

| Switch | Meaning |
|---|---|
| \rNumber | Reset the sequence to the specified number. For instance {seq photos \r10} would start the photos sequence at 10. |
| \h | Do not display the result of the field. This would be useful if you want to create a SEQ number to cross-reference but do not want the number to appear. |

## Displaying the Date and Time

Among the most frequently used fields are DATE and TIME. It is often desirable to stamp a document, or a part of a document, with the current date or time. These are such common actions that there are dedicated commands to do both: InsertDateField (Alt+Shift+D) and InsertTimeField (Alt+Shift+T).

By default Word uses the systemwide date and time formats as set using the Control Panel application to determine the format in which DATE and TIME fields will be displayed. Word will display the date according to the Short Date Format specified under the Date Format dialog box of the International settings portion of Control Panel. On that dialog box you can specify the order of the date, the separator, and whether to use leading zeros. Word will display the time according to the Control Panel Time Format dialog box. You can specify a 12- or 24-hour clock, a separator, and an optional suffix.

However, the options available in Control Panel are limited. The most flexible way to alter how the date and time are displayed in Word is to supply a special instruction known as a *date-time picture* to the field.

A date-time picture instruction is composed by combining letter arguments: M for month, d for day, y for year, h for hour in 12-hour format, H for hour in 24-hour format, m for minute. Notice that the arguments for month, minute, and hour are case sensitive.

Here is a table demonstrating the use of each of these arguments:

| Syntax | Example Field | Result |
|---|---|---|
| \@ M | {date \@ M} | 1–12 |
| \@ MM | {date \@ MM} | 01–12 |
| \@ MMM | {date \@ MMM} | Jan–Dec |
| \@ MMMM | {date \@ MMMM} | January–December |
| \@ d | {date \@ d} | 1–31 |
| \@ dd | {date \@ dd} | 01–31 |

| Syntax | Example Field | Result |
|--------|---------------|--------|
| \@ ddd | {date \@ ddd} | Mon–Sun |
| \@ dddd | {date \@ dddd} | Monday–Sunday |
| \@ yy | {date \@ yy} | 00–99 |
| \@ yyyy | {date \@ yyyy} | 1900–2040 |
| \@ h | {time \@ h} | 1–12 |
| \@ hh | {time\@ hh} | 01–12 |
| \@ H | {time\@ H} | 0–23 |
| \@ HH | {time\@ HH} | 00–23 |
| \@ m | {time\@ m} | 0–59 |
| \@ mm | (time\@ mm) | 00–59 |

You can append a further argument which controls the display of an am/pm suffix:

| Syntax | Example Field | Result |
|--------|---------------|--------|
| \@ h AM/PM | {time\@ hAM/PM} | 4AM |
| \@ h am/pm | {time\@ ham/pm} | 1pm |
| \@ h A/P | {time\@ hA/P} | 1P |
| \@ h a/p | {time\@ ha/p} | 1p |

Here are some example fields and their results:

| Field | Result |
|-------|--------|
| {date \@ "MM/dd/yy hh:mm AM/PM"} | 09/03/92 01:00 PM |
| {time \@ "h:mm am/pm"} | 1:00 pm |
| {date \@ "d MMMM yyyy"} | 3 September 1992 |

| Field | Result |
|---|---|
| {date \@ "MMM d, yyyy"} | Sep 3, 1992 |
| {date \@ "h:mm am/pm 'on' MMMM d, yyyy"} | 1:00 pm on September 3, 1992 |

Notice that you can access the time using the DATE field. Notice as well that the entire date picture is enclosed in quotation marks. Otherwise Word stops reading the date-time picture at the first space (and assumes multiple instructions rather than a single date-time picture string).

The date-time picture switch can be applied to any field that returns a date. In addition to DATE and TIME, the date-time picture switch can be used to format the result of three other fields: CREATEDATE, PRINTDATE, and SAVEDATE. A date-time picture switch is ignored if encountered in any other field.

Note: Quotation marks are usually used to mark a series of space-separated strings as a single instruction. You can also use a *hard-space* to unify separate parts of a single instruction. The hard-space is character 160 (or Chr$(160) in WordBasic) and is represented on screen (when ShowAll is on) by the degree symbol: °. So, for instance, the fields

```
{date \@ "d MMMM yyyy"}
```

and

```
{date \@ d°MMMM°yyyy}
```

are equivalent. This fact is especially useful when inserting fields with a macro. The WordBasic statement:

```
InsertField .Field = "date \@" + Chr$(34) + "d MMMM yyyy" + Chr$(34)
```

works, but is more cumbersome (and prone to typos) than the equivalent statement using hard-spaces:

```
InsertField .Field = "date \@d°MMMM°yyyy"
```

You can save your date-time picture preferences, overriding the Control Panel defaults, by creating a pair of keywords under the Microsoft Word 2.0 section of WIN.INI. The DateFormat keyword specifies the default date format:

```
DateFormat=MMMM d, yyyy
```

The TimeFormat keyword specifies the default time format:

```
TimeFormat=h:mm AM/PM
```

These keywords can be entered directly into your WIN.INI from Word on the ToolsOptionsWinIni dialog box.

## Navigating with the GOTOBUTTON Field

The GOTOBUTTON is one of four action fields. It creates a "hot-spot" which, when activated, moves the insertion point to a named bookmark (the equivalent of executing the EditGoTo command).

The syntax for GOTOBUTTON is

```
{gotobutton BookmarkName DisplayText}
```

When updated such a field inserts the DisplayText string into the document. When such a field is selected and the DoFieldClick command is executed (either by double-clicking the left mouse button or by pressing Alt+Shift+F9), the field performs an action: It moves the insertion point to the named bookmark. So, for instance, the field:

```
{gotobutton ProblemSpot Click here to return to the problem spot.}
```

would display the following text:

```
Click here to return to the problem spot.
```

Note several things about this display text. It is not contained in quotation marks: Word assumes that everything after the bookmark name is to be included in the field's display text. You can format this text in whatever manner you desire (such as color or bold or bordered) in order to make the display prompt stand out from the rest of the document.

You can include a graphic within this field to display a picture as part (or all) of the hot-spot. For example, the field

```
{gotobutton Notes            }
```

contains a picture. The picture was inserted using the InsertPicture command while editing the field. It was taken from the \WINWORD\CLIPART directory installed by Word. The file name in this case is HANDWRTNG.WMF. When updated this field would display only the graphic:

which itself would be the hot-spot. Double-clicking on this picture would move the insertion point to the bookmark named Notes.

Notice that when the picture is displayed by the field, double-clicking *does not* bring up Microsoft Draw. However, if you double-click on the picture *within* the field (that is, with the field code showing) Microsoft Draw will be loaded and the field will change to:

```
{gotobutton Notes {EMBED MSDraw  \* mergeformat}}
```

when you return from editing the picture. See Figure 11.3 for an illustration of a GOTOBUTTON that contains a picture.

**Figure 11.3**

Using a graphic within a GOTOBUTTON field

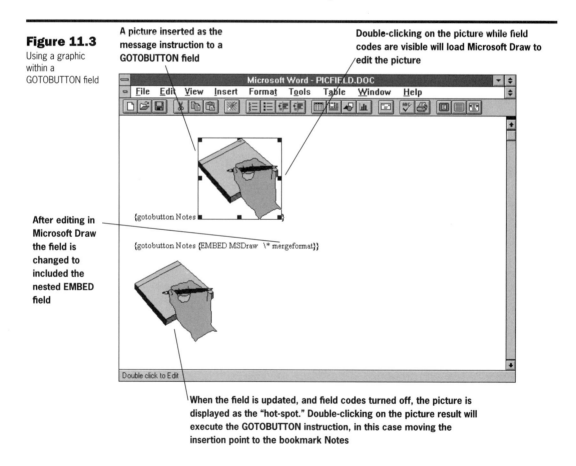

A picture inserted as the message instruction to a GOTOBUTTON field

Double-clicking on the picture while field codes are visible will load Microsoft Draw to edit the picture

After editing in Microsoft Draw the field is changed to included the nested EMBED field

When the field is updated, and field codes turned off, the picture is displayed as the "hot-spot." Double-clicking on the picture result will execute the GOTOBUTTON instruction, in this case moving the insertion point to the bookmark Notes

The GOTOBUTTON field does not support the built-in bookmarks (such as \PrevSel1 or \StartOfDocument).

If the bookmark named in a GOTOBUTTON field does not exist, you will generate an error message (the same error message posted if you try to EditGoTo a bookmark that does not exist).

The GOTOBUTTON allows you to create a document that is easily navigable by the user. This is especially useful for training documents.

## Executing Macros with the MACROBUTTON Field

The MACROBUTTON is also an action field. It has a similar syntax to GOTOBUTTON:

```
{macrobutton MacroName DisplayText}
```

This field also displays a text (or graphic) prompt when updated. When activated by DoFieldClick, it executes the named macro.

For instance, the field:

```
{macrobutton FileSave Save this file now!}
```

would display the text:

```
Save this file now!
```

and executing a DoFieldClick on this text (with a double mouse click or Alt+Shift+F9) would execute the macro FileSave. The named macro can be any user- or built-in macro. If the named macro does not exist, a beep will sound when the field is updated. When a MACROBUTTON field is unlinked (Ctrl+Shift+F9), it is removed completely (it isn't replaced by the display text as you might have expected).

The MACROBUTTON field allows you to create interactive documents. This is particularly useful for distributing macros or creating demonstration files.

## Special Effects with the EQ Field

If you include mathematical formulas in your documents, you have probably already studied both the Equation Editor application that ships with Word and the EQ field which is used to create inline equations. However, there are two uses for the EQ field that will appeal even if you have no need for complex equations.

### Overstriking Characters

One possible use for the EQ field is to *overstrike* one character with another. This allows you to create custom characters. For example, there are times when you want to make sure the capital letter "O" is never confused with the digit "0." One typographical convention specifies that the digit zero should be printed with a slash running through the 0. You can create such a "slashed zero" even if the active font does not support it by using the EQ field. The field

```
{eq \o(0,/)}
```

would create the following character:

0

You could automate the creation of this special slashed zero in either of two ways—by storing the field in a glossary entry, or by creating a macro:

```
Sub Main
InsertField .Field = "eq \o(0,/)"
End Sub
```

The advantage of the macro method is that you could assign this macro to the zero key (using the AssignKey macro listed in Chapter 7).

Note: If you want to format this slashed zero, you must apply the desired formatting *within the field* to the instruction.

### Boxing Text

You can place a box around a paragraph using the FormatBorder command or by defining a style to include borders. However, what if you want to place only a portion of a paragraph within a box? You can create a box around a portion of a paragraph by using the EQ field with the following syntax:

```
{eq \x(BoxedText)}
```

Notice that the text to box is not in quotation marks.

Here's a macro that would automatically box the current selection or the current word:

```
Sub Main
If SelType() = 2 Then
   b$ = Selection$()
Else
   CharLeft
   If Asc(Selection$()) = 32 Or Asc(Selection$()) = 13 Then
      CharRight
      WordRight 1, 1
   Else
      WordLeft 1
      WordRight 1, 1
   End If
```

```
    If Instr(Selection$(), Chr$(32)) Then CharLeft 1, 1
    b$ = Selection$()
End If
EditCut
InsertField .Field = "eq \x(" + b$ + ")"
End Sub
```

Be aware, however, that the text to box cannot exceed a single line.

## Making Smarter Fields

Although fields do not support the complex control structures found in Word-Basic, you can perform a simple conditional evaluation using the IF field. The IF field performs a logical comparison of two expressions and, like the If...Then control structure in WordBasic, performs an action dependent upon the result of the comparison. However, before demonstrating the power of the IF field, we must first introduce the concept of *nesting* fields.

A field within another field is said to be *nested*. A field can contain up to 20 nested fields. A nested field can be used to modify the containing field's instructions or its result. Here's a simple example that calculates the number of hours a document has been open by creating an expression field that divides the EDITTIME field by 60:

```
{={edittime}/60}
```

We can make this field more informative by including a QUOTE field to display a text string:

```
Hours open: 40.53
{quote "Hours open: "{={edittime}/60}}
```

Nesting fields within an IF field allow for complex conditional fields which perform different actions or display different results depending upon the value of a given expression. For example, the field:

```
{if{ref Book}="" {set Book "NewDocument"}}
```

examines the contents of the bookmark named Book and, if the bookmark is found to be empty, assigns it the value of the word NewDocument. Notice that this field displays no result. Also notice that this field has no provision for the case when the bookmark is not empty. You could make it a little smarter by adding an additional instruction:

```
{if{ref Book}="" {set Book "NewDocument"} {ref Book}}
```

This field will create a bookmark named Book if it doesn't exist or display the contents of the bookmark if it does exist.

The generalized syntax for an IF field is

```
{if Expression IfTrue IfFalse}
```

In the above example the nested field evaluation {ref Book} = " " is the expression, {set Book "NewDocument"} is the IfTrue action, and {ref Book} is the IfFalse action. Note that unlike the If…Then control in WordBasic, there are no line breaks or reserved words delimiting the IfTrue and IfFalse. They are separated, quite simply, by a space.

Note: A nested field can be broken over several lines for easier reading. For instance, the above field could be entered as:

```
{if{ref Book}=""
   {set Book "NewDocument"}
   {ref Book}
}
```

which improves legibility of the logical evaluation.

The following field evaluates the current date and displays either a message or the date:

```
{if {date \@MM/dd}="09/03" {quote "Happy Birthday!"} {date}}
```

Silly, but instructive.

Here's a more useful example. I often include the TITLE field in my headers. And then, of course, I forget to give a new document. The result is that the first printing of the document produces an incomplete header. Since the first printing is normally a draft for editing purposes, I've devised the following field that first checks to see if the document has a title. If there is no title, it displays the file name and the printing date.

If the current document has no title, the field

```
{if {title}="" "DRAFT: {filename} - Printed: {printdate}" {title}}
```

would display a string composed of the current file name and the date of printing:

```
DRAFT: CH11.DOC - Printed: 09/03/92
```

In this example the entire IfTrue instruction is contained within a pair of quotation marks. You could also write this field as:

```
{if {title}="" {quote DRAFT:°{filename}°-°Printed:°{printdate}} {title}}
```

which encloses the IfTrue instruction within a QUOTE field. Note that in this case hard-spaces are used to join the four elements of the QUOTE field.

Limitation: Because nested fields are updated from the bottom up (that is, the inner, nested fields are updated first), an action field, such as FILLIN or ASK, will always be executed, even if it would seem to be dependent upon a containing IF field. For instance, the following field:

```
{if{title}="" {title {fillin "Enter a title:"}} {title}}
```

looks like it would do the following: check if the title field of FileSummary-Info is blank; if it is, assign the result of the FILLIN field to the TITLE field; otherwise, display the title. In fact, no matter what the current title is, the FILLIN field will always be executed.

Conditional fields are often used in merge or form documents to customize the form letters depending upon the value of bookmarks. Such use of fields is documented in the *Word User's Guide*, Chapters 32–34. Here's a complex example that uses the QUOTE, ASK, IF, and REF fields to prompt the user for a name, company, and address. The point of this field is more readily seen if paragraph marks are showing, so it is reproduced as it would appear if you had selected Paragraph Marks on the ToolsOptionsView dialog box:

This field uses several neat tricks. First of all, by enclosing the three ASK fields and their corresponding conditional REF fields in a single QUOTE field, the group of statements is, in effect, turned into a single field. No extra carriage returns will be printed in the document. Secondly, the ASK field uses the field-specific switch \d, which controls the default text displayed in the input box, and sets this to nothing by sending the empty quotation mark pair: (\d" "). The most powerful part of this complex field, however, is the IF field:

```
{if{ref Name}<> "Error! Bookmark not defined." "{ref Name}¶
"}
```

The importance of this field is twofold. It demonstrates how to avoid the annoying "Error! Bookmark not defined." result when a field referencing a non-existent bookmark is updated. Simply check for that result before referencing a bookmark. The second cleverness in this field resides in the IfTrue portion of the conditional (note that it doesn't have an IfFalse portion):

```
"{ref Name}¶
"}
```

Notice that the REF field is enclosed in quotation marks. This isn't normally necessary. In this case, however, the string that is inserted into the document if the bookmark Name is not empty consists of two things: the contents of the bookmark and a carriage return (represented by the paragraph mark (¶) enclosed by the quotation marks). That is why the field spans two lines, why the closing quotation mark is on the next physical line. This allows you, for instance, to specify only a name and address, leaving out the company, without inserting an extra, blank line.

## Summary: Field Notes

Fields are discussed, in broad terms, in Chapter 41 of the *Word User's Guide*. The *Word Technical Reference* contained a chapter dedicated to fields. When this book was revised and renamed *Using WordBasic*, the field information was removed (which is logical since the new reference dealt mainly with WordBasic). However, this valuable reference information was not presented on its own or as part of the general *Word User's Guide*.

Specific discussion of individual fields can be found in the Word Help file. A document that gathers all of the Help file information in one place is available for download from the Word forum on CompuServe (WFIELD.ZIP) or as part of the *Macro Developer's Kit*.

Here are some parting thoughts on fields:

- Like WordBasic, fields are less daunting than they might at first glance appear because guiding information and details about particular fields are never far away.

- The easiest way to find out the particulars about a field is to highlight the field in question in the list of field types in InsertField and press F1 to invoke the Word Help file.

- The ability to split a document window into two panes, one displaying field codes and the other displaying field results, allows you to see the progress of complex field creation.

- Updating all fields in a document can be done at print time by setting Update Fields to on in the ToolsOptionsPrint dialog box.

- Alternatively, you can select the entire document (Ctrl+Numpad5) and execute UpdateFields (F9).

- To include a backslash in a field instruction you must insert two backslashes, for instance:

```
{include c:\\winword\\mydoc.doc}
```

■ To include text within a field instruction you must enclose it within apostrophes, for instance:

```
{date \@ "'Today is 'MMM d, yy"}
```

■ Multiple-word instruction parameters can also be unified using hard-spaces (entered with Ctrl+Shift+spacebar):

```
{date \@ MMM°d,°yy}
```

■ Conditional fields allow you to avoid error messages and extra carriage returns in form and merge documents.

In the next chapter I will build several templates to demonstrate the customization potential of all the various tools discussed in the foregoing chapters.

# Putting It All Together: Sample Templates

**W**E'VE ARRIVED AT THE POINT OF IT ALL: UNITING THE VARIOUS customization tools Word puts at our disposal into custom, task-specific templates. This chapter will step through the design and construction of six templates.

As with the other examples in this book, the templates that follow are not presented as the only, or even the best, solutions. It is impossible for any programmer to anticipate the particular (and sometimes peculiar) requirements of every user. These templates are designed according to my own (sometimes dogmatic) predilections and opinions. But they are also relatively simple, and so can be easily understood and modified, unlike some of the more complex templates that ship with Word, which often try to be all things to all people.

I have not tried to provide an example template for every type of document. I do not attempt to replace the templates supplied by Microsoft. The emphasis in the templates that follow is on manuscript preparation (rather than office automation). I hope to illustrate that even the simplest document type, such as a journal, can benefit from the flexibility inherent in Word. I want to point your thinking about template design in various useful directions and demonstrate how Word's design encourages you to consider the various customization features—the properties and pieces gathered within a template—not as discrete functions operating independently, but as a matrix of related tools that work together.

**NOTE.** *The templates that follow use the standard TrueType fonts that ship with Windows 3.1.*

## Journal

The JOURNAL.DOT template is intended to perform a single, simple task. When you open (or create) a document based on this template, the insertion point is moved to the end of the document; the date and time are inserted, formatted as heading 1; and a new, normal, paragraph is inserted.

### Styles

Since this template is intended for the creation and maintenance of a journal, the styles required are few and simple.

The main consideration in creating the styles for this template is economy: I want to display as much text on a screen as possible. Therefore the default normal style, used for body text, is defined as single-spaced 10 point Times New Roman. Paragraphs are flush left, with no first indent, with a Space Before of 0.5 line.

I make constant use of the outline facility in Word, which is why I have chosen, in this journal template, to format the date as heading 1. This allows for easier navigation (by toggling into outline view). Heading level one is formatted as 12 point bold Arial, with a Space Before of 1 line.

Headers and Footers are based on heading 1, but as 9 instead of 12 point. If you change the heading 1 font, the header and footer font will automatically change as well. Changing the normal font will not change the heading font.

| Style | Definition |
|---|---|
| header | heading 1 + Font: 9 pt, Not Bold, Space Before 0 li, Not Keep With Next, Tab stops: 3" Centered; 6" Right Flush |
| heading 1 | NextStyle: Normal, Font: Arial 12 pt, Bold, Color: Blue, Language: English (US), Flush left, Space Before 1 li, Keep With Next |
| Normal | Font: Times New Roman 10 pt, Language: English (US), Flush left, Space Before 0.5 li |

## Headers and Footers

There is no boilerplate in the body of the template. There are, however, fields defined in the headers and footers.

Since this class of documents is not intended for presentation publication, the headers and footers are designed for informational purposes.

The header uses a pair of STYLEREF fields to display the first and last date stamp on each page:

```
{styleref "heading 1"}–{styleref "heading 1" \l}
```

which would display something like:

```
9/2/92 - 3:58 am–9/7/92 - 3:58 am
```

The footer contains the date of the printing (flush left) and the page number (flush right):

```
{printdate}                              page - {PAGE}
```

## Macros

There are three macros unique to JOURNAL.DOT, all of which concern the insertion of a date stamp.

The AutoNew macro is run once, when you create a new document based upon JOURNAL.DOT. It executes AutoOpen:

```
Sub Main
ToolsMacro .Name = "AutoOpen", .Run, .Show =2
End Sub
```

The AutoOpen macro for JOURNAL.DOT switches the current view to normal (or galley); zooms the text as large as the current screen width will allow; moves to the end of the document and tests whether to insert a new paragraph; executes another macro, DateStamp; and finally, inserts a new paragraph:

```
Sub Main
ViewNormal
ViewZoomPageWidth
On Error Goto Bye
Dim dlg As FileSummaryInfo
GetCurValues dlg
If dlg.FileName = "JOURNAL.DOT" Then Goto Bye
EndOfDocument
EditGoTo "\Line"
If Asc(Selection$()) <> 13 Then
    EndOfLine
    InsertPara
End If
FormatStyle .Name = "heading 1"
ToolsMacro .Name = "DateStamp", .Run, .Show =2
EndOfLine
InsertPara
Bye:
End Sub
```

Notice that a test is made to find out if the template itself has been opened; if so, nothing is done. There are several aspects of this macro you might want to further customize. For instance, if you prefer to always work in layout mode, change ViewNormal to ViewPage.

The DateStamp macro actually inserts a date field with a custom date-time picture, and then locks the field so that it will retain the current date and time:

```
Sub Main
InsertField .Field = "date \@M/d/yy - h:mm am/pm"
PrevField
LockFields
CharRight
End Sub
```

By making this a separate macro rather than simply a part of the Auto-Open macro, you can insert a date stamp at any time. You can change the format of the date stamp by customizing the date-time picture.

JOURNAL.DOT also contains a copy of the ToggleOutline macro created in Chapter 7. If you have installed this macro globally (into NORMAL-.DOT), you can delete it from this or any of the following templates.

### Access Methods

Below is an illustration of the modified toolbar buttons contained in JOURNAL.DOT:

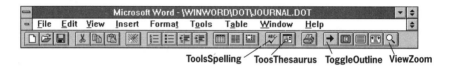

Here is a table of the keyboard assignments for JOURNAL.DOT:

| Keyboard Shortcut | Macro |
| --- | --- |
| Alt+Shift+D | DateStamp |
| Ctrl+Shift+O | ToggleOutline |

# Invoice

INVOICE.DOT provides a simple way to create an invoice. It makes use of several fields in combination with a macro to enter task date, title, hours, and rate into a table. The macro then inserts expression fields to calculate the task total, and the invoice total.

### Styles

The styles in this template were chosen to distinguish between the body elements of the invoice letter and the table of billable items.

The body text, address, and date are formatted as Times New Roman. The table text and header are formatted as Arial. Below is a table of the styles found in INVOICE.DOT.

| Style Name | Definition | Purpose |
|---|---|---|
| Address | Normal + Space After 0 li | The address of the invoice recipient |
| Date | Normal + Flush Right, Space Before 3 li After 3 li | The date of the invoice's creation |
| header | Normal + Font: Arial 12 pt, Indent: Left 4" Right -0.25" Flush Right, Space After 0 li, Border: Box (Shadowed Single), Tab stops: 3" Centered; 6" Right Flush | Used for the return address information in the first page header |
| Normal | Font: Times New Roman 10 pt, Language: (US), Flush left, Space After 0.5 li | The invoice body text |
| TableText | Normal + Font: Arial | The table text |
| Title | Normal + Bold, Line Spacing 2 li | The billable project |

Although these style divisions are useful function distinctions, the actual definitions depend entirely upon your preferences. I have not created any complex Based On or Next Style definitions. I would suggest you examine and modify the normal style definition.

Also, since an invoice is most often a single page, I have not specified header and footer information for pages beyond the first.

## Boilerplate

Of all the example templates, INVOICE.DOT depends most upon fields. Others use fields in headers and footers. The actual purpose of this template is dependent upon fields. The best way to understand what these fields accomplish is to use and examine the template. Figure 12.1(a) describes a sample invoice with field codes visible. Figure 12.1(b) describes the results of updating the template's fields.

The first page header contains the sender's name and address as specified by the ToolsOptionsUserInfo dialog box. Notice that the first line of this header is directly formatted as boldfaced.

The first line of the body of the invoice contains a DATE field. The second line contains a FILLIN field which, when updated, prompts the user for the name and address for the recipient of the invoice. The third line contains a TITLE field, which displays as the project description the document title contained in the FileSummaryInfo dialog box.

**Figure 12.1**
INVOICE.DOT
dissected with field
codes visible (a) and
with field results
visible (b)

**a)**

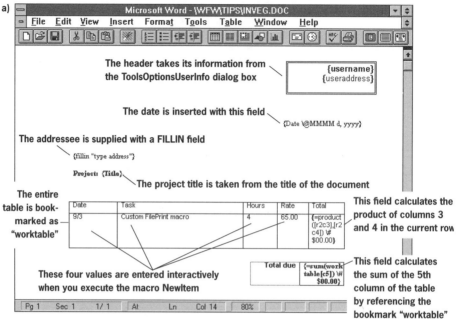

The header takes its information from the ToolsOptionsUserInfo dialog box

{username}
{useraddress}

The date is inserted with this field

{Date \@MMMM d, yyyy}

The addressee is supplied with a FILLIN field

{fillin "type address"}

Project: {Title}

The project title is taken from the title of the document

The entire table is book-marked as "worktable"

| Date | Task | Hours | Rate | Total |
|------|------|-------|------|-------|
| 9/3 | Custom FilePrint macro | 4 | 65.00 | {=product ([r2c3],[r2c4]) \# $00.00} |

This field calculates the product of columns 3 and 4 in the current row

These four values are entered interactively when you execute the macro NewItem

Total due    {=sum(worktable[c5]) \# $00.00}

This field calculates the sum of the 5th column of the table by referencing the bookmark "worktable"

**b)**

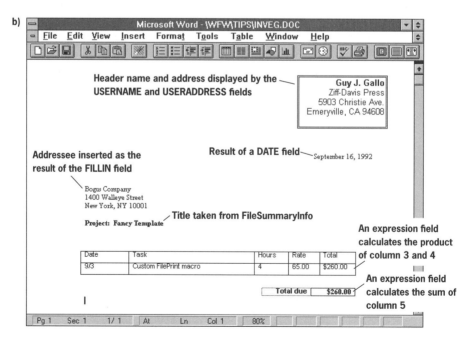

Header name and address displayed by the USERNAME and USERADDRESS fields

Guy J. Gallo
Ziff-Davis Press
5903 Christie Ave.
Emeryville, CA 94608

Addressee inserted as the result of the FILLIN field

Result of a DATE field — September 16, 1992

Bogus Company
1400 Walleye Street
New York, NY 10001

Project: Fancy Template

Title taken from FileSummaryInfo

An expression field calculates the product of column 3 and 4

| Date | Task | Hours | Rate | Total |
|------|------|-------|------|-------|
| 9/3 | Custom FilePrint macro | 4 | 65.00 | $260.00 |

Total due    $260.00

An expression field calculates the sum of column 5

The remainder of the boilerplate consists of two tables. The first contains the individual billable tasks. The last cell of each row in this table contains the following field:

```
{=product([r2c3],[r2c4]) \# $00.00}
```

This field is created and inserted by a template-specific macro named New-Item. It uses a spreadsheet-like reference—[r2c3],[r2c4]—to calculate the product of the numbers contained in columns 3 and 4 of row 2. You are not limited to a single task. That is, every time you run NewItem, a new row—with a new subtotaling field—will be created.

A second table holds the field which calculates the total due:

```
{=sum(worktable[c5]) \# $00.00}
```

The interesting thing about this field is that instead of using a spreadsheet reference, which would require the field to know how many rows and how many items there are in the invoice, this field references the entire subtotal column by using a bookmark. The table holding the individual tasks is covered by a bookmark named "worktable." You can reference all the cells of the subtotal column by combining the bookmark name with the column specification: worktable[c5].

## Macros

There are only two macros in this template. The first is an AutoNew macro:

```
Sub Main
FileSummaryInfo$
EditSelectAll
UpdateFields
ToolsMacro .Name = "NewItem", .Run, .Show = 2
End Sub
```

This macro first executes FileSummaryInfo so that you can enter a title for the current document. It then selects the entire document and updates all fields. This causes the FILLIN field to prompt you for the recipient's address. Finally, AutoNew executes the other macro in the template, NewItem:

```
Sub Main
EditGoTo "worktable"
EndOfRow
NextCell
If Not GetInput("Enter project date:") Then Goto Bye
If Not GetInput("Enter project title:") Then Goto Bye
If Not GetInput("Enter project hours:") Then Goto Bye
If Not GetInput("Enter project rate:") Then Goto Bye
x$ = Mid$(Str$(SelInfo(13)), 2)
```

```
InsertField .Field = "=product([r" + x$ + "c3],[r" + x$ + "c4]) \# $00.00"
TableSelectTable
InsertBookmark .Name = "WorkTable"
UpdateFields
EditGoTo "total"
UpdateFields
Bye:
End Sub

Function GetInput(msg$)
Begin Dialog UserDialog 340, 70
    Text 10, 6, 151, 13, msg$
    TextBox 10, 22, 319, 18, .Text
    OKButton 142, 43, 88, 21
    CancelButton 238, 43, 88, 21
End Dialog
Dim dlg As UserDialog
Choice = Dialog(dlg)
If Choice = 0 Then
    GetInput = 0
    TableDeleteCells .ShiftCells = 2
Else
    Insert dlg.Text
    NextCell
    GetInput = - 1
End If
End Function
```

NewItem moves to the table of billable items by using EditGoTo with the boilerplate bookmark "worktable," moves to the end of the table, and inserts a new row. The next four lines, all of the form:

> **If Not** GetInput(Message$) **Then Goto** Bye

call the user-function GetInput to query the user for a specific piece of information, passing as a parameter the message to display in the dialog box. If the dialog box presented by GetInput is canceled, the function removes the current row and returns false. When false is returned to the main subroutine, the macro exits. If the dialog box is not canceled, the information supplied by the user is inserted into the current cell and the insertion point is moved to the next cell.

After getting four pieces of information—date, task, hours, and rate—NewItem inserts a field that will total the amount for this row:

```
x$ = Mid$(Str$(SelInfo(13)), 2)
InsertField .Field = "=product([r" + x$ + "c3],[r" + x$ + "c4]) \# $00.00"
```

Notice that the number of the current row, which is variable with each execution of NewItem, is determined by a call to SelInfo(13).

The remainder of NewItem selects the table and redefines the bookmark "worktable," updates the fields in the task table, moves to the bookmark named "total," and updates the field which sums all the subtotals contained in column 5.

## Access Methods

Below is an illustration of the custom toolbar in INVOICE.DOT:

There is only one shortcut keystroke defined in INVOICE.DOT:

| Macro | Keyboard Shortcut |
|---|---|
| NewItem | Ctrl+Shift+N |

There is a single addition to the menu structure. The Insert menu provides another way to execute NewItem:

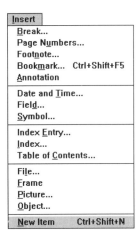

# Resume Template

The RESUME.DOT template is interesting both for what it does and what it demonstrates. It allows you to easily enter a standard format resume. What it demonstrates is how to create "side-heads," headings that are placed to the left of the subordinate body text.

See Figure 12.2 for an analysis of the styles and layout of a document based on RESUME.DOT.

**Figure 12.2**

Anatomy of RESUME.DOT

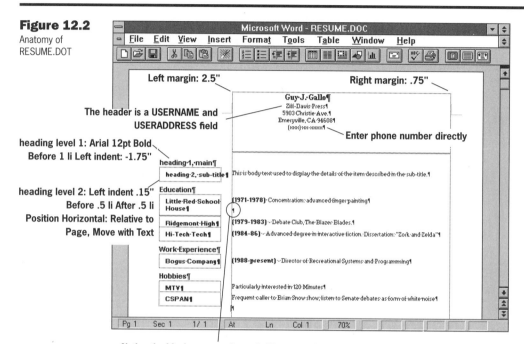

Notice the blank paragraph needed because the associated heading 2 is two lines

## Styles

There are three categories of style in RESUME.DOT: the first page header styles, the side-head styles, and the body text.

Name, Address, and AddressLast, all based upon the header style, are intended for the banner heading on the first page. The AddressLast style has a Space After of 3 lines and is, by default, applied to the resume telephone number.

| Style | Definition | Purpose |
|---|---|---|
| Address | header + Centered | The address in the first page header. |
| AddressLast | header + Centered, Space After 3 li | The last line of the address. By default this is a telephone number. |

| Style | Definition | Purpose |
|-------|-----------|---------|
| header | Normal + Indent: Left -1.75", Space Before 0 li After 0 li, Tab stops: 3" Centered; 6" Flush right | The style upon which Name, Address, and AddressLast are based. |
| heading 1 | NextStyle: heading 2: Arial 12 pt, Bold, Language: English (US), Indent: Left -1.75" Flush left, Space Before 1 li | The first of two side-heads. This heading is used to divide major categories of the resume. |
| heading 2 | NextStyle: Normal 1 + Font: 10 pt, Indent: Left 0.15", Space Before 0.5 li After 0.5 li, Position: Left Horiz. Relative To Page, 0" Vert. Relative To Horiz., Width: 1.5" | A side-head for individual items in the resume. It is positioned outside the left margin using a frame. |
| Name | header + Font: 14 pt, Bold, Centered | The first line of the banner first page header. |
| Normal | Font: Times New Roman 10 pt, Language: English (US), Flush left, Space Before 3 pt After 3 pt | Used for the body of the resume. |

## Header

The page first header contains two fields: USERNAME and USERADDRESS, formatted with the styles Name and Address, respectively. The last line of the header is intended for the contact telephone number. This line must be edited manually.

## Access Methods

Since the only macro is AutoNew and the styles used have built-in shortcut keys, there are no custom access methods.

# Manuscript

This template was designed specifically for fiction. Many publishers and agents still expect a manuscript to look like it came out of a typewriter. The publishing industry hasn't quite caught up with the electronic age. A fellow Word maven spent untold hours perfecting a template for his manuscript which made precise use of publishing style guidelines, proportionally spaced fonts, intricate and deliberate formatting for quotations, notes, equations, and the like. Theoretically, his document file could have been shipped directly to a linotronic machine and the book typeset in a matter of hours. But the publisher insisted on retyping and then hand setting the entire manuscript. Even this manuscript, which will be converted from Word for Windows to Word for the Macintosh, to a page layout program, must, according to the publisher, be void of any formatting intricacy, in double-spaced Courier 12 point.

There are, in fact, good reasons for the continued use of Courier 12 point, double-spaced for a manuscript. For one thing, it is much easier to edit. Editors think in Courier, and can more readily estimate word and page count. Therefore, MSS.DOT is completely uninteresting when it comes to font and layout. Instead it concentrates on supplying macros and access methods to ease the entry and editing of the manuscript. The fact that some find proportionally spaced fonts easier to read (as opposed to edit) is accommodated with a macro, named ToggleFormat, that switches between vanilla Courier and a two-column "book-like" proportionally spaced layout.

## Styles

The Normal style in MSS.DOT is double-spaced, 12pt Courier New, with a first line indent of 0.3".

Heading styles 1 through 3 are intended for use as part, chapter, and section headings. Heading 1 is formatted as bold 12pt Courier New, color blue, Space Before 2 li, Page Break Before, with a solid line below the paragraph. The Next Style is heading 2 (this could be changed to Normal or NormalOpen if you only use one heading level in your documents). Heading 2 is based on heading 1, with these differences: not bold, color red, and Next Style is NormalOpen.

The first paragraph of a new chapter or section should be formatted as NormalOpen. This style is identical to Normal with these exceptions: There is no first line indentation and there is a Space Before of 1.5 lines. The Next Style is Normal.

Below is a table of the significant custom or customized styles found in MSS.DOT.

| Style Name | Definition | Purpose |
|---|---|---|
| header | Normal + Font: 10 pt, Color: Blue, Indent: First 0" Right -0.5", Line Spacing Auto, Tab stops: 6.5" Right Flush | |
| heading 1 | NextStyle: heading 2, Font: Courier New 12 pt, Bold, Color: Blue, Language: English (US), Flush left, Line Spacing 1 li, Space Before 2 li, Page Break Before, Keep With Next Border: Bottom Between (Single) | Chapter or part titles |
| heading 2 | NextStyle: NormalOpen, heading 1 + Not Bold, Color: Red, Not Page Break Before, Border: Bottom Between (No Border) Border Spacing: 0 pt, Tab stops: 3" Centered | Chapter or section titles |
| heading 3 | NextStyle: NormalOpen, heading 2 + Italic, Color: Dk Red | Subsection titles |
| Normal | Font: Courier New 12 pt, Language: English (US), Indent: First 0.3" Flush left, Line Spacing 2 li | Body text |
| NormalOpen | NextStyle: Normal, Normal + Indent: First 0", Space Before 1.5 li | Body text for first paragraph of a chapter or section |
| Quotation | Normal + Italic, Color: Red, Indent: Left 1" First 0" Right 1", Line Spacing 1 li, Space Before 1 li | Extended quotations |

| Style Name | Definition | Purpose |
|---|---|---|
| SectionBreak | NextStyle: NormalOpen, Normal + Indent: First 0" Centered, Line Spacing 1 li, Space Before 2 li After 1 li, Keep With Next | For breaks within a section (often marked with a double em dash) |

## Headers and Footers

The header in MSS.DOT displays the title flush left and the most recent heading 1 flush right. For example:

```
Take Word for Windows to the Edge                                      Manuscript
```

This header manages to place text both flush left and flush right on a single line by defining a right-aligned tab setting for the header style. The paragraph itself is formatted as flush left; but there is a single right-aligned tab set at 6.5". So, by entering the first field, a tab, and the second field, the header allows both left and right flush text.

The fields that generate these results look like:

```
{title}→{if{styleref "heading 1"} <>"Error! No text of specified style in
document" {styleref 1}}¶
```

There is a neat trick in the second field code. Instead of using a simple STYLEREF field, it uses a conditional field which determines if there is a heading 1 paragraph to display. When a STYLEREF field cannot locate a paragraph of the specified style, it displays an error message: "Error! No text of specified style in document." Therefore, using an IF field, we can test if this is the result of a STYLEREF.

```
{if{styleref "heading 1"} <>"Error! No text of specified style in document"
{styleref 1}}
```

This complicated field is much the safer way to use STYLEREF. Not only is it more generally useful, since it works in a document that does not have the style in question, it also circumvents a bug which may appear in a document with multiple column breaks. If a column break coincides with a page break, a STYLEREF field in the header will produce an error on the last page before the column break.

The footer contains a PAGE field. The footer style is based on the header style, with this difference: the style contains a centered tab setting at 3" as well as the right-aligned tab setting at 6.5". This allows you to center the page number (even though the style is a left aligned paragraph). This is done by entering a tab followed by the PAGE field.

```
         →                {page}¶
```

## Revision Marking Macros

There are three macros in the MSS.DOT template that facilitate the use of revision marks: RevisionSearch, RevisionAccept, and RevisionUndo.

RevisionSearch simply looks for the next instance of revised text:

```
Sub Main
ToolsRevisionMarks .Search
End Sub
```

RevisionAccept checks to see if the current selection is a block (rather than the blinking bar insertion point), and if so, accepts any revision contained in the selection:

```
Sub Main
If SelType() = 2 Then
    ToolsRevisionMarks .AcceptRevisions
Else
    Beep
End If
End Sub
```

The revised text to be accepted can be marked manually or as a consequence of running the RevisionSearch macro.

RevisionUndo checks to see if the current selection is a block and if so reverses any revisions contained within the selection.

```
Sub Main
If SelType() = 2 Then
    ToolsRevisionMarks .UndoRevisions
Else
    Beep
End If
End Sub
```

The point of these three macros is to allow the use of revision marks without having to use the RevisionMarks dialog box to find, accept, or undo revisions.

## Toggling from Portrait to Landscape

Although editors and agents prefer typewriter-like double-spaced manuscripts, you may want to conserve paper and use an easier-to-read font when printing drafts of your manuscript. ToggleLayout changes the layout of your manuscript from the usual single-column portrait to double-column landscape. The effect is equivalent to "two-up" printing:

```
Sub Main
vp = ViewPage()
ViewNormal
```

```
Dim dlg As FormatPageSetup
GetCurValues dlg
If dlg.Orientation = 0 Then        'Toggle to landscape, two column
    FormatPageSetup .AttributeControls = 0, .ApplyPropsTo = 4, \
        .TopMargin = "1" + Chr$(34), \
        .BottomMargin = "1" + Chr$(34), \
        .LeftMargin = ".75" + Chr$(34), \
        .RightMargin = ".75" + Chr$(34), \
        .Gutter = "0" + Chr$(34)
    FormatPageSetup .AttributeControls = 0, .ApplyPropsTo = 4, \
        .Orientation = 1, \
        .PageWidth = "11 in", \
        .PageHeight = "8.5 in"
    FormatColumns .Columns = "2", \
        .ColumnSpacing = "1.5" + Chr$(34), \
        .ApplyColsTo = 4, \
        .ColLine = 1
    FormatStyle .Name = "Header", .Define
    FormatDefineStyleTabs .ClearAll
    FormatDefineStyleTabs .Position = "9.5 in", .Align = 2, .Set
    FormatStyle .Name = "Footer", .Define
    FormatDefineStyleTabs .ClearAll
    FormatDefineStyleTabs .Position = "1.75 in", .Align = 1, .Set
    FormatDefineStyleTabs .Position = "7.25 in", .Align = 1, .Set
    ViewHeaderFooter .Type = 1
    EditSelectAll
    EditClear
    ResetPara
    Call InsertSpecialPage
    ResetChar
    ClosePane
    FormatStyle .Name = "Normal", .Define
    FormatDefineStyleChar .Font = "Times New Roman", .Points = "10"
    FormatDefineStylePara .Alignment = 0, \
        .FirstIndent = ".2 in", \
        .LineSpacing = "-15 pt"
Else      'toggle to portrait, one column
    FormatPageSetup .AttributeControls = 0, .ApplyPropsTo = 4, \
        .TopMargin = "1" + Chr$(34), \
        .BottomMargin = "1" + Chr$(34), \
        .LeftMargin = "1.5" + Chr$(34), \
        .RightMargin = ".75" + Chr$(34), \
        .Gutter = "0" + Chr$(34)
    FormatPageSetup .AttributeControls = 0, .ApplyPropsTo = 4, \
        .Orientation = 0, \
        .PageWidth = "8.5 in", \
        .PageHeight = "11 in"
    FormatColumns .Columns = "1"
    FormatStyle .Name = "Header", .Define
    FormatDefineStyleTabs .ClearAll
    FormatDefineStyleTabs .Position = "6.5 in", .Align = 2, .Set
    FormatStyle .Name = "Footer", .Define
```

```
    FormatDefineStyleTabs .ClearAll
    FormatDefineStyleTabs .Position = "3 in", .Align = 1, .Set
    FormatDefineStyleTabs .Position = "6.5 in", .Align = 2, .Set
    ViewHeaderFooter .Type = 1
    EditSelectAll
    EditClear
    ResetPara
    Insert Chr$(9)
    InsertPageField
    ClosePane
    FormatStyle .Name = "Normal", .Define
    FormatDefineStyleChar .Font = "Courier New", .Points = "12"
    FormatDefineStylePara .Alignment = 0, \
        .FirstIndent = ".3 in", \
        .LineSpacing = "2 li"
End If
Bye:
If VP Then ViewPage
StartOfDocument
End Sub

Sub InsertSpecialPage
    Insert Chr$(9)
    InsertFieldChars
    Insert "="
    InsertFieldChars
    Insert "page"
    CharRight
    Insert "+"
    InsertFieldChars
    Insert "="
    InsertFieldChars
    Insert "page"
    CharRight
    Insert "- 1"
    CharRight
    Insert "*1+0"
    CharRight
    Insert Chr$(9)
    InsertFieldChars
    Insert "="
    InsertFieldChars
    Insert "page"
    CharRight
    Insert "+"
    InsertFieldChars
    Insert "="
    InsertFieldChars
    Insert "page"
    CharRight
```

```
    Insert "-1"
    CharRight
    Insert "*1+1"
End Sub
```

ToggleLayout is entirely automatic. It presents no dialog box. It first examines the orientation setting stored in FormatPageSetup. If the document is currently formatted as portrait, it changes the orientation, number of columns, footer style and information, and normal style. If the document is currently landscape, it toggles back to the normal single-column portrait.

There is one thing of particular interest in this macro: It inserts multiple page numbers for each page of the document. That is, each column is numbered as a "virtual page." This is done by the user-sub named InsertSpecial-Page. This subroutine inserts the following pair of fields into the footer:

```
{={page}+{={page}- 1}*1+0}    →    {={page}+{={page}-1}*1+1}
```

By using these fields to insert "virtual" page numbers beneath each of the two columns, the printed document will have the appearance of two pages per printed sheet.

This macro will work on any document (so, for instance, you could copy it to PLAY.DOT or SCRIPT.DOT). Since this macro will only be run occasionally, it does not have either a keyboard or toolbar access method. It does, however, appear under the Format menu.

## Utility Macros

There are two additional utility macros in MSS.DOT: ToggleOutline and ToggleRevision (both of which were created in Chapter 7).

## Access Methods

Below is an illustration of the modified toolbar buttons contained in MSS.DOT:

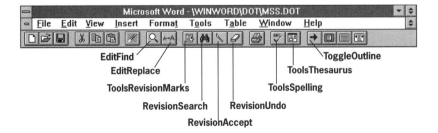

There is a single change to the menu structure in MSS.DOT. The macro ToggleLayout can be accessed from the Format menu:

Here is a table of the keyboard assignments for MSS.DOT:

| Macro | Keyboard Shortcut |
| --- | --- |
| RevisionAccept | Alt+Ctrl+A |
| ToggleRevision | Ctrl+Shift+R |
| RevisionSearch | Alt+Ctrl+S |
| RevisionUndo | Alt+Ctrl+U |
| NormalOpen | Ctrl+N |
| ToggleOutline | Ctrl+Shift+O |
| NormalStyle | Ctrl+Shift+N |

**NOTE.** *I have chosen to use Alt+Ctrl key combinations for template-specific macros to reserve the more easily accessible Ctrl+Shift combinations (which can be accessed via ToolsOptionsKeyboard) for global macros.*

## Glossaries

There is a single glossary in MSS.DOT. Named SectionBreak, this glossary will insert two em dashes, formatted with the style SectionBreak.

# Play Script

PLAY.DOT is designed to simplify the entering and editing of a standard dramatic play script. Again, the font and layout design are on the conservative side. Producers and artistic directors are not, as with book manuscripts, concerned with a standard method of calculating published page or character count. Rather, they are accustomed to judging playing time by the following formula: One page equals one minute of stage time. It's best not to strain the play's reader with fancy formatting. Better to surprise them with content.

## Styles

There are four basic paragraph styles in a play: dialogue, character name, parenthetical, and stage direction. The Normal style in PLAY.DOT is used for dialogue. It is formatted as 12pt Courier New, single-spaced. This style is applied in several ways: the normal style keyboard shortcut of Alt+Shift+Numpad5, Alt+D, or the D icon on the toolbar. The Next Style is defined as Char.

The style for character name is based upon the normal style, but with a left indent of 2.5" and a Space Before setting of 1 line. This style is applied with the keyboard shortcut Alt+C or the toolbar button C. The Next Style is defined as Dialogue.

The Paren style is designed for parenthetical remarks. Paren is formatted as italic, with an indent of 2.5". There are two shortcut keyboard combinations for the parenthetical style: One simply applies the style (Ctrl+Shift+P), the other prompts for the parenthetical text and automatically inserts the parenthesis (Alt+P). The toolbar icon P executes the latter method. The Next Style is defined as Dialogue.

The Stage style is intended for extended parentheticals or stage directions. Stage is italic, single-spaced, Space Before 1 line, left indent 2". Stage is applied either by keyboard (Alt+S) or the S icon on the toolbar. The Next Style is defined as Stage. This allows you to input multiple paragraphs of stage directions.

These styles, by clever use of the Next Style specifications, allow you to enter character name and dialogue (the most common formats in play scripts) continuously, without applying a format. That is, after typing a character name, pressing Enter positions you for dialogue; pressing Enter at the end of a line of dialogue positions you for the next character name.

Two further styles are significant and require some comment. PLAY.DOT uses heading 1 to hold the act division and heading 2 to hold the scene number. By adhering to this convention you enable two features in the template: You can then use the outlining facility to easily navigate the play script; and, when printing, the current act and scene numbers will be included in the header information.

| Style Name | Definition | Purpose |
|---|---|---|
| Char | NextStyle: Normal, Normal + Caps, Indent: Left 2.5", Space 1 li, Keep With Next, Tab stops: 2.5" | Character name. |
| header | Normal + Font: 10 pt, Color: Blue, Not Keep Lines Together, Tab stops: 3" Centered; 6" Right Flush | Note the use of tab stops at 3" and 6". This allows you to have both left and right flush text. |
| heading 1 | NextStyle: Normal, Normal + Bold, Color: Blue, Centered, Space Before 2 li After 1 li, Page Break Before, Keep With Next, Not Keep Lines Together | Act number. |
| heading 2 | NextStyle: Normal, Normal + Underline, Keep With Next, Not Keep Lines Together | Scene number. |
| Normal | NextStyle: Char Font: Courier New 12 pt, Language: English (US), Flush left, Keep Lines Together | Dialogue. |
| Paren | NextStyle: Normal, Normal + Italic, Indent: Left 2.5", Keep With Next | Parenthetical directions. |
| Stage | Normal + Italic, Indent: Left 2" Right 0.5", Space Before 1 li | Extended stage directions. |

## Header

The header contains an extraordinarily forbidding set of fields:

```
{title} →{if{styleref "heading 1"}<>"Error! No text of specified style in
document." {quote {styleref 1} - }}{if{styleref "heading 2"}<>"Error! No text
of specified style in document." {quote {styleref 2} - }}page {page}.
```

Breaking this down into a more legible format we have

```
{title}→{if
{styleref 1}<>
    "Error! No text of specified style in document."
    {quote {styleref 1} - }
}{If
{styleref 2}<>
    "Error! No text of specified style in document."
    {quote {styleref 2} - }
}page {page}.
```

In this format you can more easily see that the header consists of a TITLE field, two IF fields, and a PAGE field. The IF fields examine the result of a STYLEREF field, checking that such a style does exist and then inserting the STYLEREF result plus a hyphen. Finally, the PAGE field inserts the current page number.

This sequence of fields will result in something like:

```
Antigone                    Act One - Scene one - page 1.
```

Notice that the title is flush left and a combination of act number, scene number, and page number is flush right. The act and scene numbers will only display if you are using heading 1 and heading 2 for act and scene headlines.

## Glossaries

There are no predefined glossaries in PLAY.DOT. However, you should consider using glossaries for character names.

## Macros

Below is a table of all macros contained in PLAY.DOT:

| Macro | Purpose | Keyboard |
| --- | --- | --- |
| ApplyChar | Apply character format | Alt+C |
| ApplyDialogue | Apply dialogue format | Alt+D |
| ApplyParen | Apply parenthetical format | Alt+P |
| ApplyStage | Apply stage direction format | Alt+S |
| RevisionAccept | Accept revision | Alt+Ctrl+A |

| Macro | Purpose | Keyboard |
|---|---|---|
| RevisionSearch | Search for next revision | Alt+Ctrl+S |
| RevisionUndo | Undo revision | Alt+Ctrl+U |
| ToggleOutline | Toggle ViewOutline | Ctrl+Shift+O |
| ToggleRevision | Toggle ToolsRevisionMarks | Ctrl+Shift+R |

Three of the macros contained in PLAY.DOT simply apply a style: Apply-Char, ApplyDialogue, and ApplyStage. By creating individual macros to apply these styles we can place them on the toolbar and assign keyboard shortcuts that are not supported by the built-in shortcut key facility of FormatStyle. You will notice that the shortcut key assignment is a simple Alt plus key. Such an assignment must be made manually (using the AssignKey macro created in Chapter 7).

You will also notice that five macros that have already been discussed are included in this template: RevisionAccept, RevisionSearch, RevisionUndo, ToggleOutline, and ToggleRevision.

This leaves ApplyParen. This macro does more than simply apply the style Paren. It first determines if the current line is blank; if so, it proceeds, if not, it inserts a new paragraph. It then prompts you for the text of the parenthetical and automatically inserts the opening and closing parentheses. If you cancel the dialog box, the new paragraph is formatted as dialogue.

```
Sub Main
EditGoTo "\Line"
If Asc(Selection$()) <> 13 Then
    EndOfLine
    InsertPara
End If
Begin Dialog UserDialog 340, 70
    Text 10, 6, 151, 13, "Enter parenthetical:"
    TextBox 10, 22, 319, 18, .Text
    OKButton 142, 43, 88, 21
    CancelButton 238, 43, 88, 21
End Dialog
Dim dlg As UserDialog
Choice = Dialog(dlg)
If Choice = 0 Then
    FormatStyle .Name = "Dialogue"
ElseIf dlg.Text = "" Then
    FormatStyle .Name = "Paren"
```

```
        LineUp
        FormatParagraph .KeepWithNext = 1
        LineDown
Else
        Insert "(" + dlg.Text + ")"
        FormatStyle .Name = "Paren"
        LineUp
        FormatParagraph .KeepWithNext = 1
        LineDown
        InsertPara
End If
End Sub
```

There are two ways to format an existing paragraph as Paren without in-serting the opening and closing parentheses. You can bypass the macro Apply-Paren entirely by using the shortcut key combination defined as part of the style, Ctrl+Shift+P. Or you can execute ApplyParen and leave the edit box blank and press Enter.

You could further customize ApplyParen by providing a default paren-thetical. For instance, if your most common parenthetical is "pause," simply insert the line:

```
dlg.Text = "pause"
```

between the dimensioning of the dialog variable and displaying the dialog box:

```
Dim dlg As UserDialog
dlg.Text = "pause"
Choice = Dialog(dlg)
```

## Access Methods

Below is an illustration of the toolbar customizations contained in PLAY.DOT:

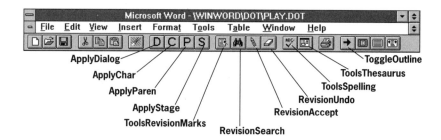

The Format menu contains the four formatting macros:

Here is a table of the keyboard assignments for MSS.DOT:

| **Macro** | **Keyboard Shortcut** |
| --- | --- |
| RevisionAccept | Alt+Ctrl+A |
| ToggleRevision | Ctrl+Shift+R |
| RevisionSearch | Alt+Ctrl+S |
| RevisionUndo | Alt+Ctrl+U |
| NormalOpen | Ctrl+N |
| ToggleOutline | Ctrl+Shift+O |
| NormalStyle | Ctrl+Shift+N |
| ApplyDialogue | Alt+D |
| ApplyChar | Alt+C |
| ApplyParen | Alt+P |
| ApplyStage | Alt+S |

# Feature Screenplay

SCRIPT.DOT is quite similar to PLAY.DOT. It is intended for the creation of feature screenplays. The format follows the guidelines established by the Writer's Guild of America.

Like play scripts, screenplays are read with an eye to playing time. Producers and script readers calculate using the same formula (one page equals one minute of screen time), and so expect a script formatted in 12 point fixed font, with generous margins.

A screenplay longer than 120 pages enters Hollywood at a distinct disadvantage. Virtually every writer panics on deadline day, trying to reformat a 140-page behemoth into a fashionably svelte manuscript. Computers make this easy. You can cheat and make your screenplays *appear* shorter by increasing the margins for action and dialogue; you can use proportionally spaced fonts. However, I advise against this for two reasons:

- No one is fooled. A script that comes in at 120 pages of 10 point Helvetica is, we all know, even producers know, actually 132 pages of script.

- It helps the actual composition of the screenplay if it is formatted according to the styles and indents contained in SCRIPT.DOT. The flow of the script, the tempo and timing, are simply easier to see, to feel; you can sense how much description is on the page, how much dialogue.

## Styles

The styles in SCRIPT.DOT are similar to those in PLAY.DOT. However, there are significant differences. The Normal style is used for action, the descriptive prose that makes up most of a screenplay, rather than dialogue. The indentations are entirely different.

One major difference between the play and screenplay templates lies in the use of heading levels. In PLAY.DOT, headings 1 and 2 were designed to hold the act and scene divisions. In stage play scripts, those divisions are normally printed. In a screenplay, act divisions are usually not printed, and scenes are numbered with a special format called a *slugline,* which contains a number and a short description of the scene's location.

However, just because the producers do not want to see the dramaturgical underpinnings doesn't mean they aren't useful to have around. So I have defined headings 1 and 2 as hidden styles, useful for organizing and outlining the screenplay, but printed only if you explicitly tell Word to do so. In SCRIPT.DOT, heading 1 is meant for the act divisions, heading 2 for the *sequence* divisions (a sequence being a related group of scenes), and heading 3 for the scene sluglines.

You do not need to use headings 1 and 2. But with a little ingenuity you can describe your screenplay in a useful, readily legible manner by using these styles.

Below is a table of the most significant custom and customized styles in SCRIPT.DOT.

| Style Name | Definition | Purpose |
|---|---|---|
| Char | NextStyle: Dialogue, Normal + Caps, Indent: Left 2.5", Keep With Next | Character name. |
| Dialogue | NextStyle: Char, Normal + Indent: Left 1.5", Space Before 0 li, Keep Lines Together | Dialogue. |
| DialogueItalic | NextStyle: Char, Dialogue + Italic | Italic dialogue. |
| header | Normal + Font: 10 pt, Color: Dk Blue, Language: (no proofing), Indent: Right - 0.5" Justified, Space Before 0 li, Tab stops: 6.75" Right Flush | Character name. |
| Heading | NextStyle: heading 3, Title + No Underline, Space Before 3 li After 2 li | A style for miscellaneous heading paragraphs (like FADE IN:). |
| heading 1 | NextStyle: heading 2 Normal + Bold Hidden, Color: Red, Keep With Next | Act division. Note this is a hidden style, meant for organizational purposes. |
| heading 2 | NextStyle: HiddenNote, Normal + Italic Hidden, Color: Red, Indent: Left 0.5" First -0.25" Right 0.25", Space Before 0.5 li, Keep With Next | Sequence division. Note this is a hidden style, meant for organizational purposes. |
| heading 3 | NextStyle: Normal, Normal + Caps, Color: Blue, Line Spacing 1 li, Space Before 1.5 li, Keep With Next, Tab stops: 0"; 1"; 6.5" Right Flush | Parenthetical directions. |

| Style Name | Definition | Purpose |
|---|---|---|
| HiddenNote | Font: Courier 10 pt, Hidden, Language: English (US), Indent: Left 1" Right 2", Flush left, Keep Lines Together, Border: Box (Single) | A hidden paragraph style meant for jotting notes. |
| Normal | Font: Courier New 12 pt, Language: English (US), Flush left, Line Spacing Exactly 1 li, Space Before 1 li | Action. |
| Paren | NextStyle: Dialogue, Normal + Indent: Left 2" First -0.1" Right 1.5", Space Before 0 li, Keep With Next | Parenthetical. Note that the first line indent of -0.1" creates a hanging indent of one character. |
| SbSChar | NextStyle: SbSDialogue, Char + Indent: Left 1" | Side by side Character name. |
| SbSDialogue | NextStyle: Normal, Normal + Line Spacing 1 li, Space Before 0 li, Keep Lines Together | Side by side dialogue. |
| Transition | NextStyle: heading 3, Normal + Caps, Color: Blue, Indent: Left 4.5" Right -0.5" | Transition break. |

## Headers

SCRIPT.DOT defines the first page header as blank. Subsequent pages display the title and the current page number using the following combination of literal text and fields:

{title}                                             page {page}

## Macros

As in PLAY.DOT, there are several macros devoted solely to applying paragraph formatting:

| Macro | Purpose |
|-------|---------|
| ApplyAction | Apply normal style |
| ApplyBreak | Apply transition break |
| ApplyChar | Apply character format |
| ApplyDialogue | Apply dialogue format |
| ApplySlugline | Apply heading 3 |
| ApplyParen | Apply parenthetical format |

The four macros used to simplify using revision marks, are also included:

| Macro | Purpose |
|-------|---------|
| RevisionAccept | Accept revision |
| RevisionSearch | Search for next revision |
| RevisionUndo | Undo revision |
| ToggleRevision | Toggle ToolsRevisionMarks |

The macros that are unique to SCRIPT.DOT are

■ *SideBySideDialog*   This macro inserts a centered table at the insertion point and formats the text within both cells as SbSChar. This allows you to immediately type the first speaker's name, press Enter (automatically formatting the next paragraph as SbSDialog), and enter the first speech. Pressing Tab moves you to the second cell of the table, where you can enter the second speaker's name and speech.

■ *NumberThisSlug*   If the current paragraph is heading 3 (the style reserved for sluglines), this macro inserts a SEQ field. The field is of the form: {seq slug}. The reason I use sequence numbering rather than either paragraph or outline numbering is simple: I can refer to the most recent sequence number by inserting a field {seq slug \r}. This allows you to insert scene numbers at both the left and right side of the slugline.

- *NumberAllSlugs*   This macro renumbers all the sluglines in the document. It gives you a choice of placing the scene number on the left, the right, or both.

- *ToggleSlugIndent*   If you place your scene numbers on the left of the slugline, you will want to run this macro. It toggles the left indent of the heading 3 style between 0" (the default) and -0.5" (which places the scene number a half an inch into the left margin).

- *StripNumbers*   This macro, accessible from NumberAllSlugs, removes all SEQ fields from the document.

## Access Methods

Below is an illustration of the custom toolbar contained in SCRIPT.DOT:

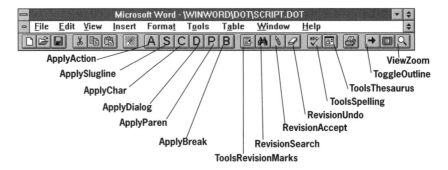

There are custom additions to three menus. The Insert menu allows you to call the SideBySideDialog macro:

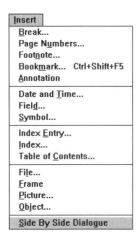

The Format menu contains items for each of the main paragraph formats:

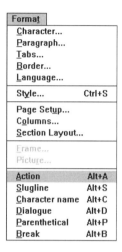

The Tools menu contains three macros related to numbering sluglines:

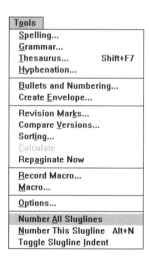

Here is a table of the keyboard assignments for SCRIPT.DOT:

| Macro | Keyboard Shortcut |
| --- | --- |
| ApplyAction (Normal) | Alt+A |
| ApplyBreak | Alt+B |

| Macro | Keyboard Shortcut |
|---|---|
| ApplyChar | Alt+C |
| ApplyDialogue | Alt+D |
| ApplyParen | Alt+P |
| ApplySlugline (heading 3) | Alt+S |
| NumberThisSlug | Alt+N |
| RevisionAccept | Alt+Ctrl+A |
| RevisionSearch | Alt+Ctrl+S |
| RevisionUndo | Alt+Ctrl+U |
| ToggleOutline | Ctrl+Shift+O |
| ToggleRevision | Ctrl+Shift+R |

## Glossaries

There are four standard abbreviations stored in the glossary of SCRIPT.DOT:

| Glossary Name | Glossary |
|---|---|
| D | DISSOLVE TO: |
| C | CUT TO: |
| I | INT. |
| E | EXT. |

# Sample Templates—Summary

Designing a template is no small matter. You must determine the font and layout requirements; consider which aspects of the document's creation or editing can be automated using fields or macros; designate a logical set of access methods that are mnemonic but do not conflict with standard assignments.

So far I have tried to elucidate the specific aspects of Word for Windows which relate to customization. In the next chapter I will discuss some potentially confusing features in Word (some might call them bugs) and present ways to optimize your configuration.

CHAPTER

13

# Miscellaneous Tips, Bugs, and Secrets

THIS CHAPTER IS A COMPENDIUM OF TRICKS, SECRETS, AND WARNINGS gathered over three years of intense exploration of Word's capacities (and limitations). The lessons to follow are not structured. They are not building to a single insight. They are presented in no particular order. Rather, I hope to give you the benefit of my sometimes frustrated experience in conquering Word.

# Oddities and Anomalies

Word is such a complicated program that often users feel humbled before it. Faced with such a powerful program, there is a danger that when a truly weird or unexpected thing happens, users will assume it was *their* fault rather than Word's. In fact, there are lots of cases where Word's behavior is less than logical. And despite my admiration for the overall design, there are many things I find infuriating (some of which I've preached on in the foregoing chapters).

## The Hidden Attribute

I'm a great fan of the hidden attribute. I love the idea of tucking little tidbits of text into a document, toggling their appearance as I type. I like the concept of a "pseudodeletion." The text formatted as hidden isn't really gone, but it's out of my way, relegated to a limbo reserved for dubious prose.

From conversations with Word's developers, it seems that the inclusion of the hidden attribute was something of an afterthought. Hidden text has been in Word for DOS for several years. The implementation of hidden text in Word for Windows demonstrates that Word for Windows is a closer cousin to Word for the Macintosh than it is to Word for DOS. In Word for DOS, the hidden attribute is one more character style and behaves quite differently than it does in Word for Windows. On the Mac, the hidden attribute was required for certain kinds of linking (that is to say, it was a kludge). When Word for Windows was created, based in large part on Word for the Mac, it inherited the implementation of hidden text from the Mac, along with some oddities and limitations.

### Direct Hidden Plus Style Hidden Equals Not Hidden

There are two kinds of formatting in Word: direct formatting (which is applied by the speed formatting keys such as Ctrl+B, Ctrl+I, and Ctrl+H) and style formatting. Since there are two ways to format text, the developers had to accommodate those instances where the same character attribute is applied with both methods to the same text. That is, what happens when you make a word bold within a paragraph that is already bold by style definition?

The answer may surprise the newcomer to Word: Bold text within a bold style becomes not bold.

Word follows this logic:

```
attribute + attribute = not attribute
```

whenever text, formatted with a given attribute, is inserted *into* a paragraph styled with the same attribute.

This is quite logical, since the point of the bold (or italic or underline) attribute is emphasis. Such attributes are used to make text stand out from the surrounding text. When pasted into surrounding text that is itself bold, the purposed emphasis is retained by toggling the inserted text from bold to not bold. The same rule also applies to other character attributes, such as underline, italic, and so on.

The problem is: This rule also applies to the hidden character attribute. Why is this a problem? Simple: Unlike the other character attributes, hidden is not intended to place emphasis on text. Once formatted as hidden, text should remain hidden no matter what, no matter how the underlying style is changed or where the hidden text is pasted. The whole point of hidden text is lost if there are any cases in which the text can be inadvertently changed to nonhidden.

To demonstrate this, create a style named Note. Format a paragraph of text as Note. Make sure that neither All nor Hidden Text is checked in the ToolsOptionsView dialog. Type a chunk of text. Select any word in the paragraph and press Ctrl+H to directly format it as hidden. Now press Ctrl+S twice to bring up the FormatStyle dialog box. Press Alt+D, Alt+C, Alt+H, Enter, Alt+A, Esc. This sequence of keystrokes changes the underlying definition of Note from nonhidden to hidden. Notice that the word previously formatted directly as hidden is now visible.

There is no way to work around this limitation. Once you know about it, however, you can more easily avoid inadvertently displaying those notes not meant for other's eyes.

### Hidden Styles

There's another oddity regarding hidden text: It is rather too easy for it to get deleted without your realizing it. My advice if you use a lot of hidden text—either paragraphs formatted with a hidden style or words directly formatted as hidden—is to make sure that Hidden Text is checked in the ToolsOptionsView dialog before doing extensive editing.

One particularly nefarious oddity can occur if you use hidden styles. It is possible to delete the first word of a nonhidden paragraph and inadvertently delete the previous hidden paragraph. Figure 13.1 shows a document based on SCRIPT.DOT that has two hidden styles (headings 1 and 2) followed by a nonhidden style (heading 3). The top pane has hidden text hidden, the lower pane is displayed for comparison's sake.

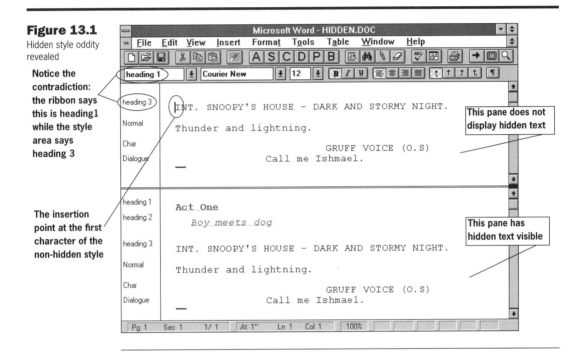

**Figure 13.1**
Hidden style oddity revealed

Notice the contradiction: the ribbon says this is heading1 while the style area says heading 3

The insertion point at the first character of the non-hidden style

Notice that the Ribbon thinks the insertion point, which is clearly poised before the first character of a heading 3 paragraph, is currently located in a heading 1 paragraph.

This may seem like a trivial inconsistency. In fact, it can cause major headaches. If you create an example document such as that shown in Figure 13.1, place the cursor at the first character of the nonhidden style and press Del; you will hear a beep and nothing will happen. Why? Because Word is confused. It knows enough to know that the insertion point is poised between two styles, one hidden and one not hidden. It will not allow you to delete the first character. However, it will not protect you if the selection is a block, rather than a blinking insertion bar.

To demonstrate, press Ctrl+Shift+Right Arrow to select the first word of the heading 3 paragraph. The Ribbon will blank (because more than one style is selected). Press Del. The two hidden paragraphs will be deleted, along with the first word of heading 3.

**DISK**
EditClear—A
replacement for the
internal EditClear
which detects
hidden text

If this sounds like a problem to you (and it will if you use a great deal of hidden text), it can be circumvented with a pair of macros to replace the built-in EditCut and EditClear commands:

```
Sub Main
If SelInfo(27) Then  EditClear$ : Goto Bye
Dim dlg As ToolsOptionsView
GetCurValues dlg
HiddenOff =   (dlg.Hidden = 0)
ShowAllOff = (dlg.ShowAll = 0)
If Hidden() And ShowAllOff And HiddenOff Then
    ToolsOptionsView .Hidden = Abs(HiddenOff)
    If MsgBox("Delete the hidden text as well?", "Confirm Edit Cut", 36) Then
        EditClear$
    Else
        Print "Toggling ShowHidden on so you can edit properly..."
    End If
Else
    EditClear$
End If
Bye:
End Sub
```

and

**DISK**
EditCut—A
replacement for the
internal EditCut
which detects

```
Sub Main
If SelInfo(27) Then  EditCut$ : Goto Bye
Dim dlg As ToolsOptionsView
GetCurValues dlg
HiddenOff =   (dlg.Hidden = 0)
ShowAllOff = (dlg.ShowAll = 0)
If Hidden() And ShowAllOff And HiddenOff Then
    ToolsOptionsView .Hidden = Abs(HiddenOff)
    If MsgBox("Delete the hidden text as well?", "Confirm Edit Cut", 36) Then
        EditCut$
    Else
        Print "Toggling ShowHidden on so you can edit properly..."
    End If
Else
    EditCut$
End If
Bye:
End Sub
```

These macros

- Check to see if the selection contains Hidden text.

- If it doesn't, cut or clear and exit.

- If the selection does contain hidden text, check to see if the user can see that it does, that is, check the current ShowAll and ShowHidden values.

■ If you can see the Hidden text, cut or clear and exit.

■ If, however, the user cannot see that hidden text is about to be deleted, the macros display the hidden material and prompt you with a dialog box to confirm that you mean to cut the hidden text as well as the visible.

This oddity can also cause mayhem if you have a macro that tests to see the style of the current paragraph. For example, the following bit of code:

```
Sub Main
While ParaDown()
    CharLeft
    MsgBox StyleName$()
Wend
End Sub
```

will post incorrect information if hidden text is not visible and it encounters a style preceded by a hidden style. It took me many hours to figure out what was going wrong when I was writing a macro to format a complex document by testing the style name of the first paragraph on every page. The solution is simple, but ugly: Make sure you are not at the first character of the paragraph by executing a CharLeft before gathering the style name.

## Revision Marks

Another feature I'm particularly fond of (as you can see from the templates presented in Chapter 12) is Revision Marking.

While revision marking is on, deleted text is displayed with a bar through each character. This character attribute looks precisely like the Strikethrough formatting available in the FormatCharacter command. Hold that thought. Text that is entered while revision marking is on can be formatted in any of five ways: nothing, bold, italic, underline, and double underline.

The interesting thing—which I consider a bug, or at minimum a failed de-sign choice—is that these apparent character formats for revised text are un-related to the identical character attributes as applied by direct formatting (with FormatCharacter) or style definition (with FormatStyle). That is to say, the "bold" applied by RevisionMarks is not the same as the "bold" applied by FormatCharacter.

To demonstrate this:

1. Open any scratch document.

2. Format any word in a document as bold.

3. Turn on RevisionMarks.

4. Set the Mark New Text With button to Bold.

**5.** Enter some text.

**6.** Execute EditFind.

**7.** Press Ctrl+B to set the Find What formatting to Bold.

**8.** Press Alt+F to Find Next.

**9.** Look puzzled when the search produces no results.

What appears to be bold on the screen (the newly inserted text) is not seen as bold by EditFind.

To compensate for this disjunction between what would seem to be identical formats (they sure look the same on the screen), the developers have hidden two new format names that can be used in the EditFind dialog box. If you press Ctrl+N, you will see the Format line beneath the Find What edit box change to New; pressing Ctrl+Q will change the format to Deleted.

Here, however, are some limitations:

If you press Ctrl+N, Ctrl+Q, you will see that the formatting description will be New, Deleted—which, of course, is not possible.

Neither format appears on the Character dialog box displayed when you select the Character button from the EditFind dialog box. One of the consequences of this is that there is no way to specify that you want to search for Deleted text from within a macro (since there is no "deleted" or "new" array item in Format-Character, there is no corresponding parameter for EditFindChar).

To make matters worse, only the New format is available in the Edit-Replace dialog box. This is a bug. It means that you cannot use the Edit-Replace command to find all instances of deleted text and change it, say, to Red, or Hidden.

Why all the fuss about what may seem arcane limitations? Take the following circumstance: You would like to format all deleted text as Hidden so you can print out the document *as if* you had accepted all revisions, but without actually removing the text. Or even more simply: You want both inserted and deleted text to be formatted with the color red (this is, after all, what is known as a "red-lining" feature).

It requires a macro, and not a very pretty one. Here's a macro to format deletions in red:

**DISK**
FormatDelRed—
Format revision
marked deleted
text as red

```
Sub Main
DelColor = 6 'Red
InsertBookmark "gtemp"
On Error Resume Next
EditFindClearFormatting
StartOfDocument
SendKeys "^q{enter}{esc}"
EditFind$
If Not EditFindFound() Then Print "No deleted found..." : Beep
```

```
CharColor DelColor
Hidden 1
While EditFindFound()
    EditFind .Find = "", .Direction = 2, .Format = 1
    CharColor DelColor
    Hidden 1
    CharRight
Wend
EditFindClearFormatting
EditGoTo "gtemp"
If ExistingBookmark("gtemp") Then InsertBookmark "gtemp", .Delete
End Sub
```

Notice that since EditFindChar cannot accept "Deleted" as a format to find, this macro must use SendKeys to set up the EditFind command.

A similar macro could be created to change all new text, no matter how it is formatted by RevisionMarks, to a color:

**DISK**
FormatNewBlue—
Format revision
marked new text as
blue

```
Sub Main
InColor = 9 'Dark blue
InsertBookmark "gtemp"
On Error Resume Next
EditFindClearFormatting
StartOfDocument
SendKeys "^n{enter}{esc}"
EditFind$
If Not EditFindFound() Then Print "No new text found..." : Beep
CharColor InColor
While EditFindFound()
    EditFind .Find = "", .Direction = 2, .Format = 1
    CharColor InColor
    CharRight
Wend
EditFindClearFormatting
EditGoTo "gtemp"
If ExistingBookmark("gtemp") Then InsertBookmark "gtemp", .Delete
End Sub
```

## ToolsCompareVersions—What Not to Expect

The ToolsCompareVersions feature compares the current document with a document chosen in the Compare Versions dialog box. At first glance this would seem a powerful feature, one that would allow you to see precisely what has changed during any given editing session, allowing you to create an "edit trail." Not so. The comparison is quite limited. ToolsCompareVersions is related to RevisionMarks, and so might be expected to do a true comparison and mark up the current document as if it had been created *from* the compare document. It doesn't. It only uses half of the RevisionMarks command, and uses that half pretty badly. What does it do then? Not much. When ToolsCompareVersions finds any difference between the current document and the compare document, it marks *the entire paragraph* as revised. This renders a comparison pretty useless if you are interested in knowing *what* has changed at a finer level than the paragraph.

Also, ToolsCompareVersions does not tell you what kind of change has been made. All differences are marked as "new text" in the source document. That is, if the compare document contains text that isn't in the current document, it is not marked as "deleted." No distinction is made between text that is "missing" from the current document and text that is "unique" to the current document. In short, ToolsCompareVersions tells you, on a paragraph level, that there is a difference; it does not tell you specifically where the difference lies within the paragraph, and it does not tell you what kind of difference (missing or unique text).

Further, ToolsCompareVersions can actually be dangerous and result in the loss of text. If you do a comparison, then execute ToolsRevisionMarks (thinking you will search for all the differences), and select Undo Revisions, *all the paragraphs with revisions will be removed from the document*. Paragraphs that are not showing on the current screen display will be deleted and you may not even know it. This is not the intended, or expected, behavior. If you do not know to immediately select EditUndo, your text can be irrevocably deleted.

My best advice is to avoid ToolsCompareVersions entirely. Its limited capabilities, combined with the danger of text loss, make it one of the major design flaws in the program. I assume it will be corrected and improved in a future version of Word. I would suggest that this is a prime candidate for Microsoft's "wish" line (see Appendix F).

## Moving the Insertion Point by Sentence

WordBasic offers two navigation commands that do not have default keyboard shortcuts and do not appear in the various lists of macros. The commands move the insertion point by sentence: SentRight and SentLeft.

To make use of these internal commands, you must create user-macros to move and select by sentence. Create the following four short macros:

SentLeft:

```
Sub Main
Super SentLeft
End Sub
```

SelSentLeft:

```
Sub Main
SentLeft 1,1
```

```
Cancel
End Sub
```

SentRight:

```
Sub Main
Super SentRight
End Sub
```

SelSentRight:

```
Sub Main
SentRight 1,1
Cancel
End Sub
```

In implementing these four new direction macros it would be nice to follow the convention used by other direction keys: one key to move by the designated unit and the same key plus Shift to move and select. It is possible to assign the SentRight and SentLeft macros to Alt+Left Arrow and Alt+Right Arrow. This would make sense. However, Alt+Shift+Left Arrow/Right Arrow are reserved for outline promotion/demotion. The next-best key combination (the one I settled upon) is Alt+Ctrl+Left Arrow/Right Arrow to move by sentence, and Alt+Ctrl+Shift+Left Arrow/Right Arrow to select by sentence.

Once the four macros are created and saved into your NORMAL-.DOT, you can run the following macro to assign them to the Alt+Ctrl and Alt+Ctrl+Shift key combinations:

```
Sub Main
ToolsOptionsKeyboard .Context = Ø, .Name = "SentLeft", .KeyCode = 1317, .Add
ToolsOptionsKeyboard .Context = Ø, .Name = "SelSentLeft", .KeyCode = 1829, .Add
ToolsOptionsKeyboard .Context = Ø, .Name = "SentRight", .KeyCode = 1319, .Add
ToolsOptionsKeyboard .Context = Ø, .Name = "SelSentRight", .KeyCode = 1831, .Add
End Sub
```

## Annotation and Footnote References

Normally, when you change a style, all instances of that style change to the new definition. This is not the case with two of the built-in styles: annotation reference and footnote reference.

If you change the style definition of a footnote or an annotation reference, prior instances will not change retroactively. Subsequent annotation or footnote references will have the new attributes.

For example, if you begin inserting footnotes with the character definition of Red and Hidden, then change it to Blue and nonhidden, the already inserted footnotes will not change to the new style.

Another manifestation of the same problem arises if you select a paragraph that contains a footnote or annotation reference and then press

Ctrl+spacebar to reset the character formatting. The attributes defined by the reference style will be lost, which can be very aggravating.

The reason for this is rather arcane, but bears some explanation. These two styles are different from all other styles in that they do not control the attributes of a paragraph. They are, in a sense, *character styles*. They control the attribute of a discrete piece of text within a paragraph.

The only way around this problem is manually to reinsert the affected annotation or footnote, not by selecting the reference, cutting, and pasting, but by opening the annotation or footnote, copying the text, and creating an entirely *new* reference.

If you have been bitten by this one, you will be pleased to find a macro named ReInsertNotes among the macros in UTILITY.DOC on the accompanying example disk. This is one of the "features" in Word 2.0 that I hope, and suspect, will be fixed in a future version.

## The Case of the Vanishing Header Information

Here's an often puzzling situation: You have the insertion point at the last paragraph of a document that has a laboriously designed header. You select File from the Insert menu to import a document from disk. All seems to go as expected—until you print or display the document in Page View: The original headers are gone, replaced by whatever header definition existed in the imported document.

This bug (or design choice) appears in other situations as well. Two documents are open. Document A is blank and contains the header definition you want to use. Document B contains text you wish had the headers in Document A. It is reasonable to think you can simply EditSelectAll the text in Document B and paste it into the waiting Document A, and instantly have the text and headers you desire in the same document. Not so. You will nuke Document A's header definition in the course of the paste. The header information in Document B is carried with the text during the paste.

What's going on? It may sound a little magical, but this is the truth: The last paragraph mark in a document has special qualities. In a sense it "contains" the header and footer information (in the same way that any paragraph mark "contains" the style information for that paragraph).

In the first case described above, insert a blank paragraph at the end of the destination document, move the insertion point from the last paragraph to the second-to-last, and proceed with the import. Your original headers will be retained.

In the second case you can protect the destination headers in one of two ways: Either, as above, make sure before the paste that the insertion point is not located at the last paragraph mark, or select everything in Document B *except* the last paragraph mark, and then paste into Document A.

There's got to be a better way. I have suggested the following to Micro-soft: If you EditSelectAll while in normal view, you do *not* select the header and footer definition, only the body text. If you EditSelectAll in Page View (where you can see the header and footer right there), you select both the body text and the header/footer information. (This is another candidate for the "wish" line. See Appendix F.)

## Proliferating TMP Files

Word creates temporary files of the form ~DOCxxyyz.TMP. These files are used by Word to keep track of changes as you edit a document (often they are, in fact, copies of the current document or template).

There are two things to know about Word's use of temporary files:

■ Unlike the temporary work files created by most programs, Word's TMP files are not stored in a specific directory.

■ Word does not always clean up after itself; the TMP files are not always deleted when Word exits.

Many programs look into the DOS environment for directions to a direc-tory where they should place temporary files. Word doesn't.

Temporary files are supposed to vanish when Word exits. Logically enough, if Word crashes, forcing you to reboot (Word, Windows, or the entire machine), the TMP files in use at the time of the crash will not be deleted. However, there are times (the logic of which eludes me still) when Word fails to clean up the TMP files even if everything shuts down properly.

One way to clean up after Word is to use the Windows File Manager's Search facility to scour your disk for leftover TMP files. Load File Manager (WINFILE.EXE) and select Search from the File menu; specify ~*.DOC in the Search For edit box; specify the root directory in the Start From edit box; and click on Search All Subdirectories. Be sure you do this only when you first load Windows. *Do not delete TMP files while Word is still running.*

## ToolsOptionsSave

There are three settings available under the ToolsOptionsSave dialog box which deserve some comment: Always Create Backup Copy, Allow Fast Saves, and Automatic Saves.

### Always Create Backup Copy

This is a systemwide setting. That is, you cannot, as you could in version 1 of Word, tell Word always to back up a specific document or class of documents. In version 2.0 you either create BAK files for all Word documents or for none.

(I would like to see three options for backups—and for the other two Save options as well: this document, all documents based on this template, and all documents. Time for a call to the Word "wish" line.)

Backups are not allowed if you have Allow Fast Saves enabled.

### Allow Fast Saves

If you check Allow Fast Saves, Word will, when possible, save the changes to the current document without writing the entire file to disk. That is, it will append a special "addendum" to the current version of the file, specifying what has changed in the document, and where. This does not affect what is displayed when you load a fast-saved document.

The major difference between a fast-saved and a normal-saved document is file size. The fast-saved document is usually larger (since it contains the original document and the edits rather than only the current state of the document).

I'm a purist. For some reason the idea of my file being a concatenation of State 1 plus a series of appended edits bothers me. I want Word to write all changes to disk. So I do not enable this option. Of course, that means I have to wait a while longer on some complex, graphic-filled documents.

Also, fast saves are only allowed if you are not creating backups (BAK files).

### Automatic Saves

Word can be told to automatically save all documents at a specified interval. You can specify from 1 to 120 minutes as the interval between automatic saves.

An automatic save does not, in fact, perform the same task as FileSave. Word does not save the documents. Rather, a temporary copy of the current state of the document is created in a specific directory. If you have an AUTOSAVE-Path defined in your WIN.INI, Word will save the temporary ASD file to that path. If you do not have an AUTOSAVE-Path setting in WIN.INI, the ASD file will be stored in the Word program directory.

This temporary file has the form: abcxyxyz.ASD. The file name appears to be a random sequence of characters. The ASD extension stands for Automatic Save Document. When you manually save, Word deletes the ASD file. If your system crashes, the last state of the ASD file will be loaded the next time you start Word.

# Optimizing Screen Display Speed

All Windows applications seem slow in drawing the screen when compared with the best DOS applications. Makes sense, considering how much more work they are doing. Still, especially for the newcomer to Windows, Word seems, at times, excruciatingly slow.

The first thing to realize when starting to optimize the screen display speed in Word is that the more sophisticated the view state, the slower the screen display. That is, Page View, which strives for an accurate reflection of the page layout as it will be printed, has much more work to do than Normal View (sometimes called Galley View). For every element added to the screen display there is a possible speed penalty. For instance, displaying table gridlines or displaying pictures instead of picture placeholders can affect screen update speed.

You should also realize that Word's screen display can be influenced by the amount of memory available. Every optional bar takes memory: the ruler, Ribbon, toolbar, status line, and scroll bars all make demands on the memory available to Word. Turning off those tools you are not using can result in a display speed increase.

Switching from Page View to Normal View provides a substantial increase in screen display. Normal View still reflects font and line breaks accurately if you activate Breaks and Fonts as Printed on the ToolsOptionsView dialog box. Character attributes, such as bold or italic, are represented accurately.

A third option, Draft View, is the fastest of three available display modes in Word. The font used is the same as the one used to display menu text (MS Sans Serif); special attributes, such as bold or italic, are all marked with underscores.

Normal View is a compromise between the layout precision of Page View and the substantially faster approximation afforded by Draft View.

In my opinion, Word's three display modes correspond to the three basic stages of composition: dumping text into the document as fast as possible (Draft View); editing the document and correcting font style, character formatting, and word spacing (Normal View); and fine-tuning the layout of a complexly formatted document (Page View).

Word in Draft View is not substantially slower (if slower at all) than DOS-based word processors. For each decrease in screen display there is a corresponding increase in functionality.

## The At and Ln Status Indicators

The status bar provides several significant pieces of information about the current location of the insertion point.

The first recessed box contains the page number, the section number, and the current page in relation to the total number of pages.

The second recessed box contains three values: At, Ln, and Col. The third value, which displays the character column holding the insertion point, is always active. The other two values, which display the location of the current line measured in inches from the top of the page and the current line number, are only available if you have Background Repagination set to on in the

ToolsOptionsGeneral dialog box and have Breaks and Fonts as Printed set to on in the ToolsOptionsView dialog box. Disabling either of these options blanks the display of At and Ln values.

Background repagination takes a small bite out of the available memory resources. It doesn't drastically affect the overall performance of Word. However, you should be aware that as with the various view elements and tools, every additional option, such as background repagination or automatic save, does come at a price, however small. If your system slows to a crawl, you can try turning all options off. If it still seems sluggish, it may be time to shut down and start over.

## Start-up Options

Word allows for several command-line parameters. As with many other programs, you can start Word with a document as the parameter:

```
WINWORD c:\winword\examples.doc
```

You can start Word with multiple document names:

```
WINWORD c:\winword\examples.doc c:\winword\pss.doc
```

More interesting is the ability to start Word with a macro as the parameter:

```
WINWORD /mFileOpen
```

The switch "/m" tells Word that the next word is not a document name, but the name of a macro. Word will load and immediately execute the named macro.

One frequent use of the /m switch is to load Word with the last document:

```
WINWORD /mFile1
```

Another useful switch allows you to tell Word not to create the default blank document:

```
WINWORD /n
```

This switch can also be used in combination with the /m directive:

```
WINWORD /mFileOpen /n
```

The result of this particular command-line is that Word will run FileOpen. If you cancel the dialog box (and thereby fail to load a document), Word will present a blank application space rather than open a default Document1.

# WIN.INI Settings

The various WIN.INI settings are described in Appendix B of the *Word User's Guide*. However, the importance of some of the keywords requires some comment. And other undocumented keywords require explanation.

### DOC-Path

The DOC-Path keyword tells Word the name of the default document directory. When you load Word it will always, no matter what the command line, move to this directory.

In my opinion this is a most inflexible way to start Word. I would recommend deleting this keyword if it exists, and exploring other ways to start Word.

### DOT-Path

The DOT-Path is an extremely important keyword. It points to the directory containing your templates. By default Word installs your templates into the same directory as the Word executable file. Using this keyword setting you can move your templates to a subdirectory. You can also have more than one directory containing templates. But most importantly, custom macros, such as the FileTemplate and SyncStyles examples in this book, often use the DOT-Path value to find and load templates. If you do not have a DOT-Path setting, create one.

Note: If you edit any of the WIN.INI settings which take a directory path designation as their value, be sure *not* to include a terminating backslash. That is, C:\WINWORD\ and C:\WINWORD are not equivalent. The latter is correct.

### BitMapMemory

This keyword sets the amount of memory allocated to hold graphic images contained in your document, measured in kilobytes. The default is 64k.

If you have the memory to spare, setting this value to 512 or 1024 can increase the speed at which pictures are displayed when scrolling through a document.

```
BitMapMemory = 1024
```

Recommended.

### CacheSize

This keyword sets the amount of memory allocated to hold nongraphic portions of your document, measured in kilobytes. The default is 64k.

If you frequently edit large documents, setting this keyword to 512 or 1024 can speed scrolling.

```
CacheSize = 1024
```

Recommended.

### NoOwnerFiles

This is an undocumented keyword. It controls the creation of a special temporary file.

Whenever you open a document, Word creates a hidden temporary file of the form: ~$FileName.DOC. This file contains the user information of the person who opened the file.

The purpose of this small file is to identify the person who has a document open. It is only meaningful if you are working on a network, or if you have multiple copies of Word loaded at the same time.

If you are (like me) a solitary user, you can stop Word from creating these temporary files by inserting the keyword:

```
NoOwnerfile = yes
```

into the Microsoft Word 2.0 section of WIN.INI.

### NoFileCache

Here is another undocumented keyword. It determines whether Word will maintain a list of the four most recently used files. By default Word tracks the last four files and places them on the File menu.

The following keyword:

```
NoFileCache = Yes
```

will disable the most recently used file list.

## Optimizing Printing

One of the most frequent complaints about Word is that it prints too slowly. Many move to Windows because it allows, theoretically, for multitasking. And, quite reasonably, they expect to be able to print one document while editing another. In fact, Windows is not all that great at allowing work to proceed while printing occurs. And Word in particular hogs the system when printing begins.

There is a trade-off. You can either print as fast as possible, hogging the system, or you can increase the total time required to print a document and allow work to proceed at the same time.

In the Print section of Control Panel you specify whether the current printer should use Print Manager to manage all printing. If the current printer is not attached to the Print Manager, printing will proceed much like it does with a DOS application: not much else can happen until printing completes.

The more common (and the default) setting is to enable Print Manager. In this case Word first *spools* the file to disk. At the same time, Print Manager is loaded to start sending the spool file to the printer. The spooling must complete before the focus returns to the document and you can continue editing (or edit another document).

There are several small ways you can improve printing from Word. First of all, realize that Word can be told where to place its temporary spool files. Many applications, including Windows, look to the DOS environment for instructions about the location of a temporary directory. The *TEMP variable* is documented in the "Optimizing Windows" chapter of the Windows user manual and in your DOS manual.

For instance, the following line, placed in your AUTOEXEC.BAT, will tell all Windows applications that look for a TEMP specification, to store temporary files in C:\TEMP:

```
Set Temp=C:\TEMP
```

Writing to a hard disk takes more time than writing to memory. Therefore, if you have a RAM disk on your system, it makes sense to point to a directory on the virtual drive (which is actually just a bunch of memory). For instance, assume you have a RAM disk designated as drive D. You can create a temporary directory, and point all applications to it, with the lines:

```
mkdir D:\TEMP
Set TEMP=D:\TEMP
```

added to your AUTOEXEC.BAT.

Spooling will take less time if you are writing the temporary file to a RAM disk.

Print Manager has three settings under the Options menu: Low Priority, Medium Priority, and High Priority. Paradoxically, setting this to High Priority will not return you to Word faster. This setting controls the amount of Windows resources devoted solely to Print Manager. This means if the priority is high in Print Manager, the spooling that is happening in Word at the same time slows down.

The best way to print a long document is to set the priority in Print Manager to low while Word is spooling, and then set it to either low or medium after spooling finishes.

Here are some summary notes about printing.

If you wish to return to Word as fast as possible, or to work in other applications while printing:

1. Make sure your printer is set to use Print Manager. This is done in the Print dialog box of the Control Panel.

2. Create a temporary directory on a RAM disk and point to it using the SET TEMP=[drive]:\PathName statement in your AUTOEXEC.BAT.

3. Set the Word application space to nonmaximized (that is, "restored"). This enables you to more easily move from Word to other applications.

4. Set Print Manager to Low Priority.

5. After spooling is complete, you can set priority to Medium. If priority is set to high, performance in all other applications will be jerky.

If you do not care how fast you return to Word, or are not interested in using other applications while printing, but are solely concerned with printing as fast as possible:

1. Disconnect the use of Print Manager from the current printer (on the Print dialog box of Control Panel).

2. Set Fast Printing Direct To Port in the Connect dialog box (found under the Print dialog box in Control Panel).

## Conclusion

We have arrived at the end of our exploration of Word's mysteries. My hope is that you can now begin to see the ways in which Word can be made more productive, more suited to your own preferences and habits. I hope that you have already begun to dissect and revise the various example macros and templates. One of the great graces of Word's design is that nothing is completely sacred. My intention has been not to provide you with canned solutions and utilities, but to provide insights into how Word can be pummeled into submission, and to adjust your thinking about the program: to set the gears in motion that will produce a uniquely customized, personalized, powerful tool for the making of sentences.

# A Listing of Word for Windows Files

The following table lists all files installed by a complete installation of Word.

| Directory | Purpose and Notes |
| --- | --- |
| C:\WINWORD | This directory contains the major components of Word for Windows. It is referenced, in WIN.INI, as the "programdir" and, by default, as the "TOOLS-path." |

| File Name | Purpose and Notes |
| --- | --- |
| macrode.exe | Dialog box editor. |
| setup.exe | Setup program; can be deleted; if deleted, adding additional Word features will require running setup from the original setup disk. |
| winword.exe | The Word program file. |
| winword.ini | Contains settings, such as user name and address; not a text file; if deleted will be rebuilt automatically. |
| wword20.inf | Data file used by setup program; can be deleted. |
| dialog.fon | Font used by dialog box. |
| spell.dll | Spelling module. |
| hyph.dll | Hyphenation module. |
| thes.dll | Thesaurus module. |
| grammar.dll | Grammar checker module. |
| wphelp.dll | WordPerfect help module. |
| readme.doc | Addendum to the documentation; can be deleted. |
| printers.doc | Notes on specific printers; can be deleted. |
| template.doc | Notes on some of the included templates; can be deleted. |
| newmacro.doc | A template that contains some useful utility macros. |
| convinfo.doc | Information about converting from various foreign formats. |
| macrocnv.doc | Information about converting macros from Word 1.x to Word 2.x. |
| graphics.doc | Information about using various graphic file formats. |
| pss.doc | A template that contains some useful macros (Product Support Services). |

**Directory** C:\WINWORD (continued)

| File Name | Purpose and Notes |
|-----------|-------------------|
| sp_am.lex | Spelling dictionary. |
| hy_am.lex | Hyphenation dictionary. |
| th_am.lex | Thesaurus data file. |
| gr_am.lex | Grammar checker data file. |
| article2.dot, datafile.dot, dissert2.dot, fax.dot letblock.dot letmdsem.dot letmodbk.dot letpersn.dot maillabl.dot memo2.dot msword.dot overhead.dot press.dot proposal.dot repland.dot repside.dot repstand.dot term2.dot | Custom templates (see Chapter 2 for a description of each). Any template you are not using can, of course, be deleted. |
| normal.dot | This template is created as soon as you define a global preference, such as a glossary, style, or macro. If deleted, all customizations stored globally will be lost. This is a good candidate for regular backup. |
| txtwlyt.cnv | Text with layout conversion module. |
| wpft5.cnv | WordPerfect conversion module. |
| wordwin1.cnv | Word for Windows 1.x conversion module. |
| worddos.cnv | Word for DOS conversion module. |
| wordmac.cnv | Word for the Macintosh conversion module. |
| rftdca.cnv | DCA conversion module. |
| xlbiff.cnv | Excel conversion module. |
| dbase.cnv | dBASE conversion module. |
| lotus123.cnv | Lotus WKS conversion module. |
| wordstar.cnv | WordStar conversion module. |
| writwin.cnv | Windows Write conversion module. |
| wp5_rtf.txt | Notes on WordPerfect conversion. |

**Directory** C:\WINWORD (continued)

| File Name | Purpose and Notes |
|---|---|
| rtf_wp5.txt | Notes on Rich Text Format. |
| pcw_rtf.txt | Notes on conversion from Word for DOS. |
| rtf_pcw.txt | Notes on conversion to Word for DOS. |
| mw5_rtf.txt | Notes on conversion from Mac Word. |
| rtf_mw5.txt | Notes on conversion to Mac Word. |
| dca_rtf.txt | Notes on conversion from DCA to RTF. |
| rtf_dca.txt | Notes on conversion from RTF to DCA. |
| 40convrt.gly | A DOS Word 4.0 glossary file to aid in conversion of glossaries to Word for Windows. |
| 50convrt.gly | A DOS Word 5.0 glossary file to aid in conversion of glossaries to Word for Windows. |
| 55convrt.gly | A DOS Word 5.5 glossary file to aid in conversion of glossaries to Word for Windows. |
| winword.hlp | The help file. |

| Directory | Purpose and Notes |
|---|---|
| C:\WINWORD\CLIPART | This directory contains several WMF (Windows Meta File) graphic files. |

| File Name | Purpose and Notes |
|---|---|
| *.WMF | If you have no need of these pictures, you can remove the files and the directory without affecting the rest of Word. |

| Directory | Purpose and Notes |
|---|---|
| C:\WINWORD\WINWORD.CBT | This is the tutorial directory. You can remove these files without affecting the rest of Word. Once they are removed, selecting Tutorial from the Help menu will result in an error message. |

| File Name | Purpose and Notes |
|---|---|
| horse.bmp | Bitmapped graphic used by tutorial. |
| winword.cbt | Tutorial module. |
| mousemv.cbt | Tutorial module. |
| grammar.cbt | Tutorial module. |

**Directory**   C:\WINWORD\WINWORD.CBT (continued)

| File Name | Purpose and Notes |
|---|---|
| cbtlib2.dll | Tutorial module. |
| buslet.doc<br>busrep.doc<br>carousel.doc<br>formlett.doc<br>market.doc<br>nepal.doc<br>newslett.doc<br>pricelis.doc<br>resume.doc<br>winners.doc | Documents used by the tutorial. |
| cbtnorm.dot | Template used by tutorial. |
| gstart.les | Getting started lesson module. |
| lword.les | Learning Word lesson module. |

| Directory | Purpose and Notes |
|---|---|
| C:\WINDOWS\MSAPPS\GRPHFLT | This directory contains the graphic conversion modules. Manually removing any of these filters or modules after a complete installation will not automatically remove the associated graphic type from the list of available graphic conversions available within Word. The list of available filters is contained in a special section of WIN.INI named "MS Graphic Import Filters." |

| File Name | Purpose and Notes |
|---|---|
| adimport.flt | AutoCAD import filter. |
| dxfimp.flt | AutoCAD import filter. |
| imdxf.dll | AutoCAD import module. |
| cgmimp.flt | Computer Graphics Metafile filter. |
| emwpg.dll | DrawPerfect export module. |
| wpgimp.flt | DrawPerfect import filter. |
| imwpg.dll | DrawPerfect import module. |
| epsimp.flt | Encapsulated Postscript filter. |
| hpglimp.flt | HP Graphic Language filter. |
| cgi_gdi.dll | Import module used by several graphic formats (AutoCAD/Micrografx Designer/Draw/DrawPerfect). |

**Directory**   C:\WINDOWS\MSAPPS\GRPHFLT (continued)

| File Name | Purpose and Notes |
| --- | --- |
| lotusimp.flt | Lotus 1-2-3 import filter. |
| drwimp.flt | Micrografx Designer/Draw import filter. |
| imdrw.dll | Micrografx Designer/Draw module. |
| pcximp.flt | PC Paintbrush filter. |
| tiffimp.flt | Tagged Image Format filter. |
| imwmf.dll | Windows Metafile import module. |
| wmfimp.flt | Windows Metafile(.WMF) filter. |
| wpgexp.flt | WordPerfect graphic export filter. |

| Directory | Purpose and Notes |
| --- | --- |
| C:\WINDOWS\MSAPPS\MSDRAW | This directory contains the MS Draw OLE application |

| File Name | Purpose and Notes |
| --- | --- |
| msdraw.exe | The MS Draw OLE application. |
| msdraw.hlp | The MS Draw help file. |
| 16colors.pal<br>17grays.pal<br>47colors.pal<br>86colors.pal<br>geni.pal | Palette files used by MS Draw. |

| Directory | Purpose and Notes |
| --- | --- |
| C:\WINDOWS\MSAPPS\MSGRAPH | This directory contains the MS Graph OLE application |

| File Name | Purpose and Notes |
| --- | --- |
| graph.exe | The MS Graph OLE application. |
| msgraph.hlp | The MS Graph Help file. |

| Directory | Purpose and Notes |
| --- | --- |
| C:\WINDOWS\MSAPPS\WORDART | This directory contains the MS WordArt OLE application |

| File Name | Purpose and Notes |
| --- | --- |
| fontfx.dll | A support module required by WordArt. |

**Directory**   C:\WINDOWS\MSAPPS\WORDART (continued)

| File Name | Purpose and Notes |
| --- | --- |
| wordart.exe | The WordArt OLE application. |
| fontfx.fnt | The WordArt font data file. |
| wordart.hlp | The WordArt help file. |

| Directory | Purpose and Notes |
| --- | --- |
| C:\WINDOWS\MSAPPS\EQUATION | This directory contains the Equation Editor OLE application |

| File Name | Purpose and Notes |
| --- | --- |
| eqnedit.exe | The equation editor OLE application. |
| eqnedit.hlp | The equation editor help file. |

## The Equation Editor

If you install the equation editor, Word will also install some necessary font files. Which font files, and where they are placed on your disk, depends upon the specifics of your configuration. There are three options.

If you are running Windows 3.1 with TrueType installed, four files will be placed in your \WINDOWS\SYSTEM directory: fences.ttf, fences.fot, mtextra.ttf, and mtextra.fot.

If you are running Windows 3.0 (or 3.1 without TrueType) and your printer is an HP Laserjet, a number of soft font files will be installed into your \PCLFONTS directory. In addition, screen fonts will be installed into your Windows directory.

If you are running Windows 3.0 (or 3.1 without TrueType) and your printer is PostScript capable, a number of soft font files will be installed into your \PCLFONTS directory. In addition, screen fonts will be installed into your Windows directory.

## OLE Applications

If you manually remove any of the four OLE applications installed by Word, you will not automatically remove that application from the list of available "objects" displayed in the InsertObject list box. When an OLE application is installed, it is "registered" systemwide. Removing it from the disk does not change this registration.

Registration information is contained in a file named REG.DAT stored in your Windows directory. The information contained in this file is also stored within WIN.INI under the "Embedding" section.

The easiest way to remove an application from REG.DAT is to load the Registration Editor (REGEDIT.EXE) that comes with Windows 3.1. Changes made to the list of registered OLE applications will appear when you next load Word.

There is another way to change the list of registered OLE applications: delete REG.DAT, edit the Embedding section of WIN.INI, and load Windows. REG.DAT will be rebuilt by Windows automatically.

# Table of Reserved Style Names

Below is a table of the 36 built-in styles:

| Style | Purpose |
|-------|---------|
| annotation reference | A pseudocharacter style which determines the character attributes of annotation reference marks. |
| annotation text | Annotation text. |
| envelopeaddress | An envelope's address information. This style becomes available for modification only after an envelope is added to the current document. |
| envelopereturn | An envelope's return address information. This style becomes available for modification only after an envelope is added to the current document. |
| footer | The document footer. |
| footnote text | Footnote text. |
| footnote reference | A pseudocharacter style which determines the character attributes of footnote reference marks. |
| header | The document header. |
| heading 1 | Outline level 1. |
| heading 2 | Outline level 2. |
| heading 3 | Outline level 3. |
| heading 4 | Outline level 4. |
| heading 5 | Outline level 5. |
| heading 6 | Outline level 6. |
| heading 7 | Outline level 7. |
| heading 8 | Outline level 8. |
| heading 9 | Outline level 9. |
| index 1 | Index level 1. |
| index 2 | Index level 2. |
| index 3 | Index level 3. |
| index 4 | Index level 4. |
| index 5 | Index level 5. |
| index 6 | Index level 6. |
| index 7 | Index level 7. |

| Style | Purpose |
|---|---|
| index heading | The Index heading. |
| line number | A pseudocharacter style which determines the style of the line numbers. |
| Normal | The default body text style. |
| Normal Indent | The default body text style plus a 0.5" left indent. |
| toc 1 | Table of Contents level 1. |
| toc 2 | Table of Contents level 2. |
| toc 3 | Table of Contents level 3. |
| toc 4 | Table of Contents level 4. |
| toc 5 | Table of Contents level 5. |
| toc 6 | Table of Contents level 6. |
| toc 7 | Table of Contents level 7. |
| toc 8 | Table of Contents level 8. |

# Table of Default Keyboard Shortcuts

Below is a table of those WordBasic commands that possess default keyboard shortcuts:

| Command | Keyboard Shortcut |
| --- | --- |
| AllCaps | Ctrl+A |
| AppMaximize | Alt+F10 |
| AppMinimize | Alt+F9 |
| AppRestore | Alt+F5 |
| Bold | Ctrl+B |
| Cancel | Esc |
| CenterPara | Ctrl+E |
| ChangeCase | Shift+F3 |
| ClosePane | Alt+Shift+C |
| CloseUpPara | Ctrl+O |
| ColumnSelect | Ctrl+Shift+F8 |
| CopyText | Shift+F2 |
| DeleteBackWord | Ctrl+Backspace |
| DeleteWord | Ctrl+Del |
| DocClose | Ctrl+F4 |
| DocMaximize | Ctrl+F10 |
| DocMove | Ctrl+F7 |
| DocRestore | Ctrl+F5 |
| DocSize | Ctrl+F8 |
| DoFieldClick | Alt+Shift+F9 |
| DoubleUnderline | Ctrl+D |
| EditClear | Del |
| EditCopy | Ctrl+C |
| EditCut | Ctrl+X |
| EditGoTo | F5 |
| EditPaste | Ctrl+V |
| EditRepeat | F4 |

| Command | Keyboard Shortcut |
| --- | --- |
| EditSelectAll | Ctrl+NumPad 5 |
| EditUndo | Ctrl+Z |
| EndOfColumn | Alt+PgDn |
| EndOfRow | Alt+End |
| ExpandGlossary | F3 |
| ExtendSelection | F8 |
| FileEditDataFile | Alt+Shift+E |
| FileExit | Alt+F4 |
| FileOpen | Ctrl+F12 |
| FilePrint | Ctrl+Shift+F12 |
| FilePrintMergeCheck | Alt+Shift+K |
| FilePrintMergeToDoc | Alt+Shift+N |
| FilePrintMergeToPrinter | Alt+Shift+M |
| FileSave | Shift+F12 |
| FileSaveAs | F12 |
| Font | Ctrl+F |
| FontSize | Ctrl+P |
| FormatStyle | Ctrl+S |
| GoBack | Shift+F5 |
| GrowFont | Ctrl+F2 |
| HangingIndent | Ctrl+T |
| Help | F1 |
| HelpContext | Shift+F1 |
| Hidden | Ctrl+H |
| IconBarMode | Shift+F10 |
| Indent | Ctrl+N |
| InsertBookmark | Ctrl+Shift+F5 |
| InsertColumnBreak | Ctrl+Shift+Enter |
| InsertDateField | Alt+Shift+D |

| Command | Keyboard Shortcut |
|---|---|
| InsertFieldChars | Ctrl+F9 |
| InsertMergeField | Alt+Shift+F |
| InsertPageBreak | Ctrl+Enter |
| InsertPageField | Alt+Shift+P |
| InsertTimeField | Alt+Shift+T |
| Italic | Ctrl+I |
| JustifyPara | Ctrl+J |
| LeftPara | Ctrl+L |
| LockFields | Ctrl+F11 |
| MenuMode | F10 |
| MoveText | F2 |
| NextField | F11 |
| NextObject | Alt+Down Arrow |
| NextWindow | Ctrl+F6 |
| NormalStyle | Alt+Shift+Numpad 5 |
| OpenUpPara | Ctrl+O |
| OtherPane | F6 |
| OutlineDemote | Alt+Shift+Right Arrow |
| OutlineMoveDown | Alt+Shift+Down Arrow |
| OutlineMoveUp | Alt+Shift+Up Arrow |
| OutlinePromote | Alt+Shift+Left Arrow |
| Overtype | Ins |
| PrevField | Shift+F11 |
| PrevObject | Alt+Up Arrow |
| PrevWindow | Ctrl+Shift+F6 |
| RepeatFind | Shift+F4 |
| ResetChar | Ctrl+spacebar |
| ResetPara | Ctrl+Q |
| RightPara | Ctrl+R |

| Command | Keyboard Shortcut |
| --- | --- |
| RulerMode | Ctrl+Shift+F10 |
| ShowAll | Ctrl+Shift+8 |
| ShrinkFont | Ctrl+Shift+F2 |
| ShrinkSelection | Shift+F8 |
| SmallCaps | Ctrl+K |
| SpacePara1 | Ctrl+1 |
| SpacePara15 | Ctrl+5 |
| SpacePara2 | Ctrl+2 |
| Spike | Ctrl+F3 |
| StartOfColumn | Alt+PgUp |
| StartOfRow | Alt+Home |
| SubScript | Ctrl++ |
| SuperScript | Ctrl+Shift++ |
| TableSelectTable | Alt+Numpad 5 |
| ToggleFieldDisplay | Shift+F9 |
| ToolsSpellSelection | F7 |
| ToolsThesaurus | Shift+F7 |
| Underline | Ctrl+U |
| UnHang | Ctrl+G |
| UnIndent | Ctrl+M |
| UnlinkFields | Ctrl+Shift+F9 |
| UnlockFields | Ctrl+Shift+F11 |
| UnSpike | Ctrl+Shift+F3 |
| UpdateFields | F9 |
| UpdateSource | Ctrl+Shift+F7 |
| ViewHeaderFooterLink | Alt+Shift+L |
| WordUnderline | Ctrl+W |

# Key Codes for ToolsMacroKeyboard

The following table lists all legal key code values that can be used by the WordBasic command ToolsOptionsKeyboard in assigning a macro to a keyboard shortcut.

This table provides more information than the one found in *Using Word-Basic*: It includes base keys omitted by Microsoft, it gives the actual key code for the modified key combinations, and it lists those key codes that possess default assignments.

| Key Name | Base Code | Ctrl (256) | Shift (512) | Ctrl+Shift (768) | Alt (1024) | Alt+Ctrl (1280) | Alt+Shift (1536) | Alt+Ctrl+ Shift (1792) |
|---|---|---|---|---|---|---|---|---|
| BackSpace | 8 | 264 DeleteBack-Word | 520 | 776 | 1032 EditUndo | 1288 | 1544 | 1800 |
| Tab | 9 | 265 | 521 | 777 | 1033 | 1289 | 1545 | 1801 |
| Numpad5 | 12 | 268 EditSelect-All | 524 | 780 | 1036 TableSelect-Table | 1292 | 1548 Normal-Style | 1804 |
| Enter | 13 | 268 InsertPage-Break | 525 | 781 InsertCol-umnBreak | 1037 | 1293 | 1549 | 1805 |
| Esc | 27 Cancel | 283 | 539 | 795 | 1051 | 1307 | 1563 | 1819 |
| Space | 32 | 288 ResetChar | 544 | 800 HardSpace | 1056 | 1312 | 1568 | 1824 |
| PgUp | 33 | 289 | 545 | 801 | 1057 StartOf-Column | 1313 | 1569 | 1825 |
| PgDn | 34 | 290 | 546 | 802 | 1058 EndOf-Column | 1314 | 1570 | 1826 |
| End | 35 | 291 | 547 | 803 | 1059 EndOfRow | 1315 | 1571 | 1827 |
| Home | 36 | 292 | 548 | 804 | 1060 StartOfRow | 1316 | 1572 | 1828 |
| Left | 37 | 293 | 549 | 805 | 1061 | 1317 | 1573 Outline-Promote | 1829 |
| Up | 38 | 294 | 550 | 806 | 1062 PrevObject | 1318 | 1574 Outline-MoveUp | 1830 |
| Right | 39 | 295 | 551 | 807 | 1063 | 1319 | 1575 Outline-Demote | 1831 |
| Down | 40 | 296 | 552 | 808 | 1064 NextObject | 1320 | 1576 Outline-MoveDown | 1832 |

| Key Name | Base Code | Ctrl (256) | Shift (512) | Ctrl+Shift (768) | Alt (1024) | Alt+Ctrl (1280) | Alt+Shift (1536) | Alt+Ctrl+ Shift (1792) |
|---|---|---|---|---|---|---|---|---|
| Insert | 45 Overtype | 301 EditCopy | 557 EditPaste | 813 | 1069 | 1325 | 1581 | 1837 |
| Delete | 46 EditClear | 302 DeleteWord | 558 EditCut | 814 | 1070 | 1326 | 1582 | 1838 |
| 0 | 48 | 304 | 560 | 816 | 1072 | 1328 | 1584 | 1840 |
| 1 | 49 | 305 | 561 | 817 | 1073 | 1329 | 1585 | 1841 |
| 2 | 50 | 306 | 562 | 818 | 1074 | 1330 | 1586 | 1842 |
| 3 | 51 | 307 | 563 | 819 | 1075 | 1331 | 1587 | 1843 |
| 4 | 52 | 308 | 564 | 820 | 1076 | 1332 | 1588 | 1844 |
| 5 | 53 | 309 | 565 | 821 | 1077 | 1333 | 1589 | 1845 |
| 6 | 54 | 310 | 566 | 822 | 1078 | 1334 | 1590 | 1846 |
| 7 | 55 | 311 | 567 | 823 | 1079 | 1335 | 1591 | 1847 |
| 8 | 56 | 312 | 568 | 824 ShowAll | 1080 | 1336 | 1592 | 1848 |
| 9 | 57 | 313 | 569 | 825 | 1081 | 1337 | 1593 | 1849 |
| A | 65 | 321 AllCaps | 577 | 833 | 1089 | 1345 | 1601 | 1857 |
| B | 66 | 322 Bold | 578 | 834 | 1090 | 1346 | 1602 | 1858 |
| C | 67 | 323 EditCopy | 579 | 835 | 1091 | 1347 | 1603 ClosePane | 1859 |
| D | 68 | 324 Double- Underline | 580 | 836 | 1092 | 1348 | 1604 InsertDate- Field | 1860 |
| E | 69 | 325 CenterPara | 581 | 837 | 1093 | 1349 | 1605 FileEdit- DataFile | 1861 |
| F | 70 | 326 Font | 582 | 838 | 1094 | 1350 | 1606 Insert- MergeField | 1862 |
| G | 71 | 327 UnHang | 583 | 839 | 1095 | 1351 | 1607 | 1863 |
| H | 72 | 328 Hidden | 584 | 840 | 1096 | 1352 | 1608 | 1864 |
| I | 73 | 329 Italic | 585 | 841 | 1097 | 1353 | 1609 | 1865 |
| J | 74 | 330 JustifyPara | 586 | 842 | 1098 | 1354 | 1610 | 1866 |

| Key Name | Base Code | Ctrl (256) | Shift (512) | Ctrl+Shift (768) | Alt (1024) | Alt+Ctrl (1280) | Alt+Shift (1536) | Alt+Ctrl+ Shift (1792) |
|---|---|---|---|---|---|---|---|---|
| K | 75 | 331 SmallCaps | 587 | 843 | 1099 | 1355 | 1611 FilePrint-Merge-Check | 1867 |
| L | 76 | 332 LeftPara | 588 | 844 | 1100 | 1356 | 1612 ViewHeader-FooterLink | 1868 |
| M | 77 | 333 UnIndent | 589 | 845 | 1101 | 1357 | 1613 FilePrint-MergeTo-Printer | 1869 |
| N | 78 | 334 Indent | 590 | 846 | 1102 | 1358 | 1614 | 1870 |
| O | 79 | 335 CloseUp-Para | 591 | 847 | 1103 | 1359 | 1615 | 1871 |
| P | 80 | 336 FontSize | 592 | 848 | 1104 | 1360 | 1616 InsertPage-Field | 1872 |
| Q | 81 | 337 ResetPara | 593 | 849 | 1105 | 1361 | 1617 | 1873 |
| R | 82 | 338 RightPara | 594 | 850 | 1106 | 1362 | 1618 | 1874 |
| S | 83 | 339 FormatStyle | 595 | 851 | 1107 | 1363 | 1619 | 1875 |
| T | 84 | 340 Hanging-Indent | 596 | 852 | 1108 | 1364 | 1620 InsertTime-Field | 1876 |
| U | 85 | 341 Underline | 597 | 853 | 1109 | 1365 | 1621 | 1877 |
| V | 86 | 342 EditPaste | 598 | 854 | 1110 | 1366 | 1622 | 1878 |
| W | 87 | 343 Word-Underline | 599 | 855 | 1111 | 1367 | 1623 | 1879 |
| X | 88 | 344 EditCut | 600 | 856 | 1112 | 1368 | 1624 | 1880 |
| Y | 89 | 345 | 601 | 857 | 1113 | 1369 | 1625 | 1881 |
| Z | 90 | 346 EditUndo | 602 | 858 | 1114 | 1370 | 1626 | 1882 |
| 0 | 96 | 352 | 608 | 864 | 1120 | 1376 | 1632 | 1888 |
| 1 | 97 | 353 Space-Para1 | 609 | 865 | 1121 | 1377 | 1633 | 1889 |

| Key Name | Base Code | Ctrl (256) | Shift (512) | Ctrl+Shift (768) | Alt (1024) | Alt+Ctrl (1280) | Alt+Shift (1536) | Alt+Ctrl+ Shift (1792) |
|---|---|---|---|---|---|---|---|---|
| 2 | 98 | 354 Space-Para2 | 610 | 866 | 1122 | 1378 | 1634 | 1890 |
| 3 | 99 | 355 | 611 | 867 | 1123 | 1379 | 1635 | 1891 |
| 4 | 100 | 356 | 612 | 868 | 1124 | 1380 | 1636 | 1892 |
| 5 | 101 | 357 Space-Para15 | 613 | 869 | 1125 | 1381 | 1637 | 1893 |
| 6 | 102 | 358 | 614 | 870 | 1126 | 1382 | 1638 | 1894 |
| 7 | 103 | 359 | 615 | 871 | 1127 | 1383 | 1639 | 1895 |
| 8 | 104 | 360 | 616 | 872 | 1128 | 1384 | 1640 | 1896 |
| 9 | 105 | 361 | 617 | 873 | 1129 | 1385 | 1641 | 1897 |
| Numpad * | 106 | 362 | 618 | 874 | 1130 | 1386 | 1642 | 1898 |
| Numpad + | 107 | 363 | 619 | 875 | 1131 | 1387 | 1643 | 1899 |
| Numpad Ins | 108 | 364 | 620 | 876 | 1132 | 1388 | 1644 | 1900 |
| Numpad - | 109 | 365 | 621 | 877 | 1133 | 1389 | 1645 | 1901 |
| Numpad . | 110 | 366 | 622 | 878 | 1134 | 1390 | 1646 | 1902 |
| Numpad / | 111 | 367 | 623 | 879 | 1135 | 1391 | 1647 | 1903 |
| F1 | 112 Help | 368 | 624 Help-Context | 880 | 1136 | 1392 | 1648 | 1904 |
| F2 | 113 MoveText | 369 GrowFont | 625 CopyText | 881 ShrinkFont | 1137 | 1393 | 1649 | 1905 |
| F3 | 114 Expand-Glossary | 370 Spike | 626 Change-Case | 882 UnSpike | 1138 | 1394 | 1650 | 1906 |
| F4 | 115 EditRepeat | 371 DocClose | 627 RepeatFind | 883 | 1139 FileExit | 1395 | 1651 | 1907 |
| F5 | 116 EditGoTo | 372 DocRestore | 628 GoBack | 884 Insert-Bookmark | 1140 AppRestore | 1396 | 1652 | 1908 |
| F6 | 117 OtherPane | 373 Next-Window | 629 | 885 PrevWindow | 1141 | 1397 | 1653 | 1909 |
| F7 | 118 ToolsSpell-Selection | 374 DocMove | 630 Tools-Thesaurus | 886 Update-Source | 1142 | 1398 | 1654 | 1910 |
| F8 | 119 Extend-Selection | 375 DocSize | 631 Shrink-Selection | 887 Column-Select | 1143 App-Minimize | 1399 | 1655 | 1911 |

| Key Name | Base Code | Ctrl (256) | Shift (512) | Ctrl+Shift (768) | Alt (1024) | Alt+Ctrl (1280) | Alt+Shift (1536) | Alt+Ctrl+ Shift (1792) |
|---|---|---|---|---|---|---|---|---|
| F9 | 120 Update-Fields | 376 InsertField-Chars | 632 ToggleField-Display | 888 Unlink-Fields | 1144 App-Maximize | 1400 | 1656 | 1912 |
| F10 | 121 MenuMode | 377 Doc-Maximize | 633 IconBar-Mode | 889 RulerMode | 1145 | 1401 | 1657 | 1913 |
| F11 | 122 NextField | 378 LockFields | 634 PrevField | 890 Unlock-Fields | 1146 | 1402 | 1658 | 1914 |
| F12 | 123 FileSaveAs | 379 FileOpen | 635 FileSave | 891 FilePrint | 1147 | 1403 | 1659 | 1915 |
| ; (semicolon) | 186 | 442 | 698 | 954 | 1210 | 1466 | 1722 | 1978 |
| + (plus) | 187 | 443 SubScript | 699 | 955 SuperScript | 1211 | 1467 | 1723 | 1979 |
| , (comma) | 188 | 444 | 700 | 956 | 1212 | 1468 | 1724 | 1980 |
| . (period) | 189 | 445 | 701 | 957 | 1213 | 1469 | 1725 | 1981 |
| / (slash) | 190 | 446 | 702 | 958 | 1214 | 1470 | 1726 | 1982 |
| ` (grave accent) | 191 | 447 | 703 | 959 | 1215 | 1471 | 1727 | 1983 |
| [ (left bracket) | 192 | 448 | 704 | 960 | 1216 | 1472 | 1728 | 1984 |
| \ (back-slash) | 220 | 476 | 732 | 988 | 1244 | 1500 | 1756 | 2012 |
| ] (right bracket) | 221 | 477 | 733 | 989 | 1245 | 1501 | 1757 | 2013 |
| ' (apostro-phe) | 222 | 478 | 734 | 990 | 1246 | 1502 | 1758 | 2014 |

Shaded areas denote key combinations that cannot be assigned to a macro

Figure D.1 describes the base key codes on a standard IBM 101-key keyboard. Since there are variations among keyboard manufacturers, some clone keyboards may not provide access to all keys, and key codes may vary; the numpad keys are particularly vulnerable to these differences.

## Figure D.1

Base key codes

Note: Numbers in boxes are with
NumLock on

# Searching for Special Characters

It is possible to search for various special character codes in EditFind or Edit-Replace. The following table lists these special characters. Additional information can be found in Chapter 12 of the *Microsoft Word User's Guide* and in the Word help file.

| Special Character | Performs This Search |
| --- | --- |
| ? | Match any character. |
| ^? | Question mark. |
| ^W or ^w | White space—any number and combination of spaces, nonbreaking spaces, tabs, end of line, end of cell, and paragraph, section, or page breaks. Note: this code is not case-sensitive. |
| ^t | Tab character. |
| ^p | Paragraph mark. |
| ^n | Newline character. |
| ^d | Page break or section break. |
| ^m | Duplicates search text. Used to search for text and replace with same text. |
| ^c | Clipboard contents. Used as replacement text. |
| ^s | Nonbreaking space. |
| ^- | Optional hyphen. |
| ^~ | Nonbreaking hyphen. |
| ^^ | Caret character. |
| ^*nnn* | ASCII character. |
| ^0*nnn* | ANSI character. |
| ^1 | Picture. |
| ^2 | Footnote reference. |
| ^5 | Annotation reference. |
| ^9 | Tab. |
| ^10 | Line feed: Chr$(10). |
| ^11 | Newline(Shift + Enter), Chr$(11). |
| ^12 | Page or section break. |
| ^13 | Carriage return: Chr$(13) + Chr$(10). |
| ^14 | Column break. |

| Special Character | Performs This Search |
|---|---|
| ^19 | Field start (opening curly brace: {). |
| ^21 | Field end (closing curly brace: }). |

**NOTE.** *The commands EditFind and EditReplace will not distinguish between a section break and a hard page break. They are both represented by either ^d or ^12. However, if you are doing the search from within a macro, you can fig-ure out what you've found by checking the section number before and after the break. For instance, the following macro will locate every break, hard page or section, and determine if it is a section break:*

```
Sub Main
StartOfDocument
EditFind .Find = "^d", .Direction = 2
While EditFindFound()
    If IsSectionBreak Then MsgBox "This is a section break"
    EditFind .Find = "^d", .Direction = 2
Wend
End Sub

Function IsSectionBreak
    CharLeft
    UpSection = SelInfo(2)
    CharRight 1, 1
    ThisSection = SelInfo(2)
    If UpSection <> ThisSection Then IsSectionBreak = - 1
End Function
```

**NOTE.** *When you search for ^19, the beginning of a field code, you must have ViewFieldCodes set to on. When this character is found, the entire field code is selected. You can combine a search for ^19 with a field name. For in-stance, searching for "^19date" would locate every DATE field. Searching for ^21, the closing curly brace that marks a field, will also result in the entire field being selected.*

# Third-Party Add-ons and Support Products

There are several useful products available that can enhance the productivity of Word. The following list is not exhaustive.

## Microsoft

Microsoft provides the following useful facilities and products of interest to Word users.

### Using WordBasic

Product: *Using WordBasic* by WexTech Systems and Microsoft.

Ordering: Microsoft End User Sales at 800-426-9400. (Part number 059-050-574.)

Price: The first copy is free; additional copies cost $15.00 each, plus tax and shipping charges.

Comments: This manual replaces the original *Word Technical Reference* (which was available from Microsoft or in bookstores for $22.95). It is both an introduction to WordBasic (with several tutorial-type examples) and a programming reference. Includes a sample disk.

Editorial: Highly recommended. It's useful. It's free. What more could you ask? Order a copy.

### Macro Developer's Kit

Though the *Using WordBasic* manual is free, for a few dollars more you can order the Macro Developer's Kit (MDK) and get several additional reference works.

The MDK includes

- *Using WordBasic* by WexTech Systems and Microsoft.

- The Developer's Handbook, also known as "The Yellow Book," which is a compilation of articles written and presented at the 1991 Microsoft Developer's Forum. It includes discussions of dynamic data exchange (DDE) with Word, WordBasic tips and tricks, and information on third-party products that can be integrated with Word.

- Fields Documentation: This article duplicates (in easier to read format) the information contained in the Word help file.

- RTF Specifications: Rich Text File format specifications used for add-on products that need to read Word for Windows files.

- Microsoft Consultant Relations Program Information: This program provides additional facilities for WordBasic developers. The MDK includes information on joining the program.

- WordBasic Update Document: Documentation on changes from Word-Basic 1.x to 2.x.

Ordering: To order the Microsoft Word for Windows Macro Developer's Kit, call 800-323-3577. From outside the U.S. call Microsoft International Customer Service at 206-936-8661 to locate the office in your area.

Price: $19.95, plus shipping and handling.

Editorial: Most of the articles in the Developer's Handbook were written for version 1.x of Word. They still provide lots of useful information. The fields documentation is conveniently formatted (it should have been included in *Using WordBasic)*, but not unique. The RTF specification is invaluable if you are writing add-on products that must read Word files. Worth the price.

### Legal Resource Kit

Microsoft has gathered several items of interest to lawyers. The Microsoft Legal Resource Kit (LRK) includes: Lexis 2000 for Windows software; an improved table of authorities macro and documentation; BRIEF.DOT and CONTRACT.DOT templates; the "Self-Guided Tour of the Legal Features in Word for Windows"; a coupon for Alki Software's legal dictionary; and a coupon for DocuComp, a DOS-based program to compare document versions.

Ordering: Call Microsoft End User Sales at 800-426-9400.

Price: Licensed owners are entitled to one free copy of the LRK.

### Microsoft Word and Bookshelf

Word and Bookshelf will interest anyone who has a CD-ROM drive. The package consists of a single CD containing Word 2.0x and Microsoft Bookshelf, a collection of seven reference works: *The American Heritage Dictionary, Bartlett's Familiar Quotations, The Concise Columbia Dictionary of Quotations, The Concise Columbia Encyclopedia, Hammond Atlas, Roget's II Electronic Thesaurus*, and *The World Almanac and Book of Facts 1992.*

Word and a CD reader application are installed onto your hard drive. Special macros allow easy access, from within Word, to the various elements of Microsoft Bookshelf.

In addition to the reference works, the CD contains a hypertext copy of the *Microsoft Word User's Guide.*

Ordering: Call Microsoft End User Sales at 800-426-9400.

Price: Of interest to readers of this book is the update price for current owners of Word: $99.00.

### Wish Line

Not long ago Microsoft instituted a "wish" line. If you have an idea for a new or improved feature, you can call this number and tell them about it.

I think this is a great tool. Much of the direction of Word is determined by the calls placed to PSS (Product Support Services), which means much effort is spent collating and digesting problems reported by new users and users who are having difficulty with the product. The wish line provides a way for positive suggestions to enter the loop.

The number is: 206-936-9474.

If you have the inclination, here's my own top ten list of wished-for features:

1. A document compare feature that does something useful.

2. Improved glossaries: among other things, fixing all font oddities and displaying glossaries segregated by context.

3. Character styles.

4. Smarter dialog boxes: triggers, drop-down lists, graphics.

5. Improved revision marking: I'd like to be able to choose the formatting to be applied to deleted and new text, such as making deleted text hidden in addition to struck through.

6. Visible bookmarks.

7. A new command for WordBasic to turn off the display during macro execution.

8. Better use of the context concept: In all macro-related dialog boxes there should be three options—Display Commands, Global Macros, and if in a template, Template Macros. Currently you can either display all the internal commands or all the macros (both global and template).

9. A macro manager utility that would allow simple moving of macros, styles, glossaries, and access methods from one template to another.

10. Any number of WordBasic improvements, such as global variables, ability to load libraries of macros, and ability to execute a macro from disk.

## Alki

Alki's MasterWord is a collection of tools, written in C and integrated via macros and DDE. It contains:

- *New File Commands*   More powerful versions of FileNew, FileTemplate, and FileSaveAs.

- *CustomBar*   A customizable toolbar that can replace or supplement the built-in toolbar.

■ *Nickname*   Assigns 1- to 4-character letter codes to styles or macros. This facility does not replace the built-in ToolsMacroKeyboard assignments.

■ *Manager*   A utility to facilitate copying macros, styles, and glossaries between templates.

■ *Template Selector*   Presents icon representations of your templates.

In addition to these tools that alter Word's interface, the full MasterWord package comes with an enhanced help file and a collection of "Handy Macros." Note: All macros are encrypted.

Ordering: To order contact:

Alki Software Corp.
219 First Ave. N.
Suite 410
Seattle, WA 98109
206-286-2600

Price: $99.95.

Alki also offers replacement dictionaries for the speller and thesaurus. The *Microsoft Comprehensive Spelling* package ($79.95) adds 74,100 medical, legal, and business terms. The *Microsoft Comprehensive Thesaurus* ($79.95) includes 600,000 synonyms.

In addition, Alki markets 13 foreign language dictionaries: English (British), French, French (Canadian), Swedish, Norwegian, Finnish, Spanish, Danish, Portuguese, Portuguese (Brazilian), German, Italian, and Dutch. The dictionaries are $99.95 each.

## Doc-To-Help

Doc-To-Help is a suite of templates designed to facilitate the creation of manuals in any of three formats (8½-by-11 inch, side heads, and 7-by-9 inch). In addition to predefined styles and layouts, these templates contain macros to format special terms, tables, and pictures. There are also macros to ease index and glossary generation.

The real magic in this package lies in its ability to take a Word for Windows document (formatted according to Doc-To-Help's rules) and turn it, virtually without intervention, into a fully featured Windows help file, with hypertext links and pop-up definitions. With Doc-To-Help you can create help files without ever having to touch the complex RTF file required by the help compiler.

Doc-To-Help ships with both Windows 3.0 and 3.1 versions of the help compiler.

Editorial: If you write technical manuals in Word, Doc-To-Help is a great set of tools. If you write technical manuals *and* create Windows help files, Doc-To-Help is indispensable.

Ordering: To order contact:

WexTech Systems, Inc.
310 Madison Ave., Suite 905
New York, NY 10017
212-949-9595

Price: $299.95

## Word-for-Word

Windows Word-for-Word, by MasterSoft, is a collection of conversion modules for foreign document formats.

The formats supported include Ami Professional 1.x, 2.0; ASCII (Smart); ASCII (Stripped); DEC DX; DisplayWrite Native & DCA/RFT; EBCDIC; Enable 1.1, 2.0, 2.15; Final Form (FFT); FrameWork III, IV; HP Advance-Write Plus; IBM Writing Assistant 1.0; InterLeaf Publisher 1.1; Lotus Manuscript 2.0, 2.1; Mass-11 Version 8.0; MultiMate 4; Navy DIF; OfficeWriter 4, 5, 6, 6.1; PeachText 5000, 2.12; PFS First Choice 1.0, 2.0; PFS: Write Version C; Professional Write 1.0, 2.0, 2.1, 2.2; Professional Write Plus; Q&A Version 3.0, 4.0; Samna Word IV & IV Plus; Total Word 1.2, 1.3; Volkswriter Deluxe 2.2; Volkswriter 3, 4; Wang PC Version 3.0; WordPerfect 5.1; WordStart 5.0, 5.5, 6.0; WordStar 2000, Release 3.0, 3.5; XyWrite III, III Plus.

Ordering: To order contact:

MasterSoft
6991 E. Camelback Rd., Suite A320
Scottsdale, AZ 85251
602-277-0900

Price: $79.95

## Gadfly Macros

Many of the macros in this book (and in UTILITY.DOC) began life as part of a package of macros called gToolBox. I distribute, via CompuServe and other electronic bulletin boards, several ShareWare macros:

■ *gToolBox*   A collection of utility macros. GTBX10.EXE.

- *ChooseDirectory*    A macro to facilitate document management. GCD30.EXE.

- *InsertLJMark*    A macro to insert a watermark into a Word document using an HP III printer. GLJMK2.EXE.

- *gScript*    A suite of templates to aid in the creation and formatting of a feature screenplay. GSF20.EXE.

    Versions of these packages are included on disk in the GTOOLS directory. Ordering: To order contact:

    Indelible, Inc.
    219 East 69th St.
    New York, NY 10021
    CompuServe: 71171,3555

## WOPR

WOPR, Woody's Office Powerpack, is a collection of WordBasic macros. The center of WOPR lies in two application macros:

- *Enveloper*    Prints envelopes with bar codes, custom envelope styles, multiple return address information.

- *TwoByFour*    Prints a Word document front and back, two pages to a sheet, two pages back and front, and booklet.

    In addition, the package includes several utility macros (a replacement for FileNew, WOPRClock, Viewer, WordCount).
    All macros come unencrypted, so they can be studied and modified.
    Ordering: To order contact:

    Pinecliffe International
    Advanced Support Group
    11900 Grant Pl.
    Des Peres, MO 63131
    800-OK-WINWORD or 314-965-5630

    Price: $49.95

## Writer's Toolkit

The Writer's Toolkit, by Systems Compatibility Corporation, is a collection of six reference works and a grammar checker.

The grammar checker is based upon The Houghton Mifflin CorrecText Grammar, Style, Punctuation and Spelling Correction System.

The six reference works are

- *The American Heritage Electronic Dictionary*
- *Roget's II Electronic Thesaurus*
- *The Houghton Mifflin Abbreviation Program*
- *The Concise Columbia Dictionary of Quotations*
- *The Dictionary of Command Knowledge*
- *Written Word III—Principles of Grammar & Style*

The Writer's Toolkit comes with macros (installed into your NORMAL-.DOT) which allow easy access to various modules.

Editorial: If you have the disk space, this could prove a useful set of tools. The grammar and spelling checker is fast, quite informative, and remarkably accurate. Though the program converts the native Word document to RTF in order to check, formatting is preserved. The one limitation I could find was that text formatted as hidden in Word is not checked at all, though it remains hidden when the processed document is returned to Word format.

Ordering: To order contact:

Systems Compatibility Corp.
401 N. Wabash, Suite 600
Chicago, IL 60611
312-329-0700

Price: $129.95

## SuperQue

Windows is not known for its speedy printing. SuperQue is a replacement for the Print Manager which speeds the processing of a print request. It does not speed the actual printing of your document; however, it does decrease the wait before control is returned to Word. SuperQue then spools the print job in the background.

A companion program, SuperText, does speed printing of graphics by using a proprietary printing technology.

Ordering: To order contact:

Zenographics
#4 Executive Cir., Suite 200

Irvine, CA 92714
714-851-6352

Price: $69.95

## MathType

The makers of the Equation Editor application that ships with Word market a more powerful version called MathType.
Ordering: To order contact:

Design Science, Inc.
4028 Broadway
Long Beach, CA 90803
213-433-0685

Price: $249.00; $89.00 for users of Word 2.x

# Reference to Tools on Disk

Below is a listing of the files found on the sample disk and a brief description of their purpose and contents.

## Macros Discussed in Chapter 7

The following macros were presented in Chapter 7 and are located in the file CH07MACS.DOC:

| Macro | Purpose |
|---|---|
| AssignKey | Assigns virtually any key combination to a macro |
| AutoCloseFileBackup | Possible AutoClose macro to copy the current file to drive A:\ |
| AutoExecBackup | Possible AutoExec macro to backup NORMAL.DOT |
| AutoExecMaximize | Possible AutoExec macro to maximize Word |
| AutoExecRestore | Possible AutoExec macro to restore Word |
| AutoOpenLastEdit | Possible AutoOpen macro to return to last edit location |
| AutoOpenInsertDateTime | Possible AutoOpen macro to date stamp last line of document |
| EditTemplate | Loads the current document template |
| FileCloseAll | Closes all open files |
| FileOpenShowAll | A possible FileOpen replacement which displays all files |
| FilePrintGeneric | Changes active printer to Generic/TTY before printing |
| FilePrintUpdate | Possible FilePrint replacement which forces an update of all fields |
| SpecialBold | Toggles special boldface |
| StripCarriageReturns | Reformats ASCII files containing carriage returns at each line end into paragraphs |
| ToggleHidden | Toggles display of hidden text |
| ToggleOutline | Toggles in and out of outline view |
| TogglePictures | Toggles display of pictures and picture placeholders |
| ToggleRevisionMarks | Toggles revision marking on and off |
| ToggleStyleArea | Toggles the display of style names on the left of the current document |
| ToggleWindow | Toggles Window split |

## Macros Discussed in Chapter 9

The following macros were presented in Chapter 9 and are located in the file CH09MACS.DOC:

| Macro | Purpose |
|---|---|
| BookmarkVar | Demonstrates how to use bookmarks as document-specific variables |
| ButtonMac | Example of how to pass a parameter to a macro that is launched with a MACROBUTTON field |
| CallMac | Calls the Startup subroutine of ParamMac with a parameter |
| DialogExample | A custom dialog box example |
| FileInfo | Demonstrates the retrieval of the contents of FileSummaryInfo |
| FileOpenShowAll | The second version of a modified FileOpen command (this version uses the dollar sign trick) |
| GlossaryVar | Example of using SetGlossVar and GetGlossVar$ to create persistent variables |
| GotoDialogEditor | Loads the dialog box editor (MACRODE.EXE) if it isn't loaded; activates it if it is |
| GotoDialogEditorTwo | Loads the dialog box editor (MACRODE.EXE) if it isn't loaded; activates it if it is (uses zDeclare) |
| ParamMac | Demo of how to call a macro with a parameter |
| PrivateINI1 | Demonstration of how to write values to a private INI file |
| PrivateINI2 | Writes, reads, and deletes private INI file keyword/value |
| TestForPane | Tests to see if the insertion point is in an annotation, footnote, or header/footer pane |
| WinINI1 | Example of how to use GetProfileString and SetProfileString to create persistent variables |
| WinINI2 | Example of how to use GetProfileString and SetProfileString to write to a private WIN.INI section |
| zDeclare | Example library of useful Declare statements |
| zLib | A collection of string handling routines |
| zLibDemo | Demonstration of the string routines found in zLib |

## Macros Discussed in Chapter 10

The following macros were presented in Chapter 10 and are located in the file CH10MACS.DOC:

| Macro | Purpose |
|---|---|
| BackUpThisDoc | Copies the current document to a backup directory |
| ControlRun | A configurable replacement for the built-in ControlRun macro that provides a command line |
| CopyMacro | Copies a macro from the current template to a loaded template |
| CreateIconSimple | Creates an icon in Program Manager to load the current document |
| CreateIconThisDoc | Creates an icon in Program Manager for the current document, presenting a list of all available groups |
| DeleteIdleStyles | Removes user-defined styles that are not active in the current document—use with caution |
| EditFindThisChar | Finds all subsequent instances of the current character formatting |
| EditFindThisPara | Finds all subsequent instances of the current paragraph formatting |
| EditFindThisStyle | Finds all subsequent instances of the current style |
| EncryptMacros | Encrypts selected macros in the current template |
| FileFindThisDir | Runs FileFind on the current directory |
| FileTemplate | Changes the template and the template options |
| InsDoubleQuote | Inserts a double smart quote |
| InsertSmartMark | Informs you if a proposed bookmark already exists |
| InsertSmarterMark | Informs you if a bookmark name already exists and proposes an incremented name |
| InsSingleQuote | Inserts a single smart quote |
| LoadMRUList | Opens all of the files in the MRU list |
| PrintListOfPages | Prints a range of pages |
| PrintOddEven | Prints all even or all odd pages |
| SyncStyles | Merges styles to and from template |
| ToggleSmartQuotes | Toggles the state of SmartQuotes |
| WinArrangeTwo | Stacks the current document atop one of the other open documents |
| WinCascadeAll | Arranges open document windows in a cascading stack |
| WinSideBySide | Arranges the current document next to one of the other open documents |

## Macros Discussed in Chapter 13

The following macros were presented in Chapter 13 and are located in the file CH13MACS.DOC:

| Macro | Purpose |
| --- | --- |
| EditClear | A replacement for the built-in EditClear command which checks to see if the selection to clear contains hidden text |
| EditCut | A replacement for the built-in EditCut command which checks to see if the selection to cut contains hidden text |
| FormatDelRed | Formats as red all text marked as deleted by Revision Marking |
| FormatNewBlue | Formats as blue all text marked as new by Revision Marking |

## Templates Presented in Chapter 12

The following example templates, each with customized styles, macros, and access methods, were analyzed in Chapter 12 and can be found on the samples disk:

| Macro | Purpose |
| --- | --- |
| JOURNAL.DOT | For maintaining a date and time stamped journal |
| INVOICE.DOT | For generating a single-page invoice |
| RESUME.DOT | For generating a formal resume, using side-heads |
| MSS.DOT | For book manuscripts (fiction or nonfiction) |
| PLAY.DOT | For dramatic play scripts |
| SCRIPT.DOT | For feature screenplays |

## UTILITY.DOC

In addition to the files described above, which contain macros that were discussed and annotated in the foregoing chapters, an additional file, named UTILITY.DOC, contains several useful macros.

### BackupTemplateMenus

As pointed out in Chapter 8, there is a potentially dangerous bug which can destroy menu customizations if the proper set of circumstances converge: With macros from multiple contexts open and "dirty," selecting FileSaveAll can inadvertently remove the custom menus in one of the contexts.

The macro BackupTemplateMenus can help guard against this danger. What it does is simple: It creates a template macro that contains the WordBasic statements that reflect *the current menu geography*. In essence, BackupTemplateMenus takes a snapshot of the current menu customizations and stores it in a macro that can be executed if the bug described above bites.

Usage: Copy BackupTemplateMenus into your NORMAL.DOT. Load a document based upon the template that contains the menu customizations you wish to protect. Select Tools, Macro and select BackupTemplateMenus (since this is not a macro you will necessarily run frequently I do not recommend assigning it to a shortcut access method). Select Run.

A new document will be created and named in the form fname.MNU. For instance, if you execute BackupTemplateMenus on a file based upon SCRIPT.DOT, the macro first creates a file named SCRIPT.MNU. This new document contains a table of the menu customizations.

BackupTemplateMenus then creates a macro in the form fnameMenus. For instance, using a SCRIPT.DOT-based document would result in a macro named SCRIPTMenus. Here is a copy of the macro SCRIPTMenus (formatted with backslashes for easier reading):

```
Sub Main
REM - menus for the template : C:\WINWORD\SCRIPT.DOT
ToolsOptionsMenus .ResetAll, .Context = 1
ToolsOptionsMenus .Name = "-", .Menu = "&Insert",\
    .MenuText = "--------------------", .Context = 1, .Add
ToolsOptionsMenus .Name = "SideBySideDialogue", .Menu = "&Insert",\
    .MenuText = "&Side By Side Dialogue", .Context = 1, .Add
ToolsOptionsMenus .Name = "-", .Menu = "Forma&t",\
    .MenuText = "--------------------", .Context = 1, .Add
ToolsOptionsMenus .Name = "ApplyNormal", .Menu = "Forma&t",\
    .MenuText = "&Action", .Context = 1, .Add
ToolsOptionsMenus .Name = "ApplySlugline", .Menu = "Forma&t",\
    .MenuText = "&Slugline", .Context = 1, .Add
ToolsOptionsMenus .Name = "ApplyChar", .Menu = "Forma&t",\
    .MenuText = "&Character name", .Context = 1, .Add
ToolsOptionsMenus .Name = "ApplyDialogue", .Menu = "Forma&t",\
    .MenuText = "&Dialogue", .Context = 1, .Add
ToolsOptionsMenus .Name = "ApplyParen", .Menu = "Forma&t",\
    .MenuText = "&Parenthetical", .Context = 1, .Add
ToolsOptionsMenus .Name = "ApplyBreak", .Menu = "Forma&t",\
    .MenuText = "&Break", .Context = 1, .Add
ToolsOptionsMenus .Name = "-", .Menu = "T&ools",\
    .MenuText = "--------------------", .Context = 1, .Add
ToolsOptionsMenus .Name = "NumberAllSlugs", .Menu = "T&ools",\
    .MenuText = "Number &All Sluglines", .Context = 1, .Add
ToolsOptionsMenus .Name = "NumberThisSlug", .Menu = "T&ools",\
    .MenuText = "&Number This Slugline", .Context = 1, .Add
ToolsOptionsMenus .Name = "ToggleSlugIndent", .Menu = "T&ools",\
    .MenuText = "Toggle Slugline &Indent", .Context = 1, .Add
End Sub
```

You can see, in this example, that the macro, after resetting all menu assignments in the template, consists entirely of ToolsOptionsMenus statements which set up custom menus.

Hint: You can use this macro as a starting point to further customize a template's menus. For instance, you could more easily change the menu text of all a template's menus by editing this macro than by using the built-in ToolsOptionsKeyboard dialog box. You could easily add additional menu assignments.

### MacroKey

MacroKey allows you to assign macros to key combinations that are not accessible using the built-in ToolsOptionsKeyboard dialog box. In addition to the Ctrl and Ctrl+Shift combinations available in the ToolsOptionsKeyboard dialog box, MacroKey allows you to assign a macro to Alt, Alt+Ctrl, Alt+Shift, and Alt+Shift+Ctrl. Note that Word reserves many of these combinations (such as Alt+T and Alt+Shift+S) for its own use. Use this macro cautiously and backup all DOT files before you experiment. Figure G.1 presents the main MacroKey dialog box.

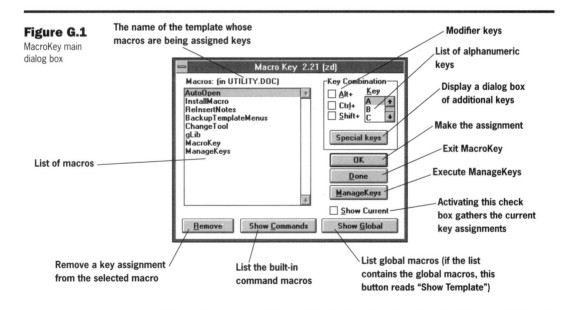

**Figure G.1**
MacroKey main dialog box

The name of the template whose macros are being assigned keys

Modifier keys

List of alphanumeric keys

Display a dialog box of additional keys

Make the assignment

Exit MacroKey

Execute ManageKeys

Activating this check box gathers the current key assignments

List of macros

Remove a key assignment from the selected macro

List the built-in command macros

List global macros (if the list contains the global macros, this button reads "Show Template")

When you select the Special keys button, you will be presented with the dialog box shown in Figure G.2.

**Figure G.2**

MacroKey's Special
Keys dialog box

The macro being given a
special key assignment

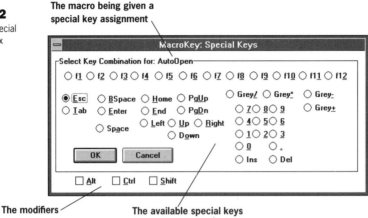

The modifiers

The available special keys

Note: The macros are not sorted. The template macros will appear in the order you created them. The built-in command macros will appear in the mysterious order in which Word's programmers arranged them.

Limitations: MacroKey will warn you if you are about to use a key combination that is already assigned to a macro. However, it will only warn you if the key combination in question is *not* one of the default assignments. That is, it must be an assignment you have made, rather than one that Word for Windows assumes is the case. For instance, if you assign F9 (the default key for the built-in command UpdateFields) to a user-macro, MacroKey will *not* warn you that it already has an assignment. If, however, F9 has already been assigned to a macro other than UpdateFields, MacroKey will detect the custom assignment and ask if you want to continue with the new assignment.

MacroKey does not warn you if you are about to use a key combination that is assigned to a style.

Legal Keys: Any combination of modifiers with F1 will always call help. So F1 isn't fair game.

NumPad 5 (the Numpad 5 that is activated by turning NumLock ON) does not accept shift characters. The NumPad 5 that is active in default state (NumLock OFF) does accept shift characters. MacroKey accounts for this oddity.

The direction keys, listed on the Special Keys dialog box, have some limitations: No direction keys (Home, End, PgUp, PgDn, Right, Left, Down, Up) can be assigned to a macro; no direction key plus Ctrl can be assigned to a macro; no direction key plus Ctrl+Shift can be assigned to a macro; the Alt key plus Up or Down is legal. The Alt key plus Left or Right is not legal; MacroKey will not allow you to assign anything to Ctrl+Alt+Del (for a fairly obvious reason).

The Show Current check box in the main dialog box will rebuild the list of macros, displaying the current key assignments (if any). This takes a significant amount of time. This function only shows key assignments made by the user, not key assignments that are internal to Word for Windows.

Requirements: Like some other utility macros, MacroKey requires that the library gLib also be installed in NORMAL.DOT.

### ManageKeys

ManageKeys is a support macro that can be called from the main MacroKey dialog box or executed alone. It lists the user-key assignments in the current context and, optionally, allows you to create a document containing a table of those key assignments. You can also delete a key assignment from within ManageKeys. Figure G.3 presents the main ManageKeys dialog box.

**Figure G.3**
ManageKeys dialog box

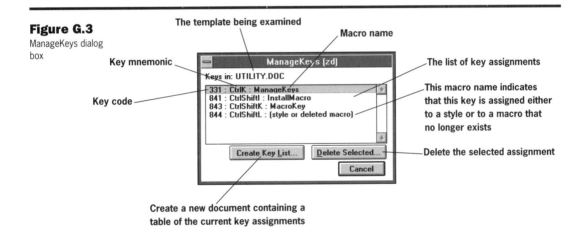

The template being examined

Macro name

Key mnemonic

The list of key assignments

Key code

This macro name indicates that this key is assigned either to a style or to a macro that no longer exists

Delete the selected assignment

Create a new document containing a table of the current key assignments

Each item in the list box contains three pieces of information:

- The key code for the key combination
- The mnemonic for the key combination
- The macro that has a key assignment

There are two buttons (aside from Cancel):

- **Create Key List**   This button will create a new document (based on NORMAL.DOT) and generate a table containing all of the key assignments.

■ **Delete Selected**   This button will remove the currently selected key assignment.

Note: Key assignments that have been made to a style, using the Format-Style command, are detected by ManageKeys; however, there is no way for WordBasic, at this point, to determine the style associated with a keyboard shortcut. It is also possible for a keyboard combination to *appear* as active when in fact the macro associated with the combination has been deleted.

If the macro name in the list is "(style or deleted macro)," then the keyboard combination is either associated with a style or associated with a macro that no longer exists. The latter can be deleted with the Delete Selected button. The style keyboard assignments will not be deleted by ManageKeys.

Requirements: Like some other utility macros, ManageKeys requires that the library gLib also be installed in NORMAL.DOT.

### ChangeTool

One of the limitations of the built-in ToolsOptionsToolbar command is that if you want to rearrange the icons in either NORMAL.DOT or a template, you have to remove and replace each one.

This macro allows you to insert a new tool and move the rest to the right, replace a tool with another, replace a tool with a space, or remove a tool altogether. See Figure G.4 for an explanation of the various parts of the Change-Tool dialog box.

**Figure G.4**

ChangeTool dialog box

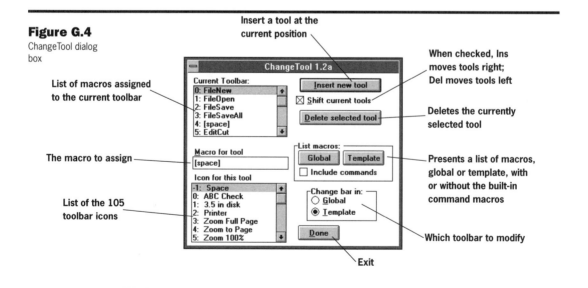

Limitations: The list of macros will not appear sorted.

Since Word for Windows dialog boxes cannot contain bitmaps, there is no way to actually include the toolbar icons. The list box in this macro displays the number of the tool (-1 to 104) and a short description.

Requirements: Like some other utility macros, ChangeTool requires that the library gLib also be installed in NORMAL.DOT.

### ReInsertNotes

If you change the style definition of a footnote or annotation reference mark, previously inserted marks will not automatically change. Subsequent mark insertions will have the new attributes.

For example, if you begin inserting footnotes with the character definition of Red and hidden, then change it to Blue and nonhidden, the already inserted footnotes will not change to the new style.

Another manifestation of this problem arises if you select a paragraph that has a footnote in it, and press Ctrl+spacebar to reset the character formatting.

The macro ReInsertNotes provides a way (albeit rather inelegant) around this buglet.

ReInsertNotes has two modes of operation: If the insertion point is currently positioned on a footnote reference or an annotation mark, ReInsertNotes will reinsert that footnote or annotation only and then stop; if the insertion point is not on a footnote reference or an annotation mark, ReInsertNotes will prompt you with the following dialog box:

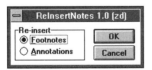

and then proceed to reinsert all of the footnotes or annotations in the document.

Requirements: Like some other utility macros, ReInsertNotes requires that the library gLib also be installed in NORMAL.DOT.

### gLib

gLib, named with my initial as its first character, is a library of subroutines and functions which have proven invaluable.

This library is used by several macros contained in gToolBox (a collection of ShareWare macros I distribute) and in some of the macros contained in UTILITY.DOC.

Here is a brief description of the subroutines and functions contained in gLib.

**ActivatePartial(Doc$)** This subroutine can be used to supplement the built-in command Activate WindowName$. The difference between the two is that this procedure only requires a partial name, whereas the built-in command requires that you know precisely what's up there on the document bar.

```
ActivatePartial("UTIL")
```

will cycle through each open window and stop at the first one whose title contains the letters "util" (not case-sensitive).

**CheckLib** This function returns the version number of gLib:

```
If glib.CheckLib Then Print "Okay"
```

**Chew$(Source$,Marker$)** This is a string function that returns the left portion of a string up to the occurrence of the marker.

The source string is truncated. So, for instance:

```
S$ = "one|two|three|four"
m$ = "|"
For x = 1 To 4
    MsgBox glib.Chew$(s$,m$)
Next x
```

would display four message boxes, containing one, two, three, and four, in sequence.

**CountChar(Source$, Char$)** This is a function that returns the number of occurrences of a specific character in a string:

```
x = gLib.CountChar("one,two,three",",")
```

would return 2.

**fExist(FullPathName$)** This function returns -1 if the specified file was found; 0 if not.

**fFileCount(FileSpec$)** This function counts the number of files in a directory:

```
DotCount = gLib.fFileCount("c:\winword\*.dot")
```

**fFileName$(b$)**   This function returns the file name portion of a full path name.

```
Name$ = gLib.fFileName$("c:\winword\normal.dot")
```

would return "normal".

**fFileNameExt$(b$)**   This function returns the file name plus extension from a full path designation.

```
Name$ = gLib.fFileNameExt$("c:\winword\normal.dot")
```

would return "normal.dot".

**fStr$(Num)**   This function returns a formatted string from an integer, stripping the padding Word places in front of a digit.

**GetDocDir$**   This function returns the directory in which a document is stored. If this function is called from within a macro pane, it returns a null string.

**GetFile(FullName$,Dir$,Default$)**   This function displays the FileOpen dialog box.

**GetPath$(Source$)**   This function strips out a path from a full file/path specification.

**GetTemplate$**   This function returns the current document's template.

**gLibInstalled(Macro$)**   This function is unique in the package. It should not be used from within the gLib macro but should be copied into any macro that calls a gLib routine.

What it does is use the same logic as MacroExist to determine if there is, in fact, a macro named gLib in the current NORMAL.DOT.

This allows you to test at the top of a macro that requires gLib if the library is installed. It displays a warning message and request for reinstallation.

If you look at almost any of the more complicated macros in gToolBox, you will see an example of how this is used.

**gMsg(Msg$,Title$)**   This subroutine displays a message with an attention sign.

**gQuery(Msg$,Title$)**   This function displays a query dialog box and returns true or false.

**HasKey(Macro$,Context)**   This function returns whether a macro in the given context has a key assignment.

**Inject$(Source$, New$, Place)**   This is a string function to insert a string within a string at a given place.

```
Name$ = gLib.Inject$(Name$("Guy Gallo", "J. ",4)
```

would return "Guy J. Gallo".

**IsMacroPane([MacroName$])**   This function returns –1 if the focus is currently on a macro editing window.

MacroName$ is an optional parameter containing the name of the macro calling the function. This is so that the warning message will be smart and tell you the name of the macro causing trouble.

**KeyDescription$(KeyCode)**   This function returns a string mnemonic for the specified key code.

**ListMacros$(Context,All)**   This is a simple function that displays a list of macros and returns the selected macro or a null string (if canceled).

It will display a list box of all macros in the specified context (0 for global and 1 for the current template).

If All is 0, then only user-macros will be displayed. If All is 1, then the built-in commands will also be displayed.

Limitation: This routine does not sort the list of user-macros. User-macros are displayed in the order they were created.

The built-in commands, for who knows what reason, are also not sorted alphabetically.

**MacroExist(Macro$)**   This function returns true or false (-1/0) if a macro exists. It takes a string argument in the same form as IsExecuteOnly. General syntax:

```
MacroExist([TemplateName:]MacroName)
```

For example:

```
MacroExist("NORMAL.DOT:GLIB")
```

If the template name is omitted, the macro will look in the current document's template first and then in the global context.

**NoSlash(Source$)**   This function checks to see if the last character in a string is a backslash and, if so, strips it off. This is useful for properly formatting a path specification for ChDir.

**Replace$(Source$, Old$, New$)**   This function replaces every occurrence in a string of one string with another string.

```
N$ = glib.Replace("h*e*l*l*o","*","_")
```

would return the string "h_e_l_l_o".

**Reverse$(Source$, Marker$)**   This function rearranges a string along a given character or group of characters. This is useful in combination with Replace$( ) when you want to change LastName,FirstName into FirstName LastName. For example:

```
Name$ = "Gallo,Guy"
Name$ = gLib.Reverse$(Name$,",")
Name$ = gLib.Replace$(Name$,",",Chr$(32))
```

After these three lines the variable Name$ would hold the string "Guy Gallo".

**SameFormat**   This function returns true if every character in the selection has the identical character attributes. If any character in the selection has a different character attribute it returns false.

**SelectSameFormatRight**   This subroutine extends the selection until it encounters a character format different from the one in effect at the starting point. This is used by ReInsertNotes. This subroutine calls another function in gLib, named SameFormat:

```
Sub SelectSameFormatRight
'Extends the selection until some part of the character formatting changes
CharRight 1, 1
While SameFormat
    CharRight 1, 1
Wend
CharLeft 1, 1
End Sub
```

A corresponding SelectSameFormatLeft could easily be implemented as well.

**Split(Source$, Marker$, First$, Second$)**   This is a subroutine that will take a string and divide it in two at a specific point.
   For example, if Source$ = "Guy+Gallo", the command

```
gLib.Split(Source$,"+",First$,Second$)
```

would return "Guy" in the variable First$, and "Gallo" in the variable Second$.

**Trim$(Source$, ZapChar$)**   This function strips a character from both sides of a string. So, for instance:

```
Pad$ = "****Test****"
Unpad$ = gLib.Trim$(Pad$,"*")
```

would return, in the variable Unpad$, the string "Test".

**Wait(Seconds)**   This subroutine is not astronomically accurate—I think it's dependent on CPU speed—but still is useful in debugging and testing macros.

# INDEX

## A

Abort buttons, displaying, 113

Abs() function, 103

accelerator keys. *See* keyboard shortcut assignments

access methods for commands

    for INVOICE.DOT, 353

    for JOURNAL.DOT, 348

    keyboard, 9–10, 60–62

    menus, 7–9, 57–60

    for MSS.DOT, 362–363

    for PLAY.DOT, 368–369

    for RESUME.DOT, 355

    for SCRIPT.DOT, 374–376

    templates for, 14

    toolbar, 10–11, 53–57

action fields, 315, 318

ActivatePartial user-subroutine, 436

active context, 16

active printers, 160

Add button for styles, 34

addition, 102

add-ons, third-party, 418–425

Add option for menu commands, 59

Add to Template check box, 34, 257

aligning dialog box items, 217

Alki, products from, 420–421

Alt key, key codes with, 410–415

alternate versions, hidden characters for, 35

ampersands (&)

    for dialog box elements, 206

    for menu speedkeys, 9, 59

am/pm suffix, 333

annotations

    bookmarks in, 195

    checking for selections in, 241, 260

    color for, 35

    {STYLEREF} in, 329

    styles for, 387–388, 435

ANSI codes, 101, 104

apostrophes (')

    for comments, 116, 144, 199–200

    typeset-quality, 290, 292–294

AppInfo$() function, 251–252, 254

application macros, 78–79

ApplyAction user-macro, 373

ApplyBreak user-macro, 373

ApplyChar user-macro, 366–367, 373

ApplyDialogue user-macro, 366–367, 373

ApplyParen user-macro, 366–368, 373

ApplySlugline user-macro, 373

ApplyStage user-macro, 366–367

Apply To: box, 24

AppMaximize() function, 149

AppRestore() function, 149

"Argument-count Mismatch (116)" message, 188

arguments, 86–87

    errors with, 188

    for fields, 324

arithmetic, 102–103, 315, 319, 325

arranging

    icons, 54–55, 434–435

    windows, 250–256

arrays and array variables, 123–124

    and dialog boxes and macros, 124–128

# ■ TO RECEIVE 5¼-INCH DISK(S)

The Ziff-Davis Press software contained on the $3^{1}/_{2}$-inch disk included with this book is also available in $5^{1}/_{4}$-inch format. If you would like to receive the software in the $5^{1}/_{4}$-inch format, please return the $3^{1}/_{2}$-inch disk with your name and address to:

**Disk Exchange**
Ziff-Davis Press
5903 Christie Avenue
Emeryville, CA 94608

# Send For Your Free Issue Today!

# IT'S FREE!

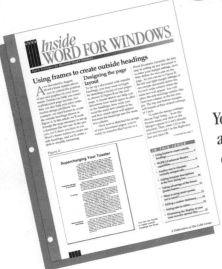

Your first issue of *Inside Word for Windows* is absolutely free! All you have to do is mail the card below.

# THE COBB GROUP
*Software Journal Publishers*

Microsoft is a registered trademark and Windows is a trademark of Microsoft Corporation.

---